Krishna Consciousness
in the West

Krishna Consciousness in the West

EDITED BY

David G. Bromley and Larry D. Shinn

Lewisburg
Bucknell University Press
London and Toronto: Associated University Presses

Associated University Presses
440 Forsgate Drive
Cranbury, NJ 08512

Associated University Presses
25 Sicilian Avenue
London WC1A 2QH, England

Associated University Presses
P.O. Box 488, Port Credit
Mississauga, Ontario
Canada L5G 4M2

The paper used in this publication meets the requirements
of the American National Standard for Permanence of Paper
for Printed Library Materials Z39.48-1984.

Library of Congress Cataloging-in-Publication Data

Krishna consciousness in the West.

Includes bibliographies and index.
1. International Society for Krishna Consciousness.
I. Bromley, David G.   II. Shinn, Larry D., 1942–   .
BL1285.84.K75   1989   294.5'44   87-47975
ISBN 0-8387-5144-X (alk. paper)

PRINTED IN THE UNITED STATES OF AMERICA

Contents

VI. *Social Response to ISKCON*

A Note on Sanskrit Terms

Since diacritical marks are not needed to understand the rather common Sanskrit terms used in the following essays, these technical words have been italicized only. Sanskrit terms that are familiar to Western readers (e.g., Brahman or karma) and those that are proper nouns are presented without italics or diacritical marks with the one exception of the historical charts that follow chapter 1.

Krishna Consciousness
in the West

I. Introduction

A Kaleidoscopic View of the Hare Krishnas in America

Larry D. Shinn
David G. Bromley

During July 1985, an unusual academic conference, under the organizing theme "Krishna Consciousness in the West: A Multidisciplinary Critique," was held in the hills of northern West Virginia. Nearly two dozen invited scholars of religion and new religious movements gathered in the Hare Krishnas' Palace of Gold in the settlement called New Vrindaban near Moundsville, West Virginia. For three days and nights these scholars discussed and debated the history, practices and development of the Hare Krishna movement in America (known officially as the International Society for Krishna Consciousness or ISKCON). The letter of invitation had stated the intent of the conference succinctly:

> The purpose of the conference is to bring together scholars from a variety of academic disciplines with a common interest generally in religious movements and specifically . . . in the Hare Krishna movement, in order to examine the movement in the broadest possible historical, comparative-religious, sociological, psychological, and theological contexts, as well as to assess its place in contemporary religiosity. (Letter dated 6 October 1984 from Subhananda dasa)

Why would scholars from a variety of academic disciplines agree to attend a conference sponsored by ISKCON and held on its "home turf"? Given the current controversies surrounding groups popularly labeled "cults," attendance at any such conference inevitably evokes questions concerning sponsorship, hidden agendas, and political implications. The participants were well aware of these issues, which have been extensively debated in academic journals. Quite simply, for the invited scholars, who in most cases knew the Krishnas through years of research contact, the conference presented a unique opportunity. It was a chance to bring together colleagues who, from their various disciplinary stances, could bring their empirical research to bear on cross-disciplinary questions related to the genesis and maturation of Hare Krishna in America. The complexity of ISKCON's structure and development have been largely obscured by the cult controversy. Furthermore, lawsuits and a current murder investigation involving a few Krishna devotees tend to cause observers to lose sight of the larger context in which most disciples live. The essays in this volume, then, offer a more comprehensive and balanced perspective on ISKCON and thus contribute more broadly to the public discussion of the diverse array of new religious movements that have been the focus of public attention.

The Hare Krishnas in America

From its inception in America, the Hare Krishna movement has been associated with the counterculture movement of the 1960s and the marginal religious movements (commonly called cults) it spawned. However, those who know the history of ISKCON are aware of its strong Indian roots and its place in the Hindu tradition as a missionary movement from Bengal in eastern India.

A. C. Bhaktivedanta Swami Prabhupada came to America in the fall of 1965. He had been a sometimes successful businessman before he adopted the ascetic life of a full-time devotee of the Hindu god Krishna in 1959. He arrived in New York City with few possessions except for copies of his English translations of the Krishna scripture called the *Bhagavata Purana*. The faith that he preached on the streets of lower Manhattan was not new with him, nor did it elevate him as the central object of veneration. Rather, Bhaktivedanta brought with him a traditional Indian devotional faith in Krishna that was made popular by the reformer Caitanya in the sixteenth century in Bengal.

Bhaktivedanta's early disciples were indistinguishable from those of other Asian gurus in America in the 1960s in terms of their countercultural affectations. The first three or four years of the Krishna movement were marked by rapid growth and a wide variety of religious practices and ways of life. However, from his very first days of preaching in Washington Square, Bhaktivedanta confronted his young listeners with traditional, undiluted devotional teachings and practices from the ancient Indian Krishna scriptures (e.g., *Bhagavad Gita* and *Bhagavata Purana*) as interpreted through the ecstatic devotionalism of Caitanya.[1]

Bhaktivedanta proclaimed Krishna to be the eternal divine being who is present to the devout believer in the recitation of his holy name. Thus, the Krishnas appeared frequently on the streets of American cities chanting the names of Krishna and singing his praises.

By 1970, the Krishna movement had become more regularized in terms of its devotional practices and temple lifestyles and thoroughly

"Indianized" in terms of its adoption of lactovegetarian diet and Indian cultural customs. Disciples wore common dress (e.g., white *dhotis* and saris or ochre robes), practiced traditional Indian rituals (e.g., regular chanting of sixteen rounds, required attendance at early morning deity worship, community reading of scriptures), and had a common appearance (e.g., shaven heads for men and covered heads for women, and traditional religious marks and beads). In most respects, the Hare Krishnas were becoming indistinguishable from many of their Indian counterparts.

During the early 1970s, ISKCON expanded to all parts of the world. Prabhupada and his disciples established settlements in his native India, Canada, and England and sent missionaries to every continent. Bhaktivedanta continued his ambitious project of translating and providing commentary for the voluminous Krishna scriptures and authored more than fifty books in the twelve years of his missionary activity after leaving India for America in 1965. During this period of expansion of ISKCON, what had begun as a charismatic and sometimes unwieldy religious movement became a more settled institution. The Governing Body Commission (GBC), initially composed of twelve senior disciples and later expanded to twenty-four, was appointed by Bhaktivedanta to oversee the worldwide business and religious affairs of ISKCON. ISKCON developed grand missionary schemes and its future seemed bright. To be sure, there were strong critics who labeled the Krishna movement a cult, but legal decisions and economic conditions appeared to insure ISKCON's future in America.

With Bhaktivedanta's death in the fall of 1977 and during the several years of transition from his leadership to that of his senior disciples, the fortunes of ISKCON changed. There were challenges within ISKCON to the eleven appointed successors who received the title of initiating gurus and who acted as both the spiritual and organizational heirs of Bhaktivedanta. The new gurus were accused of being too authoritarian, too immature spiritually, or simply too insensitive to their peers who had also been initiated by Bhaktivedanta. Very quickly, stories began to emerge about the misconduct of one guru or another. Defections by Bhaktivedanta's disciples increased and conflicts arose between many who remained. Economic difficulties associated with the book-selling activities of devotees in airports and public places forced most of the temples to adopt alternative means, sometimes questionable or illegal, to support burgeoning temple budgets.

During the transition period from Prabhupada's leadership to that of his young successors in the later 1970s, anti-cult antagonists stepped up their attack on ISKCON. Antagonism toward the Krishnas culminated in increased kidnappings of devotees by their parents with the aid of deprogrammers, the institution of numerous lawsuits against ISKCON, and renewed pressure on the media to capitalize on the Jonestown massacre by extending the fear of violence in the cults to ISKCON. All of these activities forced the Krishnas to adopt a lower profile and, sometimes, resulted in feelings of persecution that promoted antinomian behavior.

During the 1980s, the trends toward the institutional consolidation of leadership and direction for ISKCON continued. On the positive side, and in spite of the bad news that was presented almost weekly in the media about some ISKCON guru or disciple being accused of illegal or immoral behavior, ISKCON maintained its overall size in America at about twenty-five hundred full-time devotees and increased its number of disciples in Europe and India by the initiation of new devotees by the successor gurus. The Krishna mansion in Detroit received national media coverage when it was opened to the public in 1982 and displayed its opulent Indian decor. The intended spiritual heartland of ISKCON in America, New Vrindaban in Moundsville, West Virginia, became a noted tourist attraction with its Temple of Gold providing the centerpiece for many newspaper articles and television specials. Krishna farm communities from Pennsylvania to California sprang up in an attempt to recreate a mythic and idyllic past when Krishna was a cowherd in an Indian village more than three thousand years ago. Yet serious trouble was brewing inside ISKCON that now threatens its very survival in America.

On the negative side, leadership, economic, and legal/public relations issues have plagued ISKCON during the middle 1980s. First of all, six of the eleven gurus appointed to succeed Prabhupada have been expelled from the movement by the GBC. As early as 1982, the London-based guru, Jayatirtha, was accused by his godbrothers of illegal drug use and immoral conduct with women devotees. In the spring of 1983, Hansadutta, the guru of the Berkeley, California zone, was expelled by the GBC for reputed drug use and various moral violations that undercut further devotee confidence in the new gurus. By 1987, not only had six gurus been excommunicated, but one, Bhaktipada of New Vrindaban, was also under investigation along with other leaders and members of this farm community in connection with child abuse and murder allegations prompted by the murder of a fringe devotee named Steven Bryant.

With more than half of the original new gurus having breached the institutional and religious trust placed in them by ISKCON's founder, the very role of the guru has come under close scrutiny and attack within ISKCON. Reforms have been instituted in the mid-1980s in most Krishna communities that have permitted the appointment of more than two dozen new gurus, have reduced the fiscal and spiritual authority of any single guru over a geographical zone, and have eliminated the coequal status of most new gurus with the founder, Bhaktivedanta.

A second area of conflict and contention for ISKCON in the 1980s has been economic. During Bhaktivedanta's lifetime, book publishing and distribution was stressed as the central missionary and economic activity. Although various temple and private business ventures were instituted to provide acceptable means of raising funds (e.g., vegetarian restaurants or incense manufacturing), book selling in airports and public places provided a significant portion of most temples' budgets throughout much of the 1970s. However, with the anti-cult movement's increasing success after Jonestown in engendering public suspicion of all groups labeled as cults and with ISKCON's own internal leadership vacuum, many Krishna temples in the 1980s have resorted to various money-making schemes that have caused public criticism at best and have been the source of litigation at worst.

For example, many temples organized teams of devotees that sold cheap Asian reproductions as "original" oil paintings to commercial and other public institutions. Some temples have illegally sold copyrighted sports paraphernalia (T-shirts, baseball caps, etc.). Yet in spite of questionable or illegal money-making schemes, many ISKCON temples are still in deep financial trouble. Furthermore, the Krishnas' leadership and economic improprieties have sometimes led to legal actions or sensational media stories that have created even more public opposition to ISKCON than that which already existed.

The third area of ISKCON's woes in the 1980s has been increasing legal setbacks, with their attendant negative public relations effects. For instance, the 1983 Robin George brainwashing trial in Los Angeles ended with an initial $32.5 million judgment against the Krishnas in California. While the judgment was later reduced by more than half, ISKCON suffered not only the additional expense of its pending appeal, but also the diversion of its energies and resources to a defensive rearguard action. Likewise, the 1987 Boston trial of Susan Murphy and the serious allegations of murder and child abuse associated with two members of the farm settlement at New Vrindaban have undermined confidence in the future of ISKCON both inside and outside the movement. Simply put, the leadership, economic, and legal/public relations problems within and without ISKCON pose the greatest threat to ISKCON's survival in America since its inception in 1965.

Consequently, the scholars who gathered at New Vrindaban in 1985 were not ignorant of the legal and moral improprieties of some Krishna devotees or of the leadership difficulties within ISKCON and the bad public relations image ISKCON has often deserved. Rather, those in attendance had a balanced perspective of the diversity of ISKCON's devotees and communities and were less likely to be surprised at the isolated instances of moral and legal difficulties devotees and temples experience as this fledgling institution (or set of institutions) struggles to mature in a hostile environment. Thus, although the site of the conference itself, New Vrindaban, is currently under investigation as the possible home of illegal activities, the reader should not conclude that more than a few of the leaders or residents knew of the alleged immoral and illegal actions. The evidence seems to be clear that most of the citizens of New Vrindaban are sincere devotees who have given their lives to the building of this spiritual, if extravagant and touristic, temple city. In sum, care must be taken not to impute the all-too-human misbehavior of a few disciples or leaders to all devotees or to all Krishna communities.

Most important, the reader should be aware that what affects ISKCON in California or New York may have little to do with the condition and future of ISKCON in Italy or India. Although ISKCON has been an international religious movement from its inception, temples are incorporated separately and geographical zones vary in the policies and procedures that apply to various spiritual, economic, and institutional activities. The scholars whose essays are included in this volume recognize the complexity of ISKCON's personal and institutional appropriations of the Krishna faith, and, thus, the orientation of most papers is toward what is normative in ISKCON and not what is deviant or exceptional.

Participants and Perspectives

The earliest nondevotee literature on the Hare Krishnas was written by scholars who recognized the Indian roots of ISKCON. Therefore, the Krishnas were viewed by early scholars (e.g., Stillson Judah in *Hare Krishna and the Counterculture* or Francine Daner in *The American Children of Krsna*) as a missionary Hindu movement that met the psychological, social, and spiritual needs of many American youth who were disenchanted with their own culture and religion.[2] However, by the mid-1970s a burgeoning and more widely known anti-cult literature (Ted Patrick's *Let Our Children Go!* or Flo Conway and Jim Siegelman's *Snapping*) proclaimed Hare Krishna to be one of the five most "destructive cults."[3]

These opposing perspectives on the Krishna movement have persisted to the present day in the negative assessments of the more visible and popular anti-cult literature (e.g., Willa Appel's *Cults in America*) and in the less emotional work of scholars whose fieldwork and historical perspective recognizes ISKCON as a devotional Hindu missionary movement in America (Burke Rochford's *Hare Krishna in America* or Larry Shinn's *The Dark Lord*).[4] It was upon the extensive and less well-known scholarly studies of ISKCON that the New Vrindaban conference focused. This fact alone might make this book's treatment of the Hare Krishnas appear novel to the uninitiated reader. However, the summer conference, and this set of essays from it, intended to provide a richer treasure than novelty.

Because there were significant differences of opinion and perspective represented in the work of the selected participants, a primary appeal of the Krishnas' invitation to the New Vrindaban conference was that the discussions would range across a variety of disciplinary areas and among scholars not normally collected in a single academic meeting. The reader should benefit from the many hues and shades of color in the various interpretations to be found in the papers that have resulted from these earlier discussions. One commonality in all of the papers in this volume is to be found in their appreciation for the historical Indian roots of the Krishna movement, however altered by their new American missionary home.

Therefore, the Krishna conference in New Vrindaban was organized purposely around a cross-disciplinary, historical framework as its stated title suggests: "Krishna Consciousness in the West: A Multidisciplinary Critique." Of the twenty-six invited participants, twenty-two were scholars representing various disciplinary specialities, three were Krishna devotees, and one was a former devotee who is currently a graduate student in religious studies at Harvard University. Some of the scholars were invited for their historical, sociological, or psychological investigations into new religious movements, whether or not their studies focused specifically on ISKCON. Others were invited because of their knowledge of the history of American religious traditions or of ISKCON's history. Still others were invited because they were knowledgeable about Indian religious history and the place of Krishna devotion in that historical context.

Fifteen papers were presented during the three days and nights of meetings and each paper session included comments from an invited respondent who had not written a paper. Both the thoroughness of the discussion of each paper (usually lasting approximately one and a half hours) and the multidisciplinary nature of the conversations set this conference apart from yearly professional meetings of most academic groups. Throughout the conference, the only participation in the discussions by Krishna devotees was confined to the participation of the three devotees who read papers themselves.

As the invitation promised, scholars representing historical, sociological, psychological, comparative-religious, and theological perspectives all read papers on some aspect of the Hare Krishnas or their theology. Furthermore, the three Krishna devotees who read papers all were acquainted with a variety of academic perspectives through which they presented their own participant's view of the Krishna faith and the institution, ISKCON, that grows out of it. To provide a logical flow to the discussions, the conference was purposely organized around integrative themes set broadly within the historical development of ISKCON.

The multidisciplinary approach of the participants provided various creative tensions that enlivened the discussions at the conference and have provided for the reader of this book a rich and textured picture of the Hare Krishna faith and movement. Furthermore, the essential points of departure of the participants were so distinctive that these collected papers, like the conference discussions, reflect multifaceted images—a hologram that keeps changing as one assumes different spatial points. Consequently, several layers of interpretation present in these papers represent not so much conflicting views but rather views that reflect diverse beginning points.

One way to characterize the constructive tensions inherent in the papers in this volume is to recognize the poles and places on a variety of continua occupied by the authors. Their views can be classified as interpretive or expressive, external or internal, individual or collective, depending on the different methodological orientations of the authors. On one level, there are those papers that take the historical, sociological, or psychological perspective of the analyst or interpreter. Here the disciplines used to assess ISKCON interpret aspects of the life and faith of Krishna devotees according to canons of scholarship that are extrinsic to the faith assumptions of devotees. Lucy Bregman says that such analysis "makes the interpreter a 'scientific expert' who can understand other people's religiousness better than they do themselves."[5]

On a different level, some of the papers attempt to adopt the perspective of the faithful devotee, whether or not the scholar is actually a devotee. Such investigations take seriously the religious experiences of Krishna devotees and attempt to describe or assess the interior world of the Krishna faith. These studies often focus on the religious experience or conversion experience of devotees or on the logicality of the theological worldview of ISKCON. However, these intrinsic studies, which Bregman refers to as "phenomenological," still use the scholar's vocabulary and evaluative stance.[6]

Therefore, on one continuum these papers represent examples of the "interpreter versus experiencer" split that occurs between those academics or believers who use the outsider's language and categories and those who use the insider's language of faith and repeated scriptural references to describe and assess ISKCON. This bipolarity of vision is similar to that described in Robert Ellwood's *Introducing Religion: From Inside and Outside.*[7] The dichotomy is not that of the researcher versus the believer, but rather, hinges on the speaker's external or internal methodological focus.

For those whose methodological assumptions are based on disciplinary perspectives like that of psychology or sociology, a believer's faith or a religious institution's history are determined and interpreted by criteria and categories beyond the believer's universe of values and meaning. On the other hand, what Bregman calls the phenomenological approach begins by taking seriously the experience and faith of the believer. Some papers in this collection (e.g., Bromley's) reflect the disciplinary orientation of the "interpreter," whereas others (e.g., Shinn's) are driven more by the phenomenologist's attempt to take as the starting point of interpretation the experiences and worldview of the devotees themselves. Of course, most analyses included in this volume actually are located at a point some distance from any radical interpretive pole.

A second continuum of perspectives represented in this volume is that of the uncommitted outsider versus the faithful believer. One of the strengths of this collection is that scholars and devotees have both contributed their assessments of ISKCON. However, this seemingly clear dichotomy is not as stark as it first may appear. Some of the scholars who have written for this volume are empathetically disposed to the faith they are studying. Others are not. Conversely, the devotees whose papers appear in this book have to some extent modified their description of their Krishna faith by adopting the questions, categories, and vocabularies of scholars through which they communicate their own Krishna faith and practice.

Although the three days of discussion and debate in New Vrindaban were completely void of antagonistic, anti-cult sentiment on the one extreme and of proselytizing propaganda on the other, outsiders' and insiders' perspectives were quite evident. For example, the scholar-outsiders often revealed their biases in the topics they chose to discuss and in the academic rationality of their discourse (see Melton's essay). Likewise, the devotees' orientation to the centrality of the Krishna scriptures in defining the normative limits of their discussions exposed their insiders' point of view (see Deadwyler's essay). The reader will observe the sub-rosa discussions between outsiders and insiders in this volume that provide interesting and different interpretive refractions of the same issues.

Yet a third dichotomy that cuts across academic and affiliation lines in these papers is that described by Gordon Allport as the "extrinsic" versus the "intrinsic" understandings of religion and religiosity.[8]

Throughout the three days of discussion of ISKCON, various participants representing differing methodological and faith orientations vacillated between extrinsic and intrinsic understandings of Krishna devotees' faith and practice. Not once was this dichotomy of interpretations named in Allport's terms, yet participants often made a distinction between ISKCON's institutional life and practices (the extrinsic) and that of devotees' altruistic spirituality (the intrinsic). Sometimes this distinction was framed in the institutionally oriented versus the spiritually oriented individual religiosity of ISKCON devotees. Other times this popular interpretive understanding framed explanations of particular ISKCON practices such as book distribution—money motive versus preaching motive. The attentive reader will see a clear example of the intrinsic description of ISKCON in Gelberg's essay.

Of course, these continua are not to be viewed as rigidly deterministic or exclusive of each other. Rather, the reader will find that each dichotomy in its own way reveals ISKCON from the inside and from the outside. The combined effect of the papers that follow is to provide a kaleidoscopic view of a Hindu missionary movement brought to America by an aging, pious Bengali disciple of Krishna. That brightly colored picture is painted in the essays that follow.

Organization of the Volume

The first essay, by Thomas Hopkins, sets this volume in a historical context by describing the emergence of ISKCON from its Indian religious birthplace in Bengal. Hopkins carefully distinguishes the social and historical dimensions of the religious heritage of ISKCON in India from the sixteenth-century reform of Caitanya through the early twentieth-century revival of Bhaktivedanta's guru, Bhaktisiddhanta Sarasvati.

At least two critical features of ISKCON's Indian parent tradition that become critical to ISKCON's later development in America are revealed in Hopkins's historical overview. In the first place, the Gaudiya Vaisnava tradition in Bengal has been a dynamic and flexible religious movement since its inception. For example, Caitanya made clear that Krishna was a god for all people by including outcastes and Muslims in leadership positions in his movement. Likewise, when Bhaktivedanta came to America, he built on the principle of inclusiveness established by Caitanya not only by including women in his movement, but also by allowing them to live celibate lives alongside men in Krishna temples.

The second inescapable conclusion that emerges from Hopkins's essay is that ISKCON is clearly derivative of a traditional, Indian religious tradition. Hopkins shows that ISKCON's guru stood in a long line of missionary Gaudiya preachers and that the theology he preached was rooted in venerable Indian scriptural soil. Bhaktivedanta's preaching in America was a logical extension in content and style of the ministry he carried on in India for two decades before coming to America.

If Hopkins's paper represents an empathetic outsider's view of the Indian historical context out of which ISKCON comes, William Dead-wyler's (Ravindra-svarupa das) essay gives a sense of how a knowledge-able and educated young American devotee of Krishna has appropriated the Krishna faith that Bhaktivedanta brought from India. Deadwyler begins by leading the uninitiated reader through three different para-digms of how people experience time: as a linear-secular progression of events; as a cyclical-religious process of creation and destruction of the world; and as a linear-religious history of salvation.

Deadwyler uses the instructive insights of Mircea Eliade to give a framework to his own explication of how one devotee experiences the world from within the theology of Krishna. Deadwyler points out that Krishna theology turns the linear-secular notion of historical progress on its head with its insistence that what is viewed as the material advance-ment of culture is, from a spiritual point of view, actually the systematic degradation of human culture. Krishna theology then goes another step further in placing all of human history in a cosmic cyclical context (the *Yugas*) that adds an element of impermanence to all of human life and endeavor. What this means to a Krishna devotee, says Deadwyler, is that the material, worldly values and the notions of success based on those values are discredited. To be a faithful Krishna devotee is to abandon the world of one's parents and friends to the extent to which those worlds are not based on devotion to the Lord Krishna.

The positive dimension of the Krishnas' sense of time has to do with the salvation history (linear-sacred) enacted by Krishna through his many incarnations (including Caitanya) in all periods of history. From this soteriological perspective, even the material world and its cyclical framework are understood to be under Krishna's aegis. Although the Krishna devotee experiences all three temporal relationships to the world, the sacred history spawned by Krishna and in which he is the primary actor is central to the devotee's experience. Deadwyler points out that "tradition" fuses all three senses of time together in the varie-gated tapestry of a devotee's experience. Deadwyler's essay reveals how the worldview and faith that was brought from India by Bhaktivedanta has been internalized by a bright and articulate American devotee.

The next two papers set ISKCON squarely in its American context. Gordon Melton traces the ambivalent and changing attitudes of Ameri-cans toward Hinduism from 1883 to 1983. Melton shows that the initially positive and hospitable welcome Hindus received in America quickly turned to suspicion and, finally, to open hostility. Melton outlines in careful detail the riots and periods of violence that have affected Hindus and Indians of various creeds (e.g., Punjabi Sikhs) in America. After a period of relative calm in Hindu-American relations, the last two decades have witnessed a resurgence of openly hostile anti-Hindu attitudes.

With the repeal of the Asian exclusion acts in 1965, a flood of Asian religious teachers, many from India, poured into America. Bhaktivedanta and his followers were quickly stereotyped with the broad anti-cult brush that lumped all Asian groups together as dangerous and deceptive cults. Melton's essay makes the point clearly that one must put current responses to the Hare Krishnas in the historical context of anti-Hindu sentiment in America that is at least a century old.

Robert Ellwood's paper focuses more sharply than Melton's on the countercultural environment in which ISKCON grew during its early years in America. Ellwood argues that ISKCON caught the "rising tide" of the counterculture at just the right historical moment and rode it to early proselytizing successes. ISKCON utilized the counterculture's anti-technology and human potential themes as well as its psychedelic vocabulary to appeal to open-minded youth. Echoing the main theme of Stillson Judah's book, *Hare Krishna and the Counterculture* (1964), Ellwood perceives the appeal of Krishna life and faith to be linked to the counterculture values and attitudes of American youth in the 1960s.

Ellwood directs his attention toward the end of his paper to current conversion theories that his analysis finds wanting. He briefly describes two poles of interpretation used to assess cult conversions: deprivation theories and cognitive theories. He asserts that cognitive theories offer the better interpretations of Krishna conversions in the 1960s because they allow for the "inner distress" that precedes most conversions while, at the same time, giving greater weight to the positive factors of free choice and theological appeal that most Krishna conversions evidence. Ellwood's final comments on conversions lead the reader naturally to the next two essays on conversion to ISKCON.

Larry Shinn's paper explores the nature of religious conversion among the Hare Krishnas as a way of rethinking the current scholarship on religious affiliation processes. He bases his study on four years of field-work (participant observation and interviews) among the Hare Krishnas. He offers his readers two abridged conversion biographies as spring-boards to his discussion of conversion theories. The first conversion biography, that of a young woman named Sita, invites psychoanalytic interpretations based upon conflicts residing in the unconscious. Eric Erikson's and Francine Daner's understandings of conversion are outlined to provide an explication of how some persons view unconscious processes to be at work in Krishna devotees' conversions.

The second biography Shinn recounts is that of Rama, which reveals a serious spiritual quest that was promoted by counterculture disenchantment with American religious and political institutions in the late 1960s. Rama's story, therefore, prompts the investigator or interpreter to consider the conscious and conceptual (i.e., theological) elements in this young man's slow and deliberate conversion to his present Krishna faith. Using the insights of Victor Frankl and James Fowler, Shinn argues that a search for meaning that is conscious and conceptual undergirds not only Rama's conversion but that of many Krishna devotees including Sita. The thrust of Shinn's paper is to question easy reliance on anti-cult or psychoanalytic theories of conversion.

The paper by Steven Gelberg (Subhananda dasa) provides a description of how one Krishna devotee understands conversion to ISKCON. After summarizing ISKCON's historical and theological Indian devotional roots, Gelberg enumerates eight general characteristics of the convert's life. Gelberg points to intrinsic (as opposed to instrumental) motivations most devotees have as they appropriate the dualistic Krishna theology. He also provides an idealized description of the ascetic life, personalistic devotion, and transformational consciousness that attends a devotee's genuine conversion. Gelberg concludes by rehearsing the mediational, utilitarian, and evangelistic dimensions of a devotee's reborn life.

Gelberg describes a typical day in the life of a Hare Krishna devotee to allow the reader to see how the eight general characteristics of the convert's life are exemplified in daily life in a Krishna temple. The main focus of this portrayal is on the arduous and lengthy periods of devotional activity that life in a Krishna temple demands. Gelberg concludes with a suggestion that the academic study of groups like ISKCON should be more sensitive to "the personal religious cognition and experience" that underlie the externally observable behavior.

The next set of papers build on the historical and religious contexts already presented by offering a comparative analysis of ISKCON communities in India and America. The first essay in this section examines how Indian Krishna devotees accept their American counterparts. The second traces the attempt by a Hare Krishna community in rural West Virginia to simultaneously adjust to the requisites of American society and to preserve its religious commitments and Hindu culture.

Charles Brooks's essay takes the reader to the present-day Indian pilgrimage village of Vrindaban. Vrindaban is the birthplace of Krishna according to Indian scripture and today remains a thriving pilgrimage town for hundreds of thousands of Krishna devotees each year. Brooks describes the theological significance of Vrindaban as a celestial space apart from the phenomenal world, a town developed by Bengali worshippers of Krishna, and an India-wide pilgrimage center. These conceptions of Vrindaban found in religious texts and described by devotees serve as the context into which ISKCON came in the mid-1970s.

Brooks tells several stories of the interaction between ISKCON's Krishna devotees and local Vrindaban Krishna devotees. He spells out the religious and social (caste) hurdles that ISKCON had to overcome to be accepted by the indigenous populace. In a fascinating exposition, Brooks reveals how ISKCON devotees have slowly gained not only acceptance but a favored status in Vrindaban. Although caste barriers still stand in the way of full acceptance of ISKCON devotees by some local residents of Vrindaban, those barriers are sometimes overcome by the religious status accorded to ISKCON's disciples. Brooks concludes that ISKCON's devotees have achieved a permanent place for themselves in Krishna's holy city that will have an impact far beyond their relatively small numbers.

Blake Michael briefly traces the history of Vrindaban's American namesake, New Vrindaban, a community literally carved out of the West Virginia wilderness. The community's early history was one of struggle and conflict with the surrounding native residents. New Vrindaban's accommodation challenge was twofold: how to gain legitimacy within the larger societal context and how at the same time to remain faithful to traditional Hindu religious practices upon which the community was based. The residents of New Vrindaban addressed the first problem in three ways: supporting publications, conferences, and inter-religious dialogue; demonstrating an acceptance of the most fundamental American secular values (rectitude, pragmatism, hard work, and success); and undertaking ministries to Indian immigrants in America, a constituency that lent credibility, financial support, and a more conventional image to the movement. Traditional Hindu values have been defended through emphasizing the spiritual purpose of elements of religious experience with which visitors come in contact when they visit New Vrindaban: drawing on the tradition of pilgrimage, the community has been designed to attract tourists to acquaint Americans with Krishna Consciousness; serving *prasada* (food offered to the Lord, which then imparts divine grace to the humans who consume it); and creating the opportunity for visitors to see and be seen by the divine images in the temple (*darsana*), which members understand to be a religious act and to have spiritual consequences irrespective of individual intent. Though New Vrindaban's guru, Bhaktipada, has been expelled from ISKCON by the GBC, this farm and tourist community still provides a good example of the ways Krishna settlements seek American cultural legitimacy while remaining faithful to their Indian Hindu legacy.

The final three essays in this volume explore the societal reaction to ISKCON. The Saliba and Gordon papers examine the religious and mental health responses to Hare Krishna. The Bromley paper traces the development of the Anti-Cult Movement and its impact on the Hare Krishna movement.

In tracing the Christian and Jewish responses to ISKCON, John Saliba observes that the negative response of established faiths to ISKCON is not surprising. Members of new religions typically were members of a traditional faith before conversion to ISKCON. Apostasy, willful renunciation of one's faith, generates more reaction than simply assuming the status of lapsed member. Further, there is an ideological confrontation between ISKCON and established religions in which each side asserts the supremacy of its position.

Saliba finds that there are three major types of responses by established churches to new religious groups: apologetics, the most common response, which involves engaging in a debate with one or more new groups in order to defend theological positions against opposing convictions and to persuade opponents of the truth of traditional theology; "neglect," in which the established churches simply ignore the newcomers; and the development of mutual understanding and cooperation.

The primacy of apologetics is predictable in light of the interpretation of the meaning of new religions by established religions. Both Jewish and Christian churches have viewed new religions such as ISKCON as "cults." The Christian denominations have relied more on theological definitions of the term "cult," although they have incorporated pejorative elements of sociological and psychological theory (e.g., brainwashing, authoritarianism) into their depiction of "cults" as well. By contrast, the Jewish response to new religious groups has relied more heavily on the secular, coercive persuasion explanation for cult membership and has identified "cults" as the cause of family conflict and loss of individual freedom. Because ISKCON is non-Christian, there is little difficulty in refuting the validity of ISKCON's theology and declaring it a "cult" simply by comparing its beliefs with orthodox Christian tenets of faith. Linking ISKCON to the secular brainwashing based model of a cult is accomplished by identifying specific organizational characteristics (e.g., communalism) and ritualistic observances (e.g., chanting) that putatively are conducive to loss of individual "free will."

The religious explanation for the existence of ISKCON and other new religious groups and for individuals' affiliation with them does not rest solely on nefarious cultic practices, however. Saliba emphasizes that both Christian and Jewish writers identify various factors that provide fertile soil for the development of "cults," such as overemphasis on materialistic and relativistic value systems, a corresponding sense of alienation and loneliness, and a failure by Christianity and Judaism to provide youth with a solid foundation for religious life. From this perspective, the young adults who are the primary converts to ISKCON are simply responding to their own sense of disillusionment with a materialistic culture, or the counterculture, which formed in reaction to it and to the disintegration of family life and authority. Thus, in their explanations for the emergence of new religions and for conversions to them, Christian and Jewish churches accept some of the responsibility for their existence and popularity.

In concluding, Saliba stresses that the religious literature on Hare Krishna is not wholly polarized. Both the Christian and Jewish responses are variegated and contain balanced as well as rhetorical, doctrinaire positions. Although Saliba predicts that the religious response to Hare Krishna will continue to be dominated by the "anti-cult" perspective, he sees the possibility of greater dialogue between established and emergent religious traditions as well.

One of the major allegations made against Hare Krishna, as well as other new religious groups, has been that conversion and commitment to the Krishna faith and lifestyle can produce deleterious mental health effects. In a thorough exploration of the various surveys and clinical studies that address this issue, James Gordon distinguishes two different types of survey research. One set of studies begins with the psychological needs that new religions fulfill for individuals and then reports the extent of psychopathology among members of these groups. Although some of these surveys do show psychopathology among members of new religious groups, most note positive psychological benefits for members. Gordon also points out, however, that these findings do not gainsay the emotional difficulties many individuals face in breaking ties with these groups.

The second type of literature Gordon surveys begins with the assumption that new religions are pathogenic. These studies, which utilize various investigative methodologies, rely predominantly on samples of former members (often forceably removed) and retrospective accounts by these individuals. Predictably, findings from this line of research are much less sanguine about the mental health implications of membership in new religious groups. Gordon criticizes both types of surveys as unsystematic and providing little reliable data. In addition to survey research, there have been a number of clinical studies of personality characteristics of Hare Krishna members. The methodologies used in this line of research have varied from case report and informal surveys to controlled clinical/experimental studies. The most extensive and best designed of these clinical studies do not reveal any unusual pattern of dysfunction among Krishna devotees.

Although Gordon's review of the mental-health-related research on

ISKCON does not indicate that there are demonstrable pathological consequences of membership, he emphasizes that definitive conclusions cannot be formulated on the basis of existing research. Gordon identifies a number of problems characteristic of one or more of the studies he reviews. For example, they include diverse groups together in the same sample; gather data on a single group, which limits the capacity for generalization of findings; employ small samples, which raises questions about representativeness; are prone to make inferences about groups from idiosyncratic data; and fail to deal with the implications of using current and former members as data sources. Gordon concludes by arguing for more broadly based research that entails phenomenological, sociological, anthropological, and psychological approaches to ISKCON and lays out an initial agenda for such interdisciplinary research.

In the final essay in this volume David Bromley traces the strategic development of the Anti-Cult Movement and its impact on new religious movements by using controversies involving Hare Krishna to document those developments substantively. As Bromley observes, the public reaction to Hare Krishna is not unique; it is simply part of a pervasive historical pattern of hostility to new religious groups. Throughout American history, in virtually every instance when new religious groups have appeared, they have been the objects of conflict and repression. In some notable cases, such as the nineteenth-century reaction to Catholicism and Mormonism and the current reaction to cults, the public reactions have developed into major "social scares." Such social scares have been based on fears of social subversion, and "subversion mythologies" have emerged as interpretive frameworks for understanding the presumed dangers posed by the new groups.

Bromley argues that the emergence of the contemporary cult scare, like its historical predecessors, must be viewed as the product of social conflict between established institutions defending existing social arrangements and new religious movements seeking social change. In the case of contemporary new religions, the family (and specifically the families of youthful converts) was the primary locus of opposition to new religions although government, education, media, and religion also had independent reasons for opposing new religious groups. In addition, some of the more inflammatory rhetoric and radical practices of new religions fanned the flames of opposition.

The objectives of the Anti-Cult Movement consistently have been both to extricate individual members from new religious groups and to combat the groups themselves. Bromley examines the ideology of the Anti-Cult Movement and traces its strategic development using two major legal cases involving ISKCON (the Robin George and Edward Shapiro cases) that together spanned the decade between the mid-1970s and mid-1980s. Reflecting the perspective of its familial constituency, anti-cult ideology defends the occupational and domestic career socialization goals of the family and the large constellation of rational, analytic, and instrumental values that support the associated institutional arrangements. These issues energized both the George and Shapiro families to take action against ISKCON. The two cases are instructive not only because they illustrate the cultural values underpinning the anti-cult perspective but also because they demarcate vital points in the strategic development of the Anti-Cult Movement. The Shapiro case involved a coercive deprogramming from Hare Krishna, which reflected early anti-cult strategy. The George case involved a civil suit against Hare Krishna subsequent to the plaintiff's disaffiliation from the movement and relied heavily on psychiatric testimony. While both cases revolved around charges of brainwashing by Hare Krishna devotees, Bromley delineates the steady movement of the anti-cultists toward a psychopathological definition of cultic involvement and a corresponding reliance on medical/psychiatric expert testimony to document the deleterious mental health consequences of affiliation with new religious movements. The effect of this strategic evolution, Bromley asserts, is to medicalize religious deviance.

In sum, this volume offers a complex, interdisciplinary view of ISKCON that stands in sharp contrast to the stereotypical imagery generated by the current controversy surrounding new religious groups in the United States. The papers explore the richness of the Krishna religious tradition, the cross-fertilization of Indian and American cultures through the Krishna movement, the process of individual searches by youthful American devotees for personal and religious meaning through Eastern religious tradition, and the reaction to ISKCON and other Hindu religions through American history. The book thus documents both the vitality and precariousness of Krishna Consciousness in the West. Although the organizational future of ISKCON cannot be projected from these papers, taken together they provide, through a case study of a single alternative religious movement, a broad perspective on the multifaceted, dynamic process by which human beings create and recreate the symbolic reality that they inhabit.

Notes

1. For a thorough insider's portrait of Prabhupada and a clear indication of the deep Indian roots of ISKCON, see Satsvarupa dasa Goswami, *Srila Prabhupada-lilamrta*, 6 vols. (Los Angeles: Bhaktivedanta Book Trust, 1980–82).

2. See Stillson Judah, *Hare Krishna and the Counterculture* (New York: John Wiley and Sons, 1974), and Francine Jeanne Daner, *The American Children of*

Krsna: A Study of the Hare Krsna Movement (New York: Holt, Rinehart and Winston, 1976).

3. See Flo Conway and Jim Siegelman, *Snapping: America's Epidemic of Sudden Personality Change* (Philadelphia: J. B. Lippincott, 1978), and Ted Patrick and Tom Dulack, *Let Our Children Go!* (New York: Ballantine Books, 1976).

4. Willa Appel, *Cults in America: Programmed for Paradise* (New York: Holt, Rinehart and Winston, 1983); Burke Rochford, *Hare Krishna in America* (New Brunswick, NJ: Rutgers University Press, 1985); and Larry D. Shinn, *The Dark Lord: Cult Images and the Hare Krishnas in America* (Philadelphia: The Westminster Press, 1987).

5. Lucy Bregman, "The Interpreter/Experiencer Split: Three Models in the Psychology of Religion," *Journal of the American Academy of Religion* 46, no. 2 (June 1978) 119–27.

6. Ibid., pp. 128–37.

7. Robert S. Ellwood, Jr., ed., *Introducing Religion: From Inside and Outside* (Englewood Cliffs, NJ: Prentice-Hall, 1978).

8. See Gordon W. Allport, *The Individual and His Religion* (New York: Macmillan, 1950) and such contemporary extensions of his intrinsic/extrinsic categories as those of Bernard Stritka, Ralph W. Hood, Jr., and Richard L. Gorsuch, *The Psychology of Religion* (Englewood Cliffs, NJ: Prentice-Hall, 1985), pp. 18–19 and passim.

II. Emergence of ISKCON

The Social and Religious Background for Transmission of Gaudiya Vaisnavism to the West

Thomas J. Hopkins

The Social and Religious Background of Nineteenth-Century Bengal

From the middle of the eighteenth century until well into the twentieth century, Bengal was the focal point of social and religious change in India. The cause of this change, or the catalyst for it, was the introduction of British culture—more generally, Western culture—by the East India Company. The way this affected Bengal, however, and the kinds of changes that resulted, were strongly influenced by the special characteristics of Bengal society.

BENGAL BEFORE THE BRITISH

Long before the coming of the British, the social and religious patterns in Bengal had been distinctively different from those in the orthodox Hindu heartland of North India. The center of Vedic or Brahmanical orthodoxy from about 800 B.C.E. onward was the region called Aryavarta between the Ganges and Yamuna rivers. East of that region in ancient times was the kingdom of Magadha, in what is now Bihar, where around 500 B.C.E. both the Buddhist and Jaina movements began and where around 320 B.C.E. the nonorthodox Mauryan dynasty was founded. Bengal, even further to the east, was thus insulated from the full impact of Brahmanical orthodoxy for many centuries, and Buddhism—especially Mahayana Buddhism of the Tantric variety—remained strong there long after it had lost its influence in other regions of India. The theistic Hinduism that was centered on the figures of Vishnu and Shiva emerged in Bengal as elsewhere during the Gupta Empire from the fourth to the sixth centuries, but even afterward, from the eighth through the eleventh centuries, Bengal was ruled by Buddhist kings of the Pala Dynasty.

This background no doubt helps explain why, according to Bengal tradition, there were no orthodox upper-level Hindu castes in Bengal until the eleventh century of the common era. At that point, so tradition says, a local king named Adisura, himself a member of the Vaidya or physician caste of Sudra origin, became concerned about the ignorance of those who claimed to be Brahmans in his kingdom and imported five learned Brahmans and their five servants (Sudras) from the Hindu kingdom of Kananj in Aryavarta. Settled in Bengal with their families, the five Brahmans and five Sudras became the progenitors of five Brahman and five Kayastba clans respectively. To distinguish them from indigenous Brahmans, the five imported Brahmans and their descendants were classified as Kulina ("superior") Brahmans and became the clans known later by their Anglicized names (see chart 1) as the Mukherjis, Chatterjis, Bannerjis, Gangulis, and Bhattacharjis.

According to the traditional accounts, it was expected that all of the imported Sudras and their Kayastha descendants would also be given Kulina status. As it turned out, however, only four of the imported Sudras were designated as Kulinas and only three of the four remained in Bengal proper; these three produced the three main Kulina Kayastha clans of Bengal, the Mitras, Boses, and Choses, while the fourth produced the Kulina Kayastha clan of the Uhas in eastern Bengal. The fifth Sudra, the accounts tell us, was presented to King Adisura for approval like the others but refused to accept the role of a servant appropriate to a Sudra; instead, he claimed that he was superior even to the Brahmans. Having failed to meet the standard of humility appropriate to a Kulina, he was denied that status and became instead the progenitor of the highest non-Kulina Kayastha clan, the Dattas or Dutts.

We will hear more of the Dutt clan later, because it was from the Dutts that several important religious leaders emerged in the nineteenth century, including the real founder of the Krishna Consciousness movement, Bhaktivinoda Thakur (Kedarnath Dutt), and the founder of the Vedanta Society, Vivekananda (Narendranath Dutt). First, we must consider yet another source of social and religious complexity, the coming of Muslim rule to Bengal.

Muslim rule began in Bengal with the conquest of most of the region by Turko-Afghan forces near the start of the thirteenth century, and continued through a series of dynasties and changes in local circumstances until the British gained de facto control in 1765. From 1576 onward, Bengal had been an integral part of the Mughal Empire, administered by a provincial governor. Many Bengalis had converted to Islam during the centuries of Muslim domination, especially in east Bengal,

CHART 1

LEADING CASTES, CLANS, AND FAMILIES IN BENGAL IN THE 19TH AND 20TH CENTURIES

KULĪNA BRĀHMANS
(PRIESTS/TEACHERS)

THE PANCOPĀDHYĀYA, FIVE PURE BRĀHMAN CASTES BROUGHT TO BENGAL FROM KANAUJ BY ĀDIŚURA IN THE 11TH CENTURY WHEN PĀLA CONTROL WAS DECLINING; DESIGNATED AS KULĪNA BY BALĀL SENA IN THE 12TH CENTURY

UKHERJI (MUKHOPĀDHYĀYA)

HATTERJI (CAṬṬOPĀDHYĀYA)

ANNERJI (BANDHYOPĀDHYĀYA)

ANGULI (GAṄGYOPĀDHYĀYA)

HATTACHARJI (BHAṬṬĀCĀRYA)
[PŪJĀRĪS]

{ GADĀDHAR CHATTERJI (RĀMAKṚṢṆA)
    (1834-1886)
  BANKIM CHANDRA CHATTERJI [BENGALI WRITER]
    (1838-1894)

{ ISWARCHANDRA VIDYĀSAGAR (1820-1891)
  [PRINCIPAL OF SANSKRIT COLLEGE 1851-1858,
  SOCIAL REFORMER — ESP. FOR WOMEN'S RIGHTS]

↓ LOST KULĪNA STATUS ↓

NON-KULĪNA BRĀHMANS
(LANDOWNERS AND
ENTREPRENEURS)

AGORE (REFERRED TO AS "PĪRILI"
ECAUSE THEY GAVE DAUGHTERS
MARRIAGE TO MUSLIM RULERS)

DVARAKANATH TAGORE
    (1764-1846)
DEBENDRANATH TAGORE
    (1817-1905)
RABINDRANATH TAGORE
    (1861-1941)

KULĪNA KĀYASTHAS
(TRADITIONAL WRITER/
CLERICAL CASTES)

MITRA

BOSE   { RAJNARAIN BOSE
         [BRĀHMO SAMĀJ]
         SUBHAS CHANDRA BOSE
         (1897-1945)

GHOSE { AUROBIṄDO GHOSE
         (1872-1950)

NON-KULĪNA KĀYASTHAS

DUTT (DATTA)

    AKKHOY KUMAR DUTT (1820-1866)
       [EARLY BRĀHMO SAMĀJ LEADER]
    MICHAEL MADHUSUDAN DUTT (1824-1873)
       [BENGALI WRITER, CONVERTED TO CHRISTIANITY IN 1843]
    KEDARNATH DUTT (BHAKTIVINODE THAKUR) (1838-1914)
       [DISTRICT MAGISTRATE AND GAUDĪYA VAIṢṆAVA LEADER]
    NARENDRANATH DUTT (VIVEKĀNANDA) (1863-1902)
       [FOUNDER OF VEDĀNTA SOCIETY IN 1895 AND
       RAMAKRISHNA MISSION IN 1897]

↑ UPWARDLY MOBILE ↑

VAIDYAS
(TRADITIONAL ĀYURVEDIC
PHYSICIANS OF ŚŪDRA ORIGIN,
BUT ALSO RULERS —
E.G., ĀDIŚURA)

SEN   { KESHUB CHUNDER SEN
        (1838-1884)

DASGUPTA

SENGUPTA

BRĀHMAN FAMILIES
THAT HAD TAKEN
MUSLIM TITLES
AS FAMILY NAMES

OY (RĀYA)
    RAM MOHAN ROY (1772-1833)
       [FOUNDER OF BRĀHMO SAMĀJ,
       "THE FIRST MODERN INDIAN"]

HAUDHURY

AZUMDAR
    PROTAP CHUNDER MAZUMDAR (1840-1905)
       [COUSIN OF KESHUB CHUNDER SEN; REPRESENTED
       BRĀHMO SAMĀJ AT PARLIAMENT OF RELIGIONS IN
       CHICAGO IN 1893]

and the Hindu community was generally on the defensive. The Bengal Vaisnava saint Caitanya (1486–1533) had inspired a major Hindu revival early in the sixteenth century with his ecstatic devotion to Krishna, but the vitality of this movement had declined during the long period of Mughal rule. In the absence of a Hindu king to provide unity and support, Hindu institutions in general languished and the separate Hindu religious communities tended to go their way in relative isolation from each other.

The pervasive Muslim presence, combined with Muslim control of the institutions of governance and the instruments of reward, had brought about changes within Hindu society by the time the British arrived. The effects were most evident among the upper echelons of Hindu society, especially the Kulina castes, whose status depended on the preservation of ritual purity. Under Hindu rulers, they would have been among the most favored members of society as advisers, ministers, and religious functionaries serving the king. Under Muslim rulers, their access to royal power was limited and contact involved losing their ritual purity. Deprived of power, they emphasized their purity, and had become defensively conservative with regard to caste restrictions and social regulations to protect their status in the only place where it was acknowledged—the Hindu socioreligious hierarchy.

The conservatism of the elite castes, who traditionally controlled Hindu social regulations, had permeated most of Hindu society by the eighteenth century and was reflected in the current social hierarchy. Hindus who had entered into direct involvement with Muslim rulers, as some had done and were doing, had paid a price in hierarchical ranking. Some individual Hindu families such as the Tagores, for example, gave daughters in marriage to Muslim rulers and had lost their Kulina status. Other families from the elite Hindu castes had received Muslim titles such as Raya (Roy), Chaudhuri, or Mazumdar as a reward for their services and had adopted these as family names, obscuring their Hindu caste identities while enhancing their status with Muslims, and had lost whatever place they might previously have had as Kulinas. In relations with Muslims, it was clear that high-caste Hindus played a zero-sum game in which the degree of involvement with non-Hindu rulers meant a corresponding loss in Hindu social ranking.

This pattern was well established by the time the British entered Bengal as traders for the East India Company in the mid-seventeenth century under grants from the Mughal emperor and continued into the eighteenth century as the British presence increased. By the middle of the eighteenth century, the British were contending for power with local Muslim authorities, and after a successful military campaign against the provincial ruler in Bengal in 1757 they were themselves the de facto rulers. This position was confirmed in 1765 when the Company was granted the right to serve as the *Diwan,* the official revenue collector, for the by-then largely powerless Mughal empire. Given the previous pattern of Hindu response to non-Hindu rulers, it was natural that Hindus would maintain similar relations with the new *Diwan.* Only a few at first saw the differences and the advantages in the change and used it to open up new opportunities. The story of the next hundred years in Bengal is largely the story of how this group of Hindus created from those opportunities a new Hindu culture that increasingly challenged the values of the orthodox elite.

BENGAL UNDER COMPANY RULE

When the East India Company became the Diwan of Bengal, it inherited a terrible economic situation that for some time the Company and its agents made worse. Bengal had been heavily taxed to support the military campaigns carried out elsewhere in India by Aurangzeb (1658–1707), the last of the major Mughal emperors. Local power struggles after Aurangzeb's death had further disrupted the economy, and to this was added an increasing drain of wealth out of the country in British private fortunes and Company trade—the former largely due to the abuse of private trade privileges by Company agents, the latter due to the Company's concern to show a profit to its owners in England to justify the heavy investment in Bengal. When the Company took over as Diwan, it exacted heavy and nonnegotiable land revenues from the landowners in its territory even during a disastrous famine in 1770 that killed or dislocated an estimated one-third of the rural population. As hardship continued, many former landholding families were forced to transfer their land to those who could afford to make the revenue payments—in practice, mainly those Bengalis who had profited from British trade as suppliers, agents, and bankers for the Company.

The Bengalis who profited from the economic chaos of the later eighteenth century came mainly from a particular category of the Hindu population. When British rule replaced Muslim rule, the Muslim elite lost power and status and largely withdrew from direct involvement with their conquerors. The Hindu Kulina castes, both Brahmans and Kayasthas, remained aloof from the new rulers as they had from the old to preserve their upper ranks; the non-Kulina castes, on the other hand, were less concerned about purity and, in the case of families like the Tagores and Roys, were accustomed to relations with non-Hindu rulers. Recognizing the advantages of working with the Company, many of these non-Kulinas used involvement with the British to improve their economic position during the eighteenth century and emerged by the early 1800s as wealthy landowners and entrepreneurs. By then, their contacts with the British had made them aware of the value of Western culture and had started them on the path to Westernization. The more farsighted among them recognized that greater knowledge of Western culture would help assure their newly won positions, and their new wealth allowed them to pursue this goal for themselves and their children. With the motive and resources to do so, they gravitated to Calcutta, the center of Western culture in Bengal, and began to create the institutions that would give them access to what the West had to offer.

Calcutta in the early nineteenth century was the focal point of many interests. For the British, Calcutta was the center of administration for an enterprise that was still officially the Company but was increasingly coming under the control of Parliament. For the newly wealthy Hindus, Calcutta was the place where power and wealth could be gained and used in relative freedom from the restraints of orthodox Hindu society, and it was also the source of Western culture. For Christian missionaries, who were allowed to operate in Company territory after 1813, Calcutta was a place where they had access to some of the best young minds in Bengal. All of these interests came together in a concern for education, although it took some time for the various parties to agree on what form it should take. Both the Westernizing Hindus and the missionaries agreed at least that the medium should be English, and both established English language schools early in the century. By the 1840s the British administration had been won over to this view also, and by the 1850s there were numerous schools and several colleges in Calcutta providing comprehensive English education based on the British model.

Another set of problems emerged in the early nineteenth century, however, that was much more difficult to solve. Westernization was not an unmixed blessing for those Hindus who were confronted with Western culture for the first time, or whose children were beginning to be Westernized. Westernization offered these mostly non-Kulina Brahmans and Kayasthas a way to social mobility that was impossible within orthodox Hindu society, where they were and would always be ranked below the Kulinas. By sidestepping the traditional Hindu caste system, however, they were also leaving their place in the Hindu scheme of things and entering a cultural and social system in which they had no place— or, perhaps worse, competing for status with the British in a system where the British held the top places no less securely than the Kulina Brahmans and Kayasthas did in the Hindu hierarchy. If this was true socially, it was even truer religiously, because the religion that dominated the Western cultural system was Christianity. Most of the Westernizing Hindus did not want to become Christians, or have their children become Christians; that was a price they were not prepared to pay for

Westernization. What they needed was a form of Hinduism in which they could take the leading roles, a Hinduism that expressed the essence of Hinduism without its social and religious defects and was compatible with the best of Western culture: its reason, its social concern, and its ethical monotheism.

The first solution to this problem of the newly wealthy and newly Westernizing Hindus was provided by Ram Mohan Roy (1772–1833) in the form of the Brahmo Samaj, which Roy founded in 1828. Son of a non-Kulina Brahman and himself a successful entrepreneur, Ram Mohan spent a quarter century before he founded the Brahmo Samaj in search of a religious position that met his standards of reason and universality. He rejected Hindu polytheism and image worship as sectarian and sinful, and opted instead for the monotheism of the Hindu Vedanta tradition based on the *Upanishads*, which he interpreted as teaching the worship of Brahman as the sole creator and supporter of the universe. He was attracted to the ethics of Jesus, but rejected Christian Trinitarian theology, and for a few years thought that he could find the amalgam of views he sought in Unitarianism. When he realized that Unitarianism could not satisfy Hindus' needs, however, he founded the Brahmo Samaj as a rational ethical expression of Vedantic theism.

Ram Mohan's successor as leader of the Brahmo Samaj, Debendranath Tagore (1817–1905), another non-Kulina Brahman, did little to alter the basic viewpoints developed by Roy. He was just as opposed to popular Hinduism as his predecessor, just as much an enemy of image worship, and just as much committed to the formlessness of God and to reason as the test of religious truth. Nor was he alone in this, as the success of the Brahmo Samaj shows. It *did* give Hindus a way of countering attacks by Christians, it *did* give them a way of being Hindu without being subject to the control of Kulina priests, and it *did* give them a base for religious and social reform. The difficulty was that its appeal was limited almost entirely to a wealthy, reason-oriented, urban intellectual elite. It might be capable of evoking religious experience, but it was basically an intellectual religion without the mythic and emotional richness of the popular and puranic traditions.

As late as the 1860s there was as yet no equivalent effort to find religious meaning for Westernized Hindus in the popular devotional forms of Bengal Hinduism, the Sakta tradition that centered on the worship of the Goddess as Kali or Durga and the Vaisnava tradition of Caitanya—Gaudiya Vaisnavism—that centered on the worship of Krishna. Westernized Hindus who had passed through British education in Calcutta's college had nothing but disdain for what they saw as crude superstitious forms of polytheistic idol worship. These traditions themselves, on the other hand, had neither the leadership the intellec tual resources, or the practical know-how to present their views effectively to Westernized intellectuals. Nevertheless, each did find its champions: the Sakta tradition in Ramakrishna (1836–86) and Vivekananda (1863–1902), the Gaudiya Vaisnava tradition in Bhaktivinoda Thakur (1838–1914), Bhaktisiddhanta Sarasvati (1874–1937), and, last but not least, A. C. Bhaktivedanta Swami (1896–1977). The Sakta tradition is another story, although it also involves a non-Kulina Kayastha from the Dutt clan, Vivekananda. Our story concerns the Gaudiya Vaisnava tradition, and how it was shaped for its Western journey by Bhaktivinoda Thakur.

The Contribution of Bhaktivinoda Thakur

In the minds of those who went to Calcutta's British/Christian colleges or belonged to the Brahmo Samaj, Gaudiya Vaisnavism represented one of the best examples of what was wrong with traditional Hinduism. It was emotional rather than rational; it was steeped in polytheistic puranic mythology ("superstition"); it was laden with rituals centered on material images ("idols," as they had been taught to say); and, though it emphasized Krishna, it was not the rational warrior Krishna it most ardently worshiped but rather the misbehaving cowherd Krishna Gopala and his mistress Radha. One might admire its rich tradition of stories for literary purposes, but few among the educated classes were prepared to give it credence as a *religion* worthy of serious attention. Until Bhaktivinoda Thakur, the Gaudiya Vaisnava tradition in the nineteenth century had no leaders who could raise it above the level of a popular religiosity based more on heredity and habit than on understanding. This task he set himself to do; this conference and the setting in which it was held are only two of the many proofs of how successful he was.

Bhaktivinoda Thakur was born in 1838 as Kedarnath Dutt (see chart 2), son of Anandacandre Dutt, a pious and unworldly Gaudiya Vaisnava, and Jagat Mohini Devi, daughter of a wealthy Zamindar of the Mitra clan.[1] As was typical of wealthy Kayasthas of that period, Kedarnath was started early with an English education, attended high school in Calcutta at the Hindu Charitable Institution, and completed his education at Scottish Churches' College. He was thus quite representative of that large group of nineteenth-century Bengalis from non-Kulina backgrounds who had relatively high social status, an intellectual orientation, and an English education that prepared them for life under British rule.

Kedarnath began his postcollegiate career as a teacher in Orissa, where he was one of the pioneers of English education, but he also began to study law along with his teaching duties. He passed his law

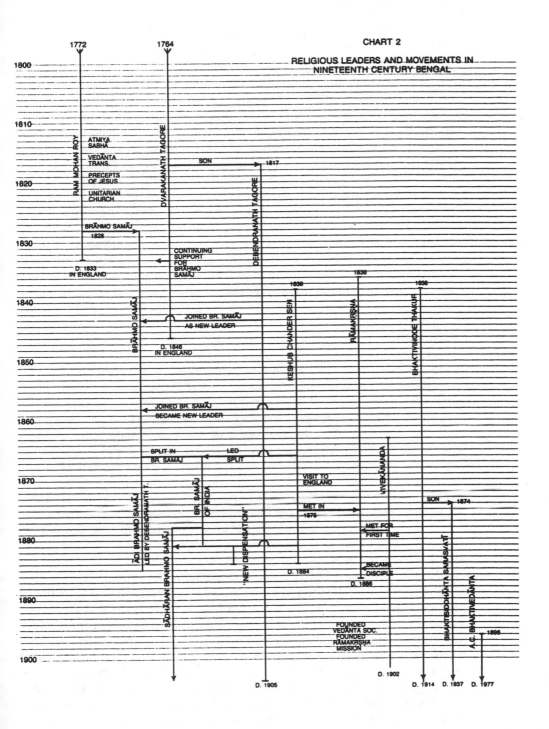

CHART 2

RELIGIOUS LEADERS AND MOVEMENTS IN
NINETEENTH CENTURY BENGAL

1772   1764

1800

1810

RAM MOHAN ROY

DVARAKANATH TAGORE

ATMIYA
SABHA

VEDĀNTA
TRANS.

SON   1817

PRECEPTS
OF JESUS

1820

UNITARIAN
CHURCH

DEBENDRANATH TAGORE

BRĀHMO SAMĀJ

1828

1830

D. 1833
IN ENGLAND

CONTINUING
SUPPORT
FOR
BRAHMO
SAMĀJ

1836

1836

1836

1840

BRĀHMO SAMĀJ

JOINED BR. SAMĀJ
AS NEW LEADER

KESHUB CHANDER SEN

RĀMAKRSNA

BHAKTIVINODE THAKUR

D. 1848
IN ENGLAND

1850

JOINED BR. SAMĀJ

BECAME NEW LEADER

1860

SPLIT IN
BR. SAMĀJ

LED
SPLIT

VISIT TO
ENGLAND

VIVEKANANDA

1870

ĀDI BRAHMO SAMĀJ
LED BY DEBENDRANATH T.

BR. SAMĀJ
OF INDIA

MET IN
1875

SON   1874

MET FOR
FIRST TIME

1880

"NEW DISPENSATION"

SĀDHĀRAN BRAHMO SAMĀJ

BECAME
DISCIPLE

D. 1884

BHAKTISIDDHĀNTA SARASVATI

A.C. BHAKTIVEDĀNTA

D. 1886

1890

FOUNDED
VEDĀNTA SOC.
FOUNDED
RĀMAKRSNA
MISSION

1896

1900

D. 1902

D. 1905   D. 1914   D. 1937   D. 1977

examinations in 1862, and in 1866 was appointed a magistrate within the Bengal provincial civil service. There he remained, with increasing rank and responsibility, until his retirement in 1894.

Kedarnath Dutt was in many ways typical of educated Indians serving the British government, holding during his career a variety of magistrate posts in Bengal, Bihar, and Orissa, including service for a time as the British-appointed overseer of the Jagannatha Temple in Puri. His principal concern as a competent and successful young magistrate was to promote the cause of British law. His interest in his own religious tradition was strictly personal, more a matter of cultural nostalgia than intellectual conviction. He did not consider Gaudiya Vaisnavism a worthy rival to Christianity and the Western intellectual tradition, nor was he alone in this opinion. In contrast to the culture confidence of the British, the Gaudiya community in general seemed to lack interest in its heritage and did little to make it available. Kedarnath was in fact unable for some years even to find a copy of the *Caitanya-caritamrta*, the great Bengali biography of Caitanya, and he had never been encouraged to study either the *Bhagavata Purana* or the writings of the Goswamis ("sages") of Vrindaban.

All of this changed in 1868, when he received from a friend a copy of both the *Caitanya-caritamrta* and the *Bhagavata Purana* with the commentary of Sridhara Swami. He plunged into these works, discovered their wealth of religious teaching, and went through a personal transformation. For the first time, he realized that there was something in the Caitanyite tradition worth preserving—and not only worth preserving, but worth promoting on a public level. This he took as his new obligation.

One of the first expressions of this new zeal is a pamphlet that Kedarnath published called *The Bhagavata: Its Philosophy, Its Ethics, and Its Theology*. It was written soon after his great discovery of "the *Bhagavat*" (the *Bhagavata Purana*), and is based on perhaps the first public lecture that he gave in 1869 to announce his new-found cause. It is clearly directed to educated Indians like himself who have lost contact with their own tradition. Written in marvelously fluent English, it is nonetheless an argument against the inroads of British education and Western cultural values and a plea for reform based on the religious insights and teachings of Caitanya, not on some modern synthetic substitute. In advocating reformation, Kedarnath does not reject the West entirely and he never loses contact with the current social and intellectual climate, but argues instead for a modern understanding of the truths to be found in the earlier tradition. This he does with a delightful style, conveying both his advocacy and his criticisms in a manner that must have contributed greatly to his success.

"Thought is progressive," he says in his statement to this Westernized audience. "The author's thoughts must have progress in the reader in the shape of correction or development. He is the best critic who can show the further development of an old thought, but a mere denouncer is the enemy of progress and consequently of Nature." The "shallow critic and the fruitless reader" are "the two great enemies of progress since they reject the treasures of the past too quickly in favor of shallow innovations." This has clearly happened, he argues, in the case of the *Bhagavata Purana*:

The *Bhagavat*, like all religious works and philosophical performances and writings of great men, has suffered from the imprudent conduct of useless readers and stupid critics. The former have done so much injury to the work that they have surpassed the latter in their evil consequence. Men of brilliant thoughts have passed by the work in quest of truth and philosophy, but the prejudice which they imbibed from its useless readers and their conduct prevented them from making a candid investigation. . . .

The *Bhagavat* has suffered alike from shallow critics both Indian and outlandish. [He knew English well enough, I think, to know what he was saying]. That book has been accused and denounced by a great number of our young countrymen who have scarcely read its contents and pondered over the philosophy on which it is founded. It is coming mostly to their imbibing an unfounded prejudice against it when they were in school. . . . We are ourselves witness of the fact. When we were in college, reading the philosophical works of the West and exchanging thought with the thinkers of the day, we had a real hatred toward the *Bhagavat*. That great work looked like a repository of wicked and stupid ideas scarcely adapted to the 19th century, and we hated to hear any arguments in its favor. With us then a volume of Channing, Parker, Emerson, or Newman had more weight than can the whole lot of the Vaishnav works. Greedily we poured over the various commentations of the Holy Bible and the labors of the Tattwa Bodhini Sabha, containing extracts from the *Upanishads* and the *Vedanta*, but no work of the Vaishnavs had any favor with us.

But when we advanced in age and our religious sentiment received development, we turned out in a manner Unitarian in our belief and prayed as Jesus prayed in the Garden. Accidentally we fell in with a work about the Great Caitanya, and on reading it with some attention in order to discern the historical position of that Mighty Genius of Nadia, we had the opportunity of gathering His explanations of the *Bhagavat* given to the wrangling Vedantist of the Benares School.

The accidental study created in us a love for all the works which we found about our Eastern Savior. We gathered with difficulty the *Kurchas* in Sanskrit, written by the disciples of Caitanya. The explanations that we got of the *Bhagavat* from these sources were of such a charming character that we procured a copy of the *Bhagavat* complete and studied its texts . . . with the assistance of the famous commentaries of Shreedhar Swami. From such study it is that we have at last gathered the real doctrines of the Vaishnavs. Oh! What a trouble to get rid of prejudices gathered in unripe years!

Kedarnath then goes on to put the position of the *Bhagavata* in proper perspective and to describe its philosophical and theological contents. He carries on in the process a running critique of other viewpoints, especially the "*mayavad* theory" of Shankaracharya (whose "barren station" he compares to the "Delhi Terminus" of Caitanya's devotional teachings) and the view of those "shallow critics" in the Brahmo Samaj and elsewhere who wanted to substitute a blend of Shankara and Christianity for the more relevant truths of the *Bhagavata* and Vaisnava devotionalism. His immediate task, as is evident from the context, was to restore the *Bhagavata Purana* and the Caitanya tradition as a whole to respectability. Even in this early writing, however, the breadth of his vision went well beyond the immediate concern for intellectual acceptance. As his conclusion indicates, the ultimate goal can be no less than a worldwide religion based on the principles of the *Bhagavata*:

> The spirit of this text goes far to honour all great reformers and teachers who lived and will live in other countries. The Vaishnava is ready to honour all great men without distinction of caste, because they are filled with the energy of God. See how universal is the religion of the *Bhagavata*. It is not intended for a certain class of Hindus alone but it is a gift to man at large in whatever country he is born and in whatever society is bred. In short, Vaishnavi is the Absolute love binding all men together into the infinite unconditioned and absolute God.

Kedarnath worked throughout the rest of his career to realize this vision, adding to his duties as a magistrate the ever more important work of developing his own religious life and promoting the cause of Gaudiya Vaisnavism. Fortunately for the tradition, he was equal to the task, as a glimpse of his awesome work schedule indicates. He went to sleep in the evening around 7:30 to 8:00, but then rose at 10:00 P.M. to light his oil lamp and write until 4:00 in the morning. After a brief rest, he would rise again at 4:30 to chant the Hare Krishna mantra on his beads. Between 7:00 and 9:30 a.m. he answered letters, read religious or philosophical works, and received callers. He then napped for a few minutes, bathed, ate breakfast, and was at the court by 10:00 a.m. From then until 5:00 P.M., with only a break between 1:00 and 2:00 P.M., he heard cases—sometimes as many as fifty a day—and wrote detailed judgments on each. Every evening after his court duties he would translate some Sanskrit religious work into Bengali by dictating to a secretary and would then bathe, eat a simple meal of rice, bread, and milk, and retire until he resumed his nightly writing schedule at 10:00 P.M.

Thanks to this demanding regimen, Kedarnath was able to write, translate, or edit nearly a hundred books from 1868 onward.[2] Publication of these and other writings became a major concern, because for far too many years there had been little attention to preserving the treasury of devotional writings from the past and there were no current editions to make them accessible. Kedarnath was devoted to recovering and publishing as much of this tradition as possible. The result was a steady stream of translations, commentaries, and expositions of Vaisnava theology including, in 1881, the founding of the journal *Sajjana-tosani* to disseminate the teachings of Caitanya. These scholarly activities did not prevent him from developing his religious life, however, for around the time he started his journal he also accepted as his *Siksa-guru* (his instructing spiritual master) the very traditional Vaishnava *sannyasin* Jagannath dasa Babaji. It was his growth in spirituality no less than his scholarship that led the Goswamis of the Vaisnava community to give him in 1886 the name Bhaktivinoda Thakur, by which he has been known to later generations.

The relationship between Kedarnath Dutt and Jagannath dasa Babaji represents an important dimension of what was happening in Bengal in the latter half of the nineteenth century. Kedarnath had scholarly competence in both Western learning and the Hindu classical tradition, whereas Jagannath dasa Babaji was anything but a scholar: he was an emotional ecstatic *babaji* of the *paramahamsa-sannyasin* type, devotional to the core, who spent most of his time doing *bhajan* and had little interest in scholarship of any kind. In their relationship, however, Jagannath dasa Babaji was the teacher and Kedarnath the student, and this example was not unique for that time and place. The saintly *sannyasin* Ramakrishna had earlier, in 1875, gained the allegiance of the Brahmo Samaj leader Keshab Chunder Sen, and was soon to acquire an even more important follower in Narendranath Dutt, better known as Vivekananda, who abandoned the Brahmo Samaj to become the first modern Hindu missionary to the West. Both symbolically and practically, these Western-educated intellectuals were affirming in the late nineteenth century a new message: that Hindus had little to learn from the West in terms of spirituality, whereas everyone—themselves included—had much to learn from Hindu spiritual masters like Jagannath dasa Babaji and Ramakrishna.

The devotional spirit so evident in Ramakrishna was somewhat obscured by Vivekananda's Vedanta orientation. Kedarnath was determined, however, that devotion remain central in the revitalized Gaudiya Vaisnava movement. To this end, he insisted in 1900 that his learned son and successor Bhaktisiddhanta Sarasvati take initiation from another pious *babaji*, Gaurakisora dasa, and in 1908, after his own guru had died, Kedarnath himself sought Gaurakisora to preside over his initiation into *sannyasin*hood. What is most impressive about this series of decisions is the apparent absence of tension between Kedarnath's two roles as a British-trained magistrate and as a pious devotee who ended his life as a *babaji*. He seems to have felt equally at ease wearing a cloth coat and doing law or wearing a *dhoti* and doing *bhajan*, and this was surely his great strength. Both the British and the *babajis* had something of value to offer. Moving between their two worlds with facility, and understanding them both, he was able to draw on each to serve the needs of devotion. This is most evident in his writings—his translations, songs, commentaries and discourses in Sanskrit, English, and Bengali—but it is also evident in the goals, principles, and practices that he passed on to his successors in the Gaudiya Vaisnava movement.

It is significant that in 1887, a year after receiving his spiritual title of Bhaktivinoda Thakur, Kedarnath established a printing press at Bhaktibhavan, his house in Calcutta, to make possible even wider distribution of Vaisnava works. Technology was not in conflict with a life of devotion but could be used to create more devotees. This principle was carried even further by his son, Bhaktisiddhanta Sarasvati, who referred to the printing press as the *brhat-mrdanga*, "the great mrdanga," because the drumbeats of an ordinary *mrdanga* can be heard for only a few blocks but the printing press can be heard around the world. Printing and distributing devotional literature was a distinctive feature of the movement from this time on, and has become, as every airport user knows, a major activity of the Krishna Consciousness organization. It is in direct accord with Kedarnath's policies that one of Bhaktivedanta Swami's first purchases in New York City was a mimeograph machine, and that establishing a publishing operation was one of his first clearly defined goals.

Kedarnath's emphasis on publishing reflected his deeply seated belief that the Vaisnava message was universal. As he said in his early lecture, the religion of the *Bhagavata* "is not intended for a certain class of Hindus alone, but is a gift to man at large in whatever country he is born." This principle was not an abstract ideal, but had practical implications. Kedarnath sent copies of his books to scholars and institutions in Europe and North America to promote the Vaisnava cause. Although there was little immediate response on record, a few German scholars expressed their appreciation and a booklet published in English in 1896 on *Caitanya*

Mahaprabhu: His Life and Precepts did end up in the libraries of McGill University and the Royal Asiatic Society in London; at least a start had been made to transcend national barriers.

Within India, the more immediate problem was social barriers. Kedarnath refused to acknowledge caste distinctions among devotees, and in particular opposed the wearing of the sacred thread by Brahmans as a sign of superiority. Although this concern for social equality was on the surface similar to that of the Brahmo Samaj and Westernized reformers in the north, Kedarnath's argument for his position was characteristically based on traditional Vaisnava religious beliefs—especially the example in the *Bhagavata Purana* of the great saint Narada who, although raised as a Sudra, was given Brahmanical status because of his learning and devotion. The Caitanyite tradition was clearly on Kedarnath's side on this issue, for Caitanya himself had argued the same case and his disciple Nityananda, the designated preacher to the masses in Bengal, had created a minor social revolution by his total disregard of caste background in the recruiting of devotees.

Kedarnath passed on his concerns for scholarship, publication, universalism, and the equality of all devotees to his son and successor in leadership, Bhaktisiddhanta Sarasvati.[3] Bhaktisiddhanta's education, directed personally by his father, gave him a scholarly knowledge of English, Sanskrit, and Bengali along with an exhaustive knowledge of devotional texts and a powerful sense of the mission to spread Krishna consciousness. In 1915, a year after his father's death, Bhaktisiddhanta established the Bhagavat Press to expand the publication of Vaisnava literature. He also maintained and even extended Kedarnath's policies of social equality, though with a reversed ritual symbolism: where his father had refused to acknowledge the sacred thread, Bhaktisiddhanta gave the sacred thread to every candidate accepted for initiation, regardless of his caste background, on the grounds that if he qualified religiously he was as good as any other Brahman. Although success was not realized until long after his death in 1937, he laid the foundation for an international Gaudiya Vaisnava mission by his appointment of a missionary to London in 1933–35 and by his directive to A. C. Bhaktivedanta Swami that he should carry the message of Krishna Consciousness to the West.

Bhaktivedanta Swami, as he himself could certainly have agreed, was simply the inheritor—well, not *simply*. He was a great person in his own right, but he was the inheritor of the revitalized Caitanyite tradition that stemmed from Kedarnath Dutt's efforts in the nineteenth century. Born in 1896 as Abhay Charan De, he completed work for his B.A. at Scottish Churches' College in Calcutta in 1920, but declined his degree as part of the Gandhian protest against British rule. Already married by the time he left college, he entered the pharmacy business to support his growing family and in 1923 became the proprietor for the Prayag Pharmacy in Allahabad. But his heart was not really in his business, and after his initiation by Bhaktisiddhanta in 1932 he turned his attention increasingly to a religious duty set by his master: to preach the message of Caitanya to English-speaking people. He founded the magazine *Back to Godhead* in 1944 to serve as a vehicle for this purpose, and produced a series of English expositions of sacred writings. His long-term goal, however, was a translation and commentary on the *Bhagavata Purana*. He began work in earnest on this project after becoming a *sannyasin* in 1959, and by 1965 had completed and published the first canto in three volumes. At that point, armed with a message and a mission, he set sail for New York City to bring Krishna consciousness to the West (see chart 3).

Bhaktivedanta Swami was seventy years old when he came to America. It was his first trip outside India, he had no money, and he had no local means of support. He did have ability, energy, and total commitment to the devotional cause, but neither these personal qualities nor conditions in America can account for his success in the next twelve years. The major factor in this success, I am convinced, was the legacy that Bhaktivedanta brought with him from Bengal, the century of effort by Kedarnath Dutt and Bhaktisiddhanta to relate the Vaisnava devotional path to the modern world. Not only did they provide the vision of a universal religion, but they had worked through many of the difficult practical questions: How Vaisnava teachings can be presented to the widest possible audience, how they can be explained to the Western mentality, how new devotees can be brought into the Caitanya movement, and how the movement can be stabilized to ensure its continuity. Almost every apparent innovation that Bhaktivedanta made can be traced back to this work of his predecessors. One particularly striking example must serve here to make the point, although many others would be readily forthcoming.

Bhaktivedanta very early began the practice of initiating his new American disciples with what is called *hari-nama* ("holy name") initiation, a ritual in which the disciple is given a religious name and a set of beads for chanting the Hare Krishna *mantra*. This stage of initiation is not unusual in itself, at least among Hindu devotional groups. What *is* unusual is the institution by Bhaktivedanta of a second stage, Brahmanical initiation, in which more advanced American disciples were given the *gayatri mantra* and invested with the sacred thread that marked them as Brahmans. This practice is in clear conflict with the orthodox Hindu view that Brahmanical status is hereditary—even more in conflict since Bhaktivedanta's death, one might add, when the American initiators have themselves become Brahmans by the same process.

CHART 3

HISTORY OF THE KRISHNA CONSCIOUSNESS MOVEMENT

CAITANYA (1486-1533) [FOUNDER OF GAUDĪYA VAIṢṆAVA MOVEMENT]

GOSWĀMĪS AT VṚNDĀVAN (1530-1592) [FIRST THEOLOGIANS OF THE MOVEMENT]

KṚṢṆADĀSA KAVIRĀJ (1530-1616): CAITANYA-CARITĀMṚTA (CA. 1615) [BIOGRAPHY OF CAITANYA]

RAM MOHAN ROY (1772-1833) [FOUNDER OF BRĀHMO SAMĀJ IN 1828; STARTED THE "BENGAL RENAISSANCE"]

(1) KEDARNATH DUTT

(BHAKTIVINODA THĀKURA)
B. 1838

- 1850 MARRIED TO FIRST WIFE

- 1860 COMPLETED COLLEGE, WENT TO ORISSA TO TEACH

- 1866 IN PROVINCIAL CIVIL SERVICE

- 1868 ACQUIRED BHĀGAVATA PUR. AND CAITANYA-CARITĀMṚTA

- 1878 STARTED SAJJANA-TOṢANI, ACCEPTED JAGANNĀTHA DĀSA BĀBĀJĪ AS ŚIKṢĀ-GURU

- 1888 LOCATED SITE OF MĀYĀPUR NEAR NAVADVĪPA

- 1896 SENT BOOK ON CAITANYA TO THE WEST

- 1908 INITIATED AS BĀBĀJĪ BY GAURAKIŚORA

D. 1914

KESHAB CHUNDER SEN (1838-1884) [BRĀHMO SAMĀJ LEADER]
BANKIM CANDRA CHATTERJEE (1838-1894) [BENGALI WRITER]

(3) BIMALA PRASADA DUTT

(BHAKTISIDDHĀNTA SARASVATĪ)
B. 1874 IN PŪRĪ, 4TH SON OF KEDARNATH DUTT

STUDIED WITH FATHER AND OTHER VAIṢṆAVA PANDITS

- 1900 TOOK INITIATION FROM GAURAKIŚORA DĀSA BĀBĀJĪ (2)

- 1915 ESTABLISHED BHAGWAT PRESS

- 1918 INITIATED SELF AS SANNYĀSIN

- 1925 FF. LED PARIKRAMAS AT HOLY PLACES IN NAVADVĪPA AND VṚNDAVANA

D. 1937

(4) ABHAY CHARAN DE

(BHAKTIVEDĀNTA SWAMĪ)
B. 1896

- 1916-20 STUDY AT SCOTTISH CHURCHES' COLLEGE IN CALCUTTA

- 1922 FIRST MEETING WITH BHAKTISIDDHĀNTA

- 1923 OPENED PRAYAG PHARMACY IN ALLAHABA

- 1932 INITIATED BY BHAKTISIDDHĀNTA

- 1944 FOUNDED BACK TO GODHEAD MAGAZINE

- 1959 INITIATED AS SANNYĀSIN

- 1963 FIRST VOLUME OF BHĀGAVATA PUBLISHED

- 1965 ARRIVED IN NEW YORK CITY, SEPT. 19

D. 1977

DISCIPLIC SUCCESSION INDICATED

BY (1) . (2) . (3) . (4)

(AFTER JAGANNĀTHA DĀSA BĀBĀJĪ)

The practice, however, is clearly based on policies established by Bhaktisiddhanta and is consistent with the inclusive spirit of Bengal Vaisnavism.

Evidence of this is the fact that Gaudiya Vaisnavas in Bengal have accepted the legitimacy of these American Brahmanical initiates and have accorded them the same ritual status as native Bengali Brahmans.[4] The more status-conscious descendants of Vrndavana Goswamis have admittedly been less willing to do so, but what this indicates most of all is that Kedarnath and Bhaktisiddhanta were influenced mainly by the tradition in Bengal that is represented by the *babajis* and by Caitanya's disciple Nityananda—who, as Ed Dimock has shown, was involved with the egalitarian and very unorthodox Tantric Vaisnava-Sahajiya movement. This historical connection is strengthened by the fact that Kedarnath himself received his *gayatri mantra* initiation from a spiritual master by the name of Vipina vihari Goswami, whom Kedarnath praised in one of his later writings as standing—as he also did by then—in the "greatly eminent" disciplic line that stemmed from Nityananda's wife, Jahnava-Devi, a prominent Sahajiya leader.

If Bhaktivedanta seemed at times to be unorthodox in terms of the Hindu tradition, it was thus because he was so true to his own tradition of Bengal Vaisnavism. The openness of that tradition goes back in Bengal to Caitanya and his disciples, especially Nityananda, and before them to the *Bhagavata Purana* and the *Bhagavada Gita*. It was the task of Kedarnath and Bhaktisiddhanta to show that it was not only compatible with the modern world but could answer many of the modern world's problems. It was Bhaktivedanta's task to bring that message to America, to plant it in a place where it would take root and flourish, and to do so without compromising the tradition and the teachers who made his work possible. Kedarnath Dutt, in an issue of *Sajjana-tosani*, looked forward to a day "when all greatly fortunate souls in countries such as England, France, Russia, Prussia and America will take up banners, kettle drums, *mrdangas* and *kartals* and thus cause the ecstatic waves of *harinam-kirtan* and the singing of Sri Caitanya Mahaprabhu's holy name to rise in the streets of their towns and cities." Thanks to Bhaktivedanta Swami, at least some part of that great vision has been realized. The astonishing thing is that a nineteenth century Indian district magistrate could have such a vision, and could prepare the way so thoroughly for its future.

Notes

1. There is no scholarly biography of Kedarnath Dutt, although there are a number of biographical accounts by disciples. Information about his life in this talk has come mainly from an undocumented biography in manuscript form

assembled by Krishna Consciousness members in India from a variety of sources that are referred to only by title and author with no dates or publication information. The sources mentioned are: Bhakti Kusuma Sraman, *Prabhupada Srila Sarasvati Thakura*; Bhakti Pradip Tirtha, *Thakur Bhaktivinoda*; Haridas Das, *Gaudiya-Vaisnava-Jivana*; Kedarnath Dutt, *Datta-Vamsa-Mala*; a genealogical account of Kedarnath's family line on his father's side, written in Sanskrit in 1876; Kedarnath Dutt, (no title given); an autobiography written in Bengali in 1887 (?); Lalita Prasad Thakur, (no title given); notes on his father's life by Kedarnath's seventh son; Paramanada Vidyaratna, *Srila Bhaktivinoda Thakura*; Satkari Chattopadhyaya Siddhanta Bhusan, *A Glimpse into the Life of Thakur Bhaktivinoda*; Sundarananda Vidyavinode, *Chatrader Sri Bhaktivinoda*; Sundarananda Vidyavinode, *Parama Guru Sri Gaurakisora*; Sundarananda Vidyavinode, *Sri Ksetra*; Sundarananda Vidyavinode, *Vaisnava-siddhante Sri-Guru-svarupa*.

2. A number of Kedarnath Dutt's writings have been published by the Gaudiya Math, although few of them are easily available. The Bhaktivedanta Book Trust, the publishing house for the Krishna Consciousness movement, has recently started publishing some of his devotional songs. The publications that I have been able to obtain are: *The Bhagavata: Its Philosophy, Its Ethics and Its Theology*, 2nd ed., ed. Bhakti Vilas Tirtha (Madras: Gaudiya Math, 1959): a discourse in two parts on the *Bhagavata Purana*, based on lectures given in 1869; *Jaiva Dharma*, trans. Bhakti Shadaka Nishkinchana and Haridas Maitra (Madras: Sree Gaudiya Math, 1971): a Purana-type theological narrative published originally in Bengali in 1893, consisting mainly of discourses on Vaisnava doctrine in response to questioners from various schools; *Srimad Bhagavad-Gita*, 3rd ed., ed. and trans. Bhakti-Pradip Tirtha (Calcutta: Gaudiya Mission, 1948): Devanagari text, *padaeccheda*, word-by-word English prose rendering and translation, and an exposition based on earlier commentaries by three Gaudiya Vaisnava *acaryas* including Kedarnath Dutt, begun while the editor-translator was serving as the first Gaudiya Vaisnava missionary to London in 1933–35; *Songs of the Vaisnava Acaryas*, ed. and trans. Acyutananda Swami (New York: Bhaktivedanta Book Trust, 1974): includes a selection of Bengali songs by Kedarnath Dutt on pp. 28–54, with English translations by an American disciple of Bhaktivedanta Swami; *The Songs of Bhaktivinoda Thakura*, prepared by Yogesvara dasa and the ISKCON Press Board of Directors with the assistance of Acyutananda Swami (ISKCON Press, 1980): an in-house publication for devotees consisting mainly of transliterations and translations of Kedarnath's *Saranagati* and *Gitavali*, both published in Bengali in 1893 that includes also a brief biography of Kedarnath by Acyutananda Swami (pp. iii–ix) and an annotated list by date of around a hundred literary works which he produced between 1849 and 1907 (pp. 151–159).

3. Some information about the life of Kedarnath's son and successor Bimala Prasad Dutt (Bhaktisiddhanta Sarasvati), especially his work in behalf of the Gaudiya Math, is provided in the first volume of the biography of Bhaktivedanta Swami that is now being prepared by Satsvarupa dasa Goswami, one of Bhaktivedanta's leading American disciples. This massively researched multivolume biography, *Srila Prabhupada-lilamrta*, will certainly be one of the most complete records of the life and work of any modern religious figure. Written in a respectful but remarkably objective style, it provides detailed accounts of Bhaktivedanta's life in India, his involvement with the Gaudiya Math, and his activities in establishing the International Society for Krishna Consciousness after he came to the United States in 1965. Thanks to the early use of tape recorders by disciples, many of his conversations and lectures in America—and the responses

of his early American contacts—are presented verbatim. The volumes of this biography so far published are: Satsvarupa dasa Goswami, *A Lifetime in Preparation: India 1896–1965, Srila Prabhupada-lilamrta*, vol. 1 (Los Angeles: The Bhaktivedanta Book Trust, 1980), with material on Bhaktisiddhanta Sarasvati in chap. 3 and 4, pp. 37–94; and Satsvarupa dasa Goswami, *Planting the Seed: New York City, 1965–1966, Srila Prabhupada-lilamrta*, vol. 2 (Los Angeles: The Bhaktivedanta Book Trust, 1980).

4. Information on the history and teaching of the Gaudiya Vaisnava can be found in the second edition of S. K. De, *Early History of Vaisnava Faith and Movement in Bengal* (Calcutta: K. L. Mukhopadhyay, 1961) and, from the perspective of a sympathetic socially conscious Western Christian, in Melville Kennedy, *The Chaitanya Movement: A Study of the Vaishnavism of Bengal* (Calcutta: Association Press, 1925). An important dimension of Bengal Vaisnavism is brought out in Edward C. Dimock, *The Place of the Hidden Moon: Exotic Mysticism in the Vaisnava-Sahajiya Cult of Bengal* (Chicago: University of Chicago Press, 1966), which makes clear the significant influence of the Tantric Vaisnava-Sahajiya tradition on the theology and social practices of Gaudiya Vaisnavism through the activities of Nityananda and his wife Jahnava-Devi (who was both a Sahajiya leader and the founder of the disciplic line into which Kedarnath Dutt was initiated centuries later).

Patterns in ISKCON's Historical
Self-Perception

William H. Deadwyler, III
(Ravindra-svarupa das)

Introduction

To understand the historical self-perception of ISKCON devotees, I would suggest three different paradigms of historical (or temporal) perception, all of which bear on the way devotees see themselves. These notions are the linear view of history in its secular form, the linear view in its religious form, and the cyclical view of history.

Historical self-consciousness, as such, is often seen as one of the hallmarks of the modern Western mind. We see ourselves as essentially historical beings, attaining self-definition in and through processes of temporal development. We are made by history, and we make history in turn. This perspective is shared by those founding fathers of modernity, Hegel, Darwin, Freud, and Marx, whose common effort is to make phenomena intelligible by examining their genesis, growth, and development.

Rudolf Otto notes that such historicism, with the associated notion of progress, developed from a uniquely Judeo-Christian sense of divine teleology:

> an interest in events as constituting a purposefully controlled and unified series. If this interest becomes secular, we have "history." The idea of teleology immanent in events then takes the place of a transcendent control, and finally this gives us a "coming-to-itself of the spirit," or maybe, the socialistic ideology of the "State of the future," or of the "triumph of civilization." But these and like leaders of the Occident would perhaps have never actually developed, had it not been for the impulse given from the beginning by God's world that has in fact the dignity of an ultimate destiny.[1]

Mircea Eliade also sees the linear view of history as a novel development in Israel, arising when prophets began to interpret catastrophic events as "negative theophanies" expressing the wrath of Yahweh. "Thus, for the first time, the prophets placed a value on history, succeeded in transcending the traditional vision of the cycle . . . and discovered a one-way time."[2] In the linear view, "historical events have a value in themselves insofar as they are determined by the will of God."[3] Thus,

> the linear attitude sees an irreversible course pointing in a definite direction, serving a definite purpose, and hence perceiving a spiritual and religious sense in history rather than a merely biological meaning.[4]

Eliade contrasts this linear view of time, in both its religious and secular forms, with the archaic notion of time as possessing a cyclical structure. Here, a simple, paradigmatic pattern—creation, gradual ontological exhaustion, destruction, creation—ceaselessly repeats itself. This view, says Eliade, expresses a "refusal of history," that is, a radical devaluation of concrete historical time as a one-way succession of novel, unrepeatable acts.[5] Although the cyclical view is characteristic of archaic man in general, it is preserved in religions of Indian origin, where it is associated soteriologically with the effort to escape or transcend time and history altogether.

The contrast between the cyclical and linear view of history has long been seen as embodying an essential difference between the religious traditions of Indian and those of Semitic origin. Otto finds this so when he compares Christianity with "India's religion of grace," the Vaisnavism of Ramanuja. Otto presents Ramanuja's vision in these words:

> *Isvara* thrones in his eternity. Deep beneath him rushes the stream of the world and humanity in *samsara,* in ever repeated circles of woeful birth and rebirth. In this world the wandering soul strolls, separated from *Isvara* by its fall and lost in the confusion of the world. Then he [*Isvara*] inclines to it in pure, undeserved grace. Out of the infinite number of the lost, he raises his own to himself. But this world of wandering rushes and runs on from one aeon to another. Never does it become the abode of the glory or the honour of God. It remains ever what it is, a *lila,* a sport of the Deity, a concatenation without goal and end—true, not without objective existence, but eternally worthless, never arriving at a fullness of worth, never *glorified* and made an abode of the kingdom and of the final dominion of God himself.[6]

Thus, we have three historical paradigms: the linear-secular, itself an outgrowth of the linear-sacred, which stands in contrast and even opposition to the cyclical-religious. But the ideas of Otto and Eliade concerning the provenance and locations of these ideas do not prepare us for what we find in ISKCON's worldview: a strongly stressed linear-sacred paradigm, containing a fully developed salvation history as well as a type of millenarianism. At the same time, the traditional cyclical paradigm is retained. It provides the context for the linear-sacred and, in addition, for an *inverted* form of the linear-secular. In this way, all three paradigms are woven together to help form the temporal self-consciousness of Krishna devotees and of ISKCON's theological worldview.

By "ISKCON's worldview" I mean that taught by Srila Prabhupada, the founder-*acarya* of the International Society for Krishna Consciousness, who, by formal lectures and informal talks, in letters, and in books, delivered the teachings of his sacred tradition—that is, the Brahma-Madhva-Gaudiya *sampradaya* ("tradition") of Caitanya's Bengal to his disciples in the West. Indeed, in bringing this tradition to the West, Prabhupada did something more than what we conventionally understand by the word "teach." He *initiated* his disciples into the tradition, thus extending the Krishna tradition both geographically and temporally.

It would be hard to overstate the importance of the idea of tradition in ISKCON's historical self-perception, and I introduce this concept as the fourth element in my analysis. As will become clear, the idea of tradition does not precisely fit any of the three temporal paradigms offered by Eliade. It combines a linear sense of time with a time-annihilating cyclical ontology expressed in theological archetypes.

Tradition

Two Sanskrit words convey the idea of tradition. The first, *parampara*, means "an uninterrupted series," "a succession." Prabhupada translates *parampara* as "disciplic succession." Such a succession is understood to be a historical chain of teachers who hand down the teaching initiated by God himself. The other word for tradition is *sampradaya*, derived from *sam-pra-/da:* "to deliver completely over to," "to transmit." There are traditionally four recognized Vaisnava *sampradayas:* the Brahma, the Rudra, the Sri, and the Kumara, each named after its founder, who, receiving enlightenment directly from the Supreme Lord, transmitted it. The notion of *parampara*, then, conveys the idea of tradition as an extended historical priestly lineage, whereas that of *sampradaya* focuses on the essentially conservative function of that tradition in an institutionalized theology.

Devotees in ISKCON are acutely conscious of their institution as a contemporary extension of the Brahma-*sampradaya*. They see themselves essentially as receivers and transmitters of an established Hindu

(Vaisnava) tradition. This consciousness of the importance of tradition was instilled in his disciples by Srila Prabhupada, who taught fidelity to tradition as a primary virtue. The tradition must be received and transmitted purely. One hears from the spiritual master, and repeats what one has heard without addition or subtraction. One must grant the spiritual master "submissive aural reception," and follow his instruction exactly. Only by so doing will one achieve success in spiritual life.

Having in this way been initiated into the tradition by his own spiritual master (who was himself initiated in the same way), Prabhupada could effectively transmit his tradition to the next generation. Prabhupada explicitly offered his spiritual lineage, the chain of spiritual masters coming down to himself, as his credentials for his status as a bona fide spiritual master and his authorization to teach and select disciples. Because he came in disciplic succession, he could initiate others into it. Furthermore, he could interpret and present Krishna scriptures (theological tradition) "as it is" (thus, his translation of the *Bhagavad-gita As It Is*).

The *Bhagavad-gita* has been read in the West, he says, for hundreds of years, but during all that time, no one understood it. For if one *understands* the discourse of Krishna, one recognizes Krishna as the Supreme Personality of Godhead and becomes his devotee; one fully surrenders to Krishna just as Arjuna did. Now that Prabhupada is presenting the *Bhagavad-gita* through the disciplic succession, people are becoming devotees of Krishna. In other words, when the teachings of Krishna are heard properly, through the disciplic succession, they possess spiritual potency. Prabhupada quotes, in this connection, from the *Padma Purana*, which says, *sampradava-vihina ye mantras te nisphala matah:* "Unless you are initiated by a bona fide spiritual master in the disciplic succession, the *mantra* that you might have received is without any effect."[7] The spiritual efficacy of the guru, then, is proof that the integrity of the chain of succession has been upheld.

We need to explore this issue of spiritual efficacy in order to grasp certain phenomenological features of the experience of tradition, features that seem, on the face of it, quite paradoxical. ISKCON's tradition, as it is experienced by devotees, imparts a consciousness of vast temporal distance, of belonging to a lineage that stretches back to remote antiquity and primordial acts, and simultaneously, it *annihilates* time. It transfers the remote past to present immediacy.

At the conclusion of the *Bhagavad-gita*, Sanjaya, who narrates the discourse between Krishna and Arjuna to the blind king Dhrtarastra, states that he has heard their discussion by the mercy of his spiritual master, Vyasa (*Bhagavad-gita* 18.75). Sanjaya was with Dhrtarastra at some distance from the Kuruksetra battlefield; nevertheless, by his guru's mercy, he could directly see and hear the encounter. Prabhupada comments on this *Gita* passage.

> This means that one has to understand Krsna not directly but through the medium of the spiritual master. The spiritual master is the transparent medium, although it is true that the experience is still direct. This is the mystery of disciplic succession. When the spiritual master is bona fide, then one can hear *Bhagavad-gita* directly, as Arjuna heard it. . . . By the grace of Vyasa, Sanjaya's senses were purified, and he could see and hear Krsna directly. One who directly hears Krsna can understand this confidential knowledge. If one does not come to the disciplic succession, he cannot hear Krsna; therefore his knowledge is always imperfect, at least as far as understanding *Bhagavad-gita* is concerned.[8]

Gaudiya Vaisnavism explains such *direct* perception by the theological principle that Krishna, being the Absolute Truth without duality, is equivalent to his name, his image, or his description. Therefore, by uttering Krishna's name or hearing Krishna's description, one can see Krishna directly, without mediation. But this direct perception of Krishna in the text takes place only when both the speaker and the listener are properly qualified spiritually. Only in that context does the text become manifest (*as it is*) and proper transmission of the text occurs.

One paradigmatic instance of this transmission is recorded in the Krishna scripture, *Srimad Bhagavatam*, when Suta Gosvami, having heard the *Bhagavatam* earlier, recites it again before the sages gathered at Naimisaryanya Forest. Suta says:

> O learned brahmanas, when Sukadeva Gosvami recited Bhagavatam there [in the presence of Emperor Pariksit], I heard him with rapt attention, and thus, by his mercy, I learned the Bhagavatam from that great and powerful sage. Now I shall try to make you hear the very same thing as I learned it from him and as I have realized it. (*Bhagavata Purana* 1.3.44)

Prabhupada comments that, "One can certainly see directly the presence of Lord Sri Krsna in the pages of *Bhagavatam*" if one hears it not from professional reciters or academic scholars, but from someone like Sukadeva Goswami, a spiritual master in disciplic succession. But Prabhupada continues,

> Simple hearing is not all: one must realize the text with proper attention. The word *nivista* means that Suta Gosvami drank the juice of *Bhagavatam* through his ears. That is the real process of receiving *Bhagavatam*. One should hear with rapt attention from the real person, and then he can at once realize the presence of Lord

Krishna on every page. The secret of knowing *Bhagavatam* is mentioned here. No one can give rapt attention who is not pure in mind. No one can be pure in mind who is not pure in action. No one can be pure in action who is not pure in eating, sleeping, fearing [i.e., defending], and mating. But somehow or other if someone hears with rapt attention from the right person, at the very beginning one can assuredly see Lord Sri Krsna in person in the pages of *Bhagavatam*.[9]

The conservative force of scriptural (i.e., theological) tradition, then, assures that every act of transmission is a virtual reinstantiation of the original revelation, a re-creation of the aboriginal transmissions, which function as models or archetypes for devotees in all places and times. The five thousand years of secular history that stand between the present and the beginning of Kaliyuga, when Krishna spoke the *Bhagavadgita* and Sukadeva Gosvami the *Srimad Bhagavatam*, are abolished in the immediacy of a spiritual encounter of Krishna in the *Gita* when it is faithfully transmitted. Also abolished are the one and a half quadrillion years that separate the present from Brahma's enlightenment by Krishna at the beginning of the creation.

But the "abolition" of time achieved by tradition does not, all the same, destroy the sense of temporal distance. Rather, the sense of distance is retained and fused with an equally strong sense of distance overcome or bridged. The concept of tradition thus requires both time and timelessness. The original, paradigmatic acts that tradition perpetuates are seen, in their first instantiation, as pregnant with the future. They are portentous, they have a temporal stance built in. So we are not (as Eliade sometimes suggests in his discussion of the repetition of archetypes) dealing with simple stasis.

Let me cite one of several instances especially significant to ISKCON devotees to show how the opposites, time and timelessness, dynamism and stasis, work in concert. These experiences of time ultimately provide the framework that allows ISKCON devotees to construct a praxis that combines both innovation and conservation.

The enlightenment of Brahma is described in *Srimad Bhagavatam*, canto 2, chapter 9. The divinity Brahma, the first created being in the universe, is born from the lotus sprouted from the navel of Vishnu, who lies on the primal waters. Coming to consciousness on that flower, Brahma is confused and perplexed, not knowing his own identity or purpose. Seeking to learn his origin, he climbs down the stem of the lotus flower, but is unsuccessful. But he hears a voice, the voice of Vishnu, repeat the two syllables "ta-pa," signifying penance or austerity. In obedience, Brahma performs penance for one thousand years of the gods, whereupon Brahma sees the Lord's transcendental abode and then the Lord himself, who with great pleasure takes Brahma by the hand (or, as Prabhupada puts it, "The Lord shook hands with Brahma"). He then speaks to Brahma four seminal verses, the seeds of *Srimad Bhagavatam*. Brahma in turn enlightens his son, the eternal sage Narada Muni, thus starting the Brahma-*sampradaya*.

In his commentary on this chapter, Prabhupada treats Brahma's enlightenment as a paradigm for the *sampradaya*. A mortal in this world finds himself thrown into existence, lost and bewildered, and cannot by his own endeavors discover his origin or purpose. But if he is fortunate, he meets the spiritual master in disciplic succession from God, who initiates him into the practices of devotional service. If the disciple is submissive and rigorously follows the order of the spiritual master, he obtains the mercy of the spiritual master and becomes purified, whereupon he comes face to face with the Supreme Lord Krishna.

Like Brahma, the devotees in his *sampradaya* ("tradition") should have a sense of mission. Having been enlightened in spiritual knowledge, they should in turn enlighten others.

> The Lord instructs Brahma in Vedic knowledge in order to diffuse this knowledge to the conditioned souls. The conditioned souls are forgetful souls in the relationship with the Lord, and thus a period of creation and the process of dissemination of Vedic knowledge are necessary activities of the Lord. Lord Brahma has a great responsibility in delivering the conditioned souls, and therefore he is very dear to the Lord.
>
> Brahma also does his duty very perfectly, not only by generating the living entities but also by spreading his party for reclaiming the fallen souls. The party is called the Brahma-*sampradaya*, and any member of this party to date is naturally engaged in reclaiming the fallen souls back to Godhead, back to home. . . . Anyone . . . preaching the mission of the Lord in the line of the Brahma-*sampradaya* is always dear to the Lord, and the Lord, being satisfied with such a preacher of the authorized bhakti cult, shakes hands with him in great satisfaction.[10]

Thus, Brahma's original enlightenment, which initiates a tradition, is seen as having significance for the future. Every subsequent spiritual master-disciple relationship in that tradition taps into that primordial enlightenment of Brahma, and reinstantiates it in new circumstances. Tradition thus effects the transcendence of time, but initiating the disciple into the tradition links him to the sacred past, the chain of succession, and instills in him the obligation to perpetuate the tradition. One looks back to the past, and forward to the future.

I have tried to give a sense of what tradition feels like to a devotee. The deep sense of tradition enables ISKCON devotees to carry on with great self-confidence and even aplomb even though they are a very small, highly deviant, highly visible minority in a culture that generally views them with deep suspicion. But the immediacy of India's Krishna tradition to the devotees, the sense of fellowship with the great teachers of the past, gives devotees their unseen support, their confident sense of belonging to a venerable religious tradition.

The steadfast adherence to tradition, inculcated through injunction to deliver the teachings exactly as they have been received, with no contributions of "mental speculation," does not convey to the modern mind any notion of vitality. The repeated exhortations of Srila Prabhupada to his disciples not to change anything, may suggest intellectual rigor mortis, and calls up an image of learning as a deadening rote-drill that stifles all creativity and originality, in which one simply mouths the words of ancient, hidebound "authorities." But, as I have tried to show, adherence to spiritual tradition, as ISKCON devotees understand and experience it, is quite different. Fidelity to tradition brings about direct spiritual realization. In that realization, what is old or ancient is experienced as vital, fresh, and new—indeed, just like Krishna himself, *purana-purusam navavauvanam ca*, "the oldest person and an ever-fresh youth" (*Brahma-samhita* 33).

Tradition is the central strand in the historical self-perception of ISKCON devotees and through it are woven the three temporal strands introduced in the beginning of this chapter. Taken together, they furnish ISKCON devotees with a complex historical outlook that fosters both conservation and innovation. Having established devotees' sense of linear time, let me now turn to those other elements.

Cyclical Consciousness

The traditional teaching of the great cycles of the ages is found in both *Bhagavad-gita* and *Srimad Bhagavatam,* and therefore it has become part of the heritage of ISKCON. According to this teaching, history moves in a succession of great cycles called *divya-yugas*. Each *divya-yuga* is composed of four ages of declining length called Satya, Dvapara, Treta, and Kali. The texts usually give their durations in divine (*divya*) years, or years of the demigods, each of which is equal to 360 human years.

	Divine years	Human years	% of total
Satya	4,800	1,728,000	40
Dvapara	3,600	1,296,000	30
Treta	2,400	864,000	20
Kali	1,200	432,000	10
TOTAL	12,000	4,320,000	100

One thousand cycles of four *yugas* (4.3 billion human years) make up one day in the life of the creator, Brahma, and each day is followed by a night of equal length, during which Brahma sleeps and most of the planets are submerged in waters of devastation. Brahma then awakes and another day of a thousand cycles commences. Three hundred sixty of these days and nights make one year of Brahma. He lives for one hundred divine years.

The duration of the life of Brahma (and his universe) is equal to one-half breath of Maha-Vishnu, a gigantic expansion of Krishna who rests in mystic slumber, floating on the primordial cloud of undifferentiated material energy. When Maha-Vishnu exhales, billions of golden seedling universes swarm out of his nostrils and skin pores, and in each of them a Brahma will be born to live his prescribed one hundred years. When Maha-Vishnu inhales, the universes are reabsorbed into his body, and the creation cycle is complete. During the inhalation there is no manifest creation, but then he exhales again, and the universes pour out. Maha-Vishnu's sleep, his deep and steady breathing, has no discernible beginning or ending.

In this vision of time, repetitive periods are packaged within periods—the *yuga* cycles within Brahma's days and nights, those in turn within the exhalations and inhalations of Vishnu. Certainly there is no sense of the creation as a whole advancing to some climactic end, although the creation of the material world does serve a divine purpose: It is the prison in the kingdom of God, a place in which those souls who reject divine service can be quarantined from the eternal kingdom of God where creation and destruction do not occur. The material world furnishes a theater of action and rehabilitation for them. A prison is needed and must be maintained, for there are souls constantly falling into the material world, just as souls are constantly being released.

Within this vast scheme, one *yuga* cycle is the smallest period, and the one that directly concerns us now. We are at this time 5,097 years into the Kali-*yuga*, the final age, of the 525th round of the *yuga* cycles in one day of Brahma's fiftieth year.

The progression of *yugas* from Satya to Kali is one of a successive decline so deeply rooted and all-pervasive that it amounts to a sort of ontological decay; the power of life itself seems to be eroded by the force of time. The character of this decline is expressed by a familiar metaphor of the four *yugas* as ages of gold, silver, copper, and iron respectively. The human lifespan, set at 100,000 in Satya-*yuga*, is diminished in each *yuga* by a factor of ten, reaching only 100 years in Kali-*yuga*, our age. Each age also brings about a reduction in the earth's productive energy, so that food loses more and more of its sustaining power, until by Kali-*yuga* people are mental, physical, moral, and spiritual runts compared with their status in the golden age. Stature, strength, stamina, memory, and intelligence are all meager. *Dharma*, the principles of religion and morality, is supported by four pillars in Satya-*yuga*: cleanliness, austerity, mercifulness, and truthfulness. In each succeeding age, one leg is removed, until, in Kali-*yuga*, *dharma* is balanced precariously on truthfulness alone, and even that erodes as the age progresses.

The defects and difficulties of the Kali-*yuga* are important and powerful themes in the first canto of *Srimad Bhagavatam*. In his commentary, (especially to that of the sixteenth chapter, "How Pariksit Received the Age of Kali"), Prabhupada sets forth with great conviction the devastating consequences of living in the Kali-*yuga*. My experience is typical of many if not most of Prabhupada's disciples. The first time I read his commentary of this portion of the *Srimad Bhagavatam*, I found this indictment of our degenerate age the most compelling and immediately convincing part. In it, Prabhupada did something quite interesting: he turned the idea of progress on its head, showing us just how, item for item, the so-called "rise of civilization," reaching new heights in modern industrial and scientific society, was in reality the progressive degeneration of real human culture in Kali-*yuga*. Even the greatest monuments of progress fell before Prabhupada's persuasive analysis. We, who even in our greatest disillusionment never doubted that the invention of writing was a great step forward, now learned that it was one more symptom of decline because in Kali-*yuga*, people's memories become so weak that everything must be written down.

The Hare Krishna movement, as Prabhupada said, offers refuge to people who are "materially exhausted." One symptom of such material exhaustion in the modern age is utter disillusionment with the various notions of progress. When the modern, secularized versions of historical teleology no longer hold out any promise, there arises, as Eliade rightly sees, such a strong sense of the meaninglessness of history that the "terror of history" becomes intolerable.[11] The position of "'historical man' (modern man), who consciously and voluntarily creates history," thus becomes unbearable.[12] The last thing one wants to do is create history. History becomes rather, as Joyce's Stephen Dedalus says, "a nightmare from which I am trying to awake."

Eliade notes how the work of such moderns as Yeats and Joyce "is saturated with nostalgia for the myth of eternal repetition and, in the last analysis, for the abolition of time." Eliade goes on to remark:

> It may be that we are witnessing a desperate attempt to prohibit the "events of history" through a reintegration of human societies within the horizon (artificial, because decreed) of archetypes and their repetition.[13]

Consequently, it may also be that Prabhupada, in introducing the Hare

Krishna movement to the West, was able to meet a quite particular psychological need, all the more so because the "horizon of archetypes and their repetition" he offered was not artificial but authentic.

The Krishna Consciousness movement, then, offers a way out of history for those who no longer want to further it. I can vividly recall the shock I felt when, as an aspiring devotee, I read in Prabhupada's writing a disparagement of those ambitious materialists who by their undertakings "unnecessarily increase the pages of history," as if "history" ought to be decently kept to a minimum! To further the progress of history, after all, means to further the degradation of Kali-*yuga*. The way out of history is simple: the devotee ceases to perform materially motivated acts. Therefore, he creates no karma and thus becomes released from the nexus of historical causality. He is liberated.

But a devotee in ISKCON ceases to perform material acts not by inaction but rather, as the *Bhagavad-gita* teaches, by performing action in devotional service, work for the satisfaction of Krishna alone. This idea of transcendental activity in the service of the Lord theologically makes possible the last strand in ISKCON's historical self-perception, namely, its engagement in a divinely mandated, world-transforming, world-spiritualizing historical mission. This sense of a salvation history is experienced as a linear-sacred time.

ISKCON and Salvation History

This final strand in ISKCON's historical self-perception places ISKCON within a vast, divinely engineered process of historical development that culminates in a spiritual millennium on earth. This strand, with its sense of temporal development and progress, has to be seen in context, counterweighted as it is by the conservation of tradition in ISKCON on the one hand and the otherworldliness and escape from history implied by the cycles of time on the other hand. But its presence in ISKCON is interesting, for according to standard opinion, it does not belong in a tradition of Indian provenance.

This historical vision is peculiar to Gaudiya Vaisnavism, because it is concerned with the advent of Sri Caitanya Mahaprabhu, the sixteenth century Bengali Krishna reformer, yet the roots of this vision are present in the teachings found in the *Bhagavad-gita* and the *Srimad Bhagavatam*, and in the followers of Caitanya the root simply develops to manifest what is seen as its actual fulfillment—the full flowering. Let me describe that vision now.

In the Gaudiya Vaisnava worldview, the linear-sacred is integrated with the cyclical. A section of the circle, sufficiently magnified, is a line. The section we are concerned with is Kali-*yuga*, this particular Kali-*yuga*.

Ordinarily, Kali-*yuga* has little to recommend it, but our present Kali-*yuga* is the one cycle out of every thousand in which Krishna descends. For that reason, the succession of *yugas* is changed: Dvapara follows Treta, and Krishna comes just at the end of Dvapara-*yuga*—in fact, Kali-*yuga* begins while he is still here, but its effects cannot manifest themselves until he leaves.

Krishna descends in this universe once in a divine day of Brahma, and Caitanya Mahaprabhu always descends in the Kali-*yuga* after Krishna's advent. Krishna's appearance gives to the world an exceptionally full and complete disclosure of divinity, a revelation rarely seen. This revelation is even further amplified or opened up by Caitanya's appearance and life.

Here we should note how, according to the *Bhagavad-gita*, an element of relativity enters into revelation. "As all surrender [*prapadyante*] unto Me," Krishna says, "I reward [*bhajami*] them accordingly. Everyone follows My path in all respects" (*Bhagavad-gita* 4.11). Krishna here states a principle of reciprocation. He reveals himself in relation to one's degree and kind of surrender. Therefore, although the absolute truth is one and unchanging, disclosure and apprehension of it by devotees and non-devotees varies.

The degree of difference in the spiritual seeing of Krishna can be illustrated by reference to the *Srimad Bhagavatam* text (1.2.11) that says the absolute truth is one and yet it is realized in three different ways: as Brahman, the all-pervading, impersonal effulgence; as the four-handed Vishnu who resides in the heart as the localized indwelling Supersoul (Paramatma); and as Bhagavan, the transcendent Supreme Personality of Godhead. All three are features of the Absolute Truth, but, as Prabhupada explains, the realizations of Brahman, Paramatma, and Bhagavan are not the same. Rather, they progress in inclusiveness and fullness, and a true devotee advances from one to the next by becoming more and more free from desires for material and spiritual self-aggrandizement.

Differences in kind of surrender are exhibited when a pure devotee like Prabhupada forms an attachment to God in some particular personal feature. Gaudiya Vaisnava *acaryas*, analyzing the divine pastimes described in scripture, have discerned a number of devotional relationships or *rasas*. They include, in order of increasing intimacy, *santa-rasa* or passive veneration; *sakhya-rasa*, service in companionship, with a sense of fractional equality; *vataslya-rasa*, service with a parental sense of nurture and protective superiority; and *madhurya-rasa*, service in the intimacy of conjugal love. God responds to these different sorts of devotees by manifesting different features or forms to each.

The manifest feature in which the Personality of Godhead enters into the most intimate and confidential of relationships is Krishna. Such intimate relationships are inhibited in the regal Narayana feature of Godhead because in that aspect God manifests his divine majesty, sovereignty, and opulence. In relationships with Narayana, there is always a sense of awe and reverence accompanied by the formalities of manners appropriate to majesty. As Narayana, God's majesty overwhelms his beauty whereas, as Krishna, his beauty defeats his majesty. Krishna sets aside all the trappings of Godhood in order to pursue intensities of love without formal constraint. Thus, Krishna reveals, as it were, the private and personal life of the Godhead, in which the most intimate fraternal, parental, and conjugal exchanges of transcendental love develop without limit.

In his function of world maintenance, God descends age after age to establish the path of religion (*Bhagavad-gita* 4.7–8). One such type of incarnation is called the *yuga-avatara*, the incarnation that teaches the *yuga-dharma*, the particular form of religious practice that is efficacious for the age. The *Srimad Bhagavatam* (12.3.52) says that whatever result was achieved in Satya-*yuga* by meditation on Vishnu, in Treta-*yuga* by performing sacrifice, in Dvapara-*yuga* by worship in the temple, is achieved in the Kali-*yuga* by chanting the name of Krishna. The idea of *yuga-dharma* is a kind of dispensationalism, and as such, it introduces another element of relativity.

What stands out in the list of *yuga-dharmas* is that these religious practices become progressively easier, which is necessary because the increasing degradation of the ages makes spiritual life harder to pursue. Therefore, in each successive age the authorized spiritual practice is, in compensation, made easier. The progressive natural decline in the *yuga* cycle is thus balanced by a progressive increase in divine mercy, so that, as things get worse (in one way), they get better (in another). As we read in the *Srimad Bhagavatam*:

> My dear King, although Kali-*yuga* is full of faults, there is still one good quality about this age. It is that simply by chanting the Hare Krsna *maha-mantra*, . . . one can become free from material bondage and be promoted to the transcendental kingdom.

Gaudiya Vaisnavas recognize Caitanya as the *yuga-avatara* who descends in Kali-*yuga* to teach the *dharma* for this age. In *Caitanya-caritamrta*, the canonical biography of Caitanya, Krsnadasa Kaviraja presents an extended scriptural proof for this contention.[14]

In the doctrine of *yuga-dharma*, the idea of an increasing simplicity of practice is already present. But in the special descents of Krishna and Caitanya, we find an exceptional development. The highest and most confidential features of divinity are increasingly disclosed. The esoteric becomes exoteric; the implicit, explicit; the hidden, manifest. At the same time, by divine grace an increasingly potent means of spiritual practice is made available. Because of this, the pool of candidates for spiritual life becomes indefinitely expanded, and the highest knowledge of the Vedas is offered to everyone, without restriction. Ironically, the worst of the ages, the Kali-*yuga*, is also the easiest in which liberation can occur.

In various places in the *Bhagavad-gita*, for example, Krishna states that the knowledge he is imparting to Arjuna is *guhyatamam*, "the most confidential" (9.1); *raja-ghuya*, "the most secret of all secrets" (9.2); *sarva-guhyatamam*, "the most confidential of all" (18.64). Yet the *Bhagavad-gita* is part of the *Mahabharata*, which is specifically intended for *stri-sudra-dvijabandhu*, women, workers, and fallen members of the twice-born castes (*Bhagavad-gita* 1.4.25), that is, those traditionally considered unqualified for spiritual life (*Bhagavata Purana* 1.4.25).

That most secret knowledge imparted in the *Bhagavad-gita* is simply to recognize fully Krishna's position as the absolute truth, the Supreme Personality of Godhead. This final conclusion (*siddhanta*) of Vedic knowledge is ordinarily extremely difficult to discern, but Krishna makes it explicit. In the *Bhagavad-gita* Krishna surveys all the major "Vedic" religious paths (*dharmas*)—the performance of sacrifice (*yajna*), the detached execution of prescribed duties and rituals (*karma-yoga*), the worship of *devatas*, the practice of meditation (*astanga-yoga*), and the pursuit of enlightenment by philosophical discrimination (*jnana-yoga*)—and declares that all are simply steps on the path to full devotion to him. As Krishna says, "By all the *Vedas* I am to be known" (*Bhagavad-gita*). Therefore, his conclusive instruction to Arjuna is to give up all these various paths, make a short work of it, and surrender to him (*Sarya-dharman parityajya man ekam saranam vraja*) (*Bhagavad-gita* 18.66).

Krishna responds to such devotion by graciously uplifting anyone who adopts it (*Bhagavad-gita* 10.10–11). Thus, the *Bhagavad-gita* says that even women, merchants, (Vaisyas), and laborers (Sudras) can attain the supreme destination (*Bhagavad-gita* 9.32). Similarly, a text in *Srimad Bhagavatam* (2.4.18) lists various barbaric and aboriginal peoples who are utterly outside the pale of "Vedic culture" and states that they can be purified by taking the shelter offered by the devotees of Krishna. Yet another text says that even a person born in a family of dog-eaters becomes eligible to perform Vedic sacrifices (*savanaya kalpate*) by uttering the name of God or by performing other activities of devotional service (*Bhagavata Purana* 3.33.7). In other words, the practices of devotional service are so spiritually potent that they can elevate the lowest person into a pure disciple of status equal to a *brahmana* (priest).

In this way, Krishna's descent revealed the most intimate and confidential pastimes of transcendental life, explicitly and clearly spelled out the highest conclusions of Vedic knowlege, and, through the potent power of *bhakti*, offered the supreme destination to everyone. Yet when Krishna again descended as Sri Caitanya and, taking the role of a devotee, taught the *yuga-dharma*, all these opportunities are extended even further. The *Caitanya-caritamrta* explains it as follows:

> The characteristics of Krsna are understood to be a storehouse of transcendental love. Although that storehouse of love certainly came with Krsna when he was present, it was sealed. But when Sri Caitanya Mahaprabhu came with His other associates of the Panca-tattva, they broke the seal and plundered the storehouse to taste the transcendental love of Krsna. The more they tasted it, the more their thirst for it grew. (Adi, 7.24).

Commenting on this verse, Prabhupada explains:

> Sri Caitanya Mahaprabhu is called *maha-vadanyavatara* [the greatly munificent incarnation] because although He is Sri Krsna Himself, He is even more favorably disposed to the poor fallen souls than Lord Sri Krsna. When Lord Sri Krsna Himself was personally present He demanded that everyone surrender unto Him and promised that He would then give one all protection, but when Sri Caitanya Mahaprabhu came to this earth with his associates, He simply distributed transcendental love of God without discrimination.[15]

The text continues:

> In distributing love of Godhead, Caitanya Mahaprabhu and His associates did not consider who was a fit candidate and who was not, nor where such distribution should or should not take place. They made no conditions. Wherever they got the opportunity the members of the Panca-tattva distributed love of Godhead. The flood of love of Godhead swelled in all directions, and thus young men, old men, women, and children were all immersed in that inundation. The Krsna consciousness movement will inundate the entire world and drown everyone, whether one be a gentleman, a rogue or even lame, invalid and blind.[16]

Elsewhere in *Caitanya-caritamrta* (*Adi*, 9), Krsnadasa Kaviraja depicts Caitanya's movement as a vast tree where Caitanya is simultaneously the trunk of the tree and the gardener who nurtures and harvests. His direct associates are the main branches. These branches grow other branches, and the tree grows to fill the world. All the limbs of the vast tree profusely produce ripened fruit, filled with the sweet nectar of pure devotion, *prema-bhakti*.

Because Sri Krsna Caitanya Mahaprabhu was the original trunk, the taste of the fruits that grew on the branches and subbranches surpassed the taste of nectar. The fruits ripened, becoming sweet and nectarean. The gardener, Sri Caitanya Mahaprabhu, distributed them without asking any price. Not considering who asked for it and who did not, nor who was fit and who unfit to receive it, Caitanya Mahaprabhu distributed the fruit of devotional service. The transcendental gardener, Sri Caitanya Mahaprubhu, distributed handful after handful of fruit in all directions, and when the poor hungry people ate the fruit, the gardener smiled with great pleasure. Lord Caitanya thus addressed the tree of devotional service.

> Since the tree of devotional service is transcendental, every one of its parts can perform the action of all the others. Although a tree is supposed to be immovable, this tree nevertheless moves. All parts of this tree are spiritually cognizant, and thus as they grew up they spread all over the world. I am the only gardener. How many places can I go? How many fruits can I pick and distribute? It would certainly be a very laborious task to pick the fruits and distribute them alone, and still I suspect that some would receive them and others would not. Therefore I order every man within this universe to accept this Krsna consciousness movement and distribute it everywhere.[17]

To spread the *yuga-dharma* in this way is one dimension of Caitanya's advent, whereas another is an even fuller disclosure of the innermost dynamics of the divine life. According to *Caitanya-caritamrta*, as Caitanya, Krishna takes on the feelings and complexions of Radharani, first among the *gopis* of Vrindavana, the highest manifestation of the feminine side of the absolute truth; she is Krishna's eternal consort, the specific embodiment of Krishna's transcendental energy of bliss. All devotional service comes under Radha's jurisdiction, for she is the best of devotees and the most beloved of Krishna. Krishna is astounded by the depth of Radha's love for him, and he realizes that by her love she tastes a bliss even greater than his. He wonders, what is it about himself that elicits such love? Therefore, Krishna, taking on the devotional feelings of Radha, manifests himself as Caitanya, in her golden complexion, and he explores and manifests *maha-bhava*, the superhuman ecstasies of Radharani.

In this way, therefore, the advent of Caitanya represents a development beyond the advent of Krishna, just as that advent represented a similar development. Here, then, is a real sense of progress, a spiritual counterbalance to the natural decline in Kali-*yuga*. Furthermore, this historical sequence is filled in by other divine descents who appeared between Krishna and Caitanya to change history, while arresting the decline in Kali-*yuga* and thus preparing the way for Caitanya.

To try to preserve spiritual culture in Kali-*yuga*, Vyasadeva edited and reduced the *Vedas* to written form, composed the Vedic supplements like the *Puranas* and *Mahabharata*, and inaugurated traditions to preserve and pass the teachings down. After this labor, he was visited at his hermitage by his guru, Narada Muni, who rebuked him for neglecting to describe fully the transcendental pastimes of Krishna, for, Narada explained, to hear and chant the glories of the Lord is so spiritually potent that it alone can save the people in Kali-*yuga*. By transmitting lower forms of religious life, specifically the practices of sense gratification regulated by scriptural injunction, Vyasa has rendered a disservice to the people of Kali-*yuga*. Narada says:

> The people in general are naturally inclined to enjoy, and you have encouraged them in that way in the name of religion. This is verily condemned and is quite unreasonable. Because they are guided under your instructions, they will accept such activities in the name of religion and will hardly care for prohibitions.[18]

Narada's prophetic words were fulfilled, for the Kali-*yuga* had not long progressed before people, in the name of Vedic sacrifice, began to become unrestricted animal killers and meat eaters. Because this practice would bring about the death of all spiritual culture, it had to be stopped, and therefore the Lord descended as the Buddha (ca. 500 B.C.), and undertook emergency action. Vigorously opposing the killing of animals, Buddha preached the doctrine of *ahimsu*, nonviolence. Because people justified such slaughter by appeal to the *Vedas*, the Buddha rejected Vedic authority. Accordingly, the Buddha was silent about transcendental matters, which made him attractive to people whose mentality had become atheistic.

Thus the Buddha stopped animal killing, but the price was the eclipse of the Vedic teachings and tradition. Therefore, at the order of Krishna, Shiva descended as Sankaracarya (A.D. 788) to take the next step in the process of restoration. To attract people steeped in Buddhist thought, Sankaracarya cleverly propounded his impersonal *mayavada* philosophy. This philosophy is, in essence, Buddhist metaphysics expounded in *Upanisadic* categories and terminology. For example, instead of the *sunya* or "emptiness" of Nargajuna, Sankara gives us undifferentiated Brahman, Brahman wholly devoid of name, form, attribute, activity, or relation, and hence cognitively identical with *sunya*. For this reason, *mayavada* philosophy is called by Prabhupada *pracchannam bauddam*, "covered Buddhism" (*Padma Purana, Uttara-khanda* 25.7). Shiva's mission has a dual purpose: on the one hand, by propounding this philosophy he promotes the degeneration of Kali-*yuga*; on the other, he brings about a partial Vedic restoration. He restores the authority of the Vedic literature, reestablishes the *brahminical* community, and forces the Buddhists to leave India.

Next came the great Vaisnava *acaryas* like Ramanuja (A.D. 1017) and Madhava (A.D. 1239), whose theistic readings of *Vedanta* and powerful preaching further prepared the way for the full restoration of spiritual culture under Caitanya Mahaprabhu.

After the preparation of his forebears just mentioned, Caitanya's appearance inaugurated a golden age of Krishna Consciousness within Kali-*yuga*. This extraordinary period is scheduled to last 10,000 years—5,000 years of increase, followed by 5,000 years of decline—after which the chanting of *Hare Krishna* will no longer be heard on this planet, and the full effects of Kali-*yuga*, held at bay, will flood back in.

ISKCON devotees are therefore convinced that Caitanya's movement is destined to become a dominant, if not *the* dominant, force in the modern world. Although Caitanya's movement, even in its first 500 years, has passed through periods of stagnation and apparent decline, the inevitable trend is upward. When necessary, Krishna sends empowered devotees to effect reform and revitalization. This process is exhibited in the case of the last three great *acaryas*—Bhaktivinoda, Bhaktisiddhanta, and Bhaktivedanta—whose work rescued the movement from eclipse, transformed it into a vital preaching organization, and launched it onto the world's stage beginning in America.

Caitanya had predicted that his movement would spread throughout the world and his name would be sung in every town and village. Bhaktivinoda Thakura had become caught up by the desire, expressed by Caitanya, to offer Krishna Consciousness to everybody. In 1885, Bhaktivinoda wrote in his journal, *Sajjana-tosani:*

> Lord Caitanya did not advent Himself to liberate only a few men in India. Rather, his main objective was to emancipate all living entities of all countries throughout the entire universe and preach the Eternal Religion. . . . There is no doubt that this unquestionable order will come to pass. . . . Very soon the unparalleled path of *hari-nama-sankirtana* will be propagated all over the world. . . . Oh, for that day when the fortunate English, French, Russian, German, and American people will take up banners, *mrdangas*, and *karatalas* and raise *kirtana* through their streets and towns! When will that day come?[19]

Prabhupada's achievement in successfully propagating Caitanya's mission outside of India fulfills the prediction of Caitanya and the desire of Bhaktivinoda Thakura. Consequently, we who are his disciples in ISKCON see our institution as historically special, a part of this momentous step toward fulfilling the destiny of Caitanya's movement and Krishna's mission of salvation. Above all, Prabhupada has charged his disciples in ISKCON with the mandate to further the progress of Caitanya's mission just as he has done, and, by so doing, work to bring about the full manifestation of 10,000 years of the golden age of Krishna Consciousness.

ISKCON has inherited this linear historical vision, presenting a salvation history in which Krishna, Vyasa, Buddha, Sankaracarya, Ramanuja, Madhva, and Caitanya are all part of a vast divine plan, a plan that later includes Bhaktivinoda, Bhaktisiddhanta, Bhaktivedanta, and ISKCON itself. Seeing themselves in the context of this sacred history, ISKCON devotees are self-conscious historical actors, makers of history. Moreover, as we have seen, this linear strand brings into play notions of change and relativity, of practice and revelation adapted to time and circumstance. There is not only real engagement with concrete history, but also a legitimate opportunity for innovation. We can contrast this strand with the notion of tradition that emphasizes preservation and conservation, the reinstantiation of the past in the present.

A verse in *Srimad Bhagavatam* describes Bhismadeva, one of the great authorities, as *dharma-jno desa-kala-vibagavit*, one who "knew perfectly all the religious principles according to time and place" (1.9.9). Srila Prabhupada comments:

> All the great *acaryas* or religious preachers or reformers of the world executed their mission by adjustment of religious principles in terms of time and place. There are different climates and situations in different parts of the world, and if one has to discharge his duties to preach the message of the Lord, he must be expert in adjusting things in terms of the time and place.[20]

In bringing Caitanya's movement to the West, Prabhupada made such adjustments. Most notably, he set the prescribed number of daily rounds of *japa* at sixteen (instead of Bhaktisiddhanta's sixty-four); he simplified ritual, especially with regard to *puja;* he created an *asrama* for unmarried women, coining the word *brahmacarini;* and he gave women disciples *brahminical* initiation with the *gayatri mantra*, hence enabling them to assume all priestly functions, including *puja*, traditionally performed by men alone.

ISKCON devotees are highly conscious of the innovative nature of

ISKCON, and, especially because many devotees have been able to spend time in India, we know very well how much we differ from traditional forms of "Hinduism." At the same time, we feel we have not left anything behind, that the full tradition has been transmitted to us, and that, by Prabhupada's grace, we have inherited everything that India's ancient spiritual heritage has to offer. We feel very old, and we feel very new.

Our weighty responsibility is to transmit what Prabhupada has given us intact to the next generation and to further the progress of Caitanya's movement. In the pages of *Srimad Bhagavatam* Srila Prabhupada has provided the blueprints for a complete spiritual civilization, and our task is to discover the ways and means to construct that civilization. We need, in that case, to be both conservative and innovative simultaneously, not securing the one at the expense of the other. Consequently, ISKCON's complex historical self-perception, uniting both tradition and a progressive linear-sacred paradigm, provides a framework for combining conservation and innovation, thus giving ISKCON both its past and its future.

Notes

1. Rudolf Otto, *India's Religion of Grace and Christianity Compared and Contrasted*, ed. Joseph M. Kitagawa (New York: Columbia University Press, 1958), p. 86.

2. Mircea Eliade, *The Myth of the Eternal Return*, trans. Willard R. Trask (Princeton: Princeton University Press, 1971), p. 104.

3. Ibid.

4. Joachim Wach, *The Comparative Study of Religion*, ed. Joseph Kitagawa (New York: Columbia University Press, 1958), p. 87.

5. Eliade, *Eternal Return*, p. 117.

6. Otto, *India's Religion of Grace*, p. 70.

7. A. C. Bhaktivedanta Swami Prabhupada, *The Science of Self-Realization* (Los Angeles: The Bhaktivedanta Book Trust, 1978), pp. 72–73.

8. A. C. Bhaktivedanta Swami Prabhupada, *The Bhagavad-gita AS IT IS* (Los Angeles: The Bhaktivedanta Book Trust, 1972), pp. 860–61.

9. A. C. Bhaktivedanta Swami Prabhupada, *Srimad Bhagavatam*, 34 vols. (Los Angeles: The Bhaktivedanta Book Trust, 1972–85), 1.1:199. Hereafter only *Bhagavatam* followed by chapter, verse, and page number will be given.

10. Ibid., 2.9, pp. 160–61.

11. Eliade, *Eternal Return*, pp. 147–54.

12. Ibid., p. 141.

13. Ibid., p. 153.

14. *Bhagavatam*, 12.3, p. 51.

15. Krsnadasa Kaviraja Gosvami, *Sri Caitanya-caritamrta*, translation and commentary by A. C. Bhaktivedanta Swami Prabhupada, 14 vols. (Los Angeles: The Bhaktivedanta Book Trust, 1974–75), *Adi-lila*, 7.24 and 2, p. 16.

16. Ibid., *Adi*, 7.23, 25, and 26.

17. Ibid., *Adi*, 9.26–27 and 29–36.

18. *Bhagavatam*, 1.5, p. 15.

19. *Sri Namamrta: The Nectar of the Holy Name*, ed. Subhananda dasa (Los Angeles: The Bhaktivedanta Book Trust, 1982).

20. *Bhagavatam*, 1.2, p. 82.

III. ISKCON in American Culture

The Attitude of Americans toward Hinduism from 1883 to 1983 with Special Reference to the International Society for Krishna Consciousness

J. Gordon Melton

The history of Hinduism in America proper can be said to have begun on 2 September 1883 when Protap Chunder Mozoomdar, the first Hindu teacher, who had arrived in Boston a few days before, delivered his initial American lecture to a small group gathered in the parlor of the widow of Ralph Waldo Emerson in Concord, Massachusetts.[1] The cordial reception he was accorded that day would be in marked contrast to the general attitude that Westerners in general and Americans in particular would demonstrate when Hinduism appeared as a movement in their countries. Mozoomdar and his colleagues who arrived during the next twenty-five years soon encountered the strong negative attitudes against India and its religion, which had been integral to both Christian and secular literature on Asia during the nineteenth century.

As one traces the rise of Hinduism to its present status as a major minority faith in America with hundreds of thousands of adherents, the hostility to its growth and spread has been more than evident. The attitude has produced a period of suppressive activity whenever a segment of the public has defined Hinduism as an immediate threat. To counter the hostility, Hindu organizations have launched public relations campaigns both to dispel negative images about India and Hindu religious practices and to champion the worthiness of Hindu thought by identifying it with the mainstream of Western thought.

The phases of interaction with the American public divide American Hindu history into four periods: from the arrival of Mozoomdar to the passing of the Oriental Exclusion Act in 1917; the period of controversies over citizenship and the *Book I* in the 1920s; a period of relative calm from

1930 to 1965; and the period of the cult wars that began soon after the recision of the Asian exclusion laws by President Lyndon Johnson.

The First Generation

Hindu thought had begun to filter into New England in the early nineteenth century. The appreciation of the *Bhagavad-gita* by the likes of Ralph Waldo Emerson became a significant element in the development of the Transcendentalist Movement and led in turn to the alignment of the Unitarian Association with Hindu reformist movements such as the Brahmo Samaj.[2] That alignment, still live today, produced the initial visit by Mozoomdar and guaranteed him at least an open hearing, the same he would receive when he returned in 1893 as one of a small handful of Hindus to address the World's Parliament of Religions in Chicago.

At the Chicago meeting, Mozoomdar, his more popular colleague, Swami Vivekananda, and other speakers would have to address prominent negative images of their homeland and their faith. Their presentations occurred in the context of the Rev. L. E. Slater's lecture in which he characterized the Indian public as "masses of people under the dominion of the priesthood, all sunk in the grossest superstition."[3] Slater's remarks, of course, simply reflected the opinion found in most nineteenth century writing on Asia and Africa. Hindus and Buddhists alike also spoke to an audience conditioned to think of America as the center of true religion (Protestantism) and not a place where heathen religion would find an audience. Methodist Bishop Jesse Peck summarized the opinions of many who listened to the Parliament's speakers, "True religion is the driving force of the nation by which God is advancing among men and subduing all things. . . . The framers of the Constitution and their successors have legislated not for Jews, Mohammedans, infidels, pagans, atheists, but for Christians . . . in other words, Christianity, as really as republicanism, is part and parcel of our laws."[4] Though rarely stated in print in recent decades, the belief in Christian America routinely affects attitudes toward Hindu Americans.

Just five years before the Parliament, a distinguished and ecumenical group of American religious scholars had compiled a one-volume encyclopedic handbook of world religion, *What the World Believes*.[5] It included India and Hinduism in its chapters on the "Pagan Nations" and, while attempting some degree of objective description, could not help but denounce what they saw as inexcusable practices. The Juggernaut festival, currently a major celebration of the Hare Krishna movement in America, was singled out because of the indignation aroused by the "horrors" of its observance. At the festival a black idol with a distended blood-colored mouth was pulled through the streets on a movable tower, under whose wheels devotees threw themselves to be crushed in an act of religious suicide. Indians were also accused of infanticide, for drowning their children in the Ganges.

At the Parliament, the youthful Vivekananda, easily the most exotic and the most popular speaker, defended the religious practices of his brothers and sisters back at home. "At the very outset," he asserted, "I may tell you that there is no polytheism in India." The missionaries distorted the picture of worship in Hinduism, and he compared the veneration of images in the Hindu temples with the use of "idols" within Christian practice. "Why does a Christian go to church? Why is the cross holy? Why is the face toward the sky in prayer? Why are there so many images in the Catholic church? Why are so many images in the minds of Protestants when they pray? My brethren, we can no more think about anything without a material image than we can live without breathing."[6] His speech, of course, did not go unnoticed by critics, both Hindu and Christian.[7]

Vivekananda left the Parliament and toured the United States for the next two years. He found enough response to form the first American Hindu organization, the Vedanta Society, in New York in 1895. On his return to India, he organized the movement in Bengal. He also found other leaders to come to the United States and head the several centers he had created. Swami Abhedananda, among the most productive writers of Vivekananda's colleagues, came to New York and Swami Turiyananda to San Francisco in 1899. Hinduism, as small as it was, had come to stay.[8]

The establishment of the first Vedanta Centers coincided with the first wave of Indian immigrants into the United States. Before 1900, no more than a few hundred people from India had come to America per decade. However, during the first decade of the new century, almost five thousand came. While not a large number in itself, as they became concentrated in a few communities, they appeared to other residents to be more numerous than they were. They also came at the very time the Asian Exclusion League had emerged on the West Coast to agitate for legal barriers against the admission of any Asians, especially Japanese and Chinese, to the United States. Although a large percentage of the new immigrants were Sikhs from the Punjab, all Indians were considered "Hindoos" by the non-Asian majority.

The "Hindoos" found jobs in the various farms and industries along the Pacific coast, where their turbans gave them a high level of visibility, especially in the smaller towns. Thus, when discharged workers saw their former jobs being given to Punjabis, who worked for less wages, they knew exactly upon whom to direct their anger. Such anger grew through the middle part of the decade, and in 1907 erupted in a series of anti-Hindoo riots. Typical was the riot in Bellingham, Washington, directed at Punjabi workers at a local sawmill. On the evening of 4 September, over four hundred men attacked the town's Hindoo residents. Some were beaten; others escaped naked into the night. The rioters sought to drive the "ragheads" out of town, and they succeeded. Similar incidents occurred in Seattle, Vancouver, Aberdeen, and Everett, Washington; Live Oak, California; and St. John, Oregon.[9]

The discussion of the Indian presence in America following the riot in Bellingham immediately tied the labor problems of the Punjabis with the several Hindu movements already active. A few voices tried to defend the riot victims. Girindra Mukerji, writing in the influential *Overland Monthly*, summarized his discussion by hesitatingly suggesting, "Who shall say, if we give in exchange, that a leaven of Hindu philosophy would not improve the humanity and even the business instinct of the strenuous American."[10] Mukerji's lone voice, however, was lost in the violent rhetoric against the phenomenon of the "turbaned tornado," the Indian equivalent to the Yellow Peril.

Writing in the same issue as Mukerji, Agnes Foster Buchannan foreshadowed the direction of the future discussion, "The Hindus and the Hindu Invasion is the latest racial problem with which we in the West have to deal. Not that it is as yet fully recognized as such." She summarized her observations by calling for new protective legal measures: "This is the propitious moment for the State Department to adopt an amendment to the Vedas and to tell our brothers of the East that while the earth is large enough for us all, there is no part of it that will comfortably accommodate both branches of the Aryan family."[11]

Within this increasingly hostile environment during the first decade of the century, Hinduism tried to grow among non-Indian Americans, and grow it did. One by one, Hindu teachers appeared and movements emerged. Some movements died after a few years, others lasted a few decades, and several remain to this day.

The first swamis not directly connected with Vivekananda arrived in 1902. Swami Rama Tirtha, a young Vedantist, landed in San Francisco, penniless and without luggage. For the next two years he lectured across the United States, appealing to Americans in part by his denunciation of the Indian caste system. While in America, he launched an organization to assist Indian students at American universities, arguing that educated youth, not missionaries, was what India needed. Unfortunately the young guru died suddenly in 1906; he drowned in the Ganges. Though only in his twenties at the time of his death, he had so inspired a few followers that they formed an organization to keep his memory alive and his writings in print.[12]

Baba Premanand Bharati, a devotee of Krishna Consciousness, began his work in New York City, where he formed the Krishna Samaj. In 1906 he attended an interfaith conference in Los Angeles, as a result of which he moved his headquarters to that city. After five years of activity, he returned to India to begin an organization there, although he seems to have had but little success. The Los Angeles Temple survived until his death in 1914.[13]

The Vedanta Society stabilized its two initial centers in New York and San Francisco (to which rural retreats were attached). New centers emerged in Boston, Washington, D.C., and Los Angeles. In 1910, Swami Abhedananda, the leader in New York, separated himself and began to work independently out of the rural center in Connecticut formerly affiliated with the New York Center.

The growth of Hinduism among non-Indians in America was only partially due to the few groups with Indian leadership. Several Americans adopted the role of Hindu teacher and had a marked effect on the spread of Hinduism within the occult/metaphysical community as well as the general public. Most important of the American "Hindus" was the lawyer William Walker Atkinson. Atkinson had moved to Chicago around the turn of the century and became a popular New Thought author and the founder of the Atkinson School of Mental Science. However, while continuing to write and teach New Thought, he assumed a second identity as Swami Ramacharacka and began to write books on Hindu thought. The first of the thirteen volumes appeared in 1903 as *Fourteen Lessons in Yoga Philosophy and Oriental Occultism.* His publisher, the Yogi Publication Society, has kept the volumes in print. So accurate is his presentation of Hinduism that, in recent years, Indian authors have quoted him as a reliable source.[14]

A second American Hindu, whose controversial activities did much to add to the negative image of Hinduism, was Pierre Bernard, who around 1909 founded the Tantrik Order in America in New York City. As a teacher of yoga and tantrism (which some would equate with its sexual aspects), Bernard took the title "Oom the Omnipotent." He quietly gathered disciples until two ex-members told the New York District Attorney and the press that Bernard had been holding them prisoner and that the Order was a cover for weekly orgies. The case was dropped when the two women disappeared. He survived the scandal, however, and began to move in socialite circles. Eventually he included some of the Vanderbilts among his followers.[15]

In 1924 he moved the Order to an estate in Nyack, New York, where despite the continuing rumors about sex and wealthy female followers, he became a respected citizen and community leader. His nephew, Theos Bernard, later wrote a thesis on yoga at Columbia University, *The*

Report of a Personal Experience (1944), which has become a classic on the topic, Hatha Yoga.[16]

A survey of the popular occult literature also reveals the presence of occultists, such as L. W. de Laurence, who assumed the role of a Hindu teacher and became one source of the popular image of swami as fortune teller. Books by the Hindu teachers, both Indian and American, circulated within the occult community and helped produce one of the few genuinely positive images of India and its religion, the popular occult notion of the mystic East as the fountain of pure occult wisdom. For most Americans, however, such books merely served to associate India with the most suspect part of American religion.

The physical violence directed toward the Indian laborers never reached the American Hindu centers,[17] though coverage of the riots reminded the public of the swamis' continued presence. During the succeeding decade, as the political movement to pass omnibus Asian exclusion legislation grew in strength, the various Hindu movements became the target of increasingly vicious attacks in books, magazines, and newspapers. The press played up incidents such as the scandal following the death of Sara Bull in 1911. This energetic follower of Vedanta left the greater part of her $500,000 estate to the Vedanta movement for charitable work in India. Her daughter, claiming that her mother had developed an unsound and disordered mind, contested the will. As evidence she called for the testimony of servants who detailed the visits of the swamis, described a meditation room complete with its pictures of overweight swamis, and recounted "seances" in which Bull and her friends sat in silence while burning incense. Based upon their description of her Hindu practices, she was declared to have been mentally incompetent; the will was overturned and all the money awarded to the daughter (who unfortunately herself died the same day that the award was made).[18]

Women took the lead in responding to the Bull trial. Typical of the articles was that by the wife of the editor of *The Methodist Quarterly Review* complaining that thousands of American women had forsaken the churches to follow heathen gods. This article was among the first to draw attention to the predominantly feminine makeup of the following of the swamis.[19] This observation, already made of Vivekananda by his critics, became a recurring theme in the writings of future critics of the Vedanta Society, who complained that Hinduism appealed primarily to bored older females.

The most substantive and among the most vicious attacks on the fledgling movement was Elizabeth A. Reed's *Hinduism in Europe and America*. Reed's two-hundred page diatribe, picking up what was to become another constant theme, accused the American swamis of preaching a misleading representation of Hinduism for the purpose of "the gathering in of foreign coin." Westerners became interested in this Americanized product without investigating its Indian foundations. Thus, to discourage any potential converts, she devoted the major portion of the volume to description of Indian Hinduism, emphasizing its worse aspects.

Reed culminated her attack by turning to those European and American fanatics who already followed the "corrupt" cult of Baba Bharati. Given the nature of their devotion, it was no wonder, she argued, they frequently ended their excursion into Hinduism in an asylum. Even though Bharati and the other swamis had yet to bring the worst of their idols, they did far worse; they enforced a slavish devotion to themselves. Followers caressed the swamis' robes and kissed their feet. Reed's final warning could have been written in the 1970s, "Let the white woman beware of the hypnotic influence of the East—let her remember that when her Guru, or god-man, has once whispered his mystic syllables into her ear and she has sworn allegiance to him, she is forever helpless in his hands."[20]

Confronted by such massive attacks, there was little that the Hindu leaders could do. In 1912 Swami Paramananda, from the Vedanta Center in Boston, began a periodical, whose purpose was to promote understanding and harmony. In its first issue, Paramananda appealed to his audience, "Uncharitableness, fanaticism and denunciation do not belong to the spiritual realm or, indeed, to true civilization; hence we should strive diligently to transcend them."[21] Hindu leaders also tried to present themselves as noncompetitive with the churches, the leaders of which had joined in the attack. Bharati, on the eve of his return to India in 1907, countered his critics by declaring, "I came not here to thrust my religion upon you, but to help you to understand your own God and your own religion. If I have talked of Krishna and the *Vedas* and Hindu philosophy, it was only to illuminate the teachings of your own Christ, to present him before you in the light of the *Vedas*, and the X-ray of our scientific philosophies."[22] Paramananda echoed similar sentiments, "The purpose of this work is not to offer a substitute for existing faiths or to foster any spirit of rivalry towards them, but to lend a friendly hand to all who earnestly seek after Truth."[23]

Their demonstrations, however, hardly slowed the tidal wave of hostile public opinion. In 1917 anti-Asian sentiment led to the passing of legislation that created the Asian Barred Zone and denied entry to immigrants from most Asian countries, including India. This law was slightly modified in 1921 by the introduction of the quota system, which allowed a trickle of immigration based upon the percentage of the number of persons of any given national origin then residing in the

United States. India's quota permitted the immigration of approximately one hundred annually.

The Asian exclusion legislation significantly blocked what would probably have been a significant growth of Hinduism. Potential teachers were, as a whole, unable to come to America. Of the organizations created before 1917, only the Vedanta Society seems to have survived into the 1920s as a viable group. But even with the low quotas, a few new gurus were able to slip through and, once in America, founded new Hindu organizations.

American Hinduism in the 1920s and 1930s

A surprising number of Hindu organizations appeared in the 1920s, a few founded by teachers who had arrived before the exclusion laws were enacted, and others founded by those who came after 1921. Besudeb Bhattacharya, better known by his religious title, Pundit Acharya, came to the United States before World War I. The author of several dramatic works, he is remembered as the founder of the Temple of Yoga, the Yoga Research Institute, and Prana Press, through which he published a number of books and pamphlets. Like Bernard, he began in New York City but moved his work to Nyack during his last years.[24]

Paramahansa Yogananda was the most important of the several swamis who arrived after 1921. This teacher of *kriya yoga* came to Boston in 1924 to attend an interfaith conference and stayed in America to found the Yogada-Satsang, later known as the Self-Realization Fellowship. His *Autobiography of a Yogi* (1946), which has enjoyed immense popularity and wide circulation, has done much in recent years to modify the harsh image of Hinduism.[25] The Self-Realization Fellowship became the largest Hindu organization in America before 1965 and, through the correspondence lessons written by Yogananda, spread Hindu teachings throughout North America.

Other popular teachers during this era included A. K. Mozumdar, whose Messianic World Message blended Christian and Hindu elements; Swami Omkar of the Santi Ashrama in Philadelphia and Los Angeles; Sri Deva Ram Sukul of the Hindu Yoga Society headquartered in Chicago; Kedarnath Das Gupta, active in the Fellowship of Faiths and leader of the Dharma Mandal; Rishi Krishnananda of the Para-Vidya Center in Los Angeles; Sant Ram Mandal of the Universal Brotherhood Temple and School of Eastern Philosophy; and Swami A. P. Mukerji of the Transcendent Science Society in Chicago. A number of Hindu teachers who did not found a separate organization became popular speakers and authored numerous titles; they included Bhagwan Singh Gyanee, Rishi Singh Grewal, and Mahasiddha Satchidananda.[26]

Anti-Hinduism in the 1920s

One would think that once the Asian exclusion legislation was in place and the growth of Hinduism effectively blocked, the small movement would have been left in relative peace. Such was not the case. Two significant anti-Hindu crusades pervaded the 1920s.

First, in 1870 the United States had passed a law that provided for the naturalization of "any alien, being a free white person who otherwise meets the requirement of the law." Under this law, the status of Indians became a matter of debate. The Asian Exclusion League considered them orientals and like the Japanese and Chinese, not eligible for citizenship. Indians, on the other hand, argued with some modest success that they were racially "caucasian" and hence "white." Some courts agreed and granted citizenship to Indians on that basis.

The issue was resolved, however, in 1923 in *United States* vs. *Bhagat Singh Thind*. In a ruling by the United States Supreme Court, Justice George Sunderland accepted the "common" understanding that not all caucasians were to be considered "white" persons. His action not only denied Thind his citizenship but led the Immigration and Naturalization Service to revoke the citizenship previously granted to other Indians.[27]

Second, the image of Hinduism for most Americans has always been intimately associated with their image of India. Throughout the nineteenth century, India had been portrayed as a backward barbaric nation whose religion was nothing more than an idolatry that included the most inhumane and immoral practices. In 1927 the reading public was reminded (in a new book, Katherine Mayo's *Mother India*), that India had not changed. The book was an immediate bestseller, going through no less than thirty-three printings in four years. M. V. Kamath, writing in the souvenir volume published by the Embassy of India on the occasion of the United States bicentennial in 1976, said of *Mother India*, "No other book about India, written either before or after, has done more to damage Indo-American understanding than this singular exercise in concentrated venom. . . . *Mother India* succeeded in prejudicing an entire generation of Americans."[28]

Almost forgotten today, Mayo unleashed her attack against almost every aspect of Indian society. She began, however, with a vivid description of a visit to a temple of Kali, where she introduced the reader to animal sacrifices and the resultant bloody rites, child brides, public health dangers, and an impotent people. She summarized her conclusions:

> Inertia, helplessness, lack of initiative and originality, lack of staying power and sustained loyalties, sterility of enthusiasm, weakness

of life vigor itself—all are traits that truly characterize the Indian not
only of today, but of long-past history. . . . His soul and body are
indeed chained in slavery. But he himself wields and hugs his
chains and with violence defends them.[29]

The total condemnation of India by Mayo could not go unanswered
and numerous responses appeared. C. S. Ranga Iyer's *Father India*,
published within months of Mayo's book, went through twelve printings
within six months.[30] American occult teacher William Estep, himself a
teacher of "Esoteric Cosmic Yogi Science," defended India and the practices of Hinduism by attacking the colonial rule of the British. He accused
Mayo of punishing a nation that was already a prisoner.[31]

Mother India became just one more obstacle for the growing American
Hindu community. They countered it with books and articles and interviews with newspaper reporters. Its lingering effects, however, were still
evident at the World Fellowship of Faiths meeting in Chicago in 1935. An
entire section, coordinated by American-Hindu leader, Kedernath Das
Gupta, extolled the virtues of India and Hinduism under the heading,
"Mother India, Fountain Head of Civilizations and Religions." Without
mentioning Mayo or her book, the different speakers answered her
charges and tried to picture India as a civilized country ravaged by
British rule and Hinduism as a religion with solutions for the world's
problems.[32]

Thirty Years of Peace

After the *Mother India* controversy spent its venom, American Hindus
were left in relative peace, having been dealt a series of blows to their
faith that could have killed it but merely left it in a weakened position.
No longer seen as a threat, Hinduism received only occasional treatment
in both the press and books on American religion. Writers generally
treated Eastern groups as religious exotica, nothing to be taken seriously
on either a theological or spiritual level. People who join such groups
were pictured as socially marginal-psychopathic, sexually maladjusted,
deviant, or social failures.

Richard Mathison's *Faiths, Cults and Sects of America* (1960), for example, treated Hinduism in his section, "California: Mecca for Cultists."
Mathison introduced his discussion of Eastern religions by noting that
California had become the home of "the unstable, the fanatic and the
plain dilly."[33] Yogananda, the guru of the luminous eyes and long wavy
hair, had settled in the "City of Psychopathic Angels." Considering the
visit of an Indian religious leader to Yogananda's center, Mathison noted
that Sri Jagadguru Shankatacharya had purchased new shoes and socks

to replace a pair that had worn out on the trip to the West. He reflected, "one could not help but note the significant message stamped on one sock toe, 'Satisfaction Guaranteed or Money Refunded.' "[34]

Arthur Orrmont treated one "Hindu" group among his collection of *Love Cults and Faith Healers*.[35] Krishna Venta, also known as Frank Penovic, founded the Fountain of the World near Chatsworth, California. This particular teacher is remembered primarily for dying in the 10 December 1958 dynamite explosion set by some ex-members upset over their wives' attachment to him. Marcus Bach, generally a very sympathetic observer of America's religious alternatives, treated Hinduism in his 1961 volume, *Strange Sects and Curious Cults*, in a section on sex cults.[36]

While people discounted American Hinduism, it was growing at a slow and modest pace, acquiring some important and articulate support (for example, Aldous Huxley, Gerald Heard, Christopher Isherwood[37]). Quite apart from the two well-known Hindu organizations, other teachers were creating a largely invisible body of believers across the United States, believers who quietly passed their religious perspectives to succeeding generations through occult interest groups and privately published books and pamphlets. The spread of courses in comparative religion in the Western institutions of higher education further assisted the growth of Hinduism. Although not a proselytizing activity, such courses created a desire in people for religious options not immediately available to them. A few adventurous souls journeyed to India to find a teacher. More awaited the arrival of teachers into their own community. A growing number of people already attached to Hindu ideas and an even larger number of the religiously dissatisfied who were open and ready for a new alternative stood in place when the Eastern gates were thrown open in 1965.

Throughout the century, but particularly in the 1930s, theosophy, through its several branches, had made a vital contribution to the growth and spread of Hinduism. In the early years it had been the major conduit for the entrance of Hindu thought into America. Indian teachers found local theosophical groups important stops on lecture tours, while members held dear the occult ideal of Eastern wisdom. Under Katherine Tingley, the American Theosophical Society developed a Raja Yoga Academy at their headquarters complex at Point Loma, California. In India, under Annie Besant, The Theosophical Society published an increasing number of books on Hindu thought, particularly on reincarnaton and karma, by far the most appealing new ideas to infiltrate the West from India.[38]

Concurrent with the *Mother India* controversy, an additional embarrassment to American Hinduism occurred unwittingly at the hands of the American Theosophical Society. Theosophists had increasingly predicted the arrival of a "world teacher," a new avatar for the modern age. In the person of young Jeddu Krishnamurti, Annie Besant and Charles Leadbeater believed they had found him, and during the mid-1920s they established the Order of the Star in the East to promote the new guru. However, in 1929, Krishnamurti announced his disbelief in his messianic role and the following year left the Theosophists. The press used the occasion for yet more ridicule of the Society.[39] After the initial scandal subsided, however, the Hindu community greatly benefited from the affair. Krishnamurti remained in the West as a teacher who attained both credibility and popularity. Though never building an organization of Krishnamurti believers, he continually traveled and lectured to ever increasing numbers of people who accepted his views. His writings are more popular than ever.[40]

The Theosophical Society and the organizations formed before World War II carried the Hindu vision in America through and after the war years up until 1965. A few new teachers, such as Yogi Gupta of the New York-based Yogi Gupta Association, arrived.[41] They led in the burgeoning of *hatha yoga* during the 1950s.[42] More important, after the war, several Americans made their way to the East to study and return as Hindu teachers, including Gurudeva Sivaya Subramuniyaswami, who in 1957 founded the Subramuniya Yoga Order, more recently renamed the Saiva Siddhanta Church.[43]

By 1965, most large American cities had at least one Hindu center and some, such as New York, Chicago, and Los Angeles, had several. Despite the Asian exclusion laws, a significant group of people who identified themselves as Hindus could be found across the United States. Though relatively small in comparison to the most conventional religious groups, they were augmented by a much larger group who were very sympathetic and open to Hindu beliefs (such as reincarnation) and practices (yoga and vegetarianism).

Since 1965

The spread of Hindu groups, practices, and ideas prepared the foundation on which a new era of American Hinduism could begin in 1965. In that year the quotas blocking immigration from Asia were removed by an amendment to the Immigration Act. Between 1871 and 1965, only 16,013 Indians had been admitted to the United States. Between 1965 and 1975, more than 96,000 were admitted, and the 1980 Census reported 387,223 Indians in the United States, the largest community (84,000) being in the New York City metropolitan area. Over fifty Hindu congregations serving first-generation Indian immigrants can currently be found in Chicago. Satyananda Ashrams, U.S.A. is typical of several Hindu organizations serving primarily Indian-Americans with centers across the United States. Hindu temple associations are currently erecting traditional Indian temple complexes at approximately twenty sites from New York to California.

This change in immigration also allowed a number of Hindu teachers to come to the United States and establish new groups consisting predominantly of new converts from among the general population. Whereas most of the new "Hindu" groups have remained local or regional in scope, the more successful—the Siddha Yoga Dham of America, the Kripalu Yoga Ashram, the Sivananda Yoga Vedanta Centers, the World Plan Executive Council—have developed a large national, even international, membership.

Religious observers and scholars were not slow to discern what was happening, though few tied the growth of Eastern religion to the 1965 change.[44] They quickly placed the Eastern religions within the context of the broadly based national revival of religious interest in the early 1970s, but supporters,[45] critics,[46] and mere observers[47] sensed that the Eastern invasion might be a special part of the wave of new religious phenomena. Throughout the 1970s, capped by Harvey Cox's book and articles in 1977, the alarm was sounded,[48] although it was not until the end of the decade that the demographic data was brought to bear on the question of the growth of Indian religion in America.[49] By that time, the major denominations in America had also become aware of the distinctive growth of their Asian-American constituency and were putting personnel and financial resources into national programmed responses.

Among the new groups, the International Society for Krishna Consciousness is not the most successful (in terms of its number of members), but has become, along with the World Plan Executive Council (the promoters of Transcendental Meditation), the best known. It was among the first of the "new" Hindu groups. A. C. Bhaktivedanta Swami, having come to America on a tourist visa just before the immigration laws were changed, was able to stay in America because of the change. Also because of the particular form of *bhakti yoga* they practiced, Krishnas, dressed in their orange robes and with their shaved heads and painted brows, became a common sight on city streets and in airports, where they danced, chanted, and solicited financial support. ISKCON became so visible to the public and the press and was so picturesque with its Indian garb and traditional temples, that pictures of Krishna devotees most frequently were used to illustrate articles on cults and new religions. Quite apart from any substantive discussion or even mention in the printed text,[50] they became the subject of numerous cartoons and provided comic relief in many movies and television shows. One could argue that during the 1970s ISKCON became the image of the typical "cult" in the public mind.

ISKCON also arose as a bridge between the more Westernized Hindu groups and the recently imported traditional Hinduism of the first-generation Indian immigrants. Although, like the Western groups, its membership consisted primarily of American-born young adults, it has been accepted as genuinely orthodox by the Indian-American community, many members of which attend Krishna temple functions in the absence of an Indian temple in their own community. With its feet in both Hindu camps, ISKCON is a fitting group for use as an illustrative model of the scope of public attitudes toward Hinduism in general.

Krishnas, The First Decade, 1965–1974

For most of the first decade after Bhaktivedanta arrived in the United States, the attitude toward him and his new groups was cordial. Not perceived as a threat, he was treated by the press as an interesting new figure in town, the leader of a marginal movement confined to such places as Greenwich Village and California. The early news reports tried to describe the Krishnas and their strange teachings and practice. Little animosity and much curiosity were evident.[51]

By 1970, more substantive treatments of the Krishnas appeared suggesting various models by which they might be better understood. The counterculture communes, which had appeared as the flower children disbanded and scattered in the 1960s, offered a model for those who looked closely at New Vrindaban.[52] A few placed the Krishnas within the larger occult community;[53] fewer still adopted the "cult" model.[54] The first scholars who looked at the Krishnas placed them within the spectrum of the "new religious experiments" that had their most visible presence in California. The studies of the "new religions" that developed around the several campuses in Berkeley, California, took the new religions model and made it the dominant one within the scholarly community.[55]

These initial shorter treatments led directly to the first two book-length studies of the movement by outsiders: J. Stillson Judah's *Hare Krishna and the Counterculture*[56] and Faye Levine's *The Strange World of the Hare Krishnas*, both of which appeared in 1974. Judah offered a very positive scholarly appraisal of ISKCON, which he viewed as a viable religious alternative that had both flowed from the counterculture of the 1960s and transcended it. Levine, a journalist, wrote after a month-long stay in the Krishna temple in New York. Adopting the "communal" model for an overall approach, she manifested only a passing awareness of the growing anti-cult movement, although, amid her final evaluations of the Krishnas, she portends what is to come:

> Logic indicates they have something going for them. . . . And yet there is something inescapably frightening about their altered personalities.
> In the end, a certain absence of humanity must be noted.[57]

The Second Decade—1974 to the Present

For the Krishnas, 1974 turned out to be a doubly important year. The secular anticult movements that had emerged in several communities around the country combined their strength to form the first national organization, the Citizens Freedom Foundation (CFF). Concurrent with their emergence, the first deprogrammings of members occurred, and the rather benign image of the Krishnas that had dominated the previous literature about the movement began to change. The Krishnas were cited by the CFF as one major cult among the many that they were against. It and the other anti-cult groups that emerged over the next few years accused the Krishnas of deception in recruiting and fundraising, brainwashing their recruits, and holding them by some form of psychological coercion. The chanting of the Hare Krishna mantra was portrayed as a mind-manipulating technique that dulls the senses, destroys the rational faculties, and, according to a few anti-cult spokespersons, actually causes physical damage.[58]

This totally negative image from the secular anti-cult movement worked in tandem with the images of Christian counter-cultists. Christians, who have long enjoyed a religious hegemony in America, had become aware of the growth of alternative religions as the Jesus People Revival spread along the West Coast in the late 1960s. As early as 1970, they had begun to publish tracts and magazine articles against the most visible of the new movements, including the Krishnas. As a whole, Christian literature provided an apologetic for Christianity and argued the truth of the Christian faith against the various alternatives. The testimonies of former members of the various groups have been a popular feature.

The first Christian book against the new Eastern religions, R. D. Clements's *God and the Gurus*, began with the images of Krishnas: "Dancing figures chant the names of Hindu gods in O'Hare Airport in Chicago."[59] As with a number of volumes to follow, Clements devoted a chapter to a description of the movement and refuted it in the light of Christian affirmations. Most Christian books have, with more or less competency, followed Clements's patterns and concentrated on informing Christian audiences of the theological differences between Christianity and Hinduism in general and Krishna Consciousness in particular. Major themes have been the nature of Jesus' uniqueness as the only Savior (not just another avatar), the incompatibility of Christianity and reincarnation, and the lack of any personal deity with whom to relate.[60] This literature describes Eastern groups as satanic, evil, and spiritual frauds, all labels whose negative emotional connotations reach far beyond the very explicit definitions of these terms as used by the best of the Christian counter-cult literature.

The decidedly negative images of the Krishnas and other new "Hindu" groups, from the secular and from the Christian literature, have combined to produce a pervasive hostility to the Krishnas in Western society in general. That attitude has been strengthened by several incidents that might, apart from the prior negative image, have been of only ephemeral concern. For example, in 1976 and 1977 wire services carried pictures of Krishnas being arrested for wearing Santa Claus suits while soliciting money at Christmastime. These arrests gave credence to older accusations of deception in fundraising at the airports. Critics accused Krishnas of failure to identify themselves properly and of accepting large bills for inexpensive literature and then refusing to give change. Such reports reinforced the image of ISKCON as a deceptive cult.[61]

More critical have been the incidents involving guns. Members, former members, and people associated with the movement have been arrested for possession of firearms. Despite its avowal of pacifism, the movement has been accused of stockpiling weapons and preparing members to use them. The accusations have received far wider coverage than any refutations. Associated with other accusations of illegal activities, from dealing in drugs to smuggling, guns are now integral to the anti-Krishna image.[62]

The extent of hostility against the Krishnas has been amply demonstrated in several incidents: the farm in West Virginia has been shot at and four Krishnas wounded (1978); the San Diego temple was firebombed (1979); and the Philadelphia temple was bombed (1984). The Philadelphia bomb was a sophisticated device with a second bomb timed to go off a few minutes after the first, possibly to kill or maim those who gathered in reaction to the first explosion. Fortunately members of the group were slow to respond and no one was injured. This level of hostility has also given sanction to the practice of deprogramming, which has been directed against the group so forcefully in the last decade. It underlay the trial of Robin George, who had been deprogrammed, filed a civil suit, and won a multimillion dollar judgment (currently on appeal).

Response to Hostility

In the face of an increasingly negative public image, the Krishnas have directed significant efforts to establish their position as a legitimate American religion and to present what they believe to be their true nature. That effort has had several very evident thrusts.

First, none of the newer religions, with the exception of the Unification Church, has been as eager to align itself with the scholarly community and accept its credentials as ISKCON. This approach was quite evident as early as 1975 in an introductory pamphlet describing ISKCON, "The Krishna Consciousness Movement Is Authorized."[63] This pamphlet, which portrayed Swami Prabhupada as an eminent scholar, spent nine of its twenty-four pages giving quote after quote from Western scholars' favorable appraisal of ISKCON's publications. The following year, ISKCON turned to the American Academy of Religion for support against the anti-cult movement. Two hundred scholars signed a document supporting the movement's authenticity as an Indian missionary movement.[64] That same year the Society counted among its membership its first two Ph.D's.[65] *Back to Godhead*, the movement's main periodical, has printed articles by nonmember scholars supportive of the movement.[66] The effort to garner the support of scholars accelerated after the appointment of a liaison between the Krishnas and the scholarly community. That appointment led directly to a major book on the movement by a commercial publisher, which presents the views of "Five Distinguished Scholars on the Krishna Movement in the West."[67]

Second, and with some success, the movement has tried to present itself as a traditional Indian religious group, not a new cult. ISKCON emphasized this theme, prominent in Krishna literature for many years, in its response to the 1979 Dole hearings on cults. At that time they issued a small pamphlet, "A Request to the Media: Please Don't Lump Us In," which attempted to distinguish the Hare Krishna movement from the "new" cults such as the Unification Church headed by Korean entrepreneur Sun Myung Moon.[68] ISKCON was defined as a denomination within Hinduism, the world's oldest religion.

Third, at the Dole hearings, the Krishnas claimed support from the several hundred thousand Indian nationals residing in the United States. Since that time they have sought to strengthen that relationship and identification. In establishing this relationship, thus identifying with a single ethnic community, the Krishnas have, whether deliberately or not, created an image of themselves as an ethnic church. And Indian-Americans have taken advantage of their presence. Those without a traditional temple have found the Krishna temples more than adequate substitutes and attend Krishna functions throughout the year.

The attachment to the Indian community has had some problems. The long-standing negative images of India and Hinduism mentioned above still exist and on occasion have arisen to block proposed expansion plans. It can also be expected that as the Indian-American community becomes more visible, latent anti-Asian sentiments, which have so far been locally confined, will surface. For example, both Hindu and Islamic communities have encountered community hostility at zoning hearings whenever they have attempted to get permits for new religious buildings. One can also expect future problems in the event that the Indian community is successful in promoting those aspects of Indian culture, such as *ayurvedic* (holistic) medicine, which Westerners find somewhat offensive.

Finally, paralleling its religious ties to India, the Society has projected an image as bearer of Vedic culture to the West. It has done this most successfully through the opening of the cultural center in Detroit, and tying it to the prominent Ford and Reuther families[69] and, concurrent with the opening of Prabhupada's Palace, the changing of the image of New Vrindaban from that of a communal farm into a site of religious pilgrimages and an educational tourist attraction.[70] On a lesser scale, smaller temples are developing minimuseums of Vedic artifacts.

Conclusion

This essay has traced the development of prominent attitudes about American Hindus during the past century and has found them to have been basically negative. The feelings against the American Hindu community have been openly expressed when first-generation Indian immigrants (always perceived by the public as Hindus) become highly visible and were seen as threatening positions of "whites," and whenever Hinduism appeared to be spreading among the "white" population. Both of these conditions occurred simultaneously in the decade before World War I and in the years since 1974.

Underlying the negative attitudes are a number of beliefs, not the least being the continuation of the ideal of a Christian America, a country whose health is predicated on its remaining basically Christian in orientation (in spite of its provisions for religious freedom) and whose duty is to Christianize and civilize the non-Western world. In relation to Hinduism, this ideal has as its counterpart a negative image of India as an extremely backward nation in both its secular and religious life, an image reinforced in recent decades by the many appeals for food to feed the starving people in India, and the drives within the mainline churches to support agricultural, educational, medical, and technological mission programs (all based on an understanding that India lacks these Western necessities).

The quantum leap in religious pluralism in the 1970s, a part of which was in the development of Eastern religion, added to the general negative attitude toward Hinduism and India. Some of the religions that were finding their first expression in the West during the 1970s were singled out as "cults." Cult, a label that carries vastly different meanings for different people, has nevertheless always been a term carrying negative connotations, be they the more scholarly ones of "social marginality"; the Christian ones of "heretical," "Satanic," or "pagan"; or the secular anti-cultist references to destructive mind control. Among the groups prominent in "cult" literature are Hindu groups.

As both a Hindu group and an organization designated as a cult, the International Society for Krishna Consciousness has had to grow and develop in a doubly hostile atmosphere. As a missionary organization, it could have expected opposition from dominant religious groups unwilling to yield their traditional place. However, it has also had to adjust to an atmosphere that has included significant secular attacks in the form of the spread of anti-Krishna literature, deprogrammings, lawsuits, and more violent incidents.

Much of the future of the ISKCON, and of other Hindu groups with predominantly "white" membership, will depend upon the waning of this hostility as the role of Asian-Americans in the society at large becomes more generally accepted. This change will be much aided by the fact that many Asian-Americans are Christians and members of mainline churches. As this lessening of tensions occurs, we may expect to see the anti-cult movement shift its emphasis away from deprogramming to less coercive forms of opposition more in keeping with our society's constitutional guarantees of religious freedom.[71]

Notes

1. Cf. Suresh Chundar Bose, *The Life of Protap Chunder Mozoomdar* (Calcutta: Nababidhan Trust, 1940).
2. On the influx of Hinduism into New England in the nineteenth century, see Arthur Christy, *The Orient in American Transcendentalism* (New York: Columbia University Press, 1932); Carl T. Jackson, *The Oriental Religions and American Thought: Nineteenth Century Explorations* (Westport, CT: Greenwood Press, 1971); J. P. Rao Rayapati, *Early American Interest in Vedanta* (London: Asia Publishing House, 1973).
3. L. E. Slater, "The Present Religious Outlook of India," in *The World's Parliament of Religions*, ed. John Henry Barrows (Chicago: Parliament Publishing Company, 1893) p. 1172.

4. Jesse T. Peck, *The Great Republic* (New York: Nelson & Phillips, 1976), p. 541.

5. George J. Hagar, ed., *What the World Believes* (New York: Gay Brothers & Company, 1888).

6. Swami Vivekananda, "Hinduism as a Religion," in *The World's Congress of Religions*, ed. J. W. Hanson (Chicago: The Monarch Book Company, 1894) pp. 366–76.

7. *Swami Vivekananda on Hinduism* (Madras: Christian Literature Society, 1895).

8. On the history of the Vedanta work in America, see Swami Gambhirananda, *History of the Ramakrishna Math and Mission* (Calcutta: Advaita Ashrama, 1957).

9. Gerald N. Hallberg, "Bellingham, Washington's Anti-Hindu Riot," *Journal of the West* 12 (1973): 163–75.

10. Girindra Mukerji, "The Hindu in America," *Overland Monthly* 51, no. 4 (April 1908): 303–8.

11. Agnes Foster Buchannan, "The West and the Hindu Invasion," *Overland Monthly* 51, no. 4 (April 1908): 308–13.

12. Cf. Puran Singh, *The Story of Swami Rama* (Lucknow: Rama Tirtha Publishing League, 1924), and Eminent Scholars of India, *Swami Rama, Various Aspects of His Life* (Lucknow: Rama Tirtha Publication League, 1939).

13. Baba Premanand Bharati, *American Lectures* (Calcutta: Indo-American Press, n.d.), and idem, *Sree Krishna, the Lord of Love* (New York: The Krishna Samaj, 1904).

14. Atkinson's works as Swami Ramacharacka include *Advanced Course in Yogi Philosophy* (Chicago: Yogi Publication Society, 1904) and *Hatha Yoga* (Oak Park, IL: Yogi Publication Society, 1905.

15. Charles Boswell, "The Great Fuss and Fume Over the Omnipotent Oom," *True* (January 1965): 31, 86–91.

16. (New York: Columbia University Press, 1943).

17. One violent incident not directly related to the riots did appreciable harm to the Vedanta Society. A deranged ex-member exploded a bomb in the San Francisco Center and killed the swami in charge of the West Coast work.

18. This story is recounted in Swami Paramananda's biography by Sara Ann Livinsky, *A Bridge of Dreams* (West Stockbridge, MA: Lindisfarne Press, 1984).

19. Mrs. Gross Alexander, "American Women Going After Heathen Gods," *The Methodist Quarterly Review* 62, no. 3 (July 1912): 495–512.

20. Elizabeth A. Reed, *Hinduism in Europe and America* (New York: G. P. Putnam's Sons, 1914), p. 131.

21. Quoted in Livinsky, *Bridge of Dreams*, p. 174.

22. Quoted in Alexander, "Heathen Gods," p. 502.

23. Livinsky, *Bridge of Dreams*, pp. 180–81.

24. Cf. Pundit Acharya, *Breath, Sleep, the Heart and Life* (Clearwater Highlands, CA: Dawn Horse Press, 1976).

25. (Los Angeles: Self-Realization Fellowship, 1946).

26. Most of these movements and teachers are discussed in Wendall Thomas's *Hinduism Invades America* (New York: Beacon Press, 1930). Also see J. Gordon Melton, *A Bibliography of Hinduism in America Prior to 1940* (Evanston, IL: Institute for the Study of American Religion, 1985).

27. "United States vs. Bhagat Singh Thind, Decided February 19, 1923," *Supreme Court Reporter* 43, no. 10 (1 April 1923): 338–42.

28. M. V. Kamath, *The United States and India. 1776–1976* (Washington, DC: The Embassy of India, 1976), p. 154.

29. Katherine Mayo, *Mother India* (New York: Blue Ribbon Books, 1927), p. 16.

30. (London: Selwyn & Blount, 1927).

31. William Estep, *An American Answers Mother India* (Excelsior Springs, MO: Super Mind Science Publications, 1929).

32. Charles Frederick Weller, *World Fellowship* (New York: Liveright Publishing Corporation, 1935), pp. 645–739.

33. (Indianapolis: Bobbs-Merrill, 1960), p. 126.

34. Ibid., p. 195.

35. (New York: Ballantine Books, 1961).

36. (New York: Dodd, Mead, 1961).

37. Christopher Isherwood, ed., *Vedanta for Modern Man* (Hollywood, CA: Vedanta Press, 1951), and idem, *Vedanta for the Western World* (Hollywood, CA: Vedanta Press, 1945).

38. Though early theosophical leader Henry S. Olcott had a well-known attachment to Buddhism and led the movement to identify with the Buddhist religion, during the twentieth century theosophy's more natural alignment with Hinduism was asserted. The adoption of significant elements of Hinduism by theosophy can be easily seen in such basic textbooks as Charles W. Leadbeater, *A Textbook of Theosophy* (Adyar: Theosophical Publishing House, 1956), and L. W. Rogers, *Elementary Theosophy* (Wheaton, IL: Theosophical Press, 1950). Theosophy's alignment with Hinduism instead of Buddhism is most clearly shown in its approach to reincarnation.

39. On the Krishnamurti affair, see Arthur H. Nethercot, *The Last Four Lives of Annie Besant* (Chicago: University of Chicago Press, 1963).

40. Most of Krishnamurti's books over the years have been privately published, but during the 1980s some titles were issued up by Harper & Row: *Krishnamurti's Journal* (1982); *The Flame of Attention* (1983).

41. Yogi Gupta, *Yoga and Long Life* (New York: Dodd, Mead, 1958).

42. The amount of literature that began to appear on *hatha yoga* has been most indicative of its spread in postwar America. See Howard R. Jarrell's *International Yoga Bibliography, 1950 to 1980* (Metuchen, NJ: Scarecrow Press, 1981).

43. Sivaya Subramuniyaswami's Church currently publishes *The New Saivite World*, one of the finest periodicals serving the inclusive Hindu community in the United States.

44. Possibly the first book on the new turn to Eastern religion was John H. Garabedian and Orde Coombs, *Eastern Religions in the Electric Age* (New York: Grosset & Dunlap, 1969).

45. Jacob Needleman, *The New Religions* (Garden City, NY: Doubleday, 1970).

46. Most of the early critical literature was produced by Christians concerned about and seeking to respond to the growth of non-Christian religion in America. The early literature consists of a number of tracts and articles in Jesus People newspapers and evangelical Christian periodicals. See, for example, Irvine Robertson, "The Eastern Mystics Are Out to Take You In," *Moody Monthly* (July – August 1973): 24–27, 47–48, and R. D. Clements, *God and the Gurus* (Downers Grove, IL: InterVarsity Press, 1975).

47. Gabriel Facke, "Going East: Neomysticism and the Christ of Faith," *The Christian Century* 88, 15 (14 April 1971); Harrison Pope Jr., *The Road East* (Boston: Beacon Press, 1974).

48. *Turning East* (New York: Simon and Schuster, 1977).

49. Maxine P. Fisher, *The Indians of New York City* (New Delhi: South Asia Books, 1980).

50. For example, M. Thomas Starkes's *No Man Goes Alone* (Atlanta: Home Mission Board, Southern Baptist Convention, 1972) has a picture of a chanting Krishna devotee as its cover art, but makes only the briefest reference to ISKCON in the text.

51. Early coverage includes Penny Ritts, "Devotee of Hindu Cult Explains Commission to Visit the West," *Butler (NY) Eagle*, 22 September 1965; James R. Sikes, "Swami's Flock Chants in Park to Find Ecstasy," *New York Times* (10 October 1966); Robert Taylor, "The Search for Godhead in Boston," *Boston Sunday Globe* (27 April 1969); and Jon Nordheimer, "Young Ascetics Honor Lord Krishna," *New York Times* (6 September 1972). See also the very sympathetic chapter on the Krishnas in Peter Rowley's, *New Gods in America* (New York: David McKay Company, 1971).

52. Robert Houriet, *Getting Back Together* (New York: Avon, 1971); W. D. Sprague, *Case Histories from the Communes* (New York: Lancer, 1972).

53. John Charles Cooper, *Religion in the Age of Aquarius* (Philadelphia: Westminster Press, 1971); John Godwin, *Occult America* (Garden City, NY: Doubleday, 1972).

54. Tracy Cabot, ed., *Inside the Cults* (Los Angeles: Holloway House Publishing Co., 1970) pp. 153–63; Christopher Evans, *Cults of Unreason* (New York: Delta, 1973).

55. ISKCON received only passing mention toward the end of Jacob Needleman's *The New Religions* (Garden City, NY: Doubleday, 1970). Marcus Bach's *Strangers at the Door* (Nashville: Abingdon, 1971) and Robert S. Ellwood, Jr.'s *Religious and Spiritual Groups in Modern America* (Englewood Cliffs, NJ: Prentice-Hall, 1973) were the first scholarly treatments of the Krishnas along with the other "new religons." Later to appear was Charles Y. Glock and Robert N. Bellah, eds., *The New Religious Consciousness* (Berkeley, CA: University of California Press, 1976).

56. (New York: John Wiley & Sons, 1974).

57. Faye Levine, *The Strange World of the Hare Krishnas* (Greenwich, CT: Fawcett Publications, 1974), p. 162.

58. Flo Conway and Jim Siegelman, *Snapping: America's Epidemic of Sudden Personality Change* (Philadelphia: Lippincott, 1978); Ted Patrick, *Let Our Children Go!* (New York: E. P. Dutton, 1976).

59. Clements, *God and the Gurus*, p. 4.

60. Major Christian responses to the Krishnas are included as chapters in Pat Means, *The Mystical Maze* (San Bernardino, CA: Campus Crusade for Christ, 1976); Jack Sparks, *The Mind Benders* (Nashville: Thomas Nelson, 1977); John P. Newport, *Christ and the New Consciousness* (Nashville: Broadman Press, 1978); Walter Martin, *The New Cults* (Santa Ana, CA: Vision House, 1980); Josh McDowell and Don Stewart, *Understanding the Cults* (San Bernardino, CA: Here's Life Publishers, 1982); and Ronald Enroth et al., *A Guide to Cults* (Downers Grove, IL: InterVarsity Press, 1983). For a Roman Catholic treatment, see William J. Whalen, *Strange Gods* (Huntington, IN: Our Sunday Visitor, 1981).

61. Deception is a major theme in Morris Yanoff's *Where is Joey?* (Chicago: Swallow Press, 1981), an attack upon ISKCON for assisting his ex-daughter-in-law's disappearance with a grandchild whose custody had been awarded to Yanoff's son.

62. The gun theme is quite evident in such articles as Alan MacRobert, "The

Krishna Question" *Boston Magazine* (December 1980): 173–74, 214–20; Michael Dorgan, "Hare Krishna, Hare Krishna, Guns 'n' Ammo, Guns 'n' Ammo," *High Times* (January 1981): 56–60, 71, 98; and the front-page story by Russell Chandler and Evan Maxwell, "Krishnas—A Kingdom in Disarray," *Los Angeles Times* (15 February 1981).

63. (Los Angeles: Bhaktivedanta Book Trust, 1975).

64. John Dart, "200 Scholars Support Hare Krishna," *Los Angeles Times* (6 November 1976).

65. "Two Ph.D.'s for KRSNA," *Back to Godhead* 11, no. 6 (1976): 10–14. One of these new doctors authored a major work in the philosophy of science under his secular name, Richard L. Thompson, *Mechanistic and Nonmechanistic Science* (Lynbrook, NY: Bala Books, 1981).

66. Diane Eck, "KRSNA Consciousness in Historical Perspective," *Back to Godhead* 14, no. 10 (1979): 26–29; Harvey Cox, "A Tribute to KRSNA Consciousness," *Back to Godhead* 12, no. 6 (June 1977): 22.

67. Steven J. Gelberg, ed., *Hare Krishna, Hare Krishna* (New York: Grove Press, 1983).

68. Subhananda dasa, *A Request to the Media: Please Don't Lump Us In* (Los Angeles: International Society for Krishna Consciousness, Office of Public Affairs, 1978).

69. Most of the coverage of the opening of the Fisher Mansion was quite positive. See, for example, Curt Suplee, "The Temple of Tomorrowland," *Washington Post* (27 May 1983). One negative reaction, which appeared locally, called it a temple consecrated to public relations: Allan Lengal, "The Tourist Trap," *Monthly Detroit* 6, no. 8 (August 1983).

70. Lynn Darling, "Krishnaland," *Washington Post* (3 September 1979).

71. The immediate future of ISKCON hinges to a large extent on the outcome of the appeal in the Robin George case. If the multimillion-dollar judgment is upheld on appeal, it would financially destroy that segment of the movement directly involved in the suit and finance future court attacks on the organization.

ISKCON and the Spirituality of the 1960s

Robert S. Ellwood

Swami Bhaktivedanta arrived in New York in the fall of 1965. From the Krishna Consciousness perspective, one could well regard that time of arrival as highly providential. For conceding all the cautions appropriate to historical speculation, it seems likely that had his mission in this country commenced even a few years—possibly a few months—earlier or later, it would have been far less fruitful. Bhaktivedanta's timing caught the powerful rising tide of what was called the counterculture, which included within its spectrum of concerns a fascination with India and an exceptional openness to exotic, consciousness-expanding spirituality. This counterculture tide carried with it many new boats, some of which have stayed afloat despite the receding of that wave.

Although it had been used before, the term "counterculture" was popularized by Theodore Roszak's *The Making of a Counter Culture* (1969).[1] Just precisely what the counterculture of the 1960s was is not easy to explain. The term counterculture, like many of the more sensational treatments of that scene in the popular media of the day, suggests a world that was more of a mirror opposite of the "establishment" than was really the case. Cynics then as now have suggested the whole phenomenon was as much created as described by sensational reporting. Yet something clearly was happening. During the 1960s, the nation, and much of the rest of the world, seemed to go from crisis to crisis and shock to shock, undergoing far-reaching sociocultural change in numerous areas, from race relations to attitudes toward the Vietnam War.

A significant part of the counterculture movement was its approach to spiritual life, which valued "high" states of consciousness, communalism, nature, and the role of spiritual master in the transmission of spirituality. It made use of exotic symbols, whether occult, Asian, or Native American, to emphasize its discontinuity with established religion. It combined a sense of alienation with a commitment to social change in the direction of vague but heartfelt ideals like love and peace, as well as specific ends ranging from sexual freedom to stopping the

Vietnam war. It had an eschatological cast in its talk of an imminent "New Age" or "Aquarian Age."

This spirituality was certainly fueled by the vogue for psychedelic drugs that swept American youth in that decade. Much has been made of the role of the hallucinogenic experience in opening up the possibility of extraordinary modes of awareness or "states of consciousness," and then of new spiritualities in incorporating such awareness into viable lifestyles through nondrug means. There is much to this argument, as the testimony of many Hare Krishnas and members of other "sixties" spiritual groups bears witness. However, the drug experience was not the only force that set apart a counterculture community in the 1960s.

First, the movement for racial equality that gathered force in the late 1950s had already set a pattern of polarization, often along generational and lifestyle as well as political lines. These social divisions were only exacerbated by the escalating war in southeast Asia, which tended to pit the same people against each other across a range of issues.

Second, and more important for our immediate purposes, the 1960s spirituality was not a new phenomenon that burst suddenly and unexpectedly on the American landscape, as startling as it may have seemed to some observers. The postwar years of the late 1940s and the 1950s were outwardly a golden age of the mainline churches, of Cardinal Spellman-style Roman Catholicism and "suburban captivity" Protestantism. But evidence also suggests a more deeply mystical current of spirituality quietly rising like water behind a dam, until the floodgates suddenly open and it streams out in torrents. Popular books of that era included Aldous Huxley's *The Perennial Philosophy* and his later *The Doors of Perception*, which was to be seminal for the psychedelic vogue in its mystical aspect. Also, Thomas Merton's *The Seven Story Mountain* recounted the conversion to Catholicism and entry into a Trappist monastery of one who would become a highly sensitive interpreter of East-West religious dialogue. The interest in Zen was another undercurrent, which was reflected in D. T. Suzuki's influential lectures at Columbia University early in the 1950s and his many books, in Alan Watts' *The Way of Zen* and other works, and in the San Francisco-based "beats," precursors of the 1960s' "hippies," who were celebrated in Jack Kerouac's lively novel, *The Dharma Bums*.

For that matter, as I have argued elsewhere, the 1950s was hardly the decade when it all began.[2] America has had a long succession of Greenwich Villages and "bohemias," where persons of spiritual and artistic bent have congregated. A clear line of apostolic succession, often through specific persons or groups, can be traced from the 1950s' and 1960s' counterspirituality back to such earlier parallels as the Theosophy, Spiritualism, and Transcendentalism of the nineteenth century. Perhaps no classic book is cited more often in the literature of counterspirituality than Thoreau's *Walden*, whose "drop-out" way of life and whose love of nature, the spiritual East, and the lonely quest struck a resonant chord in later readers. The 1960s' spiritual explosion was less a new thing than a new generation's getting in touch with some perennial American themes.

Nonetheless, it looked startling. For one thing, it was in full color; the transition from the backwoods drab or understated Zen aesthetics to the brilliant posters and light shows of the psychedelic era was like a movie switching from black and white to technicolor. The clothes, the beads, the hair were different. These symbols too carried a message—a new sense of a community called out, needing to define its boundaries like any tribe. For all the decade's blood and turmoil, it was an exciting time to be alive and above all to be young, seeing oneself as part of an apocalyptic "love generation" and harbinger of an Aquarian Age. Rightly or wrongly, part of a new generation—the postwar "baby boom" cohort coming of age—sensed itself to be profoundly different.

All this history is, for most of us, within living memory, and I will not attempt an exhaustive characterization of the 1960s' counterculture. My intention here is to point to several interpretations of its key themes and relate them to the Hare Krishna movement.

Opinions vary as to what the counterculture themes were. Some say that rock music, especially as personified by the lyrics and style of groups like the Beatles and the Grateful Dead, really ignited the counterculture and remained its profoundest bond. That is where Charles Perry Anderson starts in *The Haight-Ashbury: A History*, though he ends with a good discussion of the motifs of self-discovery, exploration of psychic "wild territory," and semiconscious fear of the "straight" world.[3]

A famous counterculture participant/commentator, Timothy Leary, in his reminiscences, *Flashbacks*, sees, as he did at the time, the psychedelic drug experience as the heart and soul of the new consciousness.[4] It freed one to "drop out" of "the system" and turn on to deeper and better realities; the new culture, in his view, was really those who shared that strange and wonderful chemically induced initiatory passage, comparable to the soul's adventures in *The Tibetan Book of the Dead*.

Theodore Roszak, in the already mentioned *The Making of a Counter Culture*, viewed antitechnology as the counterculture's deep theme. The devotees of the new age were rising up in resistance to the regimentation and dehumanization they perceived in the world being made by standard brands, multinational corporations, and computer printouts. The mysticism and new tribalism were not so much ends in themselves as human-scale counterpoints to the world of the machine.

Walter Truett Anderson, in his engaging history of the Esalen center on California's Big Sur coast, *The Upstart Spring: Esalen and the American Awakening*, stresses the importance of the "human potential" movement of which Esalen was the Vatican in those years.[5] The new freedom and new consciousness celebrated in the 1960s, he contends, were stimulated by the new view of the human self as full of a potential for radical self-expression and life-construction limned by such Esalen gurus as Abraham Maslow of Humanistic psychology and Fritz Perls of Gestalt therapy, and applied by the center's influential and controversial techniques.

Into this milieu of new dreams and new consciousnesses came Krishna Consciousness. Its public work essentially began in this country in 1966. To give an impression of how it was received in the counterculture world of 1966, we might look at one of the earliest journalistic notices it received, a story in *The East Village Other*, 15 October 1966. After observing that one of Swami Bhaktivedanta's disciples is the poet Allen Ginsburg, it quotes the confession of one new disciple about the Hare Krishna chant: "I started chanting to myself, like the Swami said, when I was walking down the street. . . . suddenly everything started looking so beautiful, the kids, the old men and women . . . even the creeps looked beautiful . . . to say nothing of the trees and flowers. It was like I'd taken a dozen doses of LSD. But I knew there was a difference. There's no coming down from this. I can always do this, anytime, anywhere. It's always with you."

"Everybody's trying to get high and stay there," another young disciple states. "Everybody's looking for an exalted state of consciousness, a way to flip out and stay out. But there's something bringing you back to the old miserable routine. Not in this. This has a snowballing effect. You can chant your way right into eternity."[6]

Another early disciple, Howard Wheeler, a one-time literature instructor at Ohio State University, tells of first taking several buttons of peyote: "It tore the doors of perception off their hinges to reveal a calming Sistine vision. . . . I actually left my body and journeyed into the universe to behold the Milky Way from an incredible distance. I discovered my real self extended beyond the body was eternal." But after he met Swami Bhaktivedanta in New York in July 1966, he learned from him that, "You don't have to take anything for your spiritual life." After beginning chanting, Wheeler "began to notice that the buildings, the people, and the sky all looked very beautiful. . . . the sound of the Supreme Lord of the Universe was passing through my body, coming upon me like a beautiful exhilarating song that had somehow been dormant, choked in me for centuries."[7]

Krishna Consciousness posters and handouts of the same years reiterate, as do many other testimonials, intentional linking of the drug high and the even greater Krishna high. One said: "STAY HIGH FOREVER. No More Coming Down. Practice Krishna Consciousness. Expand your consciousness by practicing the TRANSCENDENTAL SOUND VIBRATION. TURN ON . . . TUNE IN . . . DROP OUT."

Perhaps the ultimate high of that era was the night Swami Bhaktivedanta, after transferring to San Francisco in January of 1967, attended a "Mantra-Rock Dance" thronged with "hippies" at the famous Avalon Ballroom. Accompanied by a multimedia light show featuring slides of Krishna, conch shells and drums, with Timothy Leary and Allen Ginsberg, who spoke on stage with him, the Swami led thousands of counterculture youth, many no doubt already high, in the Hare Krishna *mantra*.[8]

By 1970 the emphasis had changed. Krishna literature spoke less of "highs," more of love, community, and issues concerned with ISKCON's institutional life. It might be possible to see a cleavage between the nature of the group's appeal in the 1960s and 1970s, and so a difference in type of person attracted: one "turned on" by the drug experience and seeking a permanent "natural high," and the other perhaps seeking more a warm and intimate community.

On the other hand, Peter Clecak, in *America's Quest for the Ideal Self: Dissent and Fulfillment in the 60s and 70s,* counters the stylish view that the 1960s were a decade of hope and spiritual buoyancy after which the "me decade" of the 1970s presented only sterility and pessimism.[9] Clecak perceives the continuities of the two periods as more important than the contrasts; both are parts of an "uncompleted chapter in American civilization." This perspective is to some extent supported by the persistence, even flourishing, during the 1970s of new religious movements that had originated in the 1960s. ISKCON is an example as are Transcendental Meditation and the Divine Light Mission, which actually reached their apogee in the 1970s. But the 1970s was a time of tighter institutionalization of the 1960s spirit, as devotees tried to package the best of that helter-skelter era for the long haul. The process is well reported for three representative religious groups in Steven Tipton's *Getting Saved from the Sixties.*

In any case, our principal concern is with Hare Krishna and the 1960s' counterculture milieu. Let us turn back to the main themes of the counterculture—rock, psychedelia, antitechnology, human potential, self-discovery, exploring psychic wild territory, fear of the straight world—suggested by several writers already cited. Without belaboring the point, it is clear that the Krishna movement had an appeal in relation to all these themes, not only a "high" to set against the drug high. The Avalon Ballroom showed the power of the Krishna chant to weave a web of magical ecstasy as surely as the top rock performers who also appeared on that stage. The "Vedic Culture" it espoused, with its cow-protection, its "plain living and high thinking," certainly set another ideal over against the world of the machine and the microchip. As for exploration and self-discovery, according to Swami Bhaktivedanta, that was what his faith was all about. The chant can take you to eternity—and beyond. Like Howard Wheeler, you can discover the song choked in you for centuries.

But why did some souls in the counterculture maelstrom turn to Krishna, whereas many others did not? Religious conversion will doubtless quite properly always remain one of those areas of human life to which a veil of mystery clings. Conversion is never exhaustively interpreted just by outside "scientific" means, for here in the conversion experience Ultimate Reality and the deep pools of human freedom and subjectivity interact. From the "inside" of any religion, why some convert and others do not may be dealt with theologically, in terms of karma or prevenient grace. Yet, even if one may not detect everything, the phenomenological observer may also at least be able to isolate some conditions through which the mysterious process of conversion tends to work.

Recent discussions along these lines have centered on two poles of interpretation for conversion, deprivation theories and cognitive theories. Deprivation in relation to conversion, as authoritatively described by Glock and Stark[10] and as admirably summarized by Gregory Johnson[11] in his discussion of early Krishna Consciousness, emphasizes comparison: the subject is consciously or unconsciously aware that others have something he does not have, or that he is lacking something in comparison to some internalized ideal. As Glock and Stark put it, "Deprivation . . . refers to any and all of the ways that an individual or group may be, or feel disadvantaged in comparison either to other individuals or groups or to an internalized set of standards."[12]

What are specific forms of deprivation in mind? One, of course, is economic deprivation, and the social degradation that usually accompanies it. Needless to say, history is full of spiritual movements of which a prima facie explanation, at least, is compensation for such worldly deprivation. Another form of deprivation is social isolation. Again, examples are not wanting of persons whose religious conversion is set against a background of poor relationships with others, whether because of psychological inadequacy or imposed conditions.

Yet most observers, not least Glock and Stark themselves, fully realize that such gross deprivation factors are far from fully explaining conversion. They do not explain why many others, equally economically deprived or socially isolated, do not embrace religious outlets. Nor do they explain those who, from the Buddha to innumerable counterculture types of upper-class background, seemingly "had it all" but gave it up for the sake of the spiritual life. For this reason these writers emphasize also "psychic deprivation," when "persons find themselves without a meaningful system of values to interpret and organize their lives."[13]

This factor, on several levels, could interpret religious commitment, especially that given to nonestablishment groups. First, there is the case of those experiencing what has been called "status inconsistency"—a situation in which one feels an inconsistency between who one knows one is inside, in terms of sensitivity and potential, and the role given one by the social order. Members of minorities or social classes virtually forced into certain occupations and economic straits, women in a highly sex-differentiated society, young people who see themselves over against a "generation gap," anyone who knows himself or herself to be quite intelligent but for one reason or another is deprived of complete formal schooling—all these are likely to sense psychic deprivation through status inconsistency. Frequently such persons are drawn to non-normative religious movements in which talents for exposition and leadership that would be closed to them in the religious "establishment" may be exercised. Understandably, their rhetoric may include jabs at those who owe ecclesiastical position to possessing the right lineage, sex, or academic degrees.

Another form of psychic deprivation, it seems to me, may be the product of traumas or shocks that disorient people sufficiently that they find themselves without values strong enough to organize their lives. The old no longer holds; they cast about desperately for something new. The tragic loss of a child may also leave one bereft of the comfortable pieties by which one had lived before; like Job, one now rejects them, but is poignantly open to something that seems stronger and more honest.

By the same token, new experiences, new visions of reality may afford so much more "data" to one's worldview as to be disorienting. Travel and education can have this effect. But in the counterculture, drug trips and all its other beauties and horrors could produce disorientation and subsequent psychic deprivation (in the sense of lacking a meaningful system of values) thick and fast. Here we are getting close to a possible background for the Hare Krishna movement in the 1960s.

Stillson Judah, in *Hare Krishna and the Counterculture*, appears to favor such an explanation in the emphasis he puts on "distress" as the controlling factor in early converts' lives. He writes, "In a large number of cases, and I suspect in most, the Krishna devotees had not discovered a satisfactory life in the counterculture. . . . They had already left the establishment with which they had been dissatisified some time ago.

They had a number of countercultural ideas that they could use to form an alternative way of life, but somehow this adventure did not give them the satisfaction they expected. They had experienced a disruption in their pattern of living, often combined with a time of distress, unhappiness, and loss of meaning often approaching despair."[14] Judah presents a series of testimonials to bear out this thesis.

Undoubtedly in a great many cases the outward pattern of a conversion process was as Judah describes. An individual, dissatisfied with the establishment, which probably meant in effect family and school, harkened to the appeal of Haight-Ashbury or some other counterculture enclave to drop out and turn on. But before long the emotional rollercoaster of drug highs and lows, easy sex, social alienation, and street rip-offs brought only sickening vertigo, and the succoring call of the Krishna *mantra* came through strong and clear.

Yet we must not forget that it is characteristic of conversion accounts to underscore the unsatisfactoriness of the convert's previous life. Judah perceptively did not overlook the fact that such converts, for all their distress, still "had a number of countercultural ideas that they could use," and one surmises that this equipment went into the choice of ISKCON as the way out. A development of that side of the process brings us to the cognitive interpretation of conversion. It stresses not so much the way conversion makes up for something that is lacking in comparison with others or an internal ideal, as the way in which it enables one to make sense out of what one has—that is, to put a worldview together. Of course, *something* is lacking, namely an overall worldview pattern, and one may certainly feel that as an emotional as well as intellectual deprivation. Indeed, the point about conversion is that in it emotional and intellectual quests are conjoined; only an answer to one will satisfy the other. But the emphasis in cognitive interpretations is put on the process as one of exploration, as one of seeking to know and subdue what Charles Perry called psychic "wild territory," rather than as one impelled negatively by an acute sense of psychic deprivation. Undeniably, the two interpretations are not inconsistent with each other and probably both had a part in the transit of many 1960s' people into Krishna Consciousness. But in the last analysis I think that the cognitive type of interpretation of conversion affords the best model. It provides a larger framework for a whole counterculture project in people's lives, in which the disorientation and despair about which Judah writes were one stage (if also often the proximate cause of initiation into Krishna Consciousness). It also takes into account what the other model cannot, the effect of the positive attractiveness of Krishnaism as worldview, practice, and community in its own right.

The basic issue is well stated by Gregory Johnson as he points to the limitations of the assumptions of deprivation theory. As he puts it, "the theory assumes that no person could join such movements unless he were somehow desperate. This is an outside-looking-in perspective. The researcher becomes an incredulous observer: " 'How could they believe such ideas and act that way? There must be something wrong with them.' Interpreted in theoretical terms, this position becomes: 'There must be something lacking in their lives.' "[15] Such a view clearly limits the freedom of persons, whether Krishnaites or others, to make real choices and prefer what they perceive as good for its own sake, rather than from deprivation. The Supreme Good may, to be sure, be a capstone worldview and practice that unites many other goods one has found and in that sense fulfills a need, but it may be arrived at through a normal human process of experiencing and choosing.

Of course, from the point of view of the anti-cult antagonists that is precisely the objection; they contend that persons joining movements like the Hare Krishnas are not exercising genuinely free choice. We cannot argue this difficult issue at length here. All I would like to point out is that, judging from the accounts of Wheeler and many others, most early converts thought they were making a free choice based on their perception of the greater good. It may be, as depth psychologists from Augustine to Freud have reminded us, that what we consider free choices are often forced by compulsions beneath the surface of the conscious mind, and that nowhere are such subterranean influences more at play than in the realm of religion. But this judgment can be extended to the motives of everyone, including anti-cultists. Whether a person interprets a choice as free is important, because that suggests a part of a process perceived as becoming a whole or free person. That process in turn has two further implications. First, it implies that one is choosing something good in its own right, as a free person would, not merely because someone else has it or because it is part of some internalized ideal painfully unrealized. Second, it implies that it is a cognitive process, because becoming whole implies making one's whole worldview consistent with all that one sees and who one believes oneself to be.

This fits in very well with a point Steven Gelberg has made. Following up on a tentative suggestion of Rodney Stark that the growth of new religious movements may not be reducible solely to sociological factors such as those he has admirably cataloged, but may also involve the fact that some theologies and worldviews are simply more plausible and communicate better, Gelberg indicates this is the case with Hare Krishna. "Vaishnava theology," he writes, "is inherently interesting (even exciting!) in that it encompasses and explores in great depth every theological and philosophical category. Its cosmology is teeming with demigods, demons, divine incarnations, heroines, and saints, inhabiting unlimitedly variegated worlds."[16] Without denying that many Westerners are, on the other hand, put off by the exoticism and complexity of this faith, it is undoubtedly the case that converts are powerfully drawn by the dreamlike beauty of its images and art; by the intoxication of its lovely myths with their vistas of time, space, and world unlimited; and by the cogency of its analysis of what is wrong with life as ordinarily lived in this particular world. If exploration of wild territory without end was a compelling drive of the counterculture in all its youthful exuberance, Krishna's universe would surely give it something to work on.

Some empirical work supports a contention that cognitive exploration is more important in interpreting counterculture conversions that psychic deprivation/disorientation due to the drug experience or any other sort of deprivation. A. M. Nicholi, for instance, in analyzing interviews with college converts to a campus nondenominational religious organization, stated that, "Drugs do not precipitate interest in the spiritual; the opposite holds true. Students turn to drugs because of an interest in the spiritual and because of a hope that drugs will meet their spiritual needs."[17] As we know, this hope is often found to fail, turning young people to other avenues of spiritual fulfillment, but the significant factor is that all this is part of a process of spiritual exploration that sets an overall cognitive tone to these experiments. Nicholi reports that after conversion the students stop drug use, and claim to acquire enhanced self-esteem, strength in controlling sexual impulses, and joy, together with lessened preoccupation with fear of death. Krishna converts report the same, as well as increased cognition of what human life and the universe is all about.

In another study of converts, Heirich compared converts to a pentecostal sect with a similar sample of Catholic nonconverts and found no difference in reports of personal stress in the two years preceding conversion.[18] On this basis he viewed conversion as a cognitive quest for clear understanding of reality rather than an attempt to handle personal stress. Other data produces some different perspectives. Enthusiasm and conviction are characteristic of new converts. Ullman observed this in a study of converts in which he found that some qualities of converts, such as inability to tolerate ambiguity in their worldview cognition, do have a background in inner stress and turmoil.[19] Nevertheless, it seems fair to assert that converts should not be stigmatized as people suffering under some great deprivation, or as people with "something wrong with them," but should rather be thought of as individuals with a highly activated need to know and to experience what they know in the widest possible arena, that of universal meaning.

Exploration was the deepest dynamic of the spiritual 1960s and is supremely epitomized in Krishna Consciousness. Like any exploration, this one often wandered, encountered dangerous beasts, and was not always successful. Still, its fundamental impetus, like that underlying all great explorers, was to know and to experience. That quest, it knew deep down, meant as always that on some level one would have to cut loose from all that was familiar, to leave one's old hometown, and find a new and abiding city situated in better advantage to truth. Some initially found that city in various hippie enclaves or communes, some in the other worlds of drug and mystical experience. Some started with a new place in the mind, like the seekers of Herman Hesse's paradigmatic *Journey to the East,* never really getting very far from home and discovering the sunrise lands to be of a nongeographical order altogether.

But for some the quest led finally to Krishna Consciousness because for them Krishna Consciousness contained all they sought: it was a new community, an opening to other worlds and ecstatically cognitive states of consciousness, a doorway to the mystic East—and, surprisingly, it was right here in America.

Notes

1. Theodore Roszak, *The Making of a Counter Culture* (Garden City, NY: Doubleday, 1969).

2. Robert Ellwood, *Alternative Altars* (Chicago: University of Chicago Press, 1979).

3. Charles Perry Anderson, *The Haight-Ashbury: A History* (New York: Random House, 1984).

4. Timothy Leary, *Flashbacks: An Autobiography* (Los Angeles: J. P. Tarcher, 1983).

5. Walter Truett Anderson, *The Upstart Spring: Esalen and the American Awakening* (Reading, MA: Addison-Wesley Publishing Co., 1983).

6. Irving Shushnick, "Save Earth Now!!" *The East Village Other* 1, no. 22 (15 October–1 November 1966): 11.

7. Robert Houriet, *Getting Back Together* (New York: Avon, 1972), pp. 335–36.

8. Satsvarupa dasa Goswami, *Only He Could Lead Them: A Biography of His Divine Grace A. C. Bhaktivedanta Swami Prabhupada* (Los Angeles: Bhaktivedanta Book Trust, 1981), 3:11–15.

9. Peter Clecak, *America's Quest for the Ideal Self: Dissent and Fulfillment in the 60s and 70s* (New York: Oxford University Press, 1983).

10. Charles Glock and Rodney Stark, *Religion and Society in Tension* (Chicago: Rand McNally, 1965).

11. Gregory L. Johnson, "An Alternative Community in Microcosm" (Ph.D. diss., Harvard University, 1973).

12. Glock and Stark, *Religion and Society in Tension,* p. 246.

13. Ibid., p. 248.

14. J. Stillson Judah, *Hare Krishna and the Counterculture* (New York: John Wiley & Sons, 1974), p. 163.

15. Johnson, "Alternative Community," pp. 89–90.

16. Steven J. Gelberg, "The Future of Krishna Consciousness in the West: An Insider's Perspective," in *The Future of New Religious Movements*, ed. Phillip Hammond and David G. Bromley (Macon, GA: Mercer University Press, 1986).

17. A. M. Nicholi, "A New Dimension of the Youth Culture," *American Journal of Psychiatry* 131 (1974): 397.

18. M. Heirich, "Change of Heart: A Test of Some Widely Held Theories About Religious Conversion," *American Journal of Sociology* 83 (1977): 653–80.

19. C. Ullman, "Cognitive and Emotional Antecedents of Religious Conversion," in *Conversion: Perspectives on Personal and Social Transformations*, ed. W. E. Conn (New York: Alba House, 1978), pp. 137–47.

IV. Conversion to ISKCON

The Search for Meaning in Conversions to ISKCON

Larry D. Shinn

Taking the Krishnas Seriously

Zwi Werblowsky, the Martin Buber Professor of History of Religions at the Hebrew University in Jerusalem and editor of *NVMEN: International Review of the History of Religions,* warns scholars who would study new religious movements ("cults"): "Students of religion are often tempted, for understandable reasons, to interrupt their serious researches and be lured in the direction of sociology of scholarly as well as pseudo-scholarly activity."[1] Professor Werblowsky's fear of misplaced scholarly efforts is shared by many of his colleagues in the field of religious studies who consider serious study of the cults a profitless venture at best and a misuse of the scholar by the cults at worst.

The mistrust for using contemporary marginal religious communities as the subject for serious religious research raises an interesting question of academic politics we will not have time to explore in this essay. However, my research for the past four years on the Hare Krishnas and other such peripheral contemporary religious groups has required me to reconsider several traditional assumptions and to explore in new ways the nature of religious conversion that would not have emerged as easily through the study of mainline church case-studies alone. Specifically, it is the insight regarding the [distinction between a conversion decision and a conversion process] afforded by five years of study of ISKCON that is the subject of this essay.

Richard Schalatter in his foreword to Clyde Holbrook's *Religion, A Humanistic Discipline* says, "The job of the humanistic scholar is to organize our huge inheritance of culture, to make the past available to the present, and to judge, as a critic, the actions of the present by the experience of the past."[2] There are those who, for various reasons, have

Portions of this essay and some of the material in it are included in chapter 7 of *The Dark Lord* (Philadelphia: Westminster Press, 1987).

judged the Hare Krishnas in America by yardsticks provided by fundamentalist and liberal religious institutions commonly known in America. Of course, the Krishnas' brand of devotional Hinduism is always found wanting in such theological comparisons. For example, Chris Elkins's *Heavenly Deception,* and Rabbi and Marsha Ruddin's *Prisoners of Paradise,* judge ISKCON's theology and religious life as deviant or dangerous according to Christian and Jewish religious values and institutions. However, anyone who knows ISKCON well is soon reminded that true humanistic scholarship must always be a two-way street. That is, not only do other religious traditions or the Krishna tradition throughout Indian history serve as a yardstick for a critique of ISKCON, but such contemporary expressions of religion as ISKCON can also require us to rethink those very theories and experiences by which we appropriate the past and thereby assess the present.

Few laypersons in America today need to be convinced of the relevance of the study of the so-called new religious movements (NRM)— especially those who would discredit the cults. Likewise, it should be clear to my academic colleagues that this paper does take seriously the notion that we who theorize about religion can learn much from those traditions in our midst, which, because of their vitality and marginality, offer us especially fruitful, living examples of the religious forms and behavior that we profess to describe and to understand. Scholars in religious studies and the humanities especially can learn much from those social scientists who have mined the fertile fields of marginal religious groups since their inception. Consequently, this paper will focus on certain psychological theories of conversion in light of five years of research on the Hare Krishnas in America and India, although it is framed in terms familiar to those at home in historical religious studies.

One of the consequences of the 1960s' and 1970s' defection by many youth from mainline religious groups or secular liberal traditions to NRMs on the margins of American society was the galvanizing of a religious pluralism in America that now includes traditions from the East.[3] This process of receiving spiritual traditions from Asia, which actually began in earnest in the nineteenth century among intellectual elites, now influences the attitudes and self-perceptions of all segments of American society. One superficial example of this point is a recent Gallup Poll in which twelve percent of American teenagers interviewed claimed allegiance to some Asian religious tradition and a greater percentage of the whole populace said they believed in reincarnation.

It would appear that the NRMs are no longer new, and that many of them, including the Hare Krishnas, are here to stay. Therefore, it is important to take seriously American youths' interest in and conversion to an alternative faith such as that of the Krishnas because these instances of clear religious choice can help us to understand the process of religious seeking that ends in conversion to any religious faith, traditional or marginal.

The three basic sources of information used for this study are personal interviews, participant observation, and selected literature on the Krishna movement and on conversion. Between 1980 and 1984 I conducted more than one hundred interviews with Krishna devotees that averaged roughly three hours each. These interviews focused on pertinent pre-Krishna events of the devotee's life story and especially on the period between the first point of contact and decision to join ISKCON—that is, when the seeker was exploring a new faith. A major segment of each interview was also given over to a description of the affiliation process that led to a conversion decision.

The ISKCON devotees interviewed ranged from five of the new gurus to kitchen cooks and temple workers. Those interviewed were divided almost evenly between men and women devotees. A total of three and a half months were spent living and participating in the life of Krishna temples and farms in America and India while interviewing devotees. Because the Krishna converts' own experiences and perceptions will guide our rethinking of some current psychological approaches to conversion, it is to one such example we now turn.

Sita Dasi

Sita Dasi (a pseudonym) was interviewed in the Washington, D.C., temple during the winter of 1981. Sita was of medium height and of dark complexion. She had long black hair tied up in a bun on the top of her head, which made her look older than her twenty-six years. She wore an Indian sari and could have passed for a Bengali woman on the streets of India. What struck one immediately about Sita was her self-assured air and easy manner and her calmness as a person. These two impressions did not prepare the listener for the story that unfolded.[4]

> The night I finally decided to commit suicide, I considered the events in my life which had brought me to this point. I was an Army brat who was born in Texas but had lived in seven or eight places throughout the United States. My family was Jewish, but seldom lived in places where there were other Jews. Consequently, whether in Texas or Washington state, I was usually the only Jew in my class. Furthermore, my family was middle-class Jewish and only attended the Synagogue on high holy days. Neither my two brothers nor I went through Bar Mitzvah or Bat Mitzvah. Consequently, I never really felt a part of my Judaism and didn't really see it as a religion at all.

My family life was pretty typical of most American homes. My two brothers and I fought a lot and our family was not particularly marked by warmth or closeness. My school life was quite normal as well. I had a good teacher in the fourth or fifth grade who really got me excited and, from that point on, was a straight "A" student. In high school I continued my good grades and got heavily into the social scene as well. I was a cheerleader, a class officer, and had my name or picture on nearly every page of our classbook in a large Baltimore high school. I had two really close friends with whom I did a lot of drugs and dating. I was really into drugs and sex, but my parents and teachers never suspected.

When I went off to the University of Maryland for college, I continued my sensual ways. My relationship with my parents improved because I was dating Jewish men almost exclusively by then. To all outside appearances, I was a successful and happy student. On the inside, however, I became more and more disenchanted with the sensual side of my life and saw that such activities were quite empty of any meaning. I began to read poets and philosophers who talked about the dark side of life and I even contemplated suicide a couple of times in my college years. My eldest brother previously had a severe reaction to LSD and never recovered completely. He finally succeeded in killing himself after several aborted attempts.

As far as my feelings toward God at this time, I presented my friends with a negative and bitter attitude and would ask, "If there is a God, why is there so much suffering in the world?" I would laugh at people being religious and all my friends thought I was a confirmed atheist. And yet every night I would pray secretly to God saying, "Please help me find the truth." No matter how intoxicated I was, I would pray. No one could have guessed from the atheistic show I put on.

During my college years I began to study Asian philosophies and more popular books like Hesse's *Siddhartha*. I stayed on at Maryland to do a Ph.D. in psychology at the University of Maryland. I continued my search for "wholeness" or "oneness" through reading about Asian religions. [I remember wanting to accept someone as a teacher and to serve someone who had the answers I sought.] I remember going to my poetry professor, whom I admired very much, and asking him why I should not commit suicide that very day. He just got red-faced and angry because he didn't feel his students had any right asking him that kind of question. By this time, however, I had already essentially made the decision that suicide was better than living life aimlessly. This feeling escalated to a fever pitch the second summer of my graduate study.

I was preparing to head up the university's freshmen orientation program and was taking graduate courses the summer I decided to take my life. I felt that my whole life was a charade and that my social facade was all that other people knew. I tried to get in touch with a high school friend who had joined the Hare Krishna movement, but the temple didn't know where he was.

When I decided that death was the only answer, I felt liberated and experienced the peace that comes with death. I remember excitedly telling my boyfriend one night, "I have the answer, the answer is suicide!" It felt right and good. My boyfriend and other friends thought I was crazy and spent the whole night with me giving me support. My whole apartment was filled with people telling me to "hang on" until the next day when I could see the school psychiatrist.

I went to the psychiatrist's office the next morning and he appeared to understand my problem but then suggested that I go to a mental hospital for the weekend. I was outraged! It was then I realized that there was no way any of my friends or teachers could understand what was wrong with me. They thought I was crazy and yet I knew exactly what my problem was. . . . I had to find some satisfaction to my deep religious questions or end my shallow life.

While at the psychiatrist's office, I insisted that he call my friend at the Krishna temple. He tried but was told my friend no longer lived in that temple. I thought of my friend because I felt that perhaps he could understand why I felt I needed to commit myself to a spiritual master or, alternatively, to kill myself. Both my friends and psychiatrist tried hard to reach my friend hoping he might be able to calm my ravings, but could not locate him.

So I left the psychiatrist's office plotting how to get rid of my friends so that I could do what I knew I must. And just as I got down to the street I ran into the Krishna friend I had been looking for. I just ran up and hugged him! He had not been alerted that I had been looking for him, and I realized that this must be Krishna's arrangement. He had just come back to Baltimore that day, but even the Baltimore temple did not know he was back in town.

I just remember that as I was hugging him I said, "I don't know what you're doing, I don't know what it is, but I want to surrender to it!" I was crying I was so happy. I just knew it was what I had to do. I just knew that I had to become a Hare Krishna devotee. I had read the *Bhagavad Gita* briefly once and had tried chanting the Krishna mantra for about five minutes once. But I knew very little about the Krishna faith or the lifestyle it entailed. I just knew I had to try it.

When my friend took me to the temple I said, "This is home." I really had committed suicide that day to my material life. . . . In my own mind I had really given up. . . . I didn't understand what it was all leading to. I just had faith in this devotee. To make my decision sound plausible to my parents, I told them I had been studying the Krishna philosophy for several years and that these people in the temple had been my friends for a long time. I knew that they would not understand. . . . Yet after six years in the movement, I am closer to my parents than I ever have been.

Psychological Perspectives on Conversion

Experiences like Sita's, which William James calls "sudden conversions," are chronicled throughout religious history. Usually, interpreters do not have the advantage of knowing what the convert's interpretation is. The conversion of Sita certainly must have appeared quite radical to her friends and family who thought she was an atheist. In a similar fashion, the Hebrew scriptures remind us of the life-altering and sudden experiences of Moses after an encounter with a burning bush and the direct vision and call of the reluctant prophet, Jeremiah. In Christian history, the radical conversion of Paul on the road to Damascus or the mass conversions on Pentecost have been duplicated by later Christians like St. Augustine or John Wesley.

Muslims believe that Muhammed had a direct vision of Allah that sparked his sudden transition from businessman to prophet, and many Sufi saints seek such life-transforming experiences for themselves. Likewise, in the Buddhist monastic traditions, the very path to salvation is essentially one of duplicating Siddhartha's experience of Nirvana that transformed him into the Buddha or Enlightened One. So too, many elite Indian schools of yoga and asceticism focus all their religious disciplines on achieving the life-altering and liberating experience of *moksa*.

Nonetheless, it has not only been the *sudden* conversion that has caught the eye of students of religion, but also the *radical* conversion that appears to be discontinuous with observable life experiences leading up to it. A classic case of the unexpected conversion is that of Paul who, while on the road to Damascus to persecute members of the new Jewish sect who were called Christians, had an experience that made *him* a Christian. All of us are likewise familiar with stories of foxhole or deathbed conversions by persons who have spent their whole lives denouncing religion. Such "crisis conversions" can be understood as an extended form of the radical variety and clearly serve as a beginning description of Sita's experience.

Some contemporary critics of the cults in America have claimed that a deceptive process they variously name brainwashing, mind control, or coercive persuasion is the cause of such dramatic conversions as that of Sita. Most of these critics claim that some formal set of brainwashing techniques akin to those described by Robert Lifton in his study of Korean war prisoners, *The Psychology of Totalism*, serves as the best explanation for all cult conversions whether radical or not. Flo Conway and Jim Siegelman's book, *Snapping: America's Epidemic of Sudden Personality Change* (1978), has excited these critics who have found in the holographic model of the brain proposed by Karl H. Pribram an explana-

tion for cult proselytizing and conversion processes based on an information onslaught and overload of the brain's normal capacities.
However, because mind control theories like that of *Snapping* would take
us far afield in this essay for little benefit, such explanations will be saved
for another setting and time. Nonetheless, conversions like that of Sita
do offer information that undercuts most of these popular and mis-
guided theories.

In any case, the primary questions addressed in this essay are, "How
do some current psychological explanations or interpretations of religious conversion approach cases like that of Sita Dasi and what more can
we learn from such instances of conversion than psychological explanations alone reveal?" We will begin with the single case of Sita Dasi
because her dramatic transformation represents a paradigmatic type of
sudden change on which lay people and scholars alike usually focus. We
will, however, meet a second Krishna devotee at a later point in the
discussion when we turn to the less dramatic types of conversion.

Because the field of conversion studies is so broad and the perspectives are so many, to recount the history of psychological, sociological,
and religious studies of conversion would require at least a book-length
study. Consequently, the choice to explore one basic set of psychological
interpretations to present several different approaches to sudden religious conversion will allow us to view Sita's conversion from varied
angles and still restrict the scope of this study.

One of the most obvious explanations of Sita's conversion comes out of
the Freudian psychological tradition. Leaving aside Freud's discredited
primal hoard theory, many persons would still agree with him that
dramatic religious conversions are best understood as infantile psychological regressions. Freud understood religious conversion as a pathology analogous to a childhood neurosis. That is, a religious crisis
resulting in conversion is actually an outbreak of previously repressed,
unconscious feelings or wishes that erupt into consciousness and dis-
rupt normal psychological functioning.

Freud's only specific study of religious conversion was published in
1928.[5] In this study, Freud reports that a young doctor was converted to
Christianity as the result of seeing an old female cadaver on a dissection
table. Freud said that this startling experience reawakened in the young
doctor oedipal feelings of jealousy and rage directed at God (the father
figure) for the sadistic and degrading treatment of the mother (represented by the old woman). Freud submits that the initial impulse of the
young physician to rebel against his father was finally resolved in capitu-
lation to that same father in the disguised form of the God of his
childhood faith.

Because Freud found the unconscious conflicts at the root of all religious conversions, he concluded that all religion was at its core an infantile regression into childhood fantasies and conflicts that led to a childish dependency. These childhood fantasies were simply disguised projections of deep-seated and unconscious wishes that finally *should* be overcome. In the *Future of an Illusion* Freud says plainly,

> A psychologist . . . makes an endeavour to assess the development of man in light of . . . a study of the mental processes of individuals during their development from child to adult. In so doing, the idea forces itself upon him that religion is comparable to a childhood neurosis, and he is optimistic enough to suppose that mankind will surmount this neurotic phase, just as so many children grow out of their similar neuroses.[6]

Freud's negative assessment of religious conversions as a pathological condition has become commonplace for most psychological interpreters who stand in his tradition. For example, Leon Salzman in 1953 and Carl Christensen in 1963 report from their studies of sudden religious conversions that they are regressive and usually stem from guilt, anger, and other such destructive preconversion attitudes.[7] Salzman recognizes gradual conversions as "progressive" because they *can* contribute to emotional maturity and development. However, he focuses his study on sudden conversions, which he calls "psychopathological conversions." In other words, a sudden religious conversion like Sita's represents a pathological state of mind.

Carl Christensen discusses the conversion of twenty-two of his patients whose experiences occurred during adolescence. He concludes that these conversion experiences are "acute hallucinatory episodes occurring within a framework of religious belief." Furthermore, he understands sudden conversions as attempts to support and reintegrate a structurally weak ego.[8] In summing up the history of psychological theories of conversion, Robert Bagwell says that religious conversions are generally understood psychologically as "an acute regression followed closely by a sudden reintegration," which may or may not be more adaptive.[9]

Although Erik Erikson allows more room for social and environmental factors to be considered by the psychologist, this renowned Harvard psychologist follows primarily in Freud's footsteps. In his book, *Young Man Luther,* Erikson applies his eight-stage psychological developmental model to Martin Luther's religious experiences. He concludes that Luther's conversion and subsequent faith were projections of his oedipal conflict with his father. That is, Luther's repressed resentment over his father's heavy-handed thwarting of his childhood initiatives resulted in a guilt that Luther projected in a stern and authoritarian Father-God. Erikson concludes his Luther study with these words:

> I have implied that the original faith which Luther tried to restore goes back to the basic trust of early infancy. In doing so I have not . . . diminished the wonder of what Luther calls God's disguise. I assume that it is the smiling face and the guiding voice of infantile parent images which religion projects onto the benevolent sky.[10]

It is precisely Erikson's psychological model that Francine Daner applies in her attempt to explain why American youth would turn to such a foreign faith as the Hare Krishnas. In her book, *The American Children of Krishna*, Daner concludes a six-page Eriksonian analysis of Krishna converts with the statement,

> The search for identity, for a definition of self, is one of the main concerns of youth today. Young people appear preoccupied with personal consciousness and experimentation, . . . The ISKCON temple provides a total-institutional setting which allows its members a well-defined structural and ideological situation into which they can fit themselves. It creates a social situation in which they can realize their identities, thereby eliminating much of the ambiguity which is generated by modern society.[11]

Applying the Freudian/Eriksonian psychological explanations used by Daner to the case of Sita's conversion yields valuable insights. First, it is clear that the severe anxiety and guilt Sita experienced before joining the Krishna temple might be explained, in part, by her family relationships. According to Sita, her mother was an impulsive, unstable authority figure. She was given to periods of severe depression spiced by fits of rage. Sita remembers her mother getting so angry at her and her brothers that she would strike out at them just prior to stomping out of the house for a cooling-off period. Sita's father was gone much of the time, making her mother the primary parent for the family. Sita's recollection of her family life was that "it was not a very warm environment."

It may well have been that unresolved and unconscious conflicts with her authoritarian mother did play some role in Sita's preconversion state of mind, but she also reports that during her first years of graduate school she and her parents had begun to understand each other and that their relationship had never been better. Furthermore, scholars have begun to be interested in the whole family picture instead of just focusing upon the way one member reflects family interactions. For example, Gordon Melton and Robert Moore in their book *The Cult Experience* caution us to consider the roles played by *all* members of the family of a cult convert.[12] Using family systems theory, Melton and Moore submit that "problem children" are often encouraged either to submit to familial discipline or to abandon the family in search of freedom and an accepting environment. Consequently, the decision to enter a deviant religious group may well reflect interactional problems throughout the whole family environment and not just in one individual family member.

Even though Sita's psychological crisis does not necessarily require one to assume either an unconscious conflict with her parents or specific role conflicts originating in the family, the particular foci provided by the psychoanalytic interpretation of religious conversion or by family systems therapy do require one to consider the motivational factors that could *unconsciously* intensify when she decided to end her life. Furthermore, that Sita was experiencing a crisis of "ego identity" as described by Erikson can hardly be doubted.[13] Certainly Sita *did* question whether any continuity existed between her image of herself and that of significant others (parents, classmates, teachers, and close friends). Nonetheless, in light of the next story, the psychoanalytic interpretation of conversion appears to be truncated and incomplete. The question then becomes whether there is a better or more inclusive way to explain both Sita's conversion process and that of Rama Dasa.

Rama Dasa

Rama Dasa makes a striking impression with his six-foot four-inch frame, blond hair, and ruddy complexion. He speaks with a confident tone in his voice and is respected greatly by his godbrothers. He had been in the movement nearly ten years when he was interviewed on a Krishna farm.

> I was born in Miami, December 7, 1950. I had two brothers and we lived a comfortable life with my parents in the suburbs. My father was a used-car dealer who provided a moderate income. Though we were not wealthy, we were a close family with a strong sense of our Jewish heritage. My parents were not practicing Jews, but I grew up with very strong pro-Jewish and pro-Israeli feelings. Though I was not trained in a religious or ascetic life, even at a very young age I was inclined toward such a life. For example, I used to hate the sight of meat, fish, and eggs, and avoided them whenever I could. When my parents forced me to eat meat I usually just threw it back up. I was attracted to poverty for myself and knew that I would never be satisfied with a purely material way of life. Furthermore, I was fanatical about personal cleanliness. For example, I always used water on my toilet paper after using the bathroom and felt dirty when I only could use toilet paper.
> I was happy in school, all the way through high school. I was on

the honor roll each term, had lots of friends, and loved to wrestle. I did smoke pot with my friends by the ninth grade, but just to find the deeper meaning of life, not just to escape. At the end of my sophomore year in high school, I hitch-hiked to California and slept on the beach. I always had this adventuresome spirit which seemed to push me to seek new experiences.

After graduation from high school, I took LSD for the first time to seek a spiritual experience. The Vietnam War was raging and as I stood back and viewed my society's material and violent values, I came to the startling realization that what I had been brought up to believe about the goodness of American life was not true! I didn't want to find the answer to the truths I was seeking through drugs, so I turned to blues music as a new avenue of exploration.

When I began college in the fall, I began to read books on religion and philosophy. I got straight A's my first year in college but really dived into my own reading the most. I was reading a lot of books on Eastern spirituality and finally was initiated into TM (Transcendental Meditation). I was not satisfied with TM but was convinced that I needed to find a spiritual guide, a guru. I quit school after that first year in college and sold my car to get money to fly to Europe. As I made my way from Europe toward India, I vowed not to smoke pot anymore. As I hitched through Holland, I was disgusted with all the free sex I saw about me and vowed not to have sex anymore. That experience occurred when a young Dutch girl offered me a place to stay one night and then tried to seduce me. I finally had to get out of bed and leave her house to wander the streets the rest of the night.

When I finally made it to New Delhi in India, I fell in love with the Indian cow. I thought, "She really is your mother!" The next time I ate meat I vomited and vowed never to eat meat again. I heard there was an International Yoga Conference in New Delhi where a large collection of gurus could be found. However, the session I attended ended with the gurus literally fighting over the microphone so they could convince the audience that their path was the best, and I left disgusted.

I headed north to Hardwar and went on to Rishikesh looking for the ashram (religious retreat) of Sivananda. I spent several days in each of several ashrams casting my Western dress aside and adopting the *lungi* and *chadar* (loin cloth and shawl) of the religious ascetic. I began my purification process by sitting beside the Ganges River for eight to ten hours a day. I ate very little and just wanted to become pure. I knew the Krishna *mantra* (prayer formula) among several mantras I had learned and would chant that or another mantra for hours on end. I found a large rock in the middle of the Ganges and would wade out to sit upon it each day for nearly a month. But I still wanted to find a guru to lead me.

I left the mountains of the north and went to Banares and lived among the Saivite (worshippers of the god Shiva) ascetics there. Then I went to Bodhgaya (place of the Buddha's enlightenment) and lived in a temple there. I traveled on to Bombay where I met the

Hare Krishnas for the first time. I saw a sign announcing a Krishna festival and went to the first night's program and heard Prabhupada speak for the first time. Several devotees descended upon me to preach to me at the end of the lecture, but I thought all religious paths led to the same goal, so why follow this Indian guru and his band of American and Indian followers? I was impressed with Prabhupada's lectures and came back each night that week arriving early so I could sit at his feet. However, I was still taking a meditation course in Bombay that was more important to me at the moment and didn't see the Krishnas anymore during that stay of Prabhupada in Bombay.

More than a year passed before I met the Krishnas and Prabhupada again. I had traveled in India from ashram to ashram and guru to guru trying to find a person I could trust to lead me spiritually. Finally, I arrived in Mathura during the birthday festival of Krishna and walked with some Indian Krishna devotees to Vrindaban (birthplace of Krishna). I met a godbrother of Prabhupada, Bon Maharaj, and stayed at his ashram for a time. I was deeply impressed with the devotion of the people of Vrindavana and felt like I was one of them—by this time I had long matted hair and looked much like any other Indian *sadhu* or seeker.

One day a busload of Krishna devotees arrived with Prabhupada and I went to their temple grounds to hear him speak again. But when I arrived, Prabhupada was singing one of the old Bengali devotional songs about Krishna and I was struck by my feeling, "This man is truly a pure devotee." I wanted to surrender to him, but was put off by the opulence of his temple and by some of the devotees who were with him. I realized that Prabhupada was the greatest guru I had met in my two years of searching in India. He answered all of my questions and everything was backed by the ancient scriptures. Furthermore, I could see that he was a living example of what he taught. Nonetheless, I was hesitant to make such a big step as surrending to him, so I went back to America.

I stayed with my parents only a short time until I left to find Prahbupada. I learned that he was in New York and was about to depart for India in only three days. I wanted to go with him and to return to Vrindaban, but he said that I should remain in America and build up new communities of devotees. I have been here ever since although it took me a full year to decide to shave my head and accept full initiation.

Shadows of Truth

[What Rama's story does is to underline a basic *conscious* dimension of all conversions that should not be ignored as we seek to understand and to explain such religious events.] The conceptual questioning and content of Rama's quest and final faith choice are perhaps more obvious in Rama's than in Sita's case. Nonetheless, a considerable amount of conscious searching took place in Sita's case of which only she and a few intimates were aware. Yet we must be careful not to insist that theological content alone is the only necessary and sufficient factor in either Rama's or Sita's conversions.

What all of the explanations of conversion reveal is the inadequacy of any one approach by itself. More important, the fact that each model has been taken by some scholars to be an explanation *sufficient in itself* gives a clearer picture of the dilemma facing anyone wishing to enter the debate. All theories of conversion are, to some extent, like the shadows on the wall of Plato's cave.[14] They are human constructs that project images of what it means to become religious that often distort as much as they reveal.

From five years of research and interviews among Hare Krishna devotees, several challenges to these conversion theories have arisen.[15] First, sudden conversions like Sita's are rare among those joining ISKCON. Less than a dozen of the one hundred twenty devotees interviewed claimed any dramatic experience or quick decision to enter a Krishna temple. The far more common pattern was for a convert to experience at least a year of occasional and unpressured contact with ISKCON coupled with some significant study of ISKCON's teachings prior to his or her decision to become a devotee and move into a temple. Rama Dasa's conversion certainly represents this pattern well (though his insistent seeking of a guru in India is not typical of most devotees). Consequently, even when psychological theories do appear to account for a sudden conversion like Sita's, they have explained the atypical, as the theories of Freud, Salzman, and Christensen do, given their biased samplings of only pathological cases of religiosity.

Second, it would appear that there are many and varied basic patterns of conversion or affiliation instead of the usually named two: sudden and gradual. The variegated patterns include various motives, differences in lengths of time before any decision to join, and idiosyncratic factors like Sita's incessant preoccupation with human suffering or Rama Dasa's single-minded seeking of a spiritual master. On the one hand, some devotees whose stories are similar to Sita's clearly escape into ISKCON before they know what life choice they have made and so that others can tell them what to believe and how to act. On the other hand, some devotees like Rama set out on a spiritual quest, and their conversion to the faith of Krishna is essentially philosophically and textually based. In short, no one model, however complex and sophisticated, can do more than cast *one* shadow on Plato's cave wall.

The third observation is really anticipated in William James's still relevant study, *The Varieties of Religious Experience*. In that book, James defines conversion this way:

> To be converted, to be regenerated, to receive grace, to experience
> religion, to gain assurance, are so many phrases which denote the
> process, gradual or sudden, by which a self hither divided, and
> consciously wrong, inferior and unhappy, becomes unified and
> consciously right, superior and happy . . . whether or not we be-
> lieve that a direct divine operation is needed to bring such a moral
> change about.[16]

James implies that conversion includes not only a *decision* to convert, but
also a *conversion process* that culminates in altered moral behavior and a
new religious life. He spells out clearly in his chapters on saintliness that
religious experiences, no matter how dramatic, do not constitute conversion—that only when the convert fully internalizes the new worldview and incorporates it into his behavior can the conversion be said to
be complete.

Consequently, a seldom noticed insight James has to offer to us is that
there is a distinction to be made between a *conversion decision* and the
conversion process, which may or may not follow such a decision. For
example, Sita decided to join the Krishna temple in a moment of emotional distress, but she also clearly underwent a conversion process
during the following years that provided answers to the questions that
had contributed consciously to her initial distress. In a different fashion,
Rama experimented with various religious lifestyles and philosophies
and did so with ISKCON before finally making a conscious choice to be
initiated. In the case of Sita, there is a clear separation between the
conversion decision and the subsequent faith-rendering process. In the
case of Rama, the two are virtually reversed.

The distinction between decision and process in conversion is assumed, though not discussed, in the recent work done on stages of
religious development by James Fowler. In *Stages of Faith*, Fowler describes six different and progressively mature types of religiosity.[17] In so
doing, Fowler talks primarily about the conversion process for those
born into a religious faith. However, Fowler's description of faith stages
is clearly consonant with the maturation process of new converts to
groups like the Krishnas.

Fowler says that the young child raised in a religious home usually
exhibits what he calls an "Intuitive-Projective" faith that is a fantasy-filled
imitation of what he or she sees in trusted adults. Subsequent to the
naive faith of the infant, five stages of religious realization follow,
culminating in what Fowler describes as the fully actualized person of
stage six. The fully mature believer has what Fowler calls a "Universaliz-
ing Faith," and becomes "a disciplined, activist *incarnation* . . . of the
imperatives of absolute love and justice."[18]

In other words, according to Fowler, a fully mature person of any faith becomes a living example of his or her particular faith. At the same time, such a person embraces, or takes account of, the world outside the religious community with all of its forms of belief and unbelief without feeling any threat to his or her own beliefs. However, between the infant's naive but trusting faith and the compassionate, mature faith lies other more or less literal, dogmatic or liberated forms of believing that tend to be exclusivistic.[19]

What is important in Fowler's analysis for our consideration of Sita's conversion is the realization that psychoanalytic or social explanations that focus on her *conversion decision* alone neglect the maturing conversion process she underwent. Likewise, Fowler's work encourages us to look at Rama's religious quest as a period of religious maturation before an actual commitment or leap of faith into ISKCON. It is clear from Rama's story that religious maturation can occur even before a converson decision—note that the choices Rama considered were radically different ones that included atheistic and theistic solutions.

Most theories of conversion will cast the shadows of the experience and worldview of those who propose them as much as of Sita or Rama. Consequently, the psychoanalysts tend to impose a predetermined interpretation of conversion on experiences like that of Sita, which may well cause us to ignore other significant dimensions of such dramatic religious decisions. When I talked with Sita six years after she became a devotee, I discovered that her conversion *decision* to enter the temple was quite different *in character* from the *conversion process* that had led to her maturing faith. Although a psychological crisis may have helped to precipitate her joining ISKCON, Sita's study of the Krishna scriptures in light of her existential questions resulted in her becoming a mature Krishna disciple who not only knew who Krishna was but worshiped him knowledgeably. Interviews with other devotees at Sita's temple confirmed the impression that Sita was among the more religiously mature of the devotees interviewed and observed. She was respected as a counselor for new women devotees, as a knowledgeable student of the Krishna scriptures, and as a good representative of ISKCON to the outside world.

What Fowler's theory of six stages of faith represents is one more shadow on our cave's wall, but its shape is dramatically different from that of most conversion theories. It requires that we take seriously the *conscious content* of Sita's distress and Rama's search and see in *both* of them a desire to build a future that is ultimately meaningful. Viktor Frankl in his book, *Man's Search for Meaning*, states well the commonality in Sita's and Rama's searches when he says, "A [person's] search for meaning is a primary force in his life and not a 'secondary rationalization' of instinctual drives. This meaning is unique and specific in that it

must and can be filled by him alone; only then does it achieve a significance that will satisfy his own will to meaning."[20]

Perhaps the most important lesson to be learned from the conversions
of American Krishna devotees is that conscious, cognitive factors often
weigh heavily in conversion decisions and are paramount in subsequent
conversion processes. Consequently, it is clear that we will miss entirely
the significance and origin of Sita's conversion and its similarity to
Rama's if we do not seek to know why it was the theology of Krishna that
finally satisfied Sita. Many have joined ISKCON in a moment of distress
only to leave at a later date unsatisfied. Only if one takes account of the
process of theological or spiritual maturation in devotees—that is, a
conversion process—will additional progress be made in explaining why
some devotees stay and others leave even though external factors appear
to be similar.

Being attentive to the theological questioning that is so obvious in
Rama's quest sensitizes us to realize that Sita's conversion decision and
process are linked by her conscious religious questioning and despair
that finally found satisfactory answers in the Hindu teachings of
Krishna. Such a perspective also explains why Sita, and most Krishna
devotees, could become a Krishna disciple but not likely a follower of the
Reverend Moon.[21]

To understand Sita's conversion as motivated in great part by factors
fully known to her (conscious factors) places a very different agenda
before the inquiring scholar than most of the theories based on unconscious factors allow. Such an approach requires that we focus on the
consciously derived decisions, motivations, and ideological processes of
the religious convert even when the intellectual component is not as
obvious as it is in the case of Rama's religious seeking. Furthermore,
such an agenda will usually include more talk about the conversion
process than any single decision to join a new faith, and inevitably turn
the researcher's attention away from social and psychological explanations alone and toward theological and philosophical considerations.

Surprising as it may seem from external appearances, a strong common denominator in most devotee conversions described in the interviews was a quest for meaning that was finally satisfied in the specific
teaching and stories of the Indians' Cowherd Krishna. Although some
unconscious factors were undoubtedly at work in greater and lesser
degrees in these conversion experiences, it is just as obvious that conscious decisions had been made to enter a new religious life by each
devotee. While most devotees recognize that they still have a considerable distance to travel on their spiritual journey, all believe that they have
consciously chosen to surrender to Krishna. It would be foolish for
scholars to ignore the devotees' own interpretations of their conversion

experiences and the lesson they can teach us about distinction between a conversion decision and a conversion process.

Notes

1. R. J. Z. Werblowsky, "Religious New and Not So New," *NVMEN: International Journal for the History of Religions* 27, no. 1 (June 1980): 155.

2. (New York: Prentice-Hall, 1963), p. vii.

3. See J. Gordon Melton and Robert L. Moore, *The Cult Experience: Responding to the New Religious Pluralism* (New York: The Pilgrim Press, 1982).

4. To share with the reader some of the immediacy of Sita's story, the following abridgment of her interview has all been set in the first person. Sita had been a member of the Washington temple for six years when this story was told.

5. Sigmund Freud, "A Religious Experience," in *The Standard Edition of the Complete Psychological Works of Sigmund Freud,* ed. and trans. James Strachey (London: Hogarth Press, 1961), pp. 169–72.

6. Sigmund Freud, *The Future of an Illusion,* trans. W. D. Robson-Scott (New York: W. W. Norton & Company, 1928), pp. 86–87.

7. Salzman, "The Psychology of Religious and Ideological Conversion," *Psychiatry* 16, no. 2 (May 1953): 177–87; and Christensen, "Religious Conversions," *Archives of General Psychiatry* 9, no. 3 (September 1963): 207–16.

8. Christensen, "Religious Conversions," p. 207.

9. Robert Bagwell, "The Abrupt Religious Conversion," *Journal of Religion and Health* 8, no. 2 (1969): 167–69.

10. Erikson, *Young Man Luther* (New York: Anchor Books, 1964), pp. 265–66.

11. Francine Jeanne Daner, *The American Children of Krishna: A Study of the Hare Krishna Movement* (New York: Holt, Rinehart and Winston, 1976), pp. 14 and 12.

12. Melton and Moore, *The Cult Experience,* pp. 65–69.

13. Erik H. Erikson, *Identity: Youth and Crisis* (New York: W. W. Norton and Company, 1968), pp. 49–50 and 165ff.

14. For Plato's description of false images of reality as symbolized by shadows on a cave's wall, see *The Republic of Plato,* trans. Allan Bloom (New York: Basic Books, 1968), pp. 193–220.

15. For two different sociological challenges to psychological approaches to NRM conversions, see Rodney Stark and William Baimbridge, "Networks of Faith: Interpersonal Bonds and Recruitment to Cults and Sects," *American Journal of Sociology* 85 (1980): 1376–95; and David Bromley and Anson Shupe, "Just a Few Years Seem Like a Lifetime: A Role Theory Approach to Participation in Religious Movements," in *Research in Social Movements: Conflict and Change,* ed. Louis Kriesberg (Greenwich, CT: JAI Press, 1979), pp. 59–85. My utilization and responses to these sociological approaches to cult conversions can be found in Larry D. Shinn, "Conflicting Networks: Guru and Friend in ISKCON," in *Genesis, Exodus, and Numbers,* ed. Rodney Stark (New York: Paragon House Publishers, 1986); and in Larry D. Shinn, "The Many Faces of Krishna," in *Alternatives to American Mainline Churches,* ed. Joseph H. Fichter (New York: Rose of Sharon Press, 1983), pp. 113–35. Both of these sociological approaches were found to be of use but also were found to be inadequate *in and of themselves* to explain the complexity of the Krishna conversions revealed in interviews and observations.

16. *The Varieties of Religious Experiences* (New York: Collier Books, 1961), p. 160.

17. James W. Fowler, *Stages of Faith: The Psychology of Human Development and the Quest for Meaning* (San Francisco: Harper and Row, 1981), pp. 119–211.

18. Ibid., p. 200.

19. Although Fowler's explication of the stages of religious maturation is valuable and suggestive, it is limited in application by the Christian set of values that underlie each of the six stages. For example, Fowler's assumptions include a theistic divinity and love and justice as signs of the completely mature faith. While Fowler is aware of the Christian focus of his study, the reader must be careful not to assume that the content of the six stages of faith would be the same for mature disciples of other faiths of the world, like ISKCON.

20. (New York: Pocket Books, 1963), p. 154.

21. For a description by Eileen Barker of a "typical Moonie" and a comparison with those interviewed in ISKCON by this author, see Larry D. Shinn, "The Many Faces of Krishna," pp. 122–25.

Exploring an Alternative Reality: Spiritual Life in ISKCON

Steven J. Gelberg
(Subhananda dasa)

Introduction

When a person enters the Hare Krishna movement, he or she enters a new world, a universe of thought and feeling quite remote from the social and cognitive norms of late twentieth-century America. In this essay, I describe that inner world of "Krishna Consciousness," with the hope of making it more comprehensible to outsiders. My focus is on the religious life of the movement, putting it in historical and theological context but, more important for our present purposes, describing it phenomenologically in an attempt to communicate a sense of the distinctive experiential ambiance within the movement.

Formally attempting this kind of in-depth exploration is worthwhile for various reasons. First, there is inherent value in comprehending a phenomenon that is as seemingly exotic and as highly stigmatized (and thus as little understood) as ISKCON devotees' religiosity. Another reason for drawing attention to spirituality in ISKCON has to do with the highly abstract nature of much social scientific thinking. In their desire to construct broad, interpretive theories about socioreligious phenomena, social scientists tend to retreat hastily from the living wellsprings of religiosity in the field to return to the safety of office and library. The requirements of intellectual abstraction can cause them to lose touch with the raw, experiential data of the lived, religious life with all its rich particularity and complexity. Theoretical formulas about why people join and commit themselves to religious movements are of dubious value if detached from a conscious sense of what it "feels like" to be a member. This essay can be viewed as an attempt, then, to provide observers of ISKCON with some "raw data" on the religious worldview and experience of a devotee, by that devotee.

Lastly, to understand the distinctive experience ISKCON offers its members is to understand something of the movement's appeal. In attempting to understand the processes of conversion and commitment to new religious movements, social scientists often underestimate the significance of individual experience, socially mediated or otherwise, for religious commitment. Rather than mount a formal theoretical argument to support this contention, I will describe, as clearly as possible, the Krishna devotee's inner world of meaning and experience, with the hope that it will make clear the fact that a religious movement can provide its members with a worldview and experience that is so filled with meaning, so absorbing and productive of personal affective transformation, that a person will become attracted and remain committed even in lieu of satisfaction of various social needs, such as those concerned with status and security. To understand ISKCON's holding power as a religious institution, it will help to get "a feel" for the aura of sacredness encountered and experienced by the seriously committed member.

Although I have mentioned the notion of religious commitment, I will not be concerned herein with the dynamics of commitment itself, either concretely or as a theoretical problem. Nor will I deal with the specific processes by which members are socialized into the Krishna Consciousness worldview and lifestyle, or with the various factors that conflict with and inhibit "pure" religiosity, such as those that come with increasing institutionalization.[1] Admittedly, a complete understanding of group-centered religiosity needs to be informed by these crucial factors, and I intend to take up these issues vis-à-vis ISKCON in the future. For the present, I wish to isolate and describe the core religious experience derived from membership in ISKCON with the conviction that this is what is most fundamental for understanding the phenomenon of Krishna Consciousness.[2]

The type of consciousness or awareness I describe here is that of one who is fully committed to and immersed in the Krishna Consciousness lifestyle and worldview—an "ideal" state of consciousness, not that of a devotee whose "pure" Krishna Consciousness is attenuated by, for instance, significant contact with the secular world or by internal religious doubt. However, this ideal does set the parameters for discipleship for hundreds of deeply committed Krishna devotees.

The basis for this study is fifteen uninterrupted years of discipleship within ISKCON. As an active member of ISKCON since 1970, and for as long before that as I can remember, I have always tried to temper the heat of experience with the cool of analysis, and so I feel I can bring something of both to bear on this subject. This particular study is not questionnaire-based, nor need it be. If it is "impressionistic," the impressions underlying it are deep, extensive, and cumulative over the many years of personal participation, observation, study, and reflection. This intuitive approach to the subject has its value. Writing on "The Participant's vs. the Observer's Frame of Reference in the Psychological Study of Religion," Joseph Havens explains that:

> The student of religion who is himself religious will be more concerned with phenomenological data for at least two reasons: his own "immersion" in the data should aid him in the evolving of constructs useful in ordering that data . . . and he will be motivated to "take seriously" such data because he himself has taken seriously similar experiences.[3]

My intention in this essay then is not to induce the reader to embrace the Krishna Consciousness worldview and experience, but to encourage him or her to "take it seriously," inasmuch as that will aid in a deeper awareness of the subject.

Historical and Theological Sources

Although ISKCON, as an incorporated institution, came into existence during the summer of 1966, it sprouted from the seeds of an Indian religious and cultural system millennia old. The seed-carrier was Srila A. C. Bhaktivedanta Swami Prabhupada, an elderly Indian scholar and *sadhu* whose mission it was to bring the consciousness of Lord Krishna to the West, as he had been instructed to do many years earlier by his own master, Bhaktisiddhanta Saraswati Goswami.[4] The seed soon grew into a sprout and by 1970 had become a sizable plant, embodying all the essentials of its native Indian tradition.

ISKCON's spiritual sources can be viewed on two levels historically. The more recent takes the form of a widespread pietistic, devotional movement originating in Bengal in the early sixteenth century and founded by the saint Sri Caitanya (1486–1534). This vital movement generally goes by the name Gaudiya (Bengal) Vaisnavism.[5]

ISKCON's Bengali spiritual roots, however, extend backward in time through Caitanya's movement to India's ancient tradition of devotional piety *(bhakti)* centered on Sri Krishna. The religious text that best embodies and communicates that tradition is the *Srimad Bhagavatam (Bhagavata Purana)*, which, along with the *Bhagavad-gita*, constitutes the principal scriptural authority for Vaisnava tradition as a whole. The essential message of these two texts is that the Krishna extolled in these texts is the Supreme Godhead and the ultimate object of worship for all humanity. The central assertion of this tradition is that Lord Krishna can be approached, realized, and pleased only through genuine, spontaneous, selfless love, *bhakti*. Both as an ideal state of consciousness and as a discipline *(sadhana)* leading to it, *bhakti* is meant:

> to destroy men's attachment to the world by shifting their affection and desire from the world to the Lord. As attachment and devotion to [the Lord] increase, attachment to the world decreases, and release from *samsara* [the cycle of repeated birth and death in the world] is possible. . . . Devotion that will bring about the necessary change of affection must occupy the whole self and absorb all of one's energies.[6]

The *Srimad Bhagavatam* is a massive text (some 18,000 verses) in which the message of devotion to Krishna—along with preliminary and subsidiary theological and philosophical topics—is presented through the mouths of venerable sages who relate richly detailed accounts of the auspicious lives and teachings of various saints and sages and of righteous kings from ancient royal dynasties, as well as of the awesome, world-protecting and world-liberating acts of numerous divine *avatars* ("incarnations"). All these beings—human, superhuman, and divine— inhabit and enliven an august spiritual civilization ("Vedic civilization") that existed on the earth in historical antiquity, but that is also primordial, eternal, and interplanetary.

It is this sacred universe in which ISKCON devotees immerse themselves and which is their ultimate, existential frame of reference. In daily communal readings (to be described later), devotees imbibe the highly developed spiritual worldview of the *Bhagavatam* and absorb its philosophical, theological, and ethical precepts into their consciousness and into their perception of reality. This potent, cognitive immersion evokes a general sense of detachment from modernity and from Western culture in particular—the more so in light of the *Bhagavatam's* assertion that the current age of humankind, the "Kali-*yuga*," is a particularly degraded period, characterized by spiritual blindness and abject materialism. The devotee sees the whole modern world, one might say, as an unpleasant intrusion into sacred time and space.

ISKCON's access into ancient Vedic-Vaisnava culture is provided through its roots in the Caitanya movement, which provides ISKCON with most of its distinctive religious characteristics. Caitanya's movement came, historically, in the context of a wider devotional renaissance, as Diana Eck explains:

> One of the most vigorous and vibrant periods of devotional piety on the Indian subcontinent began about five hundred years ago, when a new wave of this ancient *bhakti* tradition broke across north India as virtually a Protestant Reformation of the Hindu tradition. . . .

There were many poets, saints, and theologians who contributed to this era of exuberant devotion. Among them was the Bengali religious leader Sri Caitanya, who may be called the founder of the Hare Krishna movement.[7]

Sri Caitanya was a mystic, theologian and religious leader who propagated an intense, ecstatic form of devotion to Krishna. He is best known for a distinctive religious practice he revived and popularized, that of *nama-sankirtan* (congregational devotional singing of the holy names of Lord Krishna), accompanied by drums and hand-cymbals. Even within his lifetime, Caitanya was worshiped as an incarnation of Krishna (or, more precisely, of Radha and Krishna combined), who descended into human history to save the fallen souls of the age of Kali.

Caitanya commissioned several intimate followers with exceptional scholarly and devotional qualifications to compile and systematize his teachings and create a scriptural foundation for his movement. Residing in the holy town of Vrindaban, these six renowned "Goswamis" produced a large corpus of theological, metaphysical, liturgical, poetic, and dramatic writings, many of which were later recognized as religious classics.

Many other contemporary and later writers contributed to the Gaudiya Vaisnava canon as well, including Krsnadasa Kaviraj, whose biography of Sri Caitanya serves also as an encyclopedic compendium of the Gaudiya Vaisnava teaching and which is the most popular as well as the most authoritative of the many biographical works on Caitanya. This Bengali text, known as *Caitanya-caritamrta*, along with the Sanskrit *Bhakti-rasamrta-sindhu* by Rupa Goswami (of the famous six)—an analytical study of the path of *bhakti*—were translated by Srila Prabhupada, with an extensive commentary on the former. These two texts, along with the *Srimad Bhagavatam* and the *Bhagavad-gita*, constitute the essential scriptural authority for the Hare Krishna movement. It is primarily through these four texts that ISKCON members share in a system of meaning and experience that has sustained many generations of pious Vaisnavas in India.[8]

It is not possible in the space allotted here to provide even a brief survey of Caitanya Vaisnava spirituality.[9] We can, however, quote several lines from the late nineteenth-century Caitanyite saint and reformer Bhaktivinoda Thakura to convey some of the flavor of Caitanyite piety.

Give up the shackles of matter slowly. Cultivate your spirit inwards. . . . Be humble in yourself and learn to respect those who work towards spiritual attainments. Do these with your heart, mind and strength in the company of spiritual people alone, and you will see Krsna in no time.

. . . Spiritual cultivation is the main object of life. Do everything that helps it and abstain from doing anything which thwarts the cultivation of the spirit. Have a strong faith that Krsna alone protects you and none else. Admit Him as your only guardian. Do everything which you know that Krsna wishes you to do, and never think that you do a thing independently of the holy wish of Krsna. Do all that you do with humility. Always remember that you are a sojourner in this world and you must be prepared for your own home. Do your duties and cultivate *bhakti* as a means to obtain the great end of life, Krsna *priti* [love of God]. Employ your body, mind and spirit in the service of the Deity. In all your actions, worship your great Lord.[10]

With this as historical and theological background, we can now proceed to examine the particulars of spiritual life and experience in ISKCON, by analyzing eight of its characteristics, which I have enumerated as intrinsic, dualistic, ascetic, personalistic, mediational, transformational, utilitarian, and evangelistic.

General Characteristics of Spiritual Life in ISKCON

INTRINSIC

Perhaps the most noticeable characteristic of life in ISKCON is the obvious centrality and diffusion of religious orientations, concepts, language, and acts. We may use with profit Allport's concept of intrinsic (as opposed to extrinsic) orientations to religion to help define ISKCON religiosity. Whereas *extrinsic* religion is essentially instrumental and utilitarian, serving other, nonreligious ends (providing, for example, "security and solace, sociability and distraction, status and self-justification"), the *intrinsic* orientation sees religion as an end in itself. Internalized and lived fully, it "floods the whole life with motivation and meaning."[11] Krishna Consciousness is to be lived fully, totally. Devotees are, to borrow James's words, "individuals for whom religion exists not as a dull habit, but as an acute fever rather."[12]

Prabhupada often quoted the first aphorism of the *Vedanta-Sutras*, which says, *"Athato brahma-jijnas,"* indicating that human life, which texts declare is hard to come by in the course of the inexorable cycle of rebirths, is inherently and explicitly meant for the attainment of spiritual knowledge and liberation. Devotees are instructed by the *Bhagavatam* that "a human being is meant for inquiry about the Absolute Truth. Nothing else should be the goal of one's works"[13] and that one must search after the Absolute Truth "in all circumstances, in all space and time, and both directly and indirectly."[14] Furthermore, the devotee should "constantly hear about, glorify, remember and worship the Personality of Godhead with one-pointed attention."[15] Likewise, such devotional service must be "unmotivated and uninterrupted."[16] "Being completely absorbed in Me," Krishna promises in the *Bhagavad-gita*, "surely you will come to Me."[17]

This kind of urgent call to the intense religious life characterizes many Vaisnava texts and contributes to the "flavor" of ISKCON life. Those who opt for this kind of religious seriousness are often persons who describe their lives before ISKCON as being characterized by existential frustration and crisis, wherein the need for meaning in life was extremely high. Some critics of religion (including contemporary anti-cultists) characterize such feelings of existential despair as inherently pathological and pathogenic. However, most devotees would agree rather with the existential psychiatrist Victor Frankl who argues that one's search for meaning is a "primary force" in life, and that "concern, even . . . despair, over the worthwhileness of life is a *spiritual distress*" rather than a mental disease.[18] Simply put, Hare Krishna devotees are people who, often coming from a background of intense searching for meaning, have chosen to commit themselves to a religious life and practice that demands a high level of cognitive, affective, and volitional absorption.

DUALISTIC ("OTHERWORLDLY")

Along with virtually all Indian philosophical systems, ISKCON teachings present an explicit demarcation between the world of spirit and the world of matter—between the transcendent and the mundane, the self and the body—exalting the former and devaluing the latter. The material body is temporary and inherently situated to suffer. Three primary sources of suffering are: the body's innate frailties and imperfections (*adhyatmika*), inflictions by other living beings (*adhibhautika*), and natural causes (*adhidaivika*).

The soul (*atma*), on the other hand, is by nature eternal (*sat*) and full of wisdom (*chit*) and bliss (*ananda*). The soul inhabits but is distinct from the body, which is merely a "field" (*ksetram*) of activity for the soul (*Gita* 13.4) and a "city of nine gates [bodily orifices]" in which the soul resides (*Gita* 5.13). The material world itself is a temporary place that is full of miseries (*duhkhalayam asasvatam*) (*Gita* 8.15), most fundamentally the suffering of repeated birth, old age, disease, and death. Krishna texts describe the world as a prison, a conflagration, an ocean of suffering, and by many other unflattering metaphors. The material world is a false home for the soul, which is in temporary exile, as it were, from Krishna's transcendental abode.

The ISKCON devotee views the material world and society, further, as not quite fully real—dreamlike in its temporality and insubstantiality. Prabhupada writes:

> The whole material creation is a jugglery of names only . . . a bewildering creation of matter. . . . The buildings, furniture, cars . . . factories . . . atomic energy and electronics, are all simply bewildering names of material elements . . . names of no more significance than the babble of sea waves. The great kings, leaders and soldiers fight with one another in order to perpetuate their names in history. They are forgotten in due course of time, and they make a place for another era in history. But the devotee realizes how much history and historical persons are useless products of flickering time.[19]

Modern civilization has little value in its own right, but is merely "a patchwork of activities meant to cover the perpetual miseries of material existence."[20]

Such ideas as these have practical consequences for those who hold them. They bring into being what Max Weber calls "world-rejecting asceticism," a category largely appropriate to ISKCON.

> Concentration upon the actual pursuit of salvation may entail a formal withdrawal from the "world": from social and psychological ties with the family, from the possession of worldly goods, and from political, economic, artistic, and erotic activities—in short, from all creaturely interests. One with such an attitude may regard any participation in these affairs as an acceptance of the world, leading to alienation from God.[21]

This attitude accounts for the detached, communal lifestyle of fully committed devotees, who view their ashrams—communal religious centers—as "outposts" of the spiritual world and as "bases for fighting *maya* [illusion]." Unlike the "flight from the world" characteristic of what Weber calls "the contemplative mystic," the ISKCON devotee's stance is that of "rejection of the world:"[22] "His opposition to the world is psychologically felt not as a flight, but as a repeated victory over ever new temptations which he is bound to combat actively, time and again." As with other "world-rejecting" sects, ISKCON members "see themselves as instruments of a protest against society on behalf of transcendence."[23]

ASCETIC ORIENTATION

If the world and everything in it is temporary and thus not fully real, then the pleasures the world affords are also illusory and should be rejected. The concrete expression of dualistic, world-rejecting ideology in the form of active asceticism epitomizes the core of faith for many members of ISKCON. Devout members embrace a life of simplicity and austerity similar in many respects to that of some of the stricter Roman Catholic monastic orders, such as the Trappists.[24] Initiated devotees are required to observe strictly the "four regulative principles" of abstinence from: the eating of meat, fish and eggs; all forms of intoxication; illicit (nonmarital and nonprocreational) sex; and gambling and "frivolous sports" (which refer to indulgence in nondevotional, mundane entertainments including television and movies). Celibacy is required because sex is viewed as the most intense form of physical gratification; as the form of sense pleasure that most potently reinforces one's false identification with the body, it is the prime cause of the soul's bondage in the material world.

Besides the four prohibitions, there are many other practices in ISKCON that symbolically and materially express the ascetic orientation, such as shaving (males) or covering (females) of the head, wearing of simple robes, shunning of cosmetics among women, living in sparsely furnished apartments, and using sleeping bags on the floor in place of beds.

The fundamental rationale for asceticism is that the quality of one's life must conform to one's spiritual aspirations, if those aspirations are to bear fruit. Spiritual life is hardly practicable, says ascetic ideology, in the context of an undisciplined life centered on possessions and whimsical self-gratification. Ascetic practices are, in this sense, a necessary preparation for the genuine spiritual life. Worldly gratifications are a distraction from the ultimate goal of Krishna Consciousness and thus are "stumbling blocks on the path of self-realization."[25] Asceticism serves not only a preparatory function but is itself the fruit of spiritual knowledge and attainment. It is not, ultimately, stoic resignation or a policy of self-mortification by which the devotee renounces material sense pleasure, but is a response to the stark realization that such pleasures are not ultimately real. Because they "have a beginning and an end," such pleasures give rise to frustration and pain, "and so the wise man does not delight in them."[26] A renunciant may still harbor material desires but can gradually transcend them by experiencing a higher [spiritual] taste.[27]

The theme, mentioned earlier, of world-rejection as a victory over the temptation of the world (Weber) certainly includes within it the notion of asceticism as a mastery of, or a rising above, matter or nature. We find a rather eloquent expression of this idea in *The Elementary Forms of the Religious Life*, wherein Durkheim explains that a person:

never rises above himself with more brilliancy than when he subdues his own nature to the point of making it follow a way contrary to the one it would spontaneously take. By this, he distinguishes himself from all other creatures who follow blindly wherever pleasure calls them; by this, he makes a place apart for himself in the world. Suffering is the sign that certain of the bonds attaching him to his profane environment are broken; so it testifies that he is practically freed from this environment, and, consequently, it is justly considered the instrument of deliverance. So he who is thus delivered is not the victim of pure illusion when he believes himself invested with a sort of mastery over things: he really has raised himself above them, by the very act of renouncing them; he is stronger than nature, because he makes it subside. . . . the suffering which [ascetic practices] impose is not arbitrary and sterile cruelty; it is a necessary school, where men form and temper themselves, and acquire the qualities of disinterestedness and endurance without which there would be no religion.[28]

PERSONALISTIC/DEVOTIONAL/SALVATIONISTIC

This next group of characteristics concerns the devotees' conception of God and the manner in which they relate to Him. Gaudiya Vaisnava tradition has bequeathed to ISKCON devotees a conception of God that is supremely personal—no vague white light, no *Mysterium Tremendum*, no *Deus Absconditus* here. Instead, God is a wondrously beautiful youth with lotus-petal eyes, skin tinged with the hue of blue clouds, a mischievously enchanting smile, a peacock feather in His hair and a flower garland around His neck—His exquisite spiritual body composed of eternity, knowledge, and bliss. He resides in His own transcendental world, Goloka-Vrindaban, where He revels in blissful, intimate, loving "pastimes" *(lilas)* with innumerable liberated souls for all eternity (all this while simultaneously "He eternally sees, maintains and manifests the infinite universes, both spiritual and mundane").[29] In this conception, God's lordly majesty *(aisvarya)* is overshadowed by his enchanting sweetness *(madhurya)*, and He is worshiped not in awe but in love.

Devotees learn about Lord Krishna's form, qualities and pastimes primarily from an edition of the tenth canto of the *Srimad Bhagavatam*,[30] and from Prabhupada's "summary study" of Rupa Goswami's *Bhakti-rasamrta-sindhu*, published by ISKCON as *The Nectar of Devotion*.[31] Apart from such texts, Sri Krishna "appears" to his devotees in ISKCON through several other channels including His divine names (chanted daily), His *prasadam* (blessed food and flower offerings), the guru (a channel for Krishna's grace), and the "deity" (the visible image of Krishna installed and revered in the temple sanctuary).

The sacred image, called *arca-vigraha*,[32] is viewed by the devotees not as a mere symbol or representation of Krishna, but as Krishna Himself.[33] It is a form hewn from material elements (marble, brass, wood) into which the Lord has descended (invited through elaborate ritual) and in which He dwells and allows Himself to be worshiped by His devotees.[34] Periodically throughout the day, these temple images are offered ceremonial worship by trained priests, both male and female, and through much of the day are on view—available for devotional "seeing" (*darsana*)—for the devotees and the public.[35] God stands, quite literally, within the community of devotees, allowing Himself to be approached in an immediate and personal way.[36]

Krishna is, then, both highly personal and highly accessible to the devotees. They invoke Krishna's name and memory throughout the day not only in formal ritual and contemplative acts but informally—in discussion with fellow devotees—to acknowledge Krishna's protection, saving grace, and empowerment in practical ways in their daily lives.

The manner and vehicle through which the devotee relates to Krishna is simple, guileless devotion. Krishna Consciousness is attained through *bhakti yoga*, the path of devotion, wherein the devotee not only thinks of Krishna but serves Him actively, consecrating all actions to him: "All that you do, all that you eat, all that you offer and give away, as well as all austerities that you may perform, should be done as an offering unto Me."[37] Devotees view all actions done in Krishna's service as subtly and gradually evocative of love of God—that is, objective acts of devotion cumulatively evoke devotion itself. *Bhakti* is both the process and the goal.

ISKCON is salvationistic in that it sees the ultimate goal of spiritual practice as a returning "back Home, back to Godhead." As a temporary sojourner in a tragic and chaotic world, the devotee looks forward to rejoining Krishna in His eternal, blissful realm.[38] The devotee views his present life as a mere prologue, a preparation for an infinitely higher and deeper reality. Death is not feared but viewed as a launching station for transcendence: "Whoever, at the time of death, quits his body remembering Me alone, at once attains My nature. Of this there is no doubt."[39] The devotee is saved not only at the time of death, but all during his terrestrial existence. Living an enlightened life under Krishna's protection, he is released from subjective sufferings of the material world, if not from most of its objective afflictions.

MEDIATIONAL

The *Bhagavad Gita* says, "Just try to learn the truth by approaching a spiritual master. Inquire from him submissively and render service unto him. The self-realized soul can impart knowledge unto you because he has seen the truth."[40] Consequently, the devotee views his relationship with Krishna to be mediated by the spiritual master who acts, in effect, as a go-between. The guru is exemplar, guide, and conduit: a living exemplar of renunciation and devotion, a teacher of the path of devotion, and an efficacious link between the disciple and God. Krishna prefers the mediated relationship: "One who claims to be My devotee is not so. Only a person who claims to be the devotee of my devotee is actually My devotee."[41] Like a corrective lens, the guru is the "transparent via media" through which the disciple, whose spiritual vision is presently defective, can see Krishna. The guru is Krishna's emissary to the conditioned soul and has the power to act as an advocate for the disciple in his approach to God; he is also a conduit for Krishna's mercy to the disciple: "By the mercy of the spiritual master, one receives the benediction of Krishna. Without the grace of the spiritual master, one cannot make any advancement."[42]

Tradition dictates that the disciple must worship his or her guru as "the external manifestation of Krishna." The guru, for his part, is expected to renounce and "transmit" that worship on to the Lord Himself. If, however, due to pride, eogism, or attachment, he appropriates for himself that worship, he immediately becomes "opaque" and no longer can serve as an efficacious link. Scripture warns against interlopers and imposters. At the very least, a guru must have conquered all earthly desires: "[Only] a sober person who can tolerate the urge to speak, the mind's demands, the actions of anger and the urges of the tongue, belly and genitals, is qualified to make disciples."[43]

After a novitiate of six months to a year, the ISKCON devotee is formally initiated by a spiritual master of his choice or of the temple he is joining. Older members of ISKCON were initiated by Srila Prabhupada, whereas those who have joined since his death in 1977 are initiated by one of a growing number of senior disciples of Prabhupada who have themselves become gurus. The guru is very much in the center of a disciple's consciousness, because the guru fulfills the roles of educator, mentor, taskmaster, guidance counselor, and authority of ultimate recourse in practical matters for the devotee. Daily, personal contact between guru and disciple is rare in ISKCON, however, owing to the fact that not only are ISKCON gurus each responsible for hundreds of disciples, but most also have substantial administrative responsibilities in addition to maintaining and expanding their own particular missionary work. Krishna theology, however, downplays the need for extensive personal contact by stating that the guru's presence in the form of his teachings (and the disciple's living by them) is of greater importance than his mere corporeal presence.

TRANSFORMATIONAL (AND EXPERIENTIAL)

The Indologist Heinrich Zimmer points out that although Indian philosophy concerns itself with metaphysics and with human psychology and ethics, its primary concern

> has always been not information, but transformation: a radical changing of man's nature and, therewith, a renovation of his understanding both of the outer world and of his own existence; a transformation as complete as possible, such as will amount when successful to a total conversion or rebirth.[44]

Hence, the process of Krishna Consciousness is conceived as a constant endeavor for elevation from material to spiritual consciousness. Acting "with body, mind, intelligence, and even with the senses only for the purpose of purification,"[45] devotees aspire for a higher awareness that is Krishna-centered rather than self centered. Mere rational assent to the words of scripture is not sufficient because spiritual practice must eventually effect a tangible "seeing through the eyes of scripture" (*sastra-caksus*)—a deep, interior realization of its truths concerning the nature of self and reality. *Bhakti* is not mere pious sentiment, but potently productive of intuitive, mystic knowledge that "reveals everything, as the sun lights up everything in the daytime."[46]

Such inner transformation is meant to produce tangible attitudinal and behavioral changes in the devotee. While instructing Rupa Goswami on the process of *bhakti yoga*, Sri Caitanya enumerated twenty-six "transcendental qualities" that manifest in the persons of pure devotees. Devotees, he explains, are always:

> merciful, humble, truthful, equal to all, faultless, magnanimous, mild and clean. They are without material possessions, and they perform welfare work for everyone. They are peaceful, surrendered to Krsna and desireless. They are indifferent to material acquisitions and are fixed in devotional service. They completely control the six bad qualities—lust, anger, greed and so forth. They eat only as much as required, and they are not inebriated. They are respectful, grave, compassionate and without false prestige. They are friendly, poetic, expert and silent.[47]

Though this might be interpreted as a kind of Vaisnava code of ethics, devotees perceive these items as the natural psychological and behavioral fruits of Krishna-*prema*, love of Krishna, and those who manifest these qualities are held in high regard.

UTILITARIAN

A major tenet of Vaisnava theology dealing with the essential meaning of renunciation has very practical consequences for life in ISKCON.
Rupa Goswami affirms the principle succinctly in stating that "persons
eager to achieve liberation renounce things related to the Supreme
Personality of Godhead, thinking them to be material, their renunciation
is called incomplete *[phalgu]*."[48] Renunciation is defined in Krishna Consciousness not as the total rejection of material things, but as using them
in the service of their true owner, Krishna. As one cannot truly renounce
what one does not already possess (we enter the world naked and
possessionless and leave the same way), true renunciation entails renouncing the propensity to appropriate and to exploit material things
(even one's own body, senses and mind) for one's own gratification and
to restore them to their proper use. That restoration is a process of
sacralization, because matter used in Krishna's service becomes re-
spiritualized. As Prabhupada explains it, "The Absolute Truth covered
by *maya* is called matter. Matter dove-tailed for the cause of the Absolute
Truth regains its spiritual quality. Krishna Consciousness is the process
of converting the illusory consciousness into Brahman, or the Supreme."[49] The principle, then, is neither to enjoy nor to renounce the
world but to use it in Krishna's service. By this principle, a devotee can
make use of wealth and possessions and still be in a state of renunciation.

One can see this spiritual and material utilitarianism in practice in
ISKCON in its unabashed willingness to employ the fruits of material
technology in spreading its message (vehicles, computers, printing
presses, communications technology). It involves not only the use of
material objects as such, but also of the body, the senses, and the creative
instinct. One can witness this sacralizing of sense activity in the proliferating (and increasingly sophisticated) use among devotees of artistic
media such as painting, sculpture, music, dance, and drama to express
and communicate the many images, moods, and themes of Krishna
Consciousness and Vaisnava culture. This aesthetic dimension is also
evident in the construction of lavishly designed temples (such as those
in Bombay, Vrindaban, and New Vrindaban), in the use of exquisitely
designed dress and ornamentation in the decoration of the temple deities, and in the use of various sensory stimuli such as sound (bells,
conch shells, *kirtana* music), taste (sumptuous food offerings), and
aroma (incense, camphor) in the ceremonial worship of the deities.
Krishna Consciousness calls not for an extinguishing of senses and
sense activity, but rather their purification and elevation through devotional activity. Devotees are *aesthetic ascetics*.

EVANGELISTIC

Prabhupada conceived ISKCON essentially as a missionary organization, an institutional vehicle for disseminating Krishna Consciousness throughout the world. Missionary ideology lies at the heart of Caitanya theology. Because all living beings are constitutionally related to Krishna as loving servants, the devotees (those who have realized this connectedness) have a sacred duty to revive people's dormant Krishna Consciousness. As Prabhupada writes,

> A Krishna Conscious person should free himself from the clutches of *maya*, and he should also be compassionate to all others suffering in those clutches. . . . One who is interested in his own salvation is not as advanced in Krsna Consciousness as one who feels compassion for others and who therefore propagates the Krsna Consciousness Movement. . . . That is the sum and substance of the Krishna Consciousness Movement.[50]

Missionary work, or "preaching" as it is termed in ISKCON, is viewed as the supreme form of humanitarianism. Ministering to the physical needs of a person can provide temporary physical relief at best, but giving him spiritual knowledge can ultimately liberate him from the root cause of his sufferings—that is, forgetfulness of Krishna as Supreme Lord and consequent bondage in the material world.

Traveling widely on foot and chanting the names of Krishna, the sixteenth century saint Caitanya attracted thousands to his movement, always exhorting new converts to instruct whomever they met in the knowledge of Krishna and thus to liberate all persons.[51] He predicted, "In every town and village, the chanting of My name will be heard."[52]

The late nineteenth century witnessed a revival of Caitanyite missionary fervor, primarily in the person of Bhaktivinoda Thakur who, in his monthly journal *Sajjana-tosani*, in 1885, wrote longingly of a future in which fair-skinned foreigners would chant in ecstasy, with drums and cymbals, through the streets of Western cities and towns.[53]

The two forms of preaching through which ISKCON is best known to the public (and which in the movement's view are most central) are public chanting (*nama-sankirtana*) and the wide dissemination of Prabhupada's books and *Back to Godhead* magazine. Historically, ISKCON was best known by its street singing and dancing in the late 1960s and early 1970s, and by its book selling through most of the 1970s and into the 1980s. In addition to these two forms of preaching, one finds within ISKCON a fairly wide range of missionary outreach programs, including its well-known Sunday feasts (held in all its centers), large public festivals such as the *Jagannatha Ratha yatra* ("Festival of the

Chariots"), its impressive pilgrimage-cum-tourist complex in West Virginia (New Vrindaban), public distribution of sanctified food *(prasadam)*, and various video and audio productions that are disseminated to all ISKCON centers and from there to the public. In large measure, these programs are viewed by devotees not as direct recruitment strategies per se, but as means of effecting a subtle, very gradual purification of the material world by exposing it to the transcendental, transforming power of Krishna Consciousness.

Life Inside a Krishna Temple

In this section, we consider a typical day in the life of a Hare Krishna devotee. Our greatest attention is on spiritual practices proper, occurring mostly during the early hours of the morning.

Alarm clocks through the ISKCON world ring at about 4:00 A.M. After the usual cleansing of the body, the male devotee combs and ties the tuft of hair at the back of his head *(sikha)* and puts on a clean, fresh *dhoti* (lower robe) and *kurta* (long, loose shirt) while the woman devotee dresses in a sari. Both then apply soft clay from Vrindaban's sacred Yamuna River in the form of holy markings *(tilaka)* on twelve locations on the body (forehead, belly, chest, throat, right and left abdomen, right and left upper arms, and shoulders), reciting praises to Lord Viu in different names with each application (for example, *om kesavaya namah, om narayanaya namah, om madhavaya namah*). As Vaisnavas, devotees wear a Vishnu *tilaka* on their foreheads, which takes the form of a vertically elongated "U" connected to a smaller, solid dab beneath it. With the application of *tilaka*, the body has been consecrated as a temple of the Lord.

The devotee then enters the temple (or "temple room" in the more common case of converted buildings) to attend the first and most important ceremony of the day called the *mangala arati* where attendance is mandatory. The devotee bows prostrate before the image or picture of the guru and waits a few moments for the doors partitioning off the altar to open and reveal the beautiful image of the deities, still wearing their night clothes. Unless it is a small temple and community, there will be three sets of deities on the altar: Gaura-Nitai (with pictorial image of the spiritual master and his immediate predecessors); Radha and Krishna; and finally Jagannatha, Balarama, and Subhadra.[54] This early morning ceremony consists of two simultaneous events: a highly stylized ceremony performed on the altar by a priest *(pujari)* who ritually offers the deities a succession of items including incense, water, and flowers; and lively congregational singing and dancing by the devotees in attendance.

The various Sanskrit hymns and mantras are sung in antiphonal style, with a lead singer intoning each line and a chorus responding in turn.

The first and longest of the hymns, titled "Sri Sri Guv-astaka" is a group of eight stanzas glorifying the spiritual master, composed by the seventeenth-century Gaudiya Vaisnava saint Visvanstha Cakravarti Thakura. The first verse says:

> The spiritual master is receiving benediction from the ocean of mercy. Just as a cloud pours water on a forest fire to extinguish it, so the spiritual master delivers the materially afflicted world by extinguishing the blazing fire of material existence. I offer my respectful obeisances unto the lotus feet of such a spiritual master, who is an ocean of auspicious qualities.

Next, shorter prayers glorifying the specific attributes of Srila Prabhupada and of his local successor are chanted. These are followed by the *Panca-tattva mahamantra*, a verse invoking the names of Lord Caitanya and his divine associates: Sri Nityananda, Sri Advaita, Sri Gadadhara, and Srivasa Prabhu.

Finally, the famous Hare Krishna *mahamantra* is chanted: Hare Krishna, Hare Krishna, Krishna Krishna, Hare Hare / Hare Rama, Hare Rama, Rama Rama, Hare Hare. There is no set formula by which the chanting increases in tempo and volume—this depends on the mood projected by the *kirtana* leader, the size and enthusiasm of the congregation and the skills of the instrumentalists present. Generally, however, the *kirtana* begins in slow, measured cadences, a kind of staid, rhythmic, back and forth two-step. As the tempo escalates and the music and chanting grow louder, some devotees become buoyant, begin to sway, bounce, jump, leap, twirl, and perform other varieties of dance movements in response to the vibrance of the *kirtana* and to their own internal feelings. While some dance alone, others join with fellow blissful dancers in spontaneously choreographed jigs, shuffles, and snake dances. Some of the dancing is relatively routine and patterned, some highly idiosyncratic.

Theologically, the dancing and chanting is understood to be the joyful outer movement of the soul awakened to its original transcendental nature, celebrating its release from the shackles of matter, arms reaching heavenward like a child reaching for protective, loving parental embrace. The sacred dance is an act not of egoistic self-centeredness but of self-transcendence, meant not for the amusement of self and others but for the glory of God, in response to His infinite goodness and mercy.[55]

Such dancing goes on until the sound of the conch is heard, signaling the end of the *arati* ceremony on the altar. Then, while all devotees prostrate themselves, one devotee (usually the lead singer) recites standard, concluding prayers invoking the names of various gurus, saints, divinities, holy places (such as Vrindaban and Mayapur), and the sacred rivers Ganges and Yamuna and then offers "all glories to the assembled devotees." With each invocation, the devotees respond with a hearty "*jaya!*" or "all glories!" The more subdued singing of prayers to the man-lion incarnation of Vishnu, Lord Nrsimhadeva—the ferocious destroyer of demons and benign protector of devotees—concludes the entire ceremony.[56]

Directly following *mangala-arati* is a brief ceremony honoring—through obeisance, song, watering, and circumambulation—the sacred Tulasi (Basil) plant ("she" embodies a pure devotee of Krishna, to whose deity form she offers her leaves). This is followed by recitation, in unison, of the "ten offenses against the chanting of the Holy Name" (from the *Padma-Purana*), a rule assuring the proper executing (and thus the spiritual potency) of chanting. Two hours of this chanting follow.

The next major phase of early morning spiritual observances, then, is the practice of *nama-japa:* individual, rapid, verbal recitation of the Hare Krishna *mantra* on prayer beads. Devotees use the traditional string of 108 Tulasi beads (normally carried in a cloth sack around the neck), chanting one *mantra* per bead and 108 *mantras* per complete revolution (one "round"). At the time of initiation, devotees vow to chant 16 rounds daily. They are encouraged to complete all or most of their rounds during the formal *japa* period (generally between 5:00 and 7:00 A.M.); if unable to do so, they will complete their quota later on during the day.

During these two hours of the morning, ISKCON temples are abuzz with the drone of chanting, with even more individual stylistic variety than in communal singing and dancing. Some devotees chant while sitting, some standing, some pacing, some circumambulating within or outside the temple. Some chant loudly, others whisper; some recite the *mantra* monotonally, others in a sing-songy manner; some enunciate the words of the *mantra* distinctly, others hopelessly muddle them; some chant feelingly, others mechanically. It is quite a unique experience for an outsider to wander into an ISKCON temple early in the morning and hear this holy cacophonous symphony of humming, buzzing, gobbling, and warbling.

Behind all this is the belief that the mantra is nondifferent from Krishna, that it is the literal "sound incarnation" of the Lord, and thus to invoke Krishna's holy names is to directly invoke Krishna Himself. As Krishna is the supreme object of the *Vedas*,[57] His holy name contains all their knowledge,[58] and thus to chant is to become enlightened with all spiritual wisdom. The chanting of the holy name is the superlative form of religion in the current age, the *yuga-dharma*.[59] Chanting it eradicates the reactions to past sins, cleanses the heart and mind of all material desires, and ultimately brings liberation and ecstatic love for Krishna.[60]

At 7:00 A.M., all devotees reassemble in the temple for "greeting of the deities." For the previous two hours, several *pujaris*, working behind the closed doors or curtains of the altar, have been busily preparing the deities for their first public appearance of the day. Adjoining the altar is a room, or series of rooms, housing a large variety of colorful and lavish outfits for all the sets of deities (all made with great care by qualified devotee designers and seamstresses), along with other decorative paraphernalia such as crowns, turbans, feathers, necklaces, earrings and brooches (some of which might be obtained in India). Each deity or group of deities is attended by a *pujari* or priest who bathes and anoints them with various substances, dresses them in fresh daily outfits, and applies various adornments.

Promptly at 7:00 A.M., the altar doors open to reveal the effulgent and merciful Lord, all devotees bow reverently, and tape-recorded chanting of hymns from the *Brahma-samhita* scripture describing the beautiful, transcendental form of Krishna fills the temple. After all present toss flower petals and bow before each set of deities, each devotee takes three drops of *caranamrta* ("nectar from the feet")—a mixture of the substances used in bathing the deities combined with sweetened yogurt—from a special bowl.

Immediately following the greeting ceremony, devotees gather before Prabhupada's seat of honor *(Vyasasana)* and observe "worship of the guru" *(guru-puj).* While one devotee performs *arati* to a pictorial or sculpted image of Prabhupada, the others offer flowers and perform *kirtana*—in this case, responsive singing of a Bengali song by Narottama dasa Thakura, an important sixteenth-seventeenth–century Gaudiya Vaisnava poet-saint, called "Sri Guru-vandana" (Prayer to the Guru"), from a work of the name *Prema-bhakti-candrika.* The complete English translation follows:

> The lotus feet of the spiritual master are the abode of pure devotional service. I bow down to those lotus feet with great care and attention. My dear brother (my dear mind)! It is through the grace of the spiritual master that we cross over this material existence and obtain Krsna.
> Make the teachings from the lotus mouth of the spiritual master one with your heart, and do not desire anything else. Attachment to the lotus feet of the spiritual master is the best means of spiritual advancement. By his mercy all desires for spiritual perfection are fulfilled.
> He who has given me the gift of transcendental vision is my lord, birth after birth. By his mercy divine knowledge is revealed within

the heart, bestowing *prema-bhakti* and destroying ignorance. The Vedic scriptures sing of his character.

O spiritual master, ocean of mercy, and friend of the fallen souls, you are the teacher of everyone and the life of all people. O master! Be merciful unto me, and give me the shade of your lotus feet. May your glories now be proclaimed throughout the three worlds.[61]

Next on the morning schedule, at about 7:30, is a formal reading and discussion from the *Srimad Bhagavatam* conducted by one of the senior members of the temple community. Class is introduced with responsive singing of a short poem by Bhaktivinoda Thakur, "Jaya Radha-Madhava" (from his anthology *Gitvali*), which describes Krishna's *lila* in Vrindaban.[62] After responsive recitation in Sanskrit of the day's verse (led first by the instructor, then by volunteers) and responsive recitation of the word-for-word, Sanskrit-to-English, translation, the instructor reads the full English translation of the verse followed by Prabhupada's commentary. The instructor then presents his own extended comments on the subjects raised in the verse and commentary—providing illustrations from other texts, from the life of Prabhupada, and from personal experience and insight—relating, where appropriate, abstract theological and philosophical concepts to the practical day-to-day lives of the devotees. After a question-answer and discussion period, class comes to an end with the offering of obeisance.

At about 8:30 A.M., devotees partake of a communal breakfast (consisting, generally, of cereal, fruit, milk or yogurt, and chick-peas) that has earlier been offered to the deities and thus sanctified as "Krishna's mercy" (*prasadam*). During the remainder of the day, each devotee attends to his or her particular "service" (devotional work), which is assigned or assumed according both to individual ability and propensity as well as the needs of the community.

Devotees perform a wide range of functions, including temple administration (each center has a president and often a vice-president), cash-disbursement and bookkeeping, cooking, temple cleaning and maintenance, deity worship, childcare (individual and pooled), fundraising, literature distribution, and outside speaking engagements in high schools, colleges, churches, and the homes of both Indian and non-Indian congregational members. In addition to these standard activities found in all ISKCON centers, there exist a number of special programs and projects throughout ISKCON that consume devotees' energies, such as many children's schools (*gurukulas*), farms, publishing houses, international pilgrimage centers (Mayapur, Vrindaban and New Vrindaban), public relations activities, as well as various sorts of academic and artistic endeavors.

Theologically, all such activity performed for the satisfaction of Krishna is *bhakti yoga* and thus contributes to spiritual perfection. Whereas ordinary work, performed for self-gain, serves only to bind one to the material world, work for Krishna is liberating.[63] The very same work that, when performed for material gain causes bondage, brings liberation when performed, instead, for Krishna.

> O good soul, does not a thing, applied therapeutically, cure a disease which was caused by that very same thing? Thus when all a man's activities are dedicated to the service of the Lord, those very activities which caused his perpetual bondage become the [cause of liberation].[64]

The greater the devotion with which work-for-Krishna is performed, the more powerful its potential to purify and elevate the worker.

This theological view of the nature of devotional work serves, within ISKCON, to mitigate to some degree the tendency to define individual status purely in terms of hierarchical position, power, job status, and productivity (though these are also often interpreted as indications of Krishna's blessings on the sincere worker). It is ultimately not the objective work itself but the devotion with which it is performed that is pleasing to Krishna. By this spiritual logic, even the most menial work takes on a sacred quality, and Vaisnava texts are filled with examples of persons of low occupational status whose devotion *(bhakti)* makes them objects of veneration even by socially elevated persons like kings.

To return to and complete our charting of the devotees' day: after a full day's work (including free time and a mid-day break for lunch), devotees attend an evening *arati/kirtana* (optional) followed by a *Bhagavad-gita* class (also optional), and, after a light evening snack, turn in by 9:00 P.M.

Conclusion

The Hare Krishna movement embodies an absorbing religious life, rich in philosophical and theological concepts, in ritual, ethics and experience. Because of its religious vitality and the fact that it draws heavily upon a rich and long-standing religious tradition that has provided meaning and experience to many generations of religionists in India, ISKCON is bound to continue to be attractive to religious seekers drawn to its distinctive religious content and style.[65]

Although this essay has focused more on religious doctrine, ritual, and behavior than on subjective religious experience per se, we should remember that religious experience is itself largely constituted of precept and ritual deeply interiorized and "felt" and then concretized into distinct, affectively powerful ways of perceiving and conceiving reality (just as, conversely, doctrine and ritual are, in an important sense, the rational and symbolic externalization and codification of core religious experience). The attempt, therefore, has been to convey a sense of the ideological and ritual context for experience, rather than to report, empirically or impressionistically, on incidents of "higher" mystical experience. (Such phenomena certainly do exist within ISKCON, and could be treated in a future study.)

In this context, I would like to reiterate and elaborate slightly on my earlier, friendly suggestion to social scientists that they ought to take more seriously the experiential ambiance of the religious groups they wish to study. Let me preface my comments by noting that in spite of (or perhaps because of) my being a member of a religious collective, I am acutely aware that people's motives for joining, maintaining commitment within, and defecting from religious groups are almost always "mixed." Movements into, within, and out of religious institutions are hardly ever impelled by *purely* religious (God- or truth-seeking) impulses. To assert otherwise would be naive. In fact, social scientists might be surprised to discover that some Indian religious texts offer quite sophisticated analyses (sometimes with elaborate typologies) of motives affecting religious behavior, both individual and associational. Indian texts are, if anything, reflective and analytical about human religious consciousness and behavior and often are quite assiduous in their warnings against the kinds of instrumentalist, self-serving attitudes and strategies that social scientists are so adept at identifying. It can be easily admitted, then, that by its very nature institutional religious life lends itself to analysis in terms of sociological (and psychological) categories.

Such analyses cannot, however, tell the full story of human religiosity—*even sociologically*—due to the inherent reluctance of social scientists to explore the experiential religious foundations and root impulses of collective religious behavior. In discussing "The Expression of Religious Experience in Fellowship," Joachim Wach argues that religious groups contain some unique features that make them distinct from other types of human social collectives and that consequently they should be studied with appropriate sensitivities.[66] He suggests that the outward characteristics of religious groups are largely determined by the particular religious experience the group embodies because "the collective and individual relation of its members to the numen (the 'holy') is primary and the relation of the members of the group to each other is secondary" and thus:

the nature, intensity, duration, and organization of a religious group depends upon the way in which its members experience God, conceive of, and communicate with Him [in addition to] the way they experience fellowship, conceive of it, and practice it. . . . The concept of the nature and function of the members of the community will vary according to the nature of the basic religious experience. . . . It is important to realize that there is this [numinous] dimension to the notion of the religious community, because the secularized minds of many modern Westerners cannot understand it except in purely sociological terms.[67]

Wach offers specific advice to those who wish to understand the dynamics of religious collectives.

The first important concern for the student of religious groups will be to do justice to the self-interpretation of a religious communion. Full meaning is not gained where only the outward and measurable "behavior" is taken into account without regard for the meaning which concepts, attitudes, and acts are meant to convey.[68]

All this does not mean that social scientists who study religion must turn pious, much less "go native." It does suggest, however, that they would benefit greatly from developing what Rudolf Otto describes as "penetrative imaginative sympathy with what passes in the other person's mind."[69]

In closing, I would like to raise a question about the role of a movement such as ISKCON in the broader sociocultural context. Specifically, apart from whatever inherent value it has as a repository and transmitter of religious truth (and apart from its providing knowledge of and access to an important religious tradition), what is its actual or potential contribution to human culture? What possible contribution to human society can be made by people who have undertaken such an apparently radical rejection of its values and separation from its conventional life? The devotees' religious intensity itself has made them outcasts. "Essential religious ideas are so radical," writes Walter H. Clark, "that only a person who in some sense is a social deviate can follow them. . . . That which deeply criticizes life, as true religion does, must to some degree stand apart from it."[70]

However, "the man rejected by society may be in closest touch with its best interest."[71] Clark asserts that "the most essential and effective forms of religious behavior are demonstrated by only a tiny minority, a religious elite." It is this elite, these religious virtuosi, however, "who supply creative energy out of all proportion to their numbers. This influence is the 'leaven in the loaf' of which Jesus spoke."[72] Certainly, one important aspect of that leavening process lies in the practical example of spiritual discipline and attainment that religious virtuosi can provide. This theme is addressed by James Duerlinger:

> One of the major reasons so many moderns have turned toward secular rather than spiritual values is that there is nowadays so little spiritual accomplishment evidenced within the religions themselves. If man is to believe in the possibilities of his spiritual fulfillment by the use of spiritual disciplines he must be inspired to belief by the accomplishments of their seasoned practitioners.[73]

Perhaps this provision of an example of spiritual practice and transformation will be one of ISKCON's contributions to its host society—at least once public prejudice and media obfuscation subside and its example can actually be witnessed.

Another possible contribution ISKCON can make to modern society is, ironically, through its very example of separateness from it. In his book *A Rumor of Angels* (subtitled "Modern Society and the Rediscovery of the Supernatural"), Peter Berger argues that knowledge can have "definite existential consequences," specifically, that "true knowledge leads to experiences of ecstasy—of *ek-stasis,* a standing outside of the taken-for-granted routines of everyday life."[74] He laments that "modern Western man appears to have practically lost the capacity to comprehend, let alone to replicate, the ecstatic condition that the practices of various religious cults provided for their members throughout most of previous human history." He describes this lost capacity as a consequence of secularization, and identifies the resultant "denial of metaphysics" with "the triumph of triviality" in the modern world.

> How long such a shrinkage in the scope of human experience can remain plausible is debatable. In any case, it constitutes a profound impoverishment. Both in practice and in theoretical thought, human life gains the greatest part of its richness from the capacity for ecstasy, by which I do not mean the alleged experiences of the mystic, but any experience of stepping outside the taken-for-granted reality of everyday life, any openness to the mystery that surrounds us on all sides.[75]

By its very nature, life in the Hare Krishna movement entails this act of "stepping outside" of what devotees view as the colorless and futile (and self-destructive) routines of everyday life in the material world. If it does nothing else but continue to provide a viable means of *ek-stasis* or "stepping outside," and ultimately of transcendence of the world for those seeking it, it will have made no small contribution.

Notes

1. Thomas F. O'Dea, "Five Dilemmas in the Institutionalization of Religion," *Journal for the Scientific Study of Religion* 1, no. 1 (1961): 32–39.

2. Although to some extent I am framing the present discussion within social-scientific categories and language, this essay is by no means meant exclusively for social scientists. They may in fact be made uncomfortable by my implicit recognition of spirituality as an a priori category and of the religious state of mind as sui generis. If it seems that I am at times deliberately reaching for social scientific analytic categories and invoking the words of some of the discipline's stalwarts, it is only because as a member of ISKCON in regular dialogue with social scientists, I am sensitive to the need to make the experiential level of religion more accessible to those who study religion sociologically.

3. Joseph Havens, "The Participant's vs. the Observer's Frame of Reference in Psychological Study of Religion," in *Current Perspectives in the Psychology of Religion*, ed. H. Newton Maloney (Grand Rapids, MI: William B. Erdmans, 1977), pp. 110–11.

4. For an account of the events leading to Prabhupada's journey to America, see Satsvarupa dasa Goswami, *A Lifetime in Preparation: Srila-Prabhupada-lilamrta*, vol. 1 (Los Angeles: The Bhaktivedanta Book Trust, 1980).

5. According to Edward C. Dimock, the Gaudiya Vaisnava movement "is currently the strongest single religious force in the eastern part of the Indian subcontinent." See his Foreword in *Bhagavad-gita AS IT IS*, by A. C. Bhaktivedanta Swami Prabhupada (New York: Collier, 1972), p. ix. (Hereafter, cited as *Gita*.)

6. Thomas J. Hopkins, "The Social Teachings of the Bhagavata Purana," in *Krishna: Myths, Rites, and Attitudes*, ed. Milton Singer (Chicago: University of Chicago Press, 1968), pp. 8–9.

7. Diana Eck, "Krishna Consciousness in Historical Perspective," *Back to Godhead* 14, no. 10 (October 1979): 26–29.

8. For more detailed discussion on ISKCON's historical and theological relationship both with ancient *bhakti* and medieval Caitanyism, see my interviews with Thomas J. Hopkins and Shrivatsa Goswami in S. J. Gelberg, *Hare Krishna, Hare Krishna: Five Distinguished Scholars on the Krishna Movement in the West* (New York: Grove Press, 1983).

9. For book-length studies of the Caitanya movement and its theology, see S. K. De, *Early History of the Vaisnava Faith and Movement in Bengal* (Calcutta: K. L. Mukhopadhyay, 1961); A. K. Magumdar, *Caitanya: His Life and Doctrine* (Bombay: Bharatiya Vidya Bhavan, 1969); O. B. L. Kapoor, *The Philosophy and Religion of Caitanya* (New Delhi: Munshiram Manoharlal, 1977); and Melville T. Kennedy, *The Caitanya Movement: A Study of the Vaishnavism of Bengal* (Calcutta: Association Press, 1925).

10. Pandit Satkari Chattopadyaya, *A Glimpse Into the Life of Thakur Bhaktivinode* (Calcutta: Bhaktivinode Memorial Committee, 1916), p. 59.

11. Richard A. Hunt and Morton B. King, "The Intrinsic-Extrinsic Concept: A Review and Evaluation," in Malomey, *Current Perspectives in the Psychology of Religion*, p. 140.

12. William James, *The Varieties of Religious Experience* (New York: Modern Library, 1902), p. 8.

13. A. C. Bhaktivedanta Swami Prabhupada, *Srimad Bhagavatam*, 31 vols. (Los

Angeles: The Bhaktivedanta Book Trust, 1972–85), 1.2.10, p. 102. Hereafter this text will appear as *Bhagavatam* with canto, chapter, verse, and page number.

14. *Bagavatam*, 2.9.36, p. 196.

15. Ibid., 1.2.14, p. 109.

16. Ibid., 1.2.6, p. 95.

17. *Gita*, 9:34, p. 489.

18. Victor E. Frankl, *Man's Search for Meaning* (New York: Washington Square Press, 1963).

19. *Bhagavatam*, 2.1, p. 69.

20. A. C. Bhaktivedanta Swami Prabhupada, *Sri Isopanisad* (Los Angeles: The Bhaktivedanta Book Trust, 1974), p. 45.

21. Max Weber, *The Sociology of Religion* (Boston: Beacon Press, 1964), p. 166.

22. Ibid., p. 169.

23. Robert S. Ellwood, *Mysticism and Religion* (Englewood Cliffs, NJ: Prentice-Hall, 1980), p. 149.

24. Rt. Rev. Edward McCorkell, "A Monastic Encounter," *Back to Godhead*, 14, no. 12 (1979): 20–21.

25. *Gita*, 3.34, p. 200.

26. Ibid., 5.22, p. 296.

27. Ibid., 2.59, p. 145.

28. Emile Durkheim, *The Elementary Forms of the Religious Life* (New York: Free Press, 1965), p. 355.

29. These descriptions are adapted from the *Brahma-samhita* (Siddhanta Saraswati, 1932).

30. A. C. Bhaktivedanta Swami Prabhupada, *Krsna: The Supreme Personality of Godhead*, 2 vols. (Los Angeles: The Bhaktivedanta Book Trust, 1970).

31. (Los Angeles: The Bhaktivedanta Book Trust, 1982).

32. *Vigraha* means "form." As Diana Eck in *Darsan: Seeing the Divine Image in India* (Chambersburg, PA: Anima, 1981) explains, "As a noun, *vigraha* comes from a verbal root (*vi* + *grh*) which mean 'to grasp, to catch hold of.' The *vigraha* is that form which enables the mind to grasp the nature of God."

33. "The image . . . does not stand *between* the worshipper and the Lord, somehow receiving the honor properly due to the Supreme Lord. Rather, because the image is a form of the Supreme Lord, it is precisely the image that facilitates and enhances the close relationship of the worshipper and God and makes possible the deepest outpouring of emotions in worship." Ibid., p. 35.

34. Diana Eck quotes the words of the Sri Vaisnava theologian Pillai Lokacarya who writes of the Lord's mercy in appearing within the deity: "This is the greatest grace of the Lord, that being free He becomes bound, being independent He becomes dependent for all His service on His devotee. . . . In other forms the man belonged to God but behold the supreme sacrifice of Isvara; here the Almighty becomes the property of the devotee. . . . He carries Him about, fans Him, feeds Him, plays with Him—yea, the Infinite has become finite, that the child soul may grasp, understand and love Him." Ibid., p. 35.

35. "Since, in the Hindu understanding, the deity is present in the image, the visual apprehension of the image is charged with religious meaning. Beholding the image is an act of worship, and through the eyes one gains the blessings of the divine." Ibid., p. 3.

36. For a detailed theological analysis of deity worship, see William A. Deadwyler, "The Devotee and the Deity: Living a Personalistic Theology," in *God of*

Flesh/Gods of Stone: The Embodiment of Divinity in India, ed. Joanne Waghorne and Norman Cutler (Chambersburg, PA: Anima Press, 1984).

37. *Gita,* 9.27, p. 480.

38. The devotee sees his task not so much as the transformation of the world but rather the transcending of it (though the *Bhagavatam* does present a vision of a primordial and ideal God-centered society, from which one can deduce a social, economic, and political philosophy).

39. *Gita,* 8.5, p. 415.

40. Ibid., 4.34, p. 259.

41. From *Adi Purana* quoted in Prabhupada, *Nectar of Devotion,* p. 102.

42. *Sri Sri Burr-astaka* by Visvanatha Cakravarti in Prabhupada, *Songs of the Vaisnava Acaryas* (Los Angeles: The Bhaktivedanta Book Trust, 1979), pp. 18–19.

43. A. C. Bhaktivedanta Swami Prabhupada, *The Nectar of Instruction* (Los Angeles: The Bhaktivedanta Book Trust, 1975), p. 1.

44. Heinrich Zimmer, *The Philosophies of India* (Princeton: Princeton University Press, 1951), p. 4.

45. *Gita,* 5.11, p. 283.

46. Ibid., 5.16, p. 289.

47. Krsnadasa Kaviraja Gosvami, *Sri Caitanya-caritamrta,* translation and commentary by A. C. Bhaktivedanta Swami Prabhupada, 14 vols. (Los Angeles: The Bhaktivedanta Book Trust, 1974–75), Madhya-lila, 8, p. 371. Hereafter this text will be cited as *Caritamrta* section, verse, and page number.

48. Deadwyler, "Devotee and Deity."

49. *Gita,* p. 248.

50. *Bhagavatam,* 6.1, p. 126.

51. *Caritamrta,* Madhya, 3, p. 64.

52. Ibid., Madhya, 9, p. 438.

53. Brahmananda Swami, "How the Teachings of Lord Caitanya Came to the Western World," (part 2), *Back to Godhead* 68 (December 1974): 6–11.

54. "The first are the forms of Caitanya (who is also called Gauranga and Gaurahari) and his principle associate Nityananda [an incarnation of Balarama, Krishna's first emanation who appeared with Krishna in Vrindaban as His elder brother]. Radha and Krsna are the major deities worshipped by Gaudiya Vaisnavas, but we also worship the Jagannatha deities because Caitanya, who resided at Puri during the final eighteen years of his life, regularly worshipped at the Jagannatha temple and participated prominently in the ratha-yatra. . . . The form of worship has been standardized in ISKCON temples according to the procedures established for the Gaudiya Matha by Bhaktisiddhanta Sarasvati and codified in a handbook called *Arcana-paddhati,* which in turn is based upon the *Hari-bhakti-vilasa* of Sanatana Goswami [or, according to some, Gopala Bhatta Goswami]." See Deadwyler, "Devotee and Deity," p. 72.

55. Those who might view the dancing of ISKCON devotees as bizarre ought to remember that ecstatic dancing has long had a place in the religious traditions of the West such as, for instance, in the Hasidic tradition within Judaism and as reflected in this passage from Martin Luther: "Christians are a blissful people, who can rejoice at heart and sing praises, stamp and dance and leap for joy. That is well pleasing to God and doth our heart good, when we trust in God and find in Him our pride and our joyfulness. Such a gift should only kindle a fire and light in our heart, so that we should never cease dancing and leaping for joy." See Rudolf Otto, *The Idea of the Holy,* 2nd ed. (London: Oxford University Press, 1950), p. 103.

56. For an unintentionally humorous description of *arati* and *kirtana* reinterpreted as a malefic, cleverly engineered brainwashing strategem, see Flo Conway and Jim Siegelman, *Snapping: America's Epidemic of Sudden Personality Change* (New York: Delta, 1978), pp. 137–38.

57. *Gita*, 15.15, p. 712 says, "By all the *Vedas* am I to be Known." Also see *Bhagavatam* 1.2.28 which says "The ultimate object of the *Vedas* is Vasudera (Krishna)."

58. "The essence of all Vedic Knowledge . . . is included in the eight syllables [Hare Krsna, Hare Krsna]. This is the reality of all *Vedanta*. The chanting of the holy name is the only means to cross the ocean of nescience." *Caritamrta, Adi*, 2, p. 62.

59. *Harer nama, harer nama, harer namaiva kevalam / kalau nasty eva nasty eva nasty eva gatir anyatha:* "In this age of Kali there is no alternative, there is no alternative, there is no alternative for spiritual progress than the holy name, the holy name, the holy name of the Lord." *Brhan-naradiya Purana*, Ibid., p. 61.

60. For an excellent survey of Gaudiya Vaisnava theology on the holy name, see Norwin Hein, "Caitanya's Ecstasies and the Theology of the Name," in *Hinduism: New Essays in the History of Religions*, ed. Bardwell Smith (Leiden: E. J. Brill, 1976). For major ISKCON publications on the chanting of the holy name, see Subhananda dasa, *Sri Namamrta: The Nectar of the Holy Name* (Los Angeles: The Bhaktivedanta Book Trust, 1982), and Satsvarupa dasa Goswami, *Japa Reform Notebook* (Port Royal, PA: Gita-Nagari Press, 1982). The former is a lengthy compilation of Prabhupada's writings on the subject; the latter is a group of essays and reflections by the author.

61. Bhaktivedanta, *Songs of the Vaisnava Acaryas*, pp. 80–81.

62. Ibid., pp. 48–49.

63. *Gita*, 3.9, p. 170. "Work done as a sacrifice for Visnu has to be performed, otherwise work binds one to this material world. Therefore . . . perform your prescribed duties for His satisfaction, and in that way you will always remain unattached and free from bondage."

64. *Bhagavatam*, 1.5.33–34, pp. 284–85.

65. For one devotee's reflection on matters pertaining to ISKCON's future, see Steven Gelberg (Subhananda dasa), "The Future of Krishna Consciousness in the West: An Insider's Perspective," in *The Future of New Religious Movements*, ed. David Bromley and Phillip Hammond (Macon, GA: Mercer University Press, 1987).

66. Joachim Wach, *The Comparative Study of Religion* (New York: Columbia University Press, 1958), pp. 121–43.

67. Ibid., pp. 123–26.

68. Ibid., p. 129.

69. Otto, *Idea of the Holy*, p. 60.

70. Walter Houston Clark, *The Psychology of Religion* (New York: The Macmillan Company, 1958), pp. 345 and 415.

71. Ibid., p. 415.

72. Ibid., p. 418.

73. "Religion, Its Disciples, and Their Relation to Ultimate Reality," in *Ultimate Reality and Spiritual Discipline*, ed. James Duerlinger (New York: Paragon House, 1984), p. 52.

74. Peter Berger, *A Rumor of Angels* (Garden City, NY: Anchor Books, 1970), p. 28.

75. Ibid., p. 75.

V. ISKCON Communities East and West

A Unique Conjuncture: The Incorporation of ISKCON in Vrindaban

Charles R. Brooks

This paper describes the complex drama of the present-day Indian city of Vrindaban, which includes members of the International Society for Krishna Consciousness as key actors. ISKCON has become an integral part of the social and cultural scene of this Indian city, and its Krishna-Balarama temple is an important part of the sacred pilgrimage complex that is revered as the birthplace of Krishna.[1]

To understand how the integration of foreign devotees into this Indian society has taken place and to better interpret the interactions occurring there between Western and Indian devotees of Krishna, Vrindaban itself must be understood. A full understanding focuses on Vrindaban as a celestial space apart from the phenomenal world; as a town developed by the Bengal Vaisnavas and culturally shaped by the force of Krishna-*bhakti;* and as an India-wide pilgrimage destination. These elements come together as a unique conjuncture through ISKCON's presence there, and they help to formulate an interpretive framework for understanding ISKCON's acceptance by its Indian parent-city.

Although the everyday interactions between individuals occur relatively freely in Vrindaban, there is still a concern for each person's place in an overall hierarchy, and ISKCON devotees have clearly achieved a high position. Although they have not achieved true Brahman status at this point in their Vrindaban history, they have effectively altered the criteria for evaluation, not only for themselves but for others in the community. Rather than being determined by social proximity to Brahmans, status evaluation is now more often based on the quality of a person's devotion to Krishna. ISKCON has thus achieved a permanent place in the sociocultural system of Vrindaban that will continue to have an impact on the community well into the future.

Just as Krishna cannot be separated from Vrindaban, neither can ISKCON. A. C. Bhaktivedanta Swami Prabhupada, ISKCON's founder, was himself a resident of Vrindaban for some ten years before embarking on his journey west, and in 1967 brought the first of his American disciples to this North Indian pilgrimage town as part of a sweeping vision to revitalize Indian religion and spread Krishna Consciousness throughout the world. From a modest beginning with two devotees at the medieval temple of Radha-Damodara, the International Society for Krishna Consciousness has altered the cultural texture of this town, prompting one Brahman to declare the 1970s as "the decade of ISKCON in Vrindaban." The opening of the Krishna-Balarama temple complex there in 1976 gave the Hare Krishna movement a major resource for completing the complex process of conversion and culture change of its members, simultaneously providing a base from which to stage interactions with Indian pilgrims and Vrindaban residents.

For sixteen months during 1981 and 1982, I conducted anthropological fieldwork in Vrindaban to discover whether significant interactions were occurring between foreign *bhaktas* and Indians. Because many traditional Indians consider it an impossibility for foreigners to become Hindu, much less Brahman as these devotees claim to be, a paradox is created by their very presence. Empirically then, I wished to know how this conflict was being resolved in the situations of everyday life in Vrindaban, and what consequences were resulting from that resolution.

I was cautioned by both scholars and traditional Indians not to expect any significant degree of social intercourse between foreign and native Krishna groups, a doubt reflecting long-accepted notions that severe constraints embedded in the Indian sociocultural system would stifle all but the most superficial encounters. My expectations were different, however, resting upon the fundamental sociological assumption that those who occupy the same habitat sooner or later become involved in a common web of life.[2]

Today, the Krishna-Balarama temple is an integral part of Vrindaban's sacred complex, and interactions between foreign devotees and Indians occur daily in all spheres of social life. Hare Krishna devotees are not only accepted as legitimate Vaisnavas (devotees of Vishnu and Krishna) but ISKCON is also seen as an incontrovertibly vital link in the Gaudiya *sampradaya* ("tradition") of Sri Caitanya Mahaprabhu, the sixteenth-century Bengali reformer.[3]

For the anthropologist, the Vrindaban situation presents both ethnographic and ethnological problems.[4] Ethnographically an accurate description and interpretation of the day-to-day interactions between foreigners and Indians is essential to understand Vrindaban. Ethnologically there are implications in the incorporation of American devotees into Vrindaban Krishna society for broader concerns of Indian anthropology, especially the dynamics of caste and hierarchy, and the importance of pilgrimage in the overall structure of Indian society.

In this paper I show that ISKCON's success in being accepted into Vrindaban life can be explained by an in-depth understanding of the meaning of Vrindaban as it exists in the subjective consciousness of the actors, both foreign and Indian. By considering Vrindaban's importance as the symbolic locus of the activities occurring there, the contemporary social reality can be revealed as not only understandable, but also as a logical consequence of cultural and historical antecedents. This is the ethnographic focus.

Moreover, through the particular example that Vrindaban provides, another case is revealed where caste is not the primary determinant or constraint for interaction in Indian society.[5] Hierarchy, nonetheless, is a preeminent element of Indian social structure, and in Vrindaban ISKCON has effectively manipulated the hierarchy to its advantage. Although foreign devotees have not clearly achieved Brahman status at this relatively early point in their Vrindaban career, they have accomplished something that is perhaps even more significant. Through their concern for proper behavioral presentations and by arguments framed in the logic of Vaisnava texts, ISKCON devotees have won high status but not in terms of caste. They have, in effect, transformed the structural dichotomy of hierarchy from a binary opposition of Brahman/non-Brahman to one based upon devotee/nondevotee.

Dimock has pointed out that the meaning of Vrindaban exists on three interrelated levels.[6] Not only does the word refer to the cultural and linguistic region of Braj (Sanskrit *Vraja*) located along the banks of the Yamuna River in the southwestern corner of present-day Uttar Pradesh, the legendary location of Krishna's childhood and adolescence; Vrindaban also is the celestial realm where Krishna eternally conducts His transcendental affairs, and at the same time it is the ideal state of mind, which is properly the goal of every Krishna *bhakta* (devotee). The essential attribute of all of these conceptualizations is, of course, Vrindaban as the place of the intense presence of Krishna and His entourage.

Vrindaban as Celestial Space in the Phenomenal World

For both foreign and Indian devotees of Krishna, the terrestrial Vrindaban is identical with the celestial one. For, it is argued, Krishna does not exist separately from His *Dhama* (the location of His activities along with His full retinue). For the devotee, there is no doubt that Krishna manifested Himself in the earthly Vrindaban some five thousand years ago, but the equation between it and the spiritual realm rests upon more than His phenomenal presence there.

De has explained that for the Gaudiya *sampradaya*, Jiva Goswami established the identity between these two Vrindabans, drawing from Puranic sources,[7] in the following manner:

> . . . the term "terrestrial" must not be taken to imply that the earthly residence is phenomenal; it is as much nonphenomenal as the celestial abode, only it makes its appearance in the phenomenal world. . . . the only difference is that in the earthly Vrndvana Krsna is both in his Manifest *(Prakata)* and Non-manifest *(Aprakata) Lilas.* But in the unearthly Goloka he stays in his Non-manifest *Lila.* . . . In other words, there is a mystical interlapping of the infinite and the finite, of the phenomenal and the transcendental.[8]

One Vaisnava *sadhu* (sage) living on the riverbank at Cir Ghat explained to me that "Krishna never leaves here. He is always present, and if you are here also, then you are in His *lila*." Pujya Bb, another *sadhu* and key actor in the Vrindaban drama, put it this way: "If you are in Vrindaban, Krishna has called you." The fact that the Krishna devotee sees Vrindaban not merely as a sacred place, but as actually part of the spiritual realm, provides a powerful explanatory resource through which to interpret and justify almost any activity that occurs there, no matter how surprising or irrational. It is an empirical fact of my research that all but a small percentage of the total population of Vrindaban town see the physical surroundings, plants, animals, and people as part of the Holy *Dhama*, and the activities that occur there as part of Krishna's eternal pastimes.[9] Such a firm belief often results in an interpretation of events based upon a metaphysical logic that renders even contradictions understandable and violations to cultural rules acceptable. Simply put, Krishna and His *lilas* are not bound by human conceptions and understandings. The *bhakta*, then, has the option of accepting any events which occur in Vrindaban as caused directly by Krishna, although His motives may often be obscure. The following is an example of one such interpretation.

A poor but educated Brahman, Brij Bihari, was employed by Charandas, a British devotee and seven-year resident of Vrindaban, as a temporary assistant for the translation and interpretation of Hindi texts. During the course of their association, Charandas became increasingly dissatisfied with Brij's work and habits, culminating in a scene where he struck the assistant solidly with a staff. The young Brahman ran away in tears, telling all he met, especially people in the main market area, Loi Bazaar, how he had been treated by Charandas.

The initial response in the market to Brij's story was sympathy for him and animosity toward Charandas and ISKCON. Yet embedded in this spontaneous reaction was a tempering of criticism and a concession that Brij was indeed lazy and prone to bad habits. As the event receded into time, reflection by those for whom it had been significant resulted in a final interpretation that contrasts considerably with the initial reaction. Even among ISKCON's severest critics, there was a general incorporation of the events into a broader cosmological framework, the situation being seen as part of Vrindaban-*lila*. The owner of a cloth shop, for example, who once enjoyed a brisk ISKCON business but has recently fallen from favor, expressed his views in this manner:

> Some problems are there. But I am saying in confidence to you many in ISKCON are of the original *gopis* (intimate female associates of Krishna) come again in different body. This is a confidential understanding but there is some agreement. Krishna's associates in Vrindaban, all are part of Krishna's Vrindaban. We cannot understand. Charandas is crazy, Charandas is a demon—these things are heard. But he is really *avadhoot* (a holy man not bound by rules of society). Who are we feeble minds to say? We cannot understand. This is the Vrindaban; this is Krishna's *lila* always. Charandas is part. Briju is part.

This example is a direct invocation of Vrindaban's supernaturally based interpretive significance and is not an isolated case. The fact that such an interpretive device is naturally available for Indian residents to draw upon in making sense of their day-to-day activities involving foreign devotees gives ISKCON an inherent advantage in their efforts to win acceptance and attract supporters.

Despite Vrindaban's innate interpretive force, however, no instance of its application would likely occur without the foreign devotees' consistent presentation of an acceptable Vaisnava identity over time, which includes a general compliance with local norms and expectations. Goffman has shown just how important self-presentation and situation manipulation are for the achievement of desired ends in face-to-face interaction,[10] and he would likely agree that ISKCON devotees in Vrindaban are experts at "impression management."

By virtue of their socialization within ISKCON, the foreign devotees have become competent Vaisnavas even by Indian standards. Positive evaluations by Indian observers become still stronger when long-term foreign residents prove their consistency as serious devotees of Krishna, often being evaluated as more correct and energetic in their daily routine and rituals than Indian *bhaktas* themselves. For these devotees, regular, opportunistic interactions serve to integrate them deeper into the local culture, though they may sometimes be reluctant participants. Consider the following description of another devotee's encounter with a member of the merchant community, demonstrating just how interaction may serve to alter social and cultural precedents.

Prahlada das is another English devotee well known to the people of Loi Bazaar. His residence is a *dharmsala* (lodging house) just off the bazaar where he often shops for fine cottons and silks. He also has a favorite tailor there whom he regularly contracts to make *kurtas* and other garments. Although this penchant for fine clothes would seem to conflict with his devotee status, Prahlada does not claim to be a *sadhu* who has taken vows of poverty, and he is still respected as a "first class" devotee by many Brajbasis (also Brijbasi, resident of Braj). People in the bazaar observe his early morning baths in the Yamun, his making the temple rounds, his constant chanting: Prahlada's landlord often has gossip to pass on concerning his degree of renunciation and observance of spiritual practices.

Shortly before the incidents that I am about to describe occurred, the Goswami passed on to the regulars in the bazaar two items of information that served to immediately frame the events that were about to transpire. Prahlada had joined ISKCON in London at the age of thirteen and from that time had maintained celibacy—a period of twelve years. This was a significant fact because celibacy is seen in ISKCON as a chief technique for increasing the efficacy of spiritual practices and individual power. Furthermore, his celibacy served to further impress upon the Brajbasis that ISKCON devotees, and Prahlada in particular, did not fit the popularly believed stereotype that all Westerners were incorrigibly promiscuous.

Further, Prahlada had recounted to the Goswami that during a recent visit to Delhi, he was invited to dine with some peripheral ISKCON supporters who had served a mutton curry. He immediately left their house, showing that he had been greatly offended, and proclaiming that he would fast to the death before eating meat. This strong reaffirmation of his vegetarianism was another point in Prahlada's favor, for although most Brajbasis are themselves lifelong vegetarians and would never prepare or eat meat, especially within the precincts of Vrindaban, some did admit that on occasions away from the *Dhama*, they had in fact tasted mutton, chicken, and eggs. Prahlada had made it clear that under no circumstances would he be so enticed. These facts, among others, helped to create a positive image of Prahlada among Braj's townspeople, and set the stage for his being drawn deeper into Vrindaban's cultural system.

During the period of my research, the wife of Prahlada's tailor became pregnant for the first time. Because his marriage of ten years had been a barren one, he was understandably overjoyed, and saw this event as an answer to daily prayers to Krishna and various other gods and god-desses. Because Prahlada was such an important economic resource for the tailor's family, and because he was considered a friend, he was invited to eat at the tailor's home in celebration of the expected birth, still some months away.

The next day in casual conversation with another shopkeeper who deals in images and ritual paraphernalia, I learned of an interesting event that transpired during the visit. Upon Prahlada's departure, the wife had bent down to touch his feet out of respect. As is the custom, Prahlada quickly made a show of trying to prevent this ritual, gently pulling her up by the arms as she bent over, yet allowing the act to be completed. After she was again standing, Prahlada spontaneously placed his hands upon her stomach and said, "I know Krishna will bless you with a son. Krishna's blessing be yours."

Relating the incident to me, Prahlada was concerned about the story now circulating in the bazaar, thinking that his reputation might be affected due to his touching the woman, though no sexual connotation was implied. "I did it without thinking. I was rather inspired to it. It just happened."

Nothing more was said about this event until months later when the tailor's wife delivered a healthy son, and along with news of the event the people of Loi Bazaar learned that the tailor was giving Prahlada credit for the baby's being a boy. Standing beside the stoop of the tailor shop, Prahlada congratulated the tailor but at the same time delivered an admonishment: "Daoji, stop this business of saying my blessing gave you the son. It was Krishna; only Krishna provides. Celebrate a healthy son and give Krishna only the praise."

The tailor, Daoji, responded: "Jaya Radhe, Prahladaji. You gave the blessing. My family has daughters only. All my brothers only daughters, and now this son. It is Krishna's grace, but your blessing also. You must do the name-giving ceremony." Prahlada was quick to reject this new request. Most families are in a *jajmani* (patron-client) relationship with a Brahman who conducts the life-cycle rituals, including the ceremony that gives a name to a newborn child. Not only was Prahlada unfamiliar with the ritual, he was also aware that only negative repercussions would result if he usurped the *pandit's* authority, especially from the Brahman community. The tailor's response to Prahlada's objections was uncompromising: "Panditji is not so good at rituals. Always he consults the book; always he is arguing with other *pandits*. He only wants the money and I will give. You are Brahman; you wear the sacred thread, and you are a great devotee of Sri Radha. Why not?"

Surprisingly there was a strong sentiment in the bazaar supporting the tailor's request, with much discussion going on considering whether there were any absolute prohibitions against Prahlada's conducting the ritual. The general conclusion was that there were not. Moreover, the townspeople reasoned that if the *pandits* felt threatened by the foreign devotees, perhaps they would improve their services. Prahlada ultimately refused to escalate the drama by conducting the ceremony, and it was done by the family *pandit*. However, he was again invited to the tailor's home the day before the ritual to give another blessing, this time for the child. Daoji requested that Prahlada decide what the child should be called, and Prahlada complied with this request. The tailor's son was named Anupam.

This is but one instance where ISKCON devotees have taken on roles from which they would logically be excluded according to the common understanding of cultural rules. Other Vrindaban residents have openly accepted ISKCON devotees as authentic gurus, attested to by pictures on private altars. Members of ISKCON are also frequent guests in Brajbasi homes where they deliver *katha* (talks and discussions about Krishna), conduct *pujas*, and lead *kirtan* (chanting and singing). In one of the town's medieval temples, Radh-Gokulananda, an ISKCON devotee is employed as head *pujari* (priest). These cases all allude to a significant level of acceptance for ISKCON, indicating that an incorporation of Western devotees into the Vrindaban sociocultural system is occurring.

In both the cited examples, it is Vrindaban itself that provides the interpretive framework by which meaning is established. For the case that culminated in Prahlada's demand as a religious specialist for a Brajbasi family, the tailor himself was a member of the Gaudiya *sampradaya*—as are all ISKCON devotees—and it is Vrindaban's development by the founders of that sect that has largely created the town's cultural milieu. This historical component of the interpretive framework, then, must necessarily be considered.

Vrindaban and Gaudiya Vaishnavism

Today in Vrindaban there is a local organization, Sri Vrindavana Svarpo, whose slogan is *Sri Vrindavana dhama ek vana hai, nagar nahi* ("Vrindaban is a forest, not a city!"). Though its members have never experienced Vrindaban as a true forest, they desire to see it return to its "original state." They argue that a pilgrimage to Vrindaban should be a wilderness experience as it must have been until about four hundred years ago when Sri Caitanya initiated its development. Caitanya had a much different vision of the *Dhama*, however, than the members of this modern organization.

Although it was never his intention to transform the place into a city, Caitanya and his followers took as their mission a development of

Vrindaban. Caitanya hoped that the sacred sites of Krishna's *lilas* would become accessible objects of worship, that pilgrims would have adequate shelter during their *yatra* ("pilgrimage"), and that proper temples for Krishna worship would be established. This in effect would open the Holy *Dhama* to the masses, giving everyone the chance to receive its benefits. Concurrent with the establishment of a permanent and nourishing Vaisnava community created around the Six Goswamis and their disciples, Vrindaban became the main organizational and intellectual center for the new religion.

These goals reflected the underlying populist structure of Caitanya's movement, and its social implications were revolutionary. Access to God and the salvation that religion should provide was for Caitanya not to be limited to Brahmans and those who had renounced society. Because religious feeling was for him superior to complex ritual, religion was therefore not dependent on esoteric knowledge or education, which were available only to the upper classes. As Hopkins has pointed out, the *Bhaguvula Purana* (the most important Vaisnava scripture) insists that participation in religion should not be based on qualifications of birth or status but that a person's class should be determined by the characteristics he possesses.[11]

Likewise, the benefits of living in Vrindaban—a guarantee of salvation (*moksha*)—should be available to all. Furthermore, even if a person could not permanently reside in Vrindaban, which was the ideal, at least he should be able to come, stay for a while, and leave refreshed and purified, confident that a start had been made on the path to spiritual perfection.

Present-day Vrindaban with its many *ashrams*, temples, and *dharmsalas* still holds for the Indian people the image of a rural forest where the demands of everyday life can be left behind and where an experience of Krishna is still possible. The complex established by ISKCON is seen, especially by those of the Caitanya *sampradaya*, as continuing in the spirit of Caitanya and the Six Goswamis. Using their modern resources, the foreign Vaisnavas have built a place where yet another class of people can stay in relative comfort. For the Westernized, urban Indian, ISKCON has opened up the *Dhama* as never before, It is becoming common for many businesspersons, politicians, and government officials who come to Vrindaban to stay at ISKCON's Krishna-Balarama guest house.

Krishna-Balarama is a relatively new addition to the sacred complex of Vrindaban, which is still anchored to the temples built under the auspices of the original Goswamis. From a wilderness encampment, the town has grown to a present population of about 30,000 where most of the full-time residents live in Vrindaban for personal spiritual reasons, or to be involved in the direct support of the pilgrimage trade, which can handle an influx of as many as 100,000 pilgrims on the main festival days.

The early development of Vrindaban has been chronicled by Caitanya's biographers—Kavikarnapura, Vrindavana das, and Krishnadas Kaviraj—and by modern scholars as well.[12] Among modern scholars there is general agreement with De's assessment that:

> The recovery of the sacred sites of Vrndavana by the Bengal Vaisnavas and its erection into one of the religious centres of Northern India form one of the most interesting events in the history of mediaeval Vaisnavism; for the modern Vrndavana, eclipsing today the glory of the adjacent city of Mathura by its fine temples, groves, seminaries, and bathing ghats, is the creation of Bengal Vaisnavism.[13]

ISKCON's role in the town's continual development is seen by most as a logical culmination of its broader role in the spread of Krishna-*bhakti*. On numerous occasions I was reminded that in the *puranas* (Krishna scriptures) it is prophesied that *bhakti* would eventually spread to countries other than India. That the actualization of this prophesy culminates in a significant presence of foreign devotees is therefore not surprising for Vrindaban's residents, but rather a historical fulfillment of scriptural prediction.

The Bengal Vaisnavas, then, have since their inception been intent upon developing Vrindaban into a pilgrimage town wherein could be visited all the important places of Krishna's *lilas*. The institution of pilgrimage itself, therefore, provides in its own right the third meaningful element in Vrindaban's ethnographic context.

The Phenomenon of Pilgrimage in Vrindaban

Pilgrimage has been a unifying force in Indian society since at least epic times[14] and provides the final interpretive clue for understanding the dynamics of social flexibility and cultural integration in the town. Furthermore, by focusing on the information flow inherent to pilgrimage, the interactions occurring in Vrindaban can be seen to extend far beyond the boundaries of Braj.

Victor Turner has concluded that pilgrimage is a "liminal" phenomenon, one that exists outside or between the normal states and categories of social structure, and wherein transitions and transformations can easily occur.[15] For the pilgrim there is a state of spontaneous or existential "communitas" that reigns during the pilgrimage journey, a condition that relaxes the constraints of social structure, creating a condition of "anti-structure." In this communitas there is a "direct, immediate, and total confrontation of human identities which tends to make those experiencing it think of mankind as a homogeneous, unstructured, free community."[16] Interactions in this mode, then, are apt to be less patterned by normative structure and to be open to the emergence of new possibilities of relationships and meanings, fulfilling the potential of face-to-face situations.

Even in everyday situations of face-to-face interaction, "the other becomes fully real," making it "comparatively difficult to impose rigid patterns."[17] When such situations occur in the pilgrimage context, the transformative potential of face-to-face interaction is increased to an even greater degree. In their encounters with pilgrims, ISKCON devotees are therefore again confronted with an environment ideally suited for the successful presentation of Vaisnava and Brahman identities.

In Vrindaban the pilgrims themselves, participating in a state of communitas, are not only open to effective persuasion by the Western devotees, but they are also prepared for, if not expecting, a powerful personal religious experience that may in fact alter their own self-conceptions. Indeed, interactions with ISKCON devotees not only serve to confirm the reality of foreign Vaisnavas for the pilgrims, but may also instigate a revitalization of their traditional faith. For some individuals, moreover, particularly those from India's upper classes, this experience takes on such immense proportions that to call it anything but conversion would misrepresent its importance.

There are numerous examples from my data where pilgrims, through a series of interactions with Western devotees, have learned about ISKCON for the first time, or have transformed their conceptions about it and its place in the overall structure of contemporary Hinduism. Furthermore, through their interac' ons, some pilgrims have found a resolution of the conflict that they perceived existing between Hinduism and the modern world.

The motivation and disposition to engage in an activity and evaluate it as personally meaningful "is built up in the course of learning to engage in it." Consequently, "the problem becomes one of describing the set of changes in the person's conception of the activity and of the experiences it provides him."[18]

Such learning through participation in the interactions related to cultural events has long been the standard means of education in Indian society, especially for its rural majority. Norvin Hein noted in his 1972 study of the indigenous dramas of Vrindaban and Mathura that whereas "continuity in other stable advanced cultures has usually rested upon well-developed institutions of formal education," in Hindu culture this tenacity rests "upon another base . . . the existence of old, non-literary forms of Hindu education, through which the children of each generation have been trained in the lore fundamental to their culture."[19]

Consequently, it is perhaps not surprising to the Western observer that the gentle rural folk of Braj and surrounding areas who regularly visit the sacred sites and temples of Vrindaban come to the Krishna-Balarma temple with an innate reverence for the Krishna deities, the guru Swami Bhaktivedanta, and the devotees there. For them the experiences result in not so much a resolution of contradictions as a reinforcement and reaffirmation of cultural values and institutions, even though they are presented by Western actors.

During the course of his life, the rural pilgrim is likely to visit a wide range of religious shrines, some not belonging to any component of "Great Tradition" Hinduism. These may include sites and objects sacred to Sikh, Jain, Buddhist, or Muslim traditions, but due to the capacity for pilgrimage to integrate eclectic elements into a coherent, conceptual and mythological framework, no distinction or contradiction in sensed by those visiting them. As one Indian anthropologist commented, "the key paradigm of India's Hindu majority is 'cover your bases.' If there is a chance of benefit, visit any shrine, propitiate any god or saint, regardless of religious affiliation. Hinduism can incorporate them all."[20] For the devout, therefore, visiting a temple or shrine established by foreigners may yield just as potent an experience as a visit to an indigenous one. At least there is nothing lost in the effort.

Conversely, the most striking examples of meaning transformation manifested during pilgrimage occur among highly educated, Westernized Indians who, before their Vrindaban experiences, are content to put aside their practical and interpretive use of Hinduism in favor of a "scientific" worldview. But because the force of Hinduism is so all-pervasive in Indian society, a psychological tension often manifests itself in these pilgrims, and their superficial knowledge of the existence of American and European Hindus only serves to complicate the contradictions they perceive. They sometimes come to Vrindaban as cynics, classifying their visit as a vacation or educational trip, rather than pilgrimage in the true sense of the word. Still, as Turnbull has pointed out, the same liminality exists, and the potential for transformation is still there.[21] For an understanding of the processes of learning and meaning transformation that occur in this liminal environment, it is again best to consider a concrete example. The case of Marathi, an English-educated travel agent from New Delhi, provides a clear illustration.

Nominally classifying herself as a nontheist *advaitin*,[22] Marathi also claimed agnosticism during our first meeting: "Agnosticism is the only intelligent philosophical alternative." At this time she was planning a cultural tour of Agra and vicinity for a group of Belgian students and scholars, and I suggested that she might add Vrindaban to her itinerary. She agreed that this would be a novel diversion from her regular schedule. Several months later I was invited to join the tour for three days around Agra, including a day and a night in Vrindaban, with accommodations there at the Krishna-Balarama guest house.

Holding an art degree from London University, Marathi was well qualified to discuss the fine points of Mugal architecture at Fatepur Sikri and the proportional perfection of Agra's Taj Mahal. As we entered Vrindaban, however, her enthusiasm faded, as she suggested that the significant temples there were only crude medieval attempts built by unskilled artisans. It was clear she knew little of the texts that discussed the developmental importance of the temple of Govindadev or the relevance of Madana-Mohana's spire in the evolution of Hindu domes and Buddhist *stupas*. Navigating the narrow streets of Vrindaban in our air-conditioned bus, she also revealed her distaste for and apprehension of ISKCON: "These people are here for some ulterior purpose, we should be watchful of them." Arriving at the Krishna-Balarama temple, however, her mood momentarily changed as she viewed the complex for the first time. Its style reminded her of the Lake Palace at Udaipur, a structure that she admired. But as we were immersed in the circular flow of pilgrims inside the temple courtyard, her distaste returned. Pointing to an elderly man prostrating himself before an image of Bhaktivedanta, she loudly asked, "How can we win the battle over superstition when the Americans themselves are putting on this display?"

Over the course of the next three days, Marathi was involved in a series of interactions that resulted in a transformation of her attitude toward ISKCON and her own religious identity. The following four important situations provided either new information that she would ultimately evaluate as positive, or emotional reactions that would require a reevaluation of her religious outlook.

First, waiting for room assignments at the ISKCON guest house, Marathi was approached by a Dutch devotee conversant in both Hindi and Flemish. Identifying himself as our guide, Radha-Govinda offered to conduct us on a tour around the grounds before we settled in. He first took the group to a well-appointed room containing the scale model of a temple planned for Mayapur in Bengal. When completed, he explained, this would be the tallest building in India with a dome larger than St. Peter's in Rome. Marathi refused to comment about the structure, asking instead, "Is it your organization's intention to prevent India from becoming a modern country? These traditions have held us back for centuries, and now you are pushing us further back." Radha-Govinda countered: "Try to understand us without such animosity, otherwise we will remain enemies. This can never lead to good. Consider that perhaps your traditions provide everything necessary for progress. Prabhupada taught us that modern technology can be used in the service of Krishna. If Krishna is pleased with India, then India will achieve greatness."

The group was next led to ISKCON's school where an English class was in session. Radha-Govinda explained that several of the male students from Uttar Pradesh villages were studying on scholarships. "Perhaps they are doing some good after all if literacy is being increased," Marathi concluded. "Certainly education is the first step, and discipline is needed also. God knows there is discipline here.' "

Finally we were led to a visitors' lounge where a film concerning the life of Swami Bhaktivedanta was shown. At its conclusion she thanked our guide and revealed that some of her initial assumptions concerning ISKCON were in the process of revision: "Your guru was certainly an amazing man, and some of what I see here also amazes me. This is a slick film. Who produced it for you?" Radha-Govinda responded, "ISKCON. Written, filmed, edited, and produced by devotees. In our society there is the ability for every kind of project no matter how difficult. If we don't know, Krishna provides the training."

Returning to the guest house Marathi remarked, "These people are more complex than I thought. They are no dummies, I can see. With their money and dedication I'm not sure whether to be very impressed or very worried."

The events that transpired during the first afternoon in Vrindaban had served to give Marathi new information about ISKCON. After an hour's rest, the group boarded rickshaws for a tour of the town's temples. With ISKCON fresh on her mind, the upcoming evening's events would provide Marathi with a second experience, an emotional one that she was initially determined to avoid.

For two hours the group was in and out of temples for their evening *darshans* (viewing of the sacred images). The final stop was at the temple of Radha-Ramaa, the traditional seat of Gaudiya Vaisnavism in Vrindaban. In a large hall near there belonging to the temple, priests had arranged for a concert of Drupada music,[23] followed by a talk and discussion. It became apparent that Marathi had been moved by the temple *darshans* and the mass experience that *bhakti* Hinduism provides in the temple setting. She commented that unexplainably she was feeling a freshness that had escaped her since childhood. This sensation was, according to the priest, a direct result of the transcendent quality of Vrindaban, something that was impossible to escape.

Being especially affected by the temple of Radha-Ramaa, she asked the priest if she might stay overnight there to attend the 4:00 A.M. *darshan* the next day. He complied, and several others remained there as well, continuing their discussion before retiring. The conversation centered on Krishna, Vrindaban, and ISKCON's history in the town. Responding to Marathi's question about devotees, the priest said, "They are continuing the tradition of Lord Caitanya; we accept them fully as part of the *sampradaya*. They have been good for our tradition. Before Prabhupada went west, my father and I knew him here, one *sadhu* among many. But when he left for America he became empowered by Krishna. There is no other explanation; so we have joy for foreign Vaisnavas." Marathi whispered to me as she went to her room, "It's hard to believe, isn't it?"

After the first *darshan* the next morning at Radha-Ramaa, Marathi trekked with other pilgrims to Kesi Ghat for a ritual bath in the Yamun. With hair still wet, she laughed and said, "I may never leave Vrindaban. There is such peace here that I do not have in Delhi." We walked the two kilometers back to the ISKCON complex, stopping in the bazaar along the way, chatting with shopkeepers, pilgrims, and *sadhus*.

A third encounter occurred during lunch at the Krishna-Balarama restaurant where Marathi met the Krishna temple secretary, Radha Dasi, a 32-year-old American woman from the Midwest. They talked privately for most of the afternoon and became quick friends. Through her friendship with Radha Dasi, Marathi developed an affective bond that would tie Marathi to ISKCON through her regular correspondence with her new friend. Such personal relationships with devotees represent one of the primary means for recruiting new members and attracting supporters to ISKCON and similar movements.[24] For Marathi the developing of a friendship with Radha Dasi proved to be a key element in her change of attitude about the Hare Krishna movement. ·

A fourth experience occurred on Marathi's final day in Vrindaban. Our group had lunch at Vraja Academy, an institution founded by a well-known *baba* (one of the local names for a holy man) whose mission it is to preserve and disseminate Braj culture. Also in attendance were dignitaries including the district magistrate from Mathur, the former Maharaja of Kashmir, and several professors from Agra University. The *baba* lectured in fluent but sometimes convoluted English, yet his message was pointed to the religious, artistic, and cultural significance of Vrindaban as central to pan-Indian religious consciousness.[25] Due to *baba*'s speech, Marathi was certain that this old sage had gained psychic insight into her frame of mind at the beginning of her Vrindaban visit, and felt that his words were specifically directed at her. As we boarded the buses back to ISKCON for a rest before departing for Delhi, she gathered the group around her and said, "This is my apology to you for my negative attitude when we first arrived here. I did not know better, but these past days have been for me a most important education. My life has been changed, and this is not easy to admit."

With the group waiting on the bus, Marathi finally emerged from the temple office, smiling, with several books under her arm. Because I was remaining in Vrindaban, I said my goodbyes to the tour and Marathi took my hand, leading me behind the bus. Opening her handbag, she showed me two shiny images of Radha and Krishna that she had purchased in the bazaar. "They will not go into a display case," she whispered. "They will be properly worshiped every day so that I can always remember Vrindaban." Finally, she disclosed to me that she had become a life member of ISKCON by donating 3333 rupees and planned to become involved in ISKCON's Delhi activities.

Several months later I visited Marathi at her New Delhi apartment, and the Radha-Krishna deities were dressed in blue silk and decorated with jasmine garlands. "You know," she said to me, "I'm not fully a Krishna devotee, but it took Westerners to teach me about my own culture. Someday I may take *sannyasa* (the renounced order). I can live at ISKCON temples anywhere as a life member. Who knows?" Marathi continues to guide Indian and foreign tourists to destinations throughout India, and her "Agra package" always now includes a stop in Vrindaban. My last meeting with her before I returned to the United States was in Vrindaban where she was guiding a German group through the streets of the town which she now knows well; she was wearing the *tilaka* (forehead marking) of the Gaudiya Vaisnavas.

Just as Marathi has communicated her experiences in Vrindaban to members of her own social networks, other pilgrims coming from all parts of India also return with accounts of their *yatras*. All but a small percentage of Vrindaban pilgrims will visit ISKCON's Krishna-Balarama temple during their stay.[26] The communication cycle inherent in the pilgrim's journey therefore has an effect on the conceptual, symbolic, and structural systems in places far from Braj. The extended impact of Vrindaban pilgrimage warrants further study. Presently, however, I wish to consider another problem with implications for the broad understanding of the processes of social structure in modern India, the operation of caste and hierarchy in the town of Vrindaban.

Caste and Hierarchy in Vrindaban

Max Weber has stated that "caste is the fundamental institution of Hinduism. Before everything else, without caste, there is no Hindu."[27] Although this is the dominant Western conception of Indian society, anthropologists active in India have always known that the image of an inflexible, rigid order is not empirically supportable. Rather, this image is based on a reification created primarily by the requirements of British censuses.[28] Furthermore, that caste is not an indigenous term is a widely known fact. Neither *varna* nor *jati*, the two terms most commonly equated with caste adequately gloss this Western sociological concept.

Berreman[29] has shown that in urban India, *varna* and *jati* are only two categories among others that are significant in the patterning of social interactions, and the Vrindaban data fully support his findings. Moreover, the data reflect that for residents of the town, *jati* exists as only a general concept that may be based on either birth, religion, language, occupation, or regional affiliation.[30] Under such conditions an individual's "caste" rarely operates to exclude him from interactions with others.

The academic focus on caste, in any case, considers only half of the Indian social system, as Uberoi and Turner have pointed out.[31] Hindu society is most accurately described by the term *varnashrama*, which refers to a complex interweaving of the individual and society. Whereas *varna* refers to the hierarchical stratification of society, the equally important term *ashrama* refers to the stages or statuses of an individual's life. As an integrated concept, *varnashrama* does not present the image of a rigid, preexisting structure into which individuals automatically fit. Instead, the individual is an active agent in the processes that determine the course of his life.

It is in the fourth and final *ashrama*, *sannyasa*, that the person's capacity for free will is most clearly exhibited. Here he divests himself of all societal obligations and restrictions, and achieves the freedom to pursue the ultimate goal of life, spiritual perfection. Although *sannyasa* is traditionally taken in old age, this step away from society can be practically taken at any time. Wherever there is a large mendicant population, a subsequent force of egalitarianism operates to loosen the rigidity of social structure. The large number of *sadhus* in Vrindaban who have taken *sannyasa*, therefore, contributes another factor to the general deemphasis of caste in social interaction in this pilgrimage center.

Even for Dumont, who bases his explication of Indian society on an ideological conception of *varna* with its fundamental structure of purity and impurity, the opposition of "individual-in-the-world" and "individual-outside-the world" is essential for understanding Indian culture.[32] But his main point still remains that human society naturally tends toward stratification, with India exhibiting the most detailed elaboration of this fact. A concern for hierarchy—for who has the higher status—is preeminent in the Indian subcontinent.

All of the above perspectives lend support to my dual conclusion concerning the social reality of Vrindaban, especially as it relates to interactions between Western devotees and Indians: There is a freedom for any individual to engage in social intercourse with any other, thus providing the opportunity to establish status based on qualifications and consistent behavior; and yet, there exists a necessity for an individual to determine the rank of a person with whom he interacts. In the case of ISKCON, devotees often lay claim to the highest status in their interaction with natives of Vrindaban. This claim is accepted without reservation by most of the population. Only with the town's Brahman community do conflicts arise. Therefore, those situations that include Brahman actors are the most consequential for any determination of the devotee's ultimate position in the overall hierarchy.

Although Weber was incorrect to label caste as the key determinant in Indian social structure, his understanding concerning the operation of hierarchy was essentially correct: ". . . the objective situation remains unescapable; that in the last analysis, a rank position is determined by the nature of its positive or negative relation to the Brahman."[33] I have already mentioned that at this time ISKCON has not achieved Brahman status in Vrindaban. This simply means that the Brahman community has not accepted ISKCON members as social equals. The term "social" is the key here. One Brahman informant states the matter clearly: "They may be as good as Brahman, but Brahman is a social category, not a religious one. I am a Brahman because I was born a Brahman; no more, no less. The crucial questions are can the devotee eat freely with me, and can my daughters marry them. The answer to both questions is no, although personally he may be in every way better than a true Brahman."

Indeed, the two factors of commensality and intermarriage are the primary anthropological determinants of caste superiority and inferiority. In Vrindaban there are numerous examples of devotees interdining with Brahmans, and the data reflect three cases of Brahman fathers inquiring about ISKCON husbands for their daughters. These facts are empirically significant, although the verbalized position of most Brahmans remains uncompromising. Nonetheless, it is my conclusion that ISKCON devotees do possess a high status similar to that of Brahman, which they have achieved by a subtle manipulation of the very determinants of hierarchy.

Owen Lynch has shown how an untouchable group in Agra changed the criteria for their status evaluation by refusing to identify themselves as untouchable. As he explains, "A Brahman can interact with both a *kshatriya* (warrior caste) and an untouchable, but he cannot interact with a citizen since neither Brahman nor citizen is a counter status of the other. Brahmans can only interact with other castes in the caste system; citizens can only interact with other citizens in a democratic system."[34]

Similarly, a devotee interacts with other devotees, not Brahmans and Sudras. No Brahman in Vrindaban would concede that he is not also a devotee of Krishna, and when pressed, even will concede that his devotee identification is his dominant status. Furthermore, there is ample support from Vaisnava texts, especially those of the Gaudiya *sampradaya*, which equate the devotee qualitatively with the Brahman. Brahmans and ISKCON devotees have effectively debated the status issue by using this scripturally based logic: a nondevotee is no better than a Sudra, whereas a devotee is better than a Brahman (see the *Bhagavad Gita*).

It is ultimately the opinion of the majority of Vrindaban residents, including most Brahmans, that in the town a person's status can properly be determined by the quality of his devotion to Krishna.[35] ISKCON devotees have manipulated their place in the local hierarchy by the successful presentation of themselves as Krishna devotees. This subtle transformation of hierarchical patterning has been felt throughout the social structure. Two short examples illustrate this point.

A merchant recognized as a sincere *bhakta* now eats freely in a Brahman home, and the hospitality is reciprocated. The merchant credits this more tolerant atmosphere that has developed since the coming of ISKCON to the loosening of restrictions based on religious status instead of social status.

A temple priest with seven daughters also admits to changes: "It is true that I asked for Rakesh's marriage with Haridas (an ISKCON devotee). I know him almost like my own son, and he is a Brahman if I am one. But now he wants *sannyasa* (renunciation). That is the greatness of his devotion. I cannot stop his progress, but my daughter will find no better husband."

The integrating effect of Vrindaban's meaning as a celestial space, the egalitarian ideals of *bhakti* religion, the spontaneous communitas of the pilgrimage experience, and the individualism fostered by the *ashrama* of *sannyasa* create a unique sociocultural conjunction in Vrindaban with much transformative potential. Sahlins has commented that in such environments,

> . . . the relationships generated in practical action, although motivated by the traditional self-conceptions of the actors, may in fact functionally revalue those conceptions. . . . Entailing unprecedented relations between acting subjects, mutually and by relation to objects, practice entails unprecedented objectification of categories.[36]

Just so, at this Vrindaban conjuncture, devotees of the International Society for Krishna Consciousness have forged new conceptions and interpretations about a foreigner's potential in Indian society, which then reflect on the entire range of social and cultural interactions. Not only is ISKCON successfully achieving a place for itself in the Vaisnava community of Vrindaban, but concomitantly the presence of ISKCON has altered the way Vrindaban natives have reconceived their own relationships.

Summary and Conclusion

In this paper I have attempted to describe the drama of present-day Vrindaban, which includes members of the International Society for Krishna Consciousness as key actors. ISKCON has become an integral part of the social and cultural scene there, and its Krishna-Balarama temple is an important part of the sacred pilgrimage complex.

To understand how this integration has taken place and to interpret the interactions occurring there between Western devotees and Indians, I have suggested that it is Vrindaban as a social and religious society that must be understood. This understanding has three dimensions: Vrindaban as a symbolic space apart from the phenomenal world, identical with Krishna's celestial abode; Vrindaban as a town developed by the Bengal Vaisnavas and culturally shaped by the force of Krishna-*bhakti;* and Vrindaban as an India-wide pilgrimage destination. The attributes of each of these conceptual components help to formulate an interpretive framework for the evaluation of human interactions and aid in a realistic ethnographic description that approximates the subjective reality of the people who live there.

Finally, I suggested that while everyday interactions occur freely between individuals, a person's status position within the overall hierarchy is still important. ISKCON has achieved high status in Vrindaban, but its members have not yet been fully accepted as Brahmans due to the refusal of the Brahman community to accept them as social equals. Despite this one impediment, devotees have achieved a Brahman-like status by their successful behavioral presentations, which over time have effectively altered the criteria by which status is evaluated. Rather than a determination of status being based on social position in reference to Brahmans, the evaluation is now more often made based on the perceived quality of a person's devotion to Krishna. ISKCON is not only accepted as an integral part of the religious landscape of Vrindaban, but has also reshaped the very contours of that landscape.

Notes

1. The term "sacred complex" refers to an interrelated set of objects that together compose a sacred space, usually also a place of pilgrimage. Included in the sacred complex are sacred objects and their physical location, the perform-

ances that take place at these locations, and the people who participate in these performances. In Vrindaban, unlike other sacred towns, it cannot be accurately said that there is a secular part and a sacred part. Every place in the town has some sacred significance.

2. Tamotsu Shibutani, *Ethnic Stratification: A Comparative Approach* (London: Macmillan, 1965), p. 572.

3. The Gaudiya *sampradaya* is the medieval Krishna *bhakti* sect started by the Bengali ecstatic saint Caitanya. Also referred to as Bengal Vaisnavas, this *sampradaya* is the sect of Bhaktivedanta Swami, ISKCON'S founder. Because an individual belongs to the same sect as his guru, all members of ISKCON are also considered part of the Gaudiya *sampradaya*.

4. Ethnography is the task of describing and interpreting a particular cultural setting in detail. Ethnology consists of viewing the culture in structural abstraction in order to classify and compare it with other cultural settings.

5. See especially Gerald D. Berreman, "Social Categories and Social Interaction in Urban India," *American Anthropologist* 74 (1972): pp. 567–86; and Owen M. Lynch, *The Politics of Untouchability: Social Mobility and Social Change in a City in India* (New York: Columbia University Press, 1969).

6. Edward C. Dimock, *The Place of the Hidden Moon* (Chicago: University of Chicago Press, 1966), p. 169.

7. Sushil Kumar De lists the *Padma-purana* and the *Brahma-samhita* as sources that Jiva Goswami used to establish the dogma concerning the religious significance of Vrindaban. See De's *Early History of the Vaisnava Faith and Movement in Bengal* (Calcutta: Firma K. L. Mikhopayay, 1961), p. 334.

8. Ibid., pp. 334–36.

9. This statement reflects the results of informal interviews, random surveys, and questionnaires. In a questionnaire submitted to the merchants of Loi Bazaar, all but eight percent of the respondents (five out of sixty-six) agreed that Vrindaban was the same as Krishna's celestial residence. In interviews, all but one temple Brahman out of a total of twenty-two (five percent) agreed. The one dissenter commented: "When Krishna was here he kept the demons away. As soon as He left all the big demons came back. That is who is here today, the big demons."

10. See Erving Goffman's *The Presentation of Self in Everyday Life* (Garden City, NY: Doubleday Anchor Books, 1959); *Interaction Ritual: Essays on Face-to-Face Behavior* (Garden City, NY: Anchor Books, 1967); and *Relations in Public: Microstudies of the Public Order* (New York: Harper and Row, 1971).

11. Thomas Hopkins, "The Social Teachings of the *Bhagavata Purana*," *Krishna: Myths, Rites and Attitudes*, ed. Milton Singer (Honolulu, HI: East-West Center Press, 1966), pp. 11 and 18.

12. Kavikarnapura completed *Caitanya-caritamrta* nine years after Caitanya's death in 1533, giving a date to this work of 1542. Vrindavana das's *Caitanya-bhagavata* has an uncertain date but is no later than 1548. The best known of the biographies is Krishnadas Kaviraj's *Caitanya-caritamrta*, completed in 1615. Dates are based upon De, *Vaisnava Faith and Movement*, pp. 43 and 48.

13. Ibid., p. 96.

14. Diana L. Eck, *Banaras: City of Light* (New York: Alfred A. Knopf, 1982), p. 66.

15. Victor Turner, *Dramas, Fields, and Metaphors: Symbolic Action in Human Society* (Ithaca: Cornell University Press, 1974), p. 166.

16. Ibid., p. 169.

17. Peter L. Berger and Thomas Luckman, *The Social Construction of Reality: A Treatise in the Sociology of Knowledge* (Garden City, NY: Doubleday and Company, 1966), pp. 28–30.

18. Howard S. Becker, "Becoming a Marihuana User," in *Symbolic Interaction: A Reader in Social Psychology* (Boston: Allyn & Bacon, 1967), pp. 411–12.

19. Norvin Hein, *The Miracle Plays of Mathura* (New Haven: Yale University Press, 1972), p. 1.

20. Personal communication, Dr. Indra Singh, Chair, Department of Anthropology, Delhi University.

21. Colin Turnbull, "A Pilgrimage in India," *Natural History* 90 (July 1981): 14–20.

22. *Advaita* is the impersonal, nondualistic, nontheistic interpretation of the *Upanishads* and *Vedanta Sutra*, especially in the philosophical system presented by Sankara in the sixth century A.D. The Vaisnavas of Braj are united in their distaste for *advaita* because it precludes the dualistic conception of Krishna as Supreme God and man as His devotee.

23. Drupada is a musical style that according to tradition was sung at Krishna's *rasa* dance with the *gopis*. Literally meaning "fixed verse," the style was especially associated with courtly traditions of the sixteenth century. Drupada is seeing a revival in Vrindaban, through incorporation into the contemporary *rasa-lila* dramas, representing one of the surviving forms of medieval Indian culture.

24. For various studies of the Moonies and ISKCON that have made this point, see John Lofland and Rodney Stark, "Becoming a World-Savior: A Theory of Conversion to a Deviant Perspective," *American Sociological Review* 30 (1965): 862–75; Charles R. Brooks, "The Path to Krishna: Situations in the Development of American Hare Krishna Devotees," (M.A. thesis, University of Hawaii, 1979); J. Stillson Judah, *Hare Krishna and the Counterculture* (New York: John Wiley & Sons, 1974); and Burke E. Rochford, Jr., "Recruitment Strategies, Ideology, and Organization in the Hare Krishna Movement," *Social Problems* 29, no. 4 (1982): 399–409.

25. See Moti Lal Gupta, *Braj: The Centrum of Indian Culture* (Delhi: Agam Kala Prakashan, 1982).

26. Survey data indicate that ninety-eight percent of one-day pilgrims to Vrindaban visit the Krishna-Balarama temple. For pilgrims staying two or more days, only six percent fail to visit the ISKCON complex.

27. Max Weber, *The Religion of India* (New York: The Free Press, 1958), p. 29.

28. See Kenneth David, *The New Wind: Changing Identities in South Asia* (The Hague: Mouton, 1977), and Bernard S. Cohn, *India: The Social Anthropology of a Civilization* (Englewood Cliffs, NJ: Prentice-Hall, 1971).

29. See Berreman, "Social Categories."

30. In my Loi Bazaar questionnaire, response to the two questions "What is your *jati*?" and "What other *jatis* are in Vrindaban?" yielded the following percentages: *varna* categories, forty-five percent; "*jati*," or subcaste groupings, twelve percent; *sampradaya*, nineteen percent; linguistic or regional affiliation, seven percent; "Hindu," eight percent; "*sanatandharma*," nine percent.

31. J. Singh Uberoi, "Sikhism and Indian Society," *Transactions of the Indian Institute of Advanced Study* 4 (1967), and Turner, *Dramas, Fields and Metaphors*.

32. Louis Dumont, *Homo Hierarchicus* (Chicago: University of Chicago Press, 1966).

33. Weber, *Religion of India*, p. 30.

34. Lynch, *Politics of Untouchability*, p. 14.

35. In response to the question "Is it better to be Brahman or devotee of Krishna?" eighty-two percent of the total answered devotee. The devotee response for the Brahman population alone was seventy-one percent. To the question "What makes one person higher than another?" sixty-seven percent responded with an answer related to devotion to Krishna or personal characteristics. Thirty-three percent gave answers indicating status by birth.

36. Marshall David Sahlins, *Historical Metaphors and Mythical Realities: Structure in the Early History of the Sandwich Islands Kingdom* (Ann Arbor: University of Michigan Press, 1982), p. 35.

Heaven, West Virginia: Legitimation Techniques of the New Vrindaban Community

R. Blake Michael

Introduction

The foundation of the International Society for Krishna Consciousness in the mid-1960s by A. C. Bhaktivedanta Swami Prabhupada is a relatively well-known event. His impecunious arrival in New York, his simple public witness to his faith in Krishna, and his success in attracting a following from the politically or spiritually disillusioned youth of that unique decade are nearly legendary among observers of contemporary religion in America. As with most founder's legends, the stress in these accounts has been on the hardships encountered by Prabhupada and his disciples. His spiritual portrait has been enhanced by portraying the radical distinctness of the founder and his message both from the mainstream of American culture and from rival countercultural movements of the era.[1] Indeed, the founder and early followers of ISKCON were obviously and self-consciously different from and rebellious against their cultural environment.

Careful observers of the movement, however, noted rather early on that in many ways ISKCON was a movement that was learning to adapt itself to and make necessary accommodation with its cultural environment. Stillson Judah's definitive study of ISKCON in the first half of the 1970s, for example, took as one of its central theses the degree to which ISKCON represented a revitalization of certain widely shared American values, such as a strict personal moral code based on an individual's controlled self-denial. To be sure, their strict moral code included rather stringent dietary and marital sexual prohibitions, and their ascetical self-denial was no longer simply economically functional deferred gratification, but lifelong (or lives-long) denial of material gratification altogether; nonetheless, the bridges between the alien Krishna tradition and the members' "natal religions" were becoming obvious.[2]

These bridges, however, were not one-way affairs. Individuals discovered within ISKCON's teaching and practice an affirmation and intensification of certain, perhaps inchoate, values from their natal religions. For example, three of the four prohibitions of Vaisnava practice—gambling, intoxicants, illicit sex, and meat eating—also have an important place in most Western traditions, though their specific applications may differ. Furthermore, like most Western traditions, ISKCON insists on a theological vision that is personal and redemptive, not unlike that in Christian tradition. Even relatively fundamentalist Christian writers recognize the salience of the fact that "Christians and devotees alike believe in a god and a saviour who is personal."[3]

Individuals may have joined the movement because they could identify with those recognizable, though now more strongly affirmed, values. In turn, it was precisely those recognizable values and practices that came to be emphasized and displayed by the movement. That is, the movement's successful adaptation to the American environment was, to some extent, dependent on its "adoption" of or accommodation to pre-existing values and religious ideals in that environment.

There are numerous ways in which the movement's activities have served to legitimate[4] it to its larger societal context. At least three of these stand out as worthy of investigation and analysis. First, the movement has gained scholarly and theological legitimacy through its publications, through conferences, and through interreligious dialogues; second, it has "proven" itself in terms of such American secular values as rectitude, pragmatism, hard work, and success; and, third, at least some of its centers have undertaken extensive ministries to Indian immigrants in America, thereby continuing the tradition of earlier "alien" religious movements within the American "melting pot" experience.

Of course, such adaptation had its limits, lest what was unique and essential in the tradition be lost. External legitimation efforts required significant modifications in the formal social expressions of the movement and introduced some tensions between its traditional theological heritage and its contemporary forms of practice. Therefore, a need arose for an internal legitimation in the terms of the Vaisnava tradition itself. As the movement strove to remain true to its origins while adapting to and flourishing in an essentially alien environment, it was able to calm those internal tensions through appeal to traditional Hindu practices such as making pilgrimage, taking *darsana*, and taking *prasada*. In time the tension between ISKCON's Indian heritage and its American persona came to be seen as one between ISKCON's spiritual heritage and its worldly manifestation. In fact, however, the tension was nothing more or less than the growth pains of a small potentially ephemeral movement's taking root and ripening into an established and sometimes influential institution.[5]

Each of these legitimation strategies, as well as the theological reflection they engender, deserves broad investigation and comment; but, in many ways, these general patterns with ISKCON's nearly two decades of development are evidenced more specifically in the case of the Moundsville, West Virginia, pilgrimage complex and communal farm founded by the movement in 1968 and still flourishing independently two decades later. A detailed investigation of that facility and its means for achieving both external and internal legitimacy provide a useful case study of movement-wide developments.

The New Vrindaban Community

In many ways, the establishment and growth of the New Vrindaban community mirrors developments within the overall ISKCON movement during its first two decades. Admittedly, in the late 1980s, there exists a formal separation between the Governing Body Commission of ISKCON and the New Vrindaban Community. For two decades, however, no hint of separation existed and the community's development not only paralleled but often spearheaded that of ISKCON as a whole. Furthermore, despite such formal institutional disagreements, both ISKCON proper and New Vrindaban remain pioneering representatives of the Vaisnava tradition in North America. It is therefore entirely fitting that the community be analyzed as a particular manifestation of general ISKCON development.

The community began in 1968 when Kirtanananda Swami Bhaktipada (Keith Ham) arrived in rural West Virginia. He had been attracted to the area by an advertisement placed in a San Francisco newspaper by one Richard Rose, inviting people to a visit and to an ongoing intellectual exchange on his West Virginia farm. With the blessing and direction of Prabhupada, the ISKCON movement leased a small portion of the farm; and Bhaktipada, with a few other devotees, began to establish a community there.[6]

Their early efforts seem to mirror those of many rural communal experiments in the 1960s and 1970s. The emphasis was on simplicity and getting back to nature. Advanced technologies were rejected. Contacts with the outside world were minimized. Efforts were made to establish self-sufficiency by growing or manufacturing the necessities. New Vrindaban, however, differed from many other such agrarian communes in that its model for idyllic rural life was not a romanticized vision of the nineteenth-century American farm. Instead, it emulated the timeless Vedic village. The entire life of the community took as its prototype the life of traditional India, insofar as that reflected the ancient Vedic patterns for society.

An early ISKCON film celebrating the glories of New Vrindaban emphasized this simplicity of life in the pattern of Vedic culture. It showed simply clad devotees joyfully reaping the bounties of nature as they tended cattle, picked fruits and flowers, tended simple gardens, and produced handicrafts imitative of Indian ones. It praised the use of oxen for production and transportation of goods. It celebrated the re-creation, in modern America, of a society based upon Vedic spirituality and upon appropriate—that is, Vedic—technology. A later multimedia display at New Vrindaban likewise stresses the simplicity of the Vedic village emulated by the community in its early days. A recently published first-person account by one of the first residents portrays the same rustic simplicity in the early days of the community and presents Prabhupada's early advice for keeping things simple.[7] Furthermore, prohibitions against meat eating, intoxicants, illicit sex, and gambling and injunctions to *kirtana* practice, renunciation, and family relations helped to set New Vrindaban apart from other communes of the day.

New Vrindaban differed from many other agrarian communal experiments in a second important way. It survived. In fact, it not only survived; it flourished. But time brought changes in the nature of the community.

For one thing, the number of devotees living and working there gradually increased. From a mere handful, inhabiting an old farmhouse far from any improved road, the numbers expanded to more than two-hundred residents, augmented by perhaps that many more on a seasonal basis. Many could not dwell on or be supported by the original farm, so additional farms were purchased or leased, and additional residences were procured or constructed. By 1985, the community controlled approximately five thousand acres of land and utilized at least a score of large buildings (barns, workshops, dormitories, temples, and schools) and perhaps twice that many smaller residences.

Legitimation through Theological and Scholarly Dialogue

On an international level, the ISKCON movement has moved to legitimate itself within the community of scholars and particularly within the realm of theology. It has organized scholarly research projects—for example, the Vaisnava text project funded by the Smithsonian Institution; published numerous books both explicating its own scriptural tradition and raising comparative questions in relation to Christianity; encouraged its own members in their graduate study at some of the world's premier universities; sponsored conferences bringing together scholars from various disciplines to discuss topics within Vaisnava history and theology; and sought active involvement in an "ecumenical" dialogue with Christian ministers and theologians.

More specifically, within the religious context of Marshall County, West Virginia, the New Vrindaban community has sought to build bridges to its broader religious context.[8] Recognizing that it was not only in externals and in secular behavior that the commune differed from its neighbors, its leaders accepted accommodation with the environment. In the important matter of theology, the devotees espoused a tradition completely unheard of in a state where even Jews are a rarity and in a county where the ministerial association is largely Protestant. Furthermore, in contrast to the shared beliefs of major Western traditions, the devotees spoke of numerous names for gods and goddesses and celebrated the boyhood of a little cowherd. In espousing a religion that has no historical and only rather opaque theological connections to the Christian tradition, the devotees at New Vrindaban were openly inviting public ridicule and courting active censure.[9]

One area minister, who had made a sincere effort to understand Hindu philosophy and religion though overlooking the subtleties of Vaisnava theology, put it thus: "There's just nothing here which relates to the Judaeo-Christian tradition. It's *Brahman* this and *Brahman* that. I'm *Brahman*, a tree is *Brahman*, and your mother is *Brahman!* It's the whole problem of Eastern philosophy."[10] Or, in the simpler and more succinct words of erstwhile Marshall County Sheriff Robert Lightner: "When the Founding Fathers wrote about freedom of religion, they didn't have people like these in mind."[11]

The leadership of the community has not let such challenges go unanswered. In 1981, for example, they decided to seek membership in the local Ministerial Association to address some of the questions being raised about Krishna Consciousness and to open lines of communication between the community and its Christian neighbors. Bhaktipada submitted a letter of application to the association for membership. This unusual request, coming from a non-Western, non-Christian, non-Protestant organization, surprised the members of the association and divided them as to the appropriate response. Eventually, however, a compromise was worked out in which Bhaktipada withdrew his application for formal membership in the organization in return for an agreement by the association to hold at least three dialogue meetings with members of the movement in order to come to a better mutual understanding of religious and theological positions.

A conference room in the local hospital was chosen as a neutral meeting site; and a professor of religion[12] from a nearby college was brought in as a resource person and "referee." The professor began by stressing the historical roots and present strength of Vaisnava tradition in India on the one hand and the fundamentally different nature of world affirmation within Protestantism on the other. Yet, when the floor was opened to questions and to debate, such historical and theological considerations were quickly pushed aside by the association members. Instead they presented issues of a more immediate nature. For example, they sought explanations about many of the charges commonly lodged against the community—evasion of taxes, gun running, shoplifting, drug dealing, unpaid bills, and recurrently inadequate sewerage disposal; and the devotees attempted to refute or defuse each allegation. Although the rift between the two groups could not possibly have been healed by such a meeting, both groups initially emerged with a better sense of the other party's positions and with a newfound respect for their counterparts as persons.

The meeting was not, however, an unalloyed success. For their part the devotees found that their agenda for theological dialogue had been perverted to yet one more necessity for defending themselves against what they considered unsubstantiated and tedious rumors. The Ministerial Association's final perspective was even less sanguine. The devotees, through their public relations office, released to the local press accounts of the meeting and photographs of some participants.[13] The release served the Krishnas' purposes by stressing that the leaders of New Vrindaban had met on equal grounds with the Ministerial Association. Many of the ministers, for their part, had viewed the meeting as a quiet preliminary effort aimed at avoiding further ill-will and possible violence in Marshall County. Hence, they felt betrayed and used by having their proceedings publicized and their participation known.

Although a second and third formal meeting had been projected, these never took place. Continuing informal contacts, likewise, were characterized by some degree of complaint and distrust, and eventually formal contacts between the community and the association broke down entirely. Interestingly, some members of the association feel that, if dialogical contacts could be renewed, theological differences might be among the least troublesome areas. It remains the matter of lifestyle— clothing, tonsure, "uncleanliness," disregard of property maintenance, and "smell"—that is the most problematic. The community's more recent problems with murder investigations, child abuse allegations, and drug-money suspicions have exacerbated these ministerial concerns. Despite these difficulties, it should be recognized that there remain individuals on both sides who are interested in and working quietly toward providing a ministry of healing and reconciliation in this difficult situation.[14]

Another more successful, though less direct, way in which the New Vrindaban community has acted to establish its religious good faith has been through dialogical activities of a more scholarly nature and a more global scope. Again, many of these attempts are paralleled within the ISKCON movement proper, but they find particular expression at New Vrindaban. For example, the community has undertaken the publication of its own materials independent of the ISKCON Book Trust, which operates out of Los Angeles. A magazine, the *Brijabasi Spirit*, and its sister publication, *Plain Living, High Thinking*, are published from New Vrindaban,[15] primarily for devotees but also for wide distribution among scholars and interested laypersons. Several books, apparently aimed at a scholarly or quasi-scholarly audience, have been published from New Vrindaban under the logo of the Palace Press, Bhaktipada Books, or Prabhupada Books.[16]

Some of these books—for example, Hayagriva dasa (Howard Wheeler)'s *The Hare Krishna Explosion*,—seem aimed at documenting the history of both the ISKCON movement and the New Vrindaban community. Although slightly hagiographic in character, Hayagriva's first-person narrative of pivotal events in the first four years of ISKCON in America is not grossly deficient in objective historical method and is certainly valuable for its wealth of detail. Its purpose is clearly to tell the story of the movement in a favorable light but in such a manner that critically trained scholars will trust and utilize the work. Though comprehensive in its scope, approximately one-third of the volume is given over to the establishment of New Vrindaban by A. C. Bhaktivedanta Swami Prabhupada and Kirtanananda Swami Bhaktipada. It exposes the early days at New Vrindaban when the prevailing image is swarms of mosquitoes and the prevailing concern is obtaining a long-term lease on an isolated and dilapidated farmhouse. The narrative ceases with Prabhupada's 1969 departure from New Vrindaban, but already many of the later developments at that site are foreshadowed in Prabhupada's comments and instructions to the devotees. This foreshadowing may have been aimed at legitimating those later developments to an internal constituency of devotees, but the overall impact of the volume is to provide an audience of scholars with trustworthy historical material about ISKCON and its self-proclaimed flagship community, New Vrindaban.[17]

Another book published at New Vrindaban that reflects these efforts toward closer ties with the community's religious environment is Bhaktipada's *Christ and Krishna*.[18] In the foreword to that work, Bhaktipada specifically acknowledges that one of the reasons the book is needed is that most of the "pilgrims and guests" who visit New Vrindaban are Christian, and "they also want to understand how our worship relates to theirs;" the copyright page issues an explicit invitation for readers to visit the community. Approximately two-thirds of the book is a theological discourse on the nature of God, the nature of scripture, heaven and hell, proofs of God's existence, the resurrection, and so forth. Bhaktipada is skillfully consistent in his presentation of Vaisnava theology within categories intentionally more amenable to Christian discussions. The last third of the book makes the bid for legitimacy by reporting conversations with professors and groups of students visiting New Vrindaban from Harvard, Notre Dame, Ohio Wesleyan, United Theological Seminary, and others. It also reports excerpts from the aforementioned conversations with the Moundsville Ministerial Association. Overall the work serves to attract the attention of Christian readers and to leave them with a sense of Vaisnavism's legitimate place within the sphere of religious dialogue.

Perhaps brief mention should be made on one further project at New Vrindaban that helped to strengthen its ties with the scholarly community. In the summer of 1985, scholars from throughout the country assembled at New Vrindaban to share their ideas and insights on ISKCON's first two decades. Papers by devotee scholars were mingled among presentations by guests with independent scholarly reputations. Panelists ranged from Albanese to Wulff and topics covered such fields as sociological method, charismatic authority, conversion, mental health, and American religious pluralism. The presentations at the conference, in fact, provide the core of the papers included in the present collection. As such, both the conference and subsequent publication of its proceedings serve to accentuate the place of ISKCON within scholarly dialogue and the place of New Vrindaban as a focus of American Vaisnava activity.

Legitimation through Conformity to Secular Values

Nationwide, the ISKCON movement has acquired legitimacy by appealing to values within the secular or "civil religious" structure of American society. Under the rubric of service to the Lord, devotees have thrown themselves into a frenzy of activities that demonstrate their practical abilities, their humanitarian intentions, and their willingness to undertake difficult and unpleasant work. For example, in many communities they operate soup kitchens, meals-on-wheels programs, and their own free weekly temple feasts. Furthermore, their large temples and agrarian centers are showpieces of what can be accomplished through hard work dedicated to a cause. In many ways, these less explicitly theological efforts have been more successful in attaining an at least grudging acceptance from persons who may know little of Vaisnava theology and have little interest.

The community at New Vrindaban has likewise found somewhat greater success through its appeal to secular values. After all, many of the neighboring community's complaints against New Vrindaban had less to do with theology than with sanitation, security, property values, and tax and welfare rolls. Therefore, sincere attention to these concerns and pragmatic solutions to problems, real or imagined, have probably done more to gain acceptance—however grudging—from the neighboring community for New Vrindaban.

In its earliest days, the community had been restricted to a few devotees living in a remote farmhouse and posed few problems for the neighbors. Within a few short years, however, their numbers were augmented by numerous other devotees and their demands for space and other resources spilled over into satellite facilities now more often located nearer neighboring farms or on visible roadside sites. Not surprisingly, the existence and growth of a community of people hailing from all over the country and attempting to duplicate ancient Indian social and religious patterns did not long go unnoticed by their neighbors in the hills and vales of West Virginia. Here was a group of people who strove for entirely different aims and who lived vastly different styles of life in pursuit of those aims. Material success and mere physical comfort were not highly valued; "normal" gratifications of the flesh such as food, drink, and sex were rejected or restricted; and individual initiative and individual success were subordinated to the will and good of the group. Besides, their mere dress and behavior indicated that they wished to remain separate rather than fitting in with their environs.

Matters were made worse by several unfortunate incidents or alleged incidents between commune members and local persons. In one case a devotee was caught shoplifting in nearby Moundsville. In another, a house near New Vrindaban burned, fortunately without injury to anyone, and the owners rather openly accused the devotees of starting the blaze in order to force the owners to sell the land to the commune. In another instance, a sporting goods store operator alleged that the community may be heavily armed due to the amount of guns and ammunition it had purchased from him. In yet another accusation, health threats were alleged due to inadequate sewage treatment. The examples need not be multiplied but what they indicate is that frictions with nearby residents were more often over such mundane considerations rather than over matters of theology, and that any legitimacy in the eyes of neighbors would require address of these worldly matters and not just theological ratiocinations.[19]

The leadership of the community attempted to diffuse whatever grievances were false or unsubstantiated and dealt plainly and harshly with perpetrators when there had been a wrongdoing. Thus, for example, the shoplifter was not bailed out of jail, and, after his sentencing and punishment by civil authorities, was further subjected to the sanctions of the New Vrindaban community. Eventually a large sewage catchment and aeration pond was constructed, perhaps significantly, right beside the main access road to the community in plain sight of all inspectors, neighbors, and visitors.

The natives, however, were only slightly impressed by such good-faith efforts, and these pesky problems have continued to plague the community. After several years of relative peace and quiet and of slow but steady growth in acceptance by their neighbors, the community suffered from a string of public relations problems in 1985–86. In late 1985, a disenchanted community member attacked and severely injured Bhaktipada, whose near complete recovery from head injuries can probably be described as "miraculous." An individual apprehended and expelled at about the same time for carrying a loaded weapon at New Vrindaban was later found in Los Angeles apparently murdered, allegedly by another ex-devotee. The subsequent investigation and trial led not only to an indictment in that case but also to solution of a previous disappearance at New Vrindaban itself some years earlier. Inevitably suspicions of indirect involvement by community leaders, including Bhaktipada, were voiced and received considerable press attention. Two years of investigation, however, produced no proof linking the community's responsible leadership with wrongdoing. Though the faithful expect such "harrassment" to continue, they exhibit no fear that wrongdoing by the leadership will be discovered.

In a less sinister matter, devotees returning from India in the spring of 1986 infected the community with hepatitis and perhaps typhoid and necessitated a partial quarantine of the community.[20] Once again the community's leaders acted promptly and responsibly to deal with each of these problems, for example, temporarily closing the Palace's restaurant and "welcoming" a federal investigation of the murder charges,[21] but the very persistence of such problems only confirmed many of their neighbors' prejudices and fears.

The leadership of New Vrindaban also made some direct attempts to bridge the distance of the community from its neighbors. For example, its Palace Charities has operated a Food for Life program that has served an estimated fifty thousand free meals to needy area residents. On another tack, a business manager and public relations officer was brought from the Bombay temple.[22] This devotee, who holds a management degree, not only introduced organized and sound management procedures, but also became a spokesperson to the neighboring community. By using his given name, rather than his spiritual name, and by presenting himself in dress and action in a manner closer to Western norms, he attempted to appeal to those secular values that many felt had been so grievously violated. In fact, he carried the effort into the den of the community's opponents and became a member of the area Chamber of Commerce.

It may be noted that such efforts sometimes backfired and many within the Moundsville area were offended by this individual's aggressive "big city" manner. Nonetheless, his presence and perhaps his aggressiveness itself helped to establish the New Vrindaban community as a part of the Moundsville economic and, to a lesser extent, political scene. His successor's lower-profile approach seems to go over better with the locals but builds on and expands that established economic base. In the mid-1980s, for example, while Moundsville itself experienced severe economic dislocations, New Vrindaban continued to grow and flourish. In fact, the community began to hire numerous local residents in its service, construction, and landscaping operations. Those employees are not slavishly uncritical of their employers, but the overall message they carry back to the outside is that here is a community of decent, hard-working, dedicated individuals who deal fairly with their employees.[23]

Besides such direct approaches at securing a place within their social environment, the leadership of New Vrindaban has followed a less direct and less conscious path that may, in the long run, serve better to earn acceptance of their community and its way of life. That indirect path has been in their gradual opening of their lives and activities to visitors and neighbors, particularly as the commuity has begun to display and even market their skills and handiworks. For, besides the change in number and size of physical facilities, the community changed in the nature of equipment it utilized. The simple technologies of the Indian village were replaced by modern Western ways of doing things. The ox-drawn cart gave way to the four-wheel-drive pickup, and the ox-drawn plow gave way to the diesel tractor. The gentle hands of the cowherd gave way to automatic milkers, to pasteurizers, and to bulk storage facilities in the dairy barn. In fact, new dairy facilities under construction on the eastern portions of the farm will give the community the capacity to care for and milk six hundred cows per day, to chill and preserve the milk, and to process it into commercial dairy products certified for retail sale.

But perhaps most drastically, the central focus of activity in the community shifted from doing enough labor to survive while singing the praises of Lord Krishna to constructing an elaborate and unique edifice—the Palace of Gold.

The idea for this beautiful Hindu temple, or for something rather like it, is traced to a 1968 letter from Prabhupada endorsing the idea of a spiritual community at New Vrindaban and dreaming of construction of seven major temples on the hills of West Virginia reminiscent of the seven major temples of Vrindaban, India.[24] Actual plans for the Palace, however, did not begin until 1972 and then as now it was not conceived to be one of the seven main temples. Rather it was conceived and executed as a preliminary project to the main task of temple building. It was planned primarily as a residence for Prabhupada who had said that he would come to live out his days at New Vrindaban.

When construction began in 1973, the devotees had only a vague plan for a suitable residence for their spiritual master. The elaboration of those plans into an opulent edifice with marble floors, teakwood doors, crystal chandeliers, and stained glass windows was a gradual and additive process spurred along by Prabhupada's "disappearance" (death) in 1977. Concurrent with that elaboration of plans for the Palace was the development of more and more sophisticated artistic and architectural skills by the devotees. Through successes, failures, and diligent endeavors, the devoted laborers mastered techniques for marble cutting and polishing, for casting concrete, for working with stained glass and cut crystal, and for gold leafing. In fact, they went on to develop some more advanced construction technologies such as substituting cast styrofoam for cast concrete in overhead applications and culturing synthetic marble instead of cutting and polishing real stone for applications in ancillary buildings.

Besides learning techniques for the physical construction of the Palace, the devotees also had to learn how to manage the flow of people who came to view this beautiful anomaly on a West Virginia hilltop. Parking lots, a restaurant, and a comfortable guest lodge were followed by a gift shop and time-shared mountain cottages. Hence, New Vrindaban's acreage, or at least the portions of it near the Palace, have gradually taken on the appearance of a modern visitors' facility—well-equipped to meet the physical needs of the weary traveler. The simplicity of rustic life has become submerged or obscured by the development of a full-fledged tourist complex.

The complex currently includes not only the magnificent Palace of Gold but also the Radha Vrindaban Candra Temple, the comfortable guest house, the Palace Restaurant, an amphitheater, two small lakes with a swan boat altar, and ample parking. At every turn, furthermore, the visitor is informed of even grander plans. Of seven temples planned on seven nearby hills, the first has had its ground-breaking ceremony and the site is marked prominently for all visitors to see. Statuary for a "Krishna-land" theme park is to be seen at sites throughout the community, though its relocation into a landscaped park itself is yet to be begun. The occasionally used amphitheater presages a full-fledged drama center. One young elephant is harbinger of others that the community expects to acquire, train, maintain, and display. Landscaping work near the Palace has been interrupted by plans to transform the site into a massive bell tower in which will be housed both a carillon and the largest bell in the world, the "Krishna bell," currently being cast in Holland. Sketches, models, and blueprints emphasize the seriousness and the feasibility of such schemes; and the constant hum of machinery and ubiquitous signs of ongoing construction underline the commitment of the devotees to their fulfillment.

Of course, the simple existence of such structures and plans would probably not affect the way the community is viewed by its neighbors. However, the effort, the skills, and the diligence necessary to construct the Palace are virtues admired by many of the group's neighbors as well as by visitors who have come from a distance to see the remarkable Palace structure. The guided tours of the Palace are careful to point out the handiwork of the devotees. Stress is placed on the efforts of devoted tyros who, largely through trial and error, learned the complex artistic and architectural skills necessary to build the edifice. Beyond that, some visitors are permitted to visit the community's workshops where the marble, cast concrete, ironwork, furniture, crystal, tapestries, paintings, and sculptures for the Palace were fashioned and where artisans are at work on similar products for the seven additional temples projected by the community.

A guided tour of the community's workshops[25] usually involves stops at the graphic arts studio (a converted school building) and at the stained-glass shop (a converted bar). The visitor is informed that some of the artists and artisans have found their productions so highly prized that they were actually bought by outsiders. The artist[26] who painted most of the murals for the Palace later won a contract to paint a large mural in the Wheeling Civic Center. The facility acquired in working with stained glass was used to fulfill a contract from a major retailer for Tiffany style lamps. Among the less subtle arts showcased are brickmaking (25,000 per week) and sawmilling (2,000 board feet per day). This indirect appeal to the rather pervasive American evaluation of work helps to establish an appreciation for the devotees' diligence.[27]

A second but related appeal is made to the pervasive American respect for pragmatic and practical planning and forethought. This appeal is advanced by emphasizing the efforts going into planning and executing the future temples. For example, the planning department, now staffed by an erstwhile university architecture professor turned devotee[28] and equipped with the latest in computer-aided designs produced on "state-of-the-art" plotters is a showpiece of technology devoted to divine ends.[29] A similar pragmatic appeal is made by something so simple as provision of clean and adequate facilities for visitors. The restaurant and gift shop in the basement of the Palace as well as the guest lodge indicate to the visitor that these are not the same impractical, space-out people who used to chant on street corners. Rather these are level-headed, intelligent, and practical people who are building a major tourist and pilgrimage center and are providing the necessary amenities.

Furthermore, the building of the Palace has extended very real ties into the surrounding community. Despite the devotees' efforts to complete much of the work themselves, they have had to begin hiring some expert and other assistance from outside. Also, even their own productions require materials that often must be purchased from the outside. Hence, a network of financial relationships with members of the surrounding area has developed helping to give others reason for accepting the community. Perhaps this attitude is best summarized by the statement: "I might not agree with the Hare Krishnas, but there's nothing wrong with their money." Or, as the community's business manager once put it: "Let them set up a convenience store near here and they'll be fixed for life."[30]

One further example of this legitimation-through-buildings approach relates not specifically to the Palace but to the boys' school. It seems that few visitors to the community or few tourists of the Palace have been able to avoid notice of the young children, dressed Indian fashion, playing about as their mothers string flowers and shy away from contact with outsiders. The reality that an entire generation of offspring would be reared in relative isolation from mainstream society and fed on the ideas and practices of Krishna Consciousness seems infinitely more disturbing to visitors than that a handful of late adolescents or young adults should voluntarily choose a variant lifestyle. Hence, it is not surprising that charges of child neglect and child abuse have continued to plague the community. The issue of the "Children of Krishna" has even found its way into popular magazines and Sunday newspaper supplements.[31]

Of course, the community has from the beginning educated its offspring as it saw fit. It has provided sound elementary education coupled with large doses of Krishna Consciousness and smatterings of Sanskrit; but formerly such education took place in places relatively isolated from public view. As recently as 1981, the community's school for boys could be reached only by walking or by four-wheel-drive vehicle. It required a journey of some two miles through forests and cow pastures over rutted logging roads. Housed in an old farmhouse, the school had adequate but quite spartan facilities far from the gaze of or contact with outsiders. More recently, a large bar and nightclub, located near the intersection of several well-traveled roads, was purchased and converted into a school building with classrooms, dining hall, and dormitory facilities for the boys.

This building was procured because a better physical facility was needed; and its prominence to the surrounding population served to indicate the movement's good intentions, practical abilities, managerial competence, and good faith to provide for its children. Opening the school to state competency testing and to independent psychological evaluations also illustrated the community's responsible attitude toward the nurture of its children. Furthermore, the prominent private school for community children helped, for a time, allay the locals' fears that these Krishna children might be sent to public schools where their own children would be exposed to such "alien" values. Of course, it did not hurt the community's purposes that one of its recurrent sources for problematic community relations—a too close watering hole—had been eliminated in the process.

Unfortunately, the flurry of allegations and the thorough investigation that followed the Los Angeles murder revealed that there was apparently some truth to the child molestation charges. The community's leadership dismissed and placed in counseling one of the teachers in the boys' school. Furthermore, they closed, at least temporarily, the school at New Vrindaban and sent the children to public schools. How long such involvement with secular ("karmie") influences can be tolerated by the community remains to be seen. But that the community's leadership once again took decisive action to deal with internal problems can hardly escape the attention of its neighbors. Again, it may be such unspoken messages that were most effective in bridging the distance between the devotees and those neighbors.

The examples could be needlessly multiplied, but the point should be amply illustrated by now. One of New Vrindaban's more prominent and more successful strategies for establishing itself as a legitimate part of West Virginia's religious life has been not through direct religious or theological appeals but rather through appeal to certain pervasive secular values. The pragmatism, industry, relative cleanliness, diligence, openness, and perseverance of the community has earned it a grudging acceptance by its neighbors. In the words of now Marshall County Sheriff Donald Bordenkircher, "[The Krishnas] have the right to life, liberty, and the pursuit of happiness like any other American citizen."[32]

Legitimation through Service to the Immigrant Community

The third important way in which portions of the ISKCON movement have acquired legitimacy within the broader society has been in their mission to Indian immigrants. This large, well-educated, and relatively affluent segment of the American population has been relatively "unchurched." Through some of its major temples in the larger cities and through smaller "temple" houses often located near university areas, some ISKCON centers have been in the fore in establishing a network of worship and pilgrimage sites that Hinduism, by and large, was ill-equipped to provide outside the boundaries of India itself. The financial support of these immigrant families has been quite valuable to ISKCON, but the mission to them has had a second benefit as well. In a land populated by immigrants of one kind or another, this sort of mission seems somehow appropriate and harmless especially in comparison to the alternative—proselytizing of Americans into an "alien" faith. Hence, the movement's position within the estimation of American society at large is enhanced by its mission to these new Americans.

The Palace of Gold at New Vrindaban quickly attracted the attention of American natives. Newspapers and newsmagazines began featuring this cultural anomaly on a West Virginia hilltop, and tourists literally by the busload began visiting the Palace, with its gardens, restaurant, and gift shop. These tourists for the most part, however, came and saw and left. It was another type of visitor who took advantage of the guest lodge and who expressed an interest in the mountain cottages. These visitors, or perhaps more aptly pilgrims, were Indo-American Hindus who found at New Vrindaban a little corner of their native culture and native religion flourishing in America; and according to devotee estimates, Indo-American patronage of the guest lodge and cabins represents ninety to ninety-five percent of the total.

Although they may have first been attracted to visit the Palace of Gold, they are more likely to be found spending the better part of a day or weekend at the Radha Vrindaban Candra Temple located down the hill from the Palace near the guest house. This building, which enjoys its own wood-paneled elegance, is a much more functional and simpler building than the Palace. Here regular *arati* ceremonies are held several times daily, readings and lessons are scheduled regularly, and occasional religious dramas are performed.[33] Near the entrance of the building are advertised rates (ranging from $25 for *Panchamrita Snan* to $251 for a wedding) by which worshipers may endow regular performance of rituals for specified periods after their departure. Stored prominently within the building is a *ratha* for use in outdoor processions on festival days. In other words, despite its paler beauty, this temple more nearly resembles a working Hindu temple than does the more elaborate Palace. As such it serves the very real function of providing a place to worship in a manner fondly remembered by many of Indian background.

Another example of New Vrindaban's mission to the Indo-American population is its efforts to provide training in Vaisnava history and culture to the children of Indian immigrants. Its mission to these second-generation Indo-Americans is exemplified in its summer camp program.

From mid-July to mid-August, Camp Gopal flourishes on the banks of the New Yamuna River within the New Vrindaban community. It promises swimming, boating, and horseback riding along with training in *hatha yoga, mantra* meditation, *kirtanas, bhajanas,* and *pujas.* It emphasizes instruction in Vedic philosophy and vegetarian cooking as well as *darsana*s and pilgrimages to the Palace of Gold and the community's *gosala.* Of course, some of those who send their children to the camp will be ISKCON members from urban centers, but the appeal of the program, especially in its promotional literature, is plainly directed at all who revere sacred Hindu tradition. For example, in one flier on the program, all the campers depicted are apparently of Indian extraction, and unofficial estimates by community members place Indo-American participation at approximately ninety percent.

A final example of New Vrindaban's mission to Indo-Americans is the community's cow-protection program. In mailings to devotees, friends of the community, and regular visitors to New Vrindaban, the community solicits donors for its *gosala* where Lord Krishna's beloved cows will be lovingly cared for and protected from the butcher's knife. Donors are promised certificates and photographs as well as their names inscribed on plaques in the completed *gosala.* To those unfamiliar with Vaisnava theory and practice in India, such mailings appear baffling or even ludicrous, but to Indo-Americans their appeal is a familiar one. Furthermore, it is an appeal that provides reassurance that one's own cultural background may not be so out-of-place and out-of-date as mainstream American culture makes it appear. Once again immigrants are provided the opportunity to be religious in the ways that are most meaningful to them—namely, the ways they had known in childhood.[34]

The mission to Indo-Americans performed at New Vrindaban may reflect its own dynamic, growing out of the needs of that group and the desires of the community to worship as authentically as possible; but the effect of that mission has also been one of increased acceptance among non-Indo-Americans. American society has long had a vision of itself as a "melting pot" for ethnic, racial, linguistic, and religious heritages. It has learned to live with the idea that people of a particular ethnic background will continue to practice their own religious forms and that those forms pose no threat to the overall makeup of American religious and secular values so long as they remain ethnically specific. Whereas Hindu traditions may seem more bizarre to mainline Protestants than do Roman Catholic or Russian Orthodox ones, they can nonetheless be accommodated within overall American cultural patterns insofar as they represent ethnically specific traditions of a definable immigrant population. Only when such traditions begin to encroach upon established traditions by recruitment or monetary solicitation do they become a perceived threat to established societal values. Hence, to the extent that New Vrindaban directs its efforts toward Indo-Americans, its activities become more acceptable to mainstream American religiosity.[35]

Further, it is to the advantage of the community to highlight the role of Indo-Americans in its practice and support in order to find such acceptance and legitimacy in its social context. Thus many editions of *Brijabasi Spirit, Plain Living, High Thinking,* and the *Land of Krishna* newsletter contain at least a short article highlighting the role of some Indian or Indo-American within the ISKCON movement proper or at New Vrindaban in particular.[36] On the question of funding, also, the Indian solution has proved to be a helpful one. Not only have Indians been generous in their support of the community's service and building programs, but they have also provided an acceptable answer to the question often provoked by the opulence of the Palace and surroundings, "Where did the money come from?" When guests and visitors have posed this common question, one of the most acceptable answers seems to have been, "From lay followers of the movement, including many immigrant Indian professionals." That is to say, just as mainline Protestants have found it easier to accept the community so long as it was not subverting "American" youth but serving an immigrant population, so too they seem to have better accepted the movement so long as it was not diverting "our" dollars but relying upon contributions from its "natural" constituency.[37] Hence, a mission that the community has developed to a receptive target constituency has indirectly contributed to the legitimacy of the movement in the eyes of those outside that constituency.

Legitimacy within the Ancient Tradition

Each of these three approaches to legitimation to the broader society involves compromises of the distinctiveness and separateness of the Vaisnava way of life. Any genuine theological dialogue involves a willingness to consider alternative statements of the truth; and the very notion of scholarly dialogue risks opening oneself to scrutiny and criticism. The use of advanced technologies, albeit in traditional goals, necessitates contacts with a broader and supposedly "unredeemed" society and risks contamination with the views and values of that society. Even activities for the benefit of an immigrant population require marketing one's services among a group of people who have rather explicitly rejected at least some aspects of their traditional heritage in favor of contemporary American values—for example, comfort or success—and risks compromise with those views and values. With such developments New Vrindaban has had to confront a question of its identity and no longer stands utterly apart from modern Western material culture. Eventually a community that had set out to cut itself off from the material world and to spiritualize every minute of the day finds itself caught up in the same "botherations" that it had sought to avoid.

Nearly two decades into its existence, the New Vrindaban community, like the ISKCON movement proper, finds itself in a tension between, on the one hand, the necessity to organize and institutionalize itself in order to survive in an organized and institutionalized environment and, on the other hand, the necessity to preserve the uniquely non-Western, nonmodern, antimaterialism that is its spiritual heritage.[38] This tension is in no way unique; it probably occurs in some phase of institutionalization for every religious movement. But it is a position in which New Vrindaban currently finds itself.

To both devotees and visitors it is plain that some, at least apparent, discrepancy exists between the movement's teachings of antimaterialism and the opulent realities of the Palace of Gold. The simple, rural life of self-sufficient agriculture, simple handicraft, and patient cowkeeping is no more. Agricultural production may remain a mainstay of the community's economy, but it is now a highly efficient and technologically advanced agriculture. The idylls of Lord Krishna in ancient Vrindaban are little more easily imagined among the buzz of saws in the woodworking shop, the clankety-clank of bulldozers on the Appalachian slopes, and the electronic whir of cash registers in the gift shop than they are on the busy streets of a modern city.[39] The visitor to New Vrindaban is likely to wonder why a movement that disparages individual physical beauty as unimportant in comparison to the all-attractiveness of Lord Krishna should have some very attractive and well-groomed young women devotees serving as waitresses in its restaurant. Or one might wonder why a movement that eschews all use of even mild intoxicants such as coffee, tea, and soft drinks should serve these (though reputedly only in decaffeinated forms) in its restaurant and provide them in vending machines in its guest house.

These questions are not, however, confined to the outsider who visits New Vrindaban. One of the restaurant waitresses, for example, has related the spiritual questioning that her work there had occasioned. She had had doubts about the effectiveness of waiting on tables for tourists in a fully Western and materialistic environment as a form of preaching Krishna Consciousness. She concluded that her own faith had been deepened by the experience and she speculated that some of those to whom she had served *prasada* might have been led one step closer to Krishna. The very fact that she was raising such questions, however, reflects the apparent discrepancy between her ideals of Krishna Consciousness and the realities of her activities in a situation that, to some extent, compromised those ideals with a materialistic Western environment.

It should be pointed out that these doubts were expressed to another devotee and overheard by the author. The public front is generally much more cohesive; but the existence of such openly expressed doubts within the community weakens the "brainwashing" charges commonly leveled against alternative religious traditions. Community members are clearly dedicated and committed both to performing and to understanding their pious duty.[40]

The tension that both the casual visitor and the devoted follower find between ancient spiritual ideals and modern material realities at New Vrindaban is a genuine tension produced by an ongoing dynamic within the community and in its relations to its societal context. That tension, however, is not without answers from the ancient tradition itself. Historically, the community's leaders attribute some of the early isolation of the community to a misunderstanding of Prabhupada's original intention, which was not to establish a retreat but to establish a *tirtha*—a crossing point between the worldly and spiritual realms—modeled on the Vedic village. Theologically, the task of the devotee becomes the task of understanding that one is acting for Krishna in any capacity. He or she faces the same dilemma that confronted Arjuna in the *Bhagavad Gita*—how to do the unpleasant duty while remaining Krishna Conscious; and he or she finds the same answer—do the duty through detached action, yielding all results to Krishna.[41]

As a practical matter, it is once again through the Indo-American immigrant pilgrims to New Vrindaban that such answers are most powerfully demonstrated, for it is they who are theologically prepared to accept and endorse these traditional theological arguments. Specifically, the answers to both the casual visitor's sense that some aspects of New Vrindaban seem rather crassly commercialized and also to the devotees' questions about the spiritual purpose of certain occupations lie in several hallowed Hindu theories and their time-honored application to Hindu practice—namely, pilgrimage, *darsana*, and *prasada*.

Many who have visited India recall their first encounter with "tourist" agencies. Ethnocentrically assuming themselves to be "tourists" and all Indians to be local natives, Westerners are often puzzled how so many small roadside tourist agencies, bus companies, and tourist hotels can survive with only a handful of international tourists in sight. Of course, the answer is obvious, but nonetheless a lesson to be remembered. These tourist agencies are there to serve Indian tourists who have traveled from far or near to see some important sight. And as that insight begins to dawn, the Westerner is commonly further perplexed over what sights it is that the Indians are coming to see. Other than an occasional palace or a famous zoo, there often seems to be little that would warrant sightseeing. Few beach resorts, few mountain vistas, few amusement parks, and few restored historical sites seem to be the focus of these tours. Instead these tourists are there to visit revered temples, sacred waters, and other holy sites. And these tourists come not simply to view an ancient temple of architectural or historical interest but primarily to visit working temples as places of holiness and to worship there. That is to say, in India, the word "tourism" is often used to mean something more akin to the Western concept of "pilgrimage," a journey undertaken for religious or spiritual purposes.[42]

Hence when the New Vrindaban community establishes tourist facilities around its Palace and when it conducts tourists in a careful circumambulation of the sanctum (in the guise of a tour of the building's portico), it is simply providing the opportunity for the tourist to make a proper pilgrimage to a holy site as is done in thousands of sites by millions of believers every year in India. Furthermore, like the typical Indian holy place, the Palace of Gold is surrounded by statuary and artwork designed to teach religious lessons to pilgrims. That current plans call for an advance in the technology of such displays into an amusement park with animated statuary and mechanized transport does not alter the basic nature or didactic purpose of such undertakings. Thus, at New Vrindaban, as throughout India today and as throughout Christendom in a former day, tourism and pilgrimage become indistinguishable.[43]

A second Hindu doctrine that legitimizes practices at New Vrindaban is the idea of *darsana*—seeing and being seen by the divine image. Within the Hindu understanding, the divine image is charged with religious power; in fact, it is the presence of the deity itself. Therefore, visual apprehension of the image is itself a religious act. The very beholding of the image is an act of worship. Through seeing the image, one gains a religious blessing. The act of seeing is an act of divine-human communication and interaction. Bowing, praying, and other forms of obeisance are laudable and beneficial, but the mere act of physical sight of the image is the primary mode by which the contact with the divine power is effected. In fact, it does not really matter whether the visitor intends to receive such a religious blessing. For, by seeing the image, the visitor "takes *darsana*." The worshiper is a passive receptor. The deity itself, on the other hand, "gives *darsana*." The deity is the active dispenser of salvific power. In fact, in Vaisnava theory the visual form of deity, the image or *murti*, and the aural form of deity, the *mantra* are no different from deity itself. Hence seeing an image of Krishna is seeing the reality of Krishna.[44]

One should not, of course, externalize or operationalize this "seeing" too much. Some internal or spiritual condition is probably necessary for the worshiper to derive full benefit from the *darsana* experience. But it is important to note that again it is the Lord who creates that spiritual condition, not necessarily the worshiper. For example, in that most prominent of Vaisnava *darsanas*—the Krishna apocalypse of *Bhagavad Gita*, chapter eleven—it is the Lord Krishna who gives to Arjuna the special spiritual eyes to behold His true cosmic form.

> But thou canst not see Me
> With this same eye of thine own;
> I give thee a supernatural eye:
> Behold My mystic power as God![45]

The third doctrine that explains practices at New Vrindaban is the idea of *prasada*. The word literally means "grace" but often refers to those things that the Lord of His grace has given to his devotees. Specifically, proper vegetarian cooking that has been first offered to the Lord and then is "returned" to be consumed by the devotee is perceived to communicate that divine grace to the human recipient. As in the case of *darsana* it is not the recipient who makes the *prasada* holy but the Lord. The words of Sri Caitanya in Bhaktivinoda Thakura's blessing before meals reflect this doctrine.

> O My devotees, this *sak* is so delicious!
> Lord Krsna has definitely tasted it.
> At the taste of such *sak* as this,
> love of Krsna arises in the heart.
> In such love of God you should taste this *prasada*.
> Giving up all materialistic conceptions,
> and taking the Lord's *prasada*, all of you
> just chant 'Hari! Hari![46]

Therefore, the Lord "gives" *prasada* as he gives *darsana* and the worshipers "take" *prasada* as they take *darsana*. Again, it is not the worshiper who is the active agent in this process, but the Lord. Therefore, when tourists visit the Palace and dine in the Palace Restaurant, they take the Lord's *prasada*—that is, His grace is made available to them through the meal. The devotee who prepares that meal, the one who serves it, and the one who cleans the dishes afterwards are all actively engaged in the mission of the community.

Without specifically alluding to the doctrines of *darsana* or *prasada*, Bhaktipada has made the same case in perhaps clearer terms. When asked how Krishna Consciousness is presented to the visitor at New Vrindaban, he replied:

> [We present them] Krsna and Krsna's pure devotee, Srila Prabhupada, in the most attractive way we can. That's why we've built the Palace. People may come with some motive—either to see a unique place or to enjoy a vacation or for some other reason—but if they become convinced of the value of Krsna Consciousness by appreciating its beauty, that is our success. Prabhupada's Palace is to Prabhupada what a beautiful setting is to a diamond. The Palace is a means of drawing attention to Srila Prabhupada. That will benefit all humanity. . . . Because no matter how people become acquainted with Srila Prabhupada, they'll want to know more about him.[47]

With statements like this, the leadership of the community makes a clear and consistent appeal to traditional Hindu doctrine and practice for acceptance of the community and its practices within the fold of orthodox Vaisnava devotion. Although it utilizes novel forms for attracting pilgrims to take *darsana* and *prasada,* it consistently holds true to the substance of the tradition communicated through those forms.[48]

Once again, it is the Indo-Americans who make such efforts at traditional justification effective. Through that group's regular support of New Vrindaban, through its pilgrims who are so ubiquitous and prominent at the community, through their obvious enthusiasm for *darsana* of the images at *arati* times, and through other forms of participation in the life of New Vrindaban, Indo-Americans serve to certify the legitimacy of New Vrindaban within its tradition. It should also be noted that Indo-American support has been more persistent than has the tourist trade, even during New Vrindaban's disputes with ISKCON's Governing Body Commission and with secular authorities. They also promote its acceptance within the American milieu as an alien but legitimate religion appropriate at least for its immigrant clientele.

Conclusion

Nearing the end of its second decade, the Vaisnava community at New Vrindaban finds itself at the difficult crossroad that confronts many religious movements as they develop into full-fledged, well-established institutions. New Vrindaban must in some way appeal to, justify itself to, legitimate itself to, or simply get along with the neighbors in its social environment. It has experienced marginal success by approaching that problem directly and engaging ministers, scholars, and others in historical and theological dialogue. Indirect strategies, however, seem to have been more successful in bridging the difficulties. The community's efforts to work hard in pursuit of a goal and its exhibition of a certain pragmatism in its accomplishment of those goals appeal to many secular values of the surrounding society. In this sense New Vrindaban has nudged a begrudging acceptance from its neighbors in much the same way that other communal endeavors have done during nearly two centuries of American religious pluralism. Additionally, the community has enjoyed considerable success in presenting itself as a mission to an immigrant population of Indo-Americans, and that image too has found resonance with traditional American responses to pluralism.

Each victory in achieving acceptance from the broader community, however, has brought compromises in certain exotic and archaic Hindu values, which are commonly deemed spiritual, with contemporary contextual values, which are commonly deemed materialistic. The community has had to find ways to remain true to its "spiritual" genius while demonstrating success within its "materialistic" environment.

The community's own understanding of this dilemma is that it is not a question of spiritual versus material nature per se but of worldly versus divine purpose. Those things that are utilized for a divine purpose become dematerialized—as it were, spiritualized. Those objects or techniques that are dedicated to spreading Krishna Consciousness become no longer ordinary objects of the world but spiritually legitimate tools dedicated to a holy end.

Of course, left unchecked, such a purely teleological ethic can give rise to problematic individual actions, such as those that have recently provoked criminal investigation of certain devotees and ex-devotees. But, properly understood within the historical Vaisnava tradition, it becomes no more than a license to utilize legitimate modern techniques in propagation of an ancient truth. Those techniques remain subject to the behavioral rules evolved by the tradition over centuries of development and must accord with the goals of piety, not of property. The tradition's sacred texts explain and restrict such spiritualized actions:

> Except action for the purpose of worship,
> This world is bound by actions;
> Action for that purpose, son of Kunti,
> Perform thou, free from attachment (to its fruits).[49]

The actual devices for such internal or traditional legitimation of novel religious forms and technologies lie easily at hand in the common Hindu practices of pilgrimage, *darsana*, and *prasada*. The purpose of the community then is to acquaint tourists (or pilgrims) with Krishna Consciousness. Whatever devices may attract people to come and see the divine image—comfortable guest quarters, a fine restaurant, a beautiful

Palace—are acceptable because they have a divine purpose. In fact the current direction of Bhaktipada's plans lies toward a syncretism of the finest expressions of Western culture with those of Indian culture for the expression of an eternal, transcultural truth. To that end, plans are being made for inclusion of the world's largest pipe organ in the planned Radha Vrindaban Candra Temple of Understanding.[50]

> In whatsoever way any come to Me,
> In that same way I grant them favor.
> My path follow
> Men altogether, son of Prtha.[51]

In light of the community's position in tension between these two poles of legitimacy without and legitimacy within, the construction of the Palace seems an absolute stroke of genius and the rush of Westerners as well as Indo-Americans to its portals a godsend. It would be quite difficult to discern whether the original motivation for that construction was purely pious or consciously intended to achieve such legitimation; it is clear that in the minds of most devotees the motivation was purely a desire to fulfill the will of God expressed in the words of Prabhupada. Perhaps Hayagriva dasa's unpublished comment best summarizes the community's resolution on this issue.

> In the beginning, we were not so concerned with our "image" in American culture—our purpose was to please Srila Prabhupada. Coming from the iconoclastic 1960s, we were hardly the type to start a religious amusement park, or a *tirtha*, or to even proselytize. We just followed Srila P.s desires, and eventually his plan is manifesting. It is destiny. It is Krsna's desire. We can but choose to serve as instruments in its fulfillment.[52]

Whether built as a result of divine inspiration or of cold calculation, the Palace and temples serve as perfect displays for the community's commitment to dedicated labor while still putting service of divine purposes before selfish gain. Furthermore, these symbols of the movement's pious devotion endure beyond the ill-conceived actions of individuals or the bad publicity of the moment. In this way, New Vrindaban succeeds in the eyes of the world and at the same time succeeds in the eyes of the pious.

Notes

1. See, for example, Satsvarupa dasa Goswami, *Srila Prabhupada-lilamrta: A Biography of His Divine Grace A. C. Bhaktivedanta Swami Prabhupada*, 6 vols. (Los Angeles: The Bhaktivedanta Book Trust, 1980–83).

2. See J. Stillson Judah, *Hare Krishna and the Counterculture* (New York: John Wiley & Sons, 1974), esp. pp. 182–97; Harvey Cox, *Turning East* (New York: Simon and Schuster, 1977); Larry D. Shinn, "The Many Faces of Krishna," in *Alternatives to American Mainline Churches,* ed. Joseph H. Fichter (New York: Rose of Sharon Press, 1983), pp. 113–35; Larry D. Shinn, *The Dark Lord: Cult Images and the Hare Krishnas in America* (Philadelphia: Westminster Press, 1987).

3. J. Isamu Yamamoto, "Hare Krishna (ISKCON)," in *A Guide to Cults & New Religions,* ed. Ronald Enroth (Downers Grove, IL: InterVarsity Press, 1983), p. 100.

4. "Legitimate" and "legitimation" are being used here in their general sociological sense of "justifying" or "authorizing," and not in their literal juristic sense of "making legal." Contrast the excellent though dated summary of the latter problem by Leo Pfeffer, "The Legitimation of Marginal Religions in the United States," in *Religious Movements in Contemporary America,* ed. Irving I. Zaretsky and Mark P. Leone (Princeton: Princeton University Press, 1974), pp. 9–26.

5. The so-called "Neibuhr–Pope hypothesis" classically located in H. Richard Niebuhr, *The Social Sources of Denominationalism* (New York: Henry Holt, 1929), and subsequently elaborated by numerous others.

6. The best source to date on early New Vrindaban is Hayagriva dasa, *The Hare Krishna Explosion: The Birth of Krishna Consciousness in America 1966–1969* (n.p. [Moundsville, WV]: Palace Press, 1985), esp. pp. 223–340.

7. See Prabhupada's advice in his early correspondence with Kirtanananda Swami and Hayagriva dasa in the latter's account, *Hare Krishna Explosion,* pp. 235ff.

8. Similar efforts at local integration by other movements are discussed by Charles L. Harper, "Cults and Communities: The Community Interfaces of Three Marginal Religious Movements," *Journal for the Scientific Study of Religion* 21 no. 1 (1982): 26–38.

9. Satsvarupa dasa's vol. 5, *Let There Be a Temple,* reflects the similar cultural barriers that the largely Western ISKCON devotees encountered when they undertook to build a temple in Bombay, India, though there it was not on theology but on ethnicity that most disputes arose.

10. Stated, in the presence of the author, by an unidentified member of the Moundsville Ministerial Association.

11. Quoted by Linda K. Lanier, "America's Cults: Gaining Ground Again," U. S. News & World Report (8 July 1982): 39.

12. Yours truly.

13. Further public relations use of this encounter can be found in Kirtanananda Swami Bhaktipada, *Christ and Krishna; The Path of Pure Devotion* (n.p. [Moundsville, WV]: Bhaktipada Books, 1985), pp. 169–73.

14. The preceding assessments were expressed by some members of the association in telephone conversations during 1982 and in an informal meeting during June 1986.

15. (Hare Krishna Ridge, Moundsville, WV. Palace Press/ Bhaktipada Books, periodically).

16. Recent or forthcoming titles include Prabhupada's *Dialectical Spiritualism, Light of the Bhagavata, Bhagavad-Gita AS IT IS,* Bhaktipada's *Christ and Krishna, Eternal Love, The Song of God, A History of the Great Planet Earth,* Hayagriva dasa's *Hare Krishna Explosion, Vrindaban Days,* Yamuna devi's *Lord Krishna's Cuisine,* and the staff's *New Vrindaban Community: A Photographic History.*

17. Unfortunately, legal considerations have led to substitutions for the names of some individuals, impairing but not destroying the book's historical utility.

18. (Moundsville, West Virginia: Palace Press, 1984).

19. These problems were among those discussed during the 1981 dialogue session with the Ministerial Association.

20. *Moundsville Daily Echo* 91, 45 (7 May 1986); 91, 53 (16 May 1986); 91, 59 (23 May 1986); 91, 64 (30 May 1986); and 91, 69 (5 June 1986). A fiery summary of these events and subsequent accusations appears in *Rolling Stone* 497 (9 April 1987): 53–58, 78–82. The accusations continue at *New York Times* (17 June 1987): 9.

21. *The Delaware (OH) Gazette* (UPI) (18 June 1986): 13; (19 June 1986): 10; (3 December 1986): 16; and (7 January 1987): 8. The refutations continue at *Wheeling (WV) Intelligencer* (UPI) (18 June 1987) and *Wheeling (WV) News-Register* (18 June 1987): 1.

22. Mahabuddhi (né Randy Stein), B.S.B.A. San Diego State University.

23. Assessment based upon unsystematic but frank interviews with five employees during 1986 June.

24. Hayagriva dasa, *Hare Krishna Explosion*, pp. 235ff. and *Brijabasi Spirit* n.d. [1982]. 9.

25. Formerly, such tours were encouraged, but increased tourist traffic and liability considerations make them less readily available.

26. Muralidhara dasa (né Mark Missman), who studied art at Northwest Missouri State University.

27. A published version of this appeal appears in Dravida dasa, "The People Who Built the Palace," *Back to Godhead: The Magazine of the Hare Krishna Movement* 16, no. 7 (1981): 16–21.

28. Murti dasa holds a degree in architecture from the University of Southern California and studied briefly under Frank Lloyd Wright.

29. Computerization is discussed in *Plain Living, High Thinking* (April 1984): 14 and 20–22.

30. Actually two families have attempted to follow this advice with varying results. One family, after significant consultation with their minister, purchased a convenience store just outside the community's boundaries, and seems to enjoy a healthy business not only from local residents but also from tourists coming to New Vrindaban and occasionally from community members themselves. Another family, still owning land within the heart of the community on the road to the Palace, opened a small restaurant and prominently advertised hot dogs, chili, and so forth. Perceiving a direct challenge to their own values within the heart of the community itself, the leadership forbad devotees and non-devotee employees from frequenting the establishment and consequently its economic viability is in doubt.

31. Hillary Johnson, "Children of a Harsh Bliss," *Life* 3, no. 4 (April 1980): 44–51, and Gary Marshall, "Children of Krishna," *Something Extra* (1 October 1980): 7–12. See also *Rolling Stone* 497 (9 April 1987): 82.

32. Interview on West Virginia Public Radio, 6 June 1986.

33. A drama troupe, The Brijabasi Players, also makes itself available to educational and artistic associations for performances of dramas based on Vedic literature as well as contemporary morality plays. The troupe was featured at the West Virginia Cultural Center Theater's Festival of India program in October 1985.

34. Western versus immigrant reactions to a similar scheme at an ISKCON

farm in Pennsylvania can be seen in the letters to the editor of *Hinduism Today* 8, no. 1 (January 1986): 2 and 8, no. 2 (1 March 1986): 2.

35. What is implied here is that twentieth-century American religiosity is developing along the lines of "Hindu–Buddhist–Muslim" just as the nineteenth century initiated the pattern set forth by Will Herberg, *Protestant–Catholic–Jew: An Essay in American Sociology* (New York: Doubleday & Company, 1955).

36. For example, "Friend of the Month. Dr. Radha Krishna Mahajan," *Brijabasi Spirit* (n.d. [1982]): 27; "Bhattacharya performs *puja* for Srila Bhaktipada," *New Vrindaban: Land of Krishna* 2, no. 6 (February 1986): 2; and "Master Plan II: Twenty Indian architects and engineers team up to work on the Krishnaland project," *Plain Living, High Thinking* (April 1984): 24–27.

37. Less prominently discussed, for obvious reasons, is the community's Christmas season "merchandising" missions on street corners and in shopping malls nationwide, which actually account for a large portion of the devotees' own living expenses and contributions to the community. Both these methods may now have superseded direct solicitation as discussed by James T. Richardson, "Financing the New Religions: Comparative and Theoretical Considerations," *Journal for the Scientific Study of Religion* 21, no. 3 (September 1982): 255–68; David G. Bromley and Anson D. Shupe, Jr., "Financing the New Religions: A Resource Mobilization Approach," *Journal for the Scientific Study of Religion* 19, no. 3 (September 1980): 227–39; and others. Furthermore, both "merchandising" and direct solicitation risk the perennial charge that devotees misrepresent themselves ("lie") in their fundraising activity. Indo-American support minimizes such charges.

38. This tension is often heightened beyond the internal logic of Vaisnava theology by the legacy of Swami Vivekananda's famous challenge to the "materialistic" West from the "spiritual" East. See the cogent passages in *Sources of Indian Tradition*, ed. Wm. Theodore de Bary (New York: Columbia University Press, 1958), 11: 94–107.

39. The tension is well symbolized by the recent construction of a new residence for Bhaktipada far from the tourist din and perhaps fittingly quite near the original farmhouse where the community began in the late 1960s. Of course, concern for Bhaktipada's safety was also a consideration in the choice of the site.

40. A published effort to deal with the same problem is Bhavisyat dasa, "Devotion to Krishna or Big Business?" *New Vrindaban: Land of Krishna* 3, no. 6 (April 1986): 6.

41. Paraphrase of unpublished comments by Hayagriva dasa in correspondence with the author.

42. A marvelous recent work on pilgrimage to the holiest of Indian sites is Diana L. Eck, *Banaras: City of Light* (New York: Alfred A. Knopf, 1982).

43. In fact, a similar "Hindu Disneyland" has recently opened oceanside in Madras. *Hindusim Today* 8, no. 2 (1 March 1986): 28.

44. Paraphrase of unpublished comments by Hayagriva dasa in correspondence with the author. Two recent discussions of this doctrine are Diana L. Eck, *Darsan: Seeing the Divine Image in India* (Chambersburg, PA: Anima Books, 1981), and Joanne Punzo Waghorne and Norman Cutler, eds., *Gods of Flesh, Gods of Stone: The Embodiment of Divinity in India* (Chambersburg, PA: Anima Books, 1985).

45. *Bhagavad-gita* 11.8. Franklin Edgerton's translation of *na tu mam sakyase drastum / anenaiva svacaksusa / divyam dadami te caksuh / pasya me yogam aisvaram.*

46. *Songs of the Vaisnava Acaryas*, trans. A. C. Bhaktivedanta Swami Prabhupada et al. (Los Angeles: Bhaktivedanta Book Trust, 1974), pp. 46–47.

47. "Pioneer for a Spiritual Community," *Back to Godhead: The Magazine of the Hare Krishna Movement* 16, no. 7 (1981): 28.

48. In fact, Bhaktipada has recently been embroiled in controversy with the GBC apparently over the question of adherence to traditional patterns of practice rather than adaptation to more "modern" norms. The controversy has led to a "severance" of formal ties between ISKCON's GBC and the New Vrindaban community though it is far from clear what will be the outcome of the controversy. The details are opaque; but see, for example, Kirtanananda Swami Bhaktipada, *On His Order* (n.p. [Moundsville, WV]: n.p. [Bhaktipada Books], n.d. [1986]). Similarly, New Vrindaban's outreach to Indo-Americans is not universally characteristic of ISKCON centers.

49. *Bhagavad-gita* 3.9. Edgerton's translation of *yajnarthatkarmano 'nyatra / loko 'yam karmabandhanah / tadartham karma kaunteya / muktasanqah samacara.*

50. Oral communication from Bhaktipada in June 1986.

51. *Bhagavad-gita* 4.11. Edgerton's translation of *ye yatha mam prapadyante / tams tathaiva bhajamy aham / mama vartmanuvartante / manusyah partha sarvasah.*

52. Correspondence with the author.

VI. Social Response to
ISKCON

Christian and Jewish Religious Responses to the Hare Krishna Movement in the West

John A. Saliba

The presence of new religious movements in the West has been one of the issues that many Christians and Jews have had to face since the early 1970s. To Jews and Christians alike, the evangelization of, and recruitment from, their membership was not something new. The mainline Christian churches have long been subjected to the proselytizing campaigns of newer Christian churches like the Mormons and the Seventh Day Adventists. Jews, on the other hand, have always felt themselves threatened by a larger religious and cultural environment and have tended to be on the alert against missionary endeavors. The impact of the current religious movements has been felt not merely because of their extensive propaganda drives and media coverage but also because many of them draw their religious and philosophical ideology from religious traditions alien to the Judeo-Christian context. To many religious leaders, the presence of Eastern groups in the West seems like an organized missionary effort to propagate pagan beliefs and practices outside their native foreign lands.

The reaction to the new cults has been thoroughly analyzed and surveyed by Bromley, Shupe, and Oliver under the rubric of "anti-cult movement."[1] Briefly, these scholars point out that both secular and religious models have been employed by those involved in this movement and that within each model two metaphors—namely, possession (brainwashing) and deception—have been developed to explain the rise and spread of the new cults and to draw up a plan for counteracting their influence. In essence the anti-cult movement starts from the assumption that cults are a religious and/or social menace. Its main goals are, therefore, aimed at warning people of the cultic threat, at counteracting the influence of the cults by whatever means available, and at trying to "reconvert," whether by some form of persuasion, counseling, or deprogramming, those who have fallen victims to their sway.

Religious Responses to the Cults

In this paper we direct our attention to the specifically religious responses to the new cults, namely those that stem from the perception of
the new religious movements as a challenge, or as an alternative, to one's
religious tradition. When a person becomes negligent of, or simply
abandons, the faith of his or her upbringing, relatives and friends, as
well as religious leaders and instructors, apparently find it easier to
come to grips with the new situation. People who do not practice the
religion of their parents may be called "lapsed," but their line with
tradition is not conceived as being irrevocably broken. Theological concepts, such as that of "sin," and "human weakness," can be brought in to
explain their present condition, and hopes for their return can be readily
nourished. Conversion to another religion is, however, a clear statement
of preference and has an element of finality about it. In theological
terms, it is apostasy, a willful renunciation or repudiation of one's faith,
and creates the need to safeguard one's value system and to reassert the
truth of one's religious dogmas. Many parents of cult members have
been led to explore the tenets of their faith and to reexamine their own
religious commitment with mixed results. Some have grown stronger in
their faith, others have become more sympathetic and tolerant of others,
and a few have felt an attraction toward the new religious involvement of
their offspring. Religious leaders have bewilderedly asked what went
wrong in their religious education programs, which did not prevent the
defection of some of the members of their church or synagogue, and
have proposed ways of remedying the situation.

   That Jews and Christians should react negatively to the presence of
religious movements should not come as a surprise. Contact and conflict
between religions have occurred frequently throughout the history of
humankind. We suggest that, in part at least, the reaction to the new
movements can be viewed as an aspect of the meeting between religious
ideologies. Three possible ways of responding to different religions, old
or new, can be traced, the first of which corresponds, to a large degree,
to the anti-cult movement. In religious terminology it can be labeled the
apologetic approach. Here, emphasis is placed on the need to engage in
debate in order to defend one's theological position against opposing
convictions and to persuade one's opponents of the overriding truth of
one's theological statements. In this approach arguments are drawn up
showing how one's religious dogmas are the correct, or orthodox, ones,
and reasons are put forward to discredit other beliefs. Thus, Jewish
writers[2] have found it necessary to rebut the interpretation of scriptural
passages used by the Jews for Jesus in their evangelization methods,
whereas Christians[3] have argued vehemently in support of the doctrines

of the Trinity and divinity of Christ against the position propounded by, for example, The Way International. To many Jewish and Christian writers the very study of other religions or cults is considered a necessary step to successful apologetics. Several Christians[4] have dwelt on certain Eastern religious beliefs and practices that could be used to belittle, discredit, and ridicule those who have joined an Eastern religious movement. Pushed to its extreme manifestation, the apologetic approach has in the past often provided justification for persecutions and open warfare, and it is sometimes used today to rationalize the open hostility that has characterized the anti-cult movement.

Not all religious responses to the new cults, however, can be described as "anti-cult." Two other religious interpretations are, in fact, marked by the absence of most of the rhetoric and activities characteristic of the contemporary anti-cult movement. The first is distinguished by relative neglect. Christian denominations have survived side by side for centuries with little knowledge of each others' traditions and have shown even less awareness of, and interest in, other major religions. Until recently Christian education and theology has had little to say about other religions.[5] Various theories on the place of world religions were the subject of debate among some theologians and never reached the general membership. Most of the mainline Christian churches have disregarded or ignored the presence of the new religious movements. Few directives[6] have been issued and the clergy are largely uninformed. Implicit in this neglect may lie the conviction that the new cults may not be religiously of any great significance and that their impact is minimal or simply ephemeral.

Another possible way to relate to other religions and new cults is to further mutual understanding and possible cooperation. The model adopted here is that of dialogue, an approach that has been actively and officially pursued for the last two decades by the World Council of Churches and by the Vatican Secretariat for non-Christians. Although this general approach of dialogue and cooperation with world religions has found an acceptable place in the theology of the mainline Christian churches, its application to the new religions has not been systematically considered. The recent legal suit against the Reverend Moon[7] illustrates the *modus operandi* of such cooperation. In this case several Christian churches united in support of a so-called cult to uphold the constitutional rights that all religions in the United States enjoy. Dialogue and cooperation have been either largely repudiated by fundamentalists or else interpreted as a means to evangelize and convert non-Christians, or as a possible approach to lure cult members back to their previous church affiliation. It must be conceded that the approach that encourages dialogue and cooperation presents serious difficulties to those whose personal lives have been deeply affected by the new cults.

We will first examine in some depth the apologetic approach because this has been the dominant one. The religious or theological definition of a cult and the factors associated with its emergence and spread will be described. The specific objections to the Hare Krishna movement and the reasons given for its success will then be explored. Finally a brief outline of the as yet undeveloped alternate dialogue method will be presented.

Religious Definitions of a "Cult"

In an attempt to respond more effectively to this conceived threat, Christians and Jews have labored to draw up a definition of a cult and to outline its features. Christian observers of the cults have largely opted for a theological definition. Cults are first and foremost systems of belief that deny basic orthodox dogmas, like the Trinity, and contradict biblically revealed truths, like the divinity of Christ. Walter Martin's definition of a cult is typical of Christian writers. He states[8] that a cult is "a group, religious in nature, which surrounds a leader or a group of teachings which either denies or misinterprets essential biblical doctrine." Parallel lists of Christian and cultic beliefs and practices are drawn up with the intention of showing that the differences are substantial and that the acceptance of cultic ideology is nothing else but a formal repudiation of Christianity. Attached to some of the perfectly obvious theological statements about cultic belief systems are several derogatory connotations and accusations. Cults are judged to be counterfeit spiritualities and spurious religious systems. They are often explained as a manifestation of satanic forces, and they thus represent metaphorically the cosmic struggle between good and evil that augurs the apocalyptic end of time.[9]

Both psychological and sociological arguments have been used by Christian writers to buttress their theological positions. From a psychological perspective a cult is an exploitive and deceptive system of brainwashing and mind control achieved by heavy behavioral conditioning and hypnotic techniques.[10] Its effects are simply devastating. People who join have their thoughts manipulated and their egos destroyed. After a while members forfeit their interest in, and use of, logical thought, and lose contact with reality. They degenerate into "spiritual zombies." Cults are extremely demanding, exacting heavy sacrifices that might include the neglect or refusal of medical aid, thus adding serious physical problems to the psychological damage already caused by the narrow and restrictive environment. To those who maintain that cult members are possessed or under the influence of satanic forces, such psychological results are what one might, after all, expect.

From a sociological standpoint the cults are beset with serious difficulties. One of their main features is the emergence of an authoritarian leader who, claiming divine revelation or knowledge, exacts loyalty of, and submission from, all his disciples.[11] Cults are therefore closely knit social groups or systems that are kept together by discipline and regimentation. Their life is tightly structured and controlled by their leaders. Group solidarity is enhanced by legalistic codes and esoteric creeds and by the inculcation of narrow mentality that separates and isolates members from the outside world, which is vividly depicted as a hostile environment.[12] What appears to be a sociological aspect of cultic phenomena is given a religious interpretation. Cults distort the religious community and twist obedience to God into subservience to a self-proclaimed prophet.

Whereas the Christian description of a cult brings to the fore theological differences between orthodox Christianity and the cult's ideology, the Jewish definition focuses on the pejorative psychological and sociological aspects of cult involvement. Jews have highlighted the devastating effects cults have on family life, which is seen as central to religious life itself. Margaret Singer's theory[13] that a cult is a manipulative group that brainwashes its members by techniques of indoctrination, thought control, and hypnosis figures prominently in Jewish definitions.[14] Jewish writers do not compare in detail their faith with that of the new religious movements. But they do criticize them for believing that the end of the world is at hand and for promoting a secretive and mysterious atmosphere. The cultic philosophy is one where the end justifies the means. The psychological features ascribed to a cult and the social dynamics that are believed to operate in the group are almost identical to those alluded to in Christian writings.

Jewish definitions of a cult seem to emphasize two features: the separation of the cult member from his or her cultural and familial roots, and the harm done to the individual's freedom and integrity. To religious Jews the first is a violation of a divine ordinance, and the second impinges on one's God-given inherent rights.

Why Do Cults Flourish?

Given this negative picture of a cult, one wonders why they would arise in the first place, and why any young adult would even consider joining them. There are two broad reasons proposed by Jews and Christians alike to explain the resurgence of the new movements and to account for their popularity. The first reason is the general cultural and social conditions of Western civilization, and the second is the religious situation. Many religious writers see an intrinsic conflict between the secular and the sacred, between the cultural and religious aspects of one's life. There seems to be agreement that the stress on material values, which is characteristic of modern Western civilization, is at the very root of the problem. Many contemporary young adults no longer find strength, certainty, and comfort in traditional faith because they live in a society where the mood of relativity predominates and where scientific progress may have created more problems than it has solved.[15] Our society, which has apparently rejected the foundations of religious belief and which frowns on public manifestation of religious behavior, no longer offers a base for building a community where love, fellowship, and acceptance are the norm. Jewish writers in particular[16] are preoccupied with family life, which they see eroding through lack of discipline and authority.

These social, antireligious conditions are psychologically affecting many people, especially the young, who are experiencing the normal identity problems of late adolescence.[17] Such dissatisfied people have to deal with the major problems of alienation and loneliness and are searching for spiritual fulfillment. It is, moreover, argued that the present mood in Western culture has contributed to the success of Eastern religions because these have preserved values that a scientifically oriented West has neglected and have encouraged philosophical relativism, especially in religious matters.[18]

The presence of the cults also indicates that all is not well with Christianity and Judaism, both of which must have, in part at least, failed to give a solid religious formation to their respective members. The result is that people may not have their religious needs fulfilled, whereas others have a shallow understanding and knowledge of their faith. Gordon Lewis's remarks on the older Christian "cults" have been applied also to the contemporary cultic scene. He complains[19] that "the enthusiasm and sacrifice of the cults shame us. Their educational vision and their extensive use of modern methods of propagandizing the masses have left many of us far behind. More diligent in calling and giving, they reveal elements of truth and life we have neglected."

There is also agreement among Jews that Judaism has been greatly influenced by Americanization, modernization, and secularism[20] with the deplorable result that Jewish life has been trivialized. One hears the constant lament that Jewish education is both inadequate and insufficient.[21] Many Jews are criticized for being attached and committed solely to their cultural traditions with the result that the spiritual life of Judaism is at a low ebb.

Religious Evaluations of the Hare Krishna Movement

The attitudes and statements of most Christian and Jewish writers on the Hare Krishna movement have been dominated by their suspicion of cults in general. ISKCON is at times taken as an example of a pagan, un-Christian cult or of a loosely defined social group where deception and indoctrination keep members under the strict control of a despotic ruler who masquerades as a guru.

Most Christian literature on ISKCON portrays the Christian fundamentalist view of Eastern religions,[22] a view which restricts revelation to the Bible and salvation only to those who have formally accepted the Christian faith. Hinduism is presented as an idolatrous religious system to be shunned, if not abhorred. Relying heavily on Stillson Judah's study[23] of ISKCON, most of the current comments on the movement start by placing it within the framework of the Hindu religion, more specifically within the fundamentalist or Tantric tradition.[24]

The main attack against the Hare Krishna movement is directed toward its basic teachings. ISKCON is said to be a religion of incredible myths and fantastic doctrines that are irrational and primitive. Its beliefs are inconsistent and its philosophy unrealistic, unintelligible, and absurd.[25] Moreover, the movement is seen as an insidious and deceitful challenge to Christianity because of its claim that it has no desire to change a person's traditional allegiance while still maintaining its universal missionary goal and proposing Krishna Consciousness as the fulfillment of Christianity.[26] Its assertion that it is compatible with the Bible and Christianity is categorically denied. In fact most, if not all, of the teachings of the Bible cannot be reconciled with those of ISKCON.[27] It is debatable whether the devotees of Krishna are guilty of practicing idolatry.[28]

The Hare Krishna devotees are further criticized for their continuous mantra chanting, which, besides being unbiblical, is the method by which they are brainwashed and kept in a state of trance and mind control.[29] ISKCON's rigid monastic life has also been negatively interpreted. Its restrictions on sexual activity even within marriage are deemed frustrating and degrading, its vegetarian cuisine is malnutritious, its structured daily schedule leaves those who live in temples practically no responsibility, and its strictly disciplined temple life keeps them in a state of mental conditioning and deprives them of human freedom.[30] Such a system, which dominates the intellectual and emotional life of devotees, requires an absolute leader who is perceived as an unscrupulous person who assumes divine power, if not divine nature. Swami Prabhupada, like other contemporary gurus and religious leaders, has been accused of being inaccessible to his own devotees and of living a life of leisure and luxury in direct opposition to what he demands of his followers. Christian evangelical literature tends to leave one with the impression that cult leaders, including Swami Prabhupada, are basically immoral individuals who insist on fundraising for social and educational projects that never get started and who take advantage of those naive youngsters who are infatuated by their actions and ideas.[31] Behind such accusations lies the implicit judgment that ISKCON, despite its claim to the contrary, is not really a religious or spiritual organization and that its leader's religious claims are false. There are some exceptions to this condemnation of Swami Prabhupada. Yamamoto,[32] for instance, gives a much more objective and dispassionate account of ISKCON's founder whose movement, he believes, is certainly not a "rip-off."

The communal lifestyle of the devotees has frequently come under heavy fire. The most often heard complaints about them is that they have "dropped out of the world"[33] and have lost all interest in works of charity and social issues. ISKCON has been sharply criticized for undermining the traditional family and child education system and for creating and encouraging tensions between devotees and their parents.[34] This rejection of society has the effect of making the devotees rather hostile, a hostility expressed in the popular accusation that the Hare Krishna movement is essentially a violent one, as the stockpiling of weapons, especially in its West Virginia Temple, proves beyond a shadow of a doubt.[35] These practices are judged to be in direct conflict with Christian principles.

The Jewish response to the Hare Krishnas has been less thorough. ISKCON is regularly presented as a typical example of a destructive cult and the need to refute its religious doctrines and rituals is not strongly felt. Hence, one will not find in Jewish literature lengthy comparisons between ISKCON and Judaism. The major religious criticisms against the Hare Krishna movement have been that its members pay homage to a host of traditional, pagan Hindu gods and that their leader Swami Prabhupada is also worshipped.[36] Its philosophy and practices are incompatible with Judaism. It is, however, the social behavior of the Hare Krishna devotees that has aroused the anger of the Jews. Members of ISKCON behave like social outcasts who encourage hostility and violent behavior and who have turned their temple in West Virginia into a weapons cache. They avoid the ordinary pastimes of American culture, like sports and watching television, and, above all, they are forcibly cut off from their families. Women play an inferior role and are subservient to men in practically everything. Like their Christian counterparts the tendency of Jewish leaders is to see ISKCON as antagonistic to religion because, among other things, the devotees are deceptive in their soliciting of funds and in their recruitment practices.[37] A few Jewish writers[38] do point out, however, that their "religion is not corrupt or exploitive."

The charge of brainwashing is probably the strongest one brought by Jewish writers. Rudin and Rudin[39] express the popular viewpoint when they adopt Conway and Siegelman's theory of conversion to cultism. In agreement with Christian writers, Jewish commentators on ISKCON think that the chanting of the Hare Krishna *mantra* is clear evidence that the devotees are brainwashed and then maintained in this state of indoctrination by the continuous repetition of the *mantra* aided by a regimented life that lacks nutrition and medical care. Although it has been conceded that the Hare Krishna devotees may "appear to be happy," it is still concluded that there are many "vegetables" and "basket cases" in their temples. Unlike Christian apologists, however, Jews do not, as a rule, interpret this alleged state of brainwashing as a sign of satanic possession of influence.

Who Joins ISKCON and Why?

When one reads the negative accounts of the Hare Krishna movement one is left wondering why anybody would decide to commit oneself to such a harmful organization. Both Christian and Jewish commentators make serious attempts to resolve the issue of why young adults, raised and educated in the religious tradition of their parents, find any of the cults, particularly those of Eastern origin, attractive.

Probably the most common reason given to explain why young adults join the movement is that it provides an alternative to a materialistic society.[40] Western culture has become dominated by scientific technology and consumerism, which aim at material comfort and efficiency and which are inclined to ignore spiritual needs and aspirations. This has led to anxiety and disillusionment and to the desire to escape to a less worldly-oriented environment. ISKCON offers an antimaterialistic lifestyle in which individuals no longer crave material goods and are no longer motivated by competition for success.

A second reason advanced to explain why the Hare Krishna movement has established a foothold in American society is the existence of the counterculture. Judah[41] points out that the Krishna preconverts had joined the counterculture of the 1960s and, finding it unsatisfying, had been searching for an alternative lifestyle. Becoming a member of the movement meant that one was not only abandoning the counterculture of drug abuse and sexual indulgence but also expressing symbolically a rejection of American values and family heritage.

A third reason for joining ISKCON is that young adults have become disillusioned and frustrated with their churches, to which they feel no deep commitment and whose beliefs they have largely rejected.[42] Harvey Cox[43] has suggested that "perhaps Christianity and Judaism have allowed themselves to be identified with the values of accumulation, profit, performance, success and material gain." With little or no attachment to the tradition of their upbringing, many young adults, in search of self-development and spiritual experience, have discovered in ISKCON's lifestyle those spiritual values that they had abandoned or never quite possessed and that were not visibly portrayed by the traditional churches.

Several sociological and psychological reasons are also adduced to explain the success of the Hare Krishna movement. In an age and culture where family life and authority are disintegrating, those who join the movement find warmth and friendship in a supportive community where the lines of authority are clear and rigid and where people can openly express and share religious goals.[44] Although the social benefits of joining the Hare Krishna movement may sound, at first sight, desirable and beneficial, the psychological effects on those who join leave no doubt that membership is a hazard to one's mental health. The typical psychological profile of a young adult who enters the Hare Krishna temple is that of a distraught and disturbed person who has lost his or her attachment to tradition. Alienated from society and religion, such a person is unable to cope with life. With little strength and imagination and with no ambition, he or she tends to be lonely and isolated. The success of ISKCON depends on maladjusted and discontented people who are vulnerable to the strong and overbearing advances of enthusiastic devotees.[45] Membership in the group does nothing but hide or aggravate the new members' weak psychological state of being. It should be stressed that the detrimental social and psychological consequences of cult involvement are readily envisaged as being directly linked with false religious beliefs and bizarre rituals.

The tendency of both Christians and Jews is to explain the breakdown of religious values as being partly responsible for the success of the Hare Krishna movement, which offers a poor substitute for the individual's spiritual nourishment. Churches and synagogues should, if they want to counteract the success of the cults, make greater efforts to see that their members are given spiritual nourishment. The major solutions that both Christians and Jews have suggested to counteract the activity of the cults have been to underline the importance of religious education as a preventive measure and to engage in counterevangelization. Many have opted for, or at least considered, the use of legal means or deprogramming to return their offspring to the fold.

Balanced Views of ISKCON

Notwithstanding this general tendency to consider the new religious movements (ISKCON included) in a negative light, there are a few Christian and Jewish writers who, even though they favor the apologetic approach, are beginning to realize that sweeping indictments of the cults, condemning them one and all, are unrealistic. It is sometimes conceded that voluntary defection from the cults is a frequent occurrence, because the members have not been conditioned or programmed to such a degree that they are turned into mindless robots.[46] It would further be unfair to associate many of the new religious groups with the popular notion of a cult as a system of brainwashing and deception controlled by a leader who abuses power because physical coercion is lacking. Besides, one has to consider the possibility that cult members may have experienced a genuine religious conversion.[47] With these reflections in mind, the image of a cult member as a diabolically possessed or deceived individual ceases to be viable, which opens the way for relating to Hare Krishna devotees on an equal basis.

Both the legality and morality of deprogramming are now being questioned. The Lutheran Council in the United States of America warns that, besides being illegal, some deprogramming methods can be as destructive as the cult experience.[48] Some Christians have begun to wonder whether a warlike outlook toward the cults truly reflects their own genuine commitment to the Christian faith. Yamamoto has expressed this concern more forcefully than most writers. "It is a sad commentary on Christians," he writes, "when we followers of Christ look upon Krishna devotees with ridicule and derision, remarking how weird and strange they are. This is tragic in view of Christ's admonition that we are to be light to a dark world, salt to a starved people and love to crying hearts."[49]

On a more positive note, several authors have underscored the opportunity to learn from the cults.[50] Cults express the human concern for authentic religious values and have a right to their belief systems. There are indications that ISKCON is being recognized as a true religious movement in which divine revelation may have taken place.[51] Those who adhere to a much more restrictive view of revelation may still admit that the proper Christian response should be characterized more by understanding and sympathy than by violent acts perpetrated in the name of God or religion.

The Jewish reaction to the new movements also contains some balanced reflections and opinions. The influence of the cults on Jewish life may have, admittedly, been blown out of proportion. Jews often face serious problems of identity and survival. In point of fact, the Jewish community loses more young adults to suicide than to the Hare Krishna movement. ISKCON may not be such a terrifying cult. Moreover, the contention that the chanting of the Hare Krishna *mantra* causes brainwashing or induces hypnosis, and the depiction of Swami Prabhupada as a wanton guru in absolute control of his devotees' lives have been occasionally questioned.[52] Strong denunciations of deprogramming as being non-Jewish in ideology have started to surface within the Jewish community.[53]

These reflections suggest that perhaps Jews and Christians are realizing that there is something amiss with the way they are responding to the new movements—a way that is at times reminiscent of a holy war to be waged either in counterevangelism or in the courtrooms. These drastic measures have not achieved any permanent success, nor have they effectively dealt with, much less solved, some of the major issues that the presence of the new religious movements has brought to the fore.

Dialogue Between World Religions

Several authors have seen the new movements in the context of an increasingly pluralistic society in the West.[54] Both Christians and Jews are thus faced with an interaction between their respective religious traditions and Eastern religions on a scale never before encountered in history. The rather exclusive theologies that have pervaded both communities are now being reviewed. Christians and Jews are taking a broader ecumenical perspective to other religions and fostering a relationship of dialogue. In Christian theology one frequently starts by assuming that all religions share in a common essence, no matter how distorted this might have become in the course of history.[55]

While granting that there are serious differences that divide communities of faith, it is admitted that revelation and truth are present in all religions. Stressing mutually shared beliefs and collaborating on various fronts, rather than competition for members, become the primary goals in the relationship between the different religious groups.

One can observe a similar ecumenical spirit also among Jewish thinkers. Because of the Emancipation, Jews started to make frequent contacts with people of diverse faiths and, therefore, felt that they had to develop new ways of responding to the plurality of which they now were a small part. One way of counteracting religious ethnocentricity has been to regard religious truth as inherent in human reason and hence as available to all religions. Mendelssohn, for example, takes this position and goes on to argue that Jews do not possess the exclusive revelation leading to salvation. Both reason and the desire to safeguard freedom of conscience favor the existence of a pluralistic world in which no one asserts one's position over another's.[56] Fackenheim points out that the Jewish fear and condemnation of idolatry may have been responsible for their clannish mentality. But no living religion in our age can be regarded as idolatrous.[57] The doors for dialogue with IKSCON, a branch of Hinduism, are, therefore, open.

Several Jewish scholars[58] have emphasized the need for religions to maintain their identity and to renew themselves. The world's religions are a concrete witness of the many ways one can respond to God. Because the goals, ideals, and practices of many religions often overlap, they should act as partners and join forces in a spiritual battle against secularity.

Dialogue with ISKCON

This same model has been employed to promote an understanding of, and to form the basis of a better relationship with the Hare Krishna movement. Several Christian writers have pointed out that there are some similarities between Christianity and ISKCON. Charismatic and conservative Christians insist on a literal interpretation of sacred writings, generally adopt a rather anti-intellectual stance, and stress the need for a direct religious experience—qualities found also in ISKCON. Belief in a personal God who is a savior and who elicits complete devotion and total commitment is central in both religions.[59] There is thus a common ground between the two religious groups that can be used to further understanding and cooperation. One of the more important points of contact is monastic life.[60] Much of the austere life of the Hare Krishna devotees can be better understood in the light of the Christian monastic or puritanical tradition.

The suggestion that one could promote a dialogue with the members of ISKCON is also found explicitly in Christian evangelical literature, even though it has sometimes been adopted as a way of reaching out to those who have abandoned their faith.[61] No matter what position one takes regarding the relations between ISKCON and the established religions, theologians are becoming aware that ridicule is counterproductive behavior, intolerance is hardly a Christian virtue, and diatribe is not readily reconcilable with the Christian imperative of love.

Jewish writers have compared the Hare Krishna devotees with the Hassidic Jews, especially in their ideas regarding authority, their value of community, and their observance of strict rules. On a more theoretical level there is a point of contact between the Jewish *pinyele yid*, the spark that exists in every Jewish soul, and the Hare Krishna belief that after one makes contact with a spiritual master, a seed is planted in one's heart.[62]

Conclusion

The two models of apologetics and dialogue are to a large degree at odds with each other. Truly enough, they both assume that the religious and cultural conditions may be partly responsible for the rise and success of the new cults that are filling a religious vacuum that the churches and synagogues should never have allowed to occur in the first place. They both encourage the development of better religious education programs to meet the spiritual aspirations of young adults. They are based, however, on quite different assumptions about the place of one's own religion in the complex and varied religious traditions of the world. They disagree strongly on the significance and possible impact of the new movements and on the type of direct measures that should be taken to respond to them.

The apologetic approach to the cults has been dominant in Christian and Jewish circles for a number of reasons. First, it provides a model for interpreting, and reacting to, conversion to other religious traditions. Apologetics offers a concrete method for defending and reaffirming one's own religious belief system. It also appears to be the only solution to stem defections and the most reliable action one can take to reclaim members. Many of the so-called anti-cult activities have been undertaken with religious intent. Kidnapping and deprogramming a member of the Hare Krishnas can easily be conceived as pious acts of salvation and exorcism. The main liability of this model is that, pushed to its extreme form, it ceases to be, as several Jewish and Christian writers are realizing, a truly "religious" response to the cults.

The second model of dialogue has the advantage that it seeks understanding and possible cooperation against a common enemy, namely the materialistic and ungodly cultural environment. It could readily be proposed as an ideal religious solution to the spread of new religions in a culture that, though dominated by Judeo-Christian ideology, has emphasized religious liberty and has embraced the concept of religious pluralism without discrimination. From a Christian standpoint it could be argued that it promotes many Christian virtues, such as tolerance, kindness, and good neighborly relations. Its main flaw is that it has no convincing way of coping with the evangelical efforts of the cults and much less with the converts these have succeeded in attracting.

For these reasons Christian and Jewish religious reactions to the new cults are likely to remain both dominated by apologetic arguments and influenced by the anti-cult movement. Developments within the cults themselves will certainly have an impact, for better or for worse, on some of the hostile attitudes and belligerent actions described in this paper. Those cults that will, in the years ahead, achieve a measure of respectability and become self-contained religious systems and less blatantly evangelical in their recruitment techniques will probably not continue to elicit the same intense counterevangelism and forceful apologetics. Whether the Hare Krishna movement is heading in this direction remains to be seen.

Notes

1. Anson Shupe and David Bromley, *The New Vigilantes: Deprogrammers, Anti-Cultists, and the New Religions* (Beverly Hills, CA: Sage Publications, 1980).
2. Rabbi Balfour Brickner, "Christian Missionaries and Jewish Response," *Jewish Digest* 25 (Summer 1978): 10–19.
3. John Juedes, "Wierwille's Way with the Word," *Journal of Pastoral Practice* 4 (1980): 89–120.
4. Bob Larson, *Larson's Book of Cults* (Wheaton, IL: Tyndale, 1982), p. 71.
5. For some various Christian response to other religions, see John Hicks and Brian Hebblethwaite, eds., *Christianity and Other Religions* (Philadelphia: Fortress Press, 1981); and Paul F. Knitter, *No Other Name? A Critical Survey of Christian Attitudes Toward the World Religions* (New York: Orbis, 1985). One should also note that until relatively recent times the treatment of world religions in Christian theology came under apologetics.
6. The Lutheran Church seems to be one major exception because its various synods and committees have issued a number of statements on the new cults. See especially Ballard Pritchett, *Religious Cults* (Minneapolis, MN: The American Lutheran Church, 1976); Philip H. Lochhaas, *Hare Krishna: ISKCON* (St. Louis, MO: Lutheran Missouri Synod, n.d.); and Luther Council in the United States of America, *Deprogramming* (Chicago: 1977). The Pennsylvania Conference on Interchurch Cooperation issued a warning on the dangers of the cults in its 1979 meeting.
7. Herbert Richardson, ed., *Constitutional Issues in the Case of Reverend Moon: Amicus Briefs Presented to the United States Supreme Court* (Lewiston, NY: Edwin Mellen Press, 1985).
8. Walter Martin, *The New Cults* (Santa Ana, CA: Vision House, 1980), pp. 79–103.
9. Ronald Enroth et al., *A Guide to Cults and New Religions* (Downers Grove, IL: InterVarsity Press, 1983), p. 16.
10. The psychological features are usually cited without much reference to justifying sources. None of the writers seems to have had more than casual contact with cult members. See Hubert F. Beck, *How to Respond to the Cults* (St. Louis, MO: Concordia Publishing House, 1977), pp. 7–10; Una McManus and John Cooper, *Dealing with Destructive Cults* (Grand Rapids, MI: Zondervan, 1984), pp. 113–15; Larson, *Larson's Book of Cults*, p. 28; Carl T. Uehling, "Religion's Pied Pippers," *The Lutheran* (15 September 1976): 12; Richard Kyle, "The Cults: Why Now and Who Gets Caught?" *Journal of the American Scientific Affiliation* 33, no. 2 (June 1981): 94; and Enroth et al., *A Guide to Cults and New Religions*, pp. 17–

18. This view has received some official recognition (see statement issued by the Pennsylvania Conference on Interchurch Cooperation).

11. Josh McDowell and Don Stewart, *Understanding the Cults* (San Bernardino, CA: Here's Life, 1982), p. 27.

12. Larson, *Larson's Book of Cults*, pp. 18–21.

13. Margaret Thaler Singer, "Coming out of the Cults," *Psychology Today* 12, no. 8, (1979): 72; and Louis West and Margaret Thaler Singer, "Cults, Quacks and Non-professional Therapies," *Comprehensive Textbook of Psychiatry*, ed. H. Kaplan, A. Freedman, and B. Sadock (Baltimore: Williams and Wilkins, 1980), 3: 3246.

14. James A. Rudin and Marcia R. Rudin, *Prison or Paradise? The New Religious Cults* (Philadelphia: Fortress Press, 1980), pp. 16–18; and B'nai B'rith International, *How Much Do You Really Know About Those 'Religious' Cults?* (New York: n.d.).

15. William J. Petersen, *Those Curious New Cults* (New Canaan, CT: Keats, 1973), pp. 12–18; R. Medroff, "Cult Groups in Israel," *Jewish Digest* 29 (November 1982): 52.

16. Michael Appell, "Cult Encounters," *Moment* 4, no. 1 (1978): 20; Rabbi Jehudah Fine, "Interview," *Update* 8, no. 4 (December 1982): 89.

17. Idy B. Gitelson and Edward J. Reed, "Identity Status of Jewish Youth Pre- and Post-Cult Involvement," *Journal of Jewish Communal Service* 57 (1981): 318.

18. Martin, *The New Cults*, pp. 30–31.

19. Gordon Lewis, *Confronting the Cults.* (Nutley, NJ: Presbyterian and Reformed Publishing Co., 1977).

20. Marc Silver and Barbara Pash, "Cults," *Baltimore Jewish Times* (3 June 1977): 31–32; and Steven Jacobs, "Are Your Children Immune from Missionaries?" *Jewish Digest* 23 (December 1977): 10.

21. Rudin and Rudin, *Prison or Paradise?*, pp. 148–49.

22. Larson, *Larson's Book of Cults*, pp. 71–82, depicts a fairly stereotyped position. Though his view is not typical of theologians in most mainline churches, it is still, by and large, the popular view of Hinduism. Philip H. Lochhaas, *How to Respond to the Eastern Religions* (St. Louis, MO: Concordia, 1979), p. 8, states that the religions of the East are religions of despair. Leon McBeth, *Strange New Religions* (Nashville, TN: Broadman, 1977), p. 44, calls ISKCON "a religion of despair." Finally in his survey of Christian attitudes to world religions, Knitter evaluates this "conservative evangelical model" (*No Other Name?* pp. 75).

23. Stillson J. Judah, *Hare Krishna and the Counterculture*, (New York: Wiley and Sons, 1974).

24. It is not easy to find direct references to Tantrism in ISKCON. There is, however, some Tantric influence on the Vaisnavites (see B. Walker, *The Hindu World* (New York: Praeger, 1968), 2: 483. Judah, *Hare Krishna and the Counterculture*, pp. 22 and 24, maintains that the Hare Krishna movement depends also on Tantric texts.

25. Jack Sparkes, *The Mind Benders: A Look at Current Cults*, 2nd ed. (Nashville, TN: Nelson, 1977), pp. 112–21; Lowell D. Streiker, *The Cults are Coming* (Nashville, TN: Abingdon, 1978), p. 95.

26. McBeth, *Strange New Religions*, p. 36.

27. This is a touchy issue, especially among fundamentalist Christians who restrict revelation to the Judeo-Christian scriptures. See, for example, Martin, *The New Cults*, pp. 96–91; McBeth, *Strange New Religions*, p. 45; Kenneth Boa, *Cults, World Religions and You* (Wheaton, IL: Victor, 1979), p. 186; Pat Means, *The*

Mystical Maze (San Bernardino, CA: Campus Crusade for Christ, 1976), pp. 154–56; Isamu J. Yamamoto, "Hare Krishna (ISKCON," in *A Guide to Cults and New Religions*, ed. Enroth et al., p. 1011; and William Wood, "Who's This 'Harry' Krishna?" *Covenanter Witness* (19 November 1975): 6–7. To what degree the biblical argument is valid and effective can be debated (see Diana Eck, "Dialogue with the New Religious Movements," *Current Dialogue* 5 [Summer 1983]: 13, who states that such arguments have no place in the dialogue between religions).

28. Larson, *Larson's Book of Cults*, p. 4, for instance, states that the pagan worship in the Hare Krishna temples is plain idolatry. Habel G. Verghese, *Search for Inner Peace* (Van Nuys, CA: Bible Voice, 1977), p. 57, and McDowell and Stewart, *Understanding the Cults*, p. 51, are of the same opinion. On the other hand, Yamamoto, "Hare Krishna (ISKCON)," p. 99, and John P. Newport, *Christ and the New Consciousness* (Nashville, TN: Broadman, 1978), p. 32, hold that the Hare Krishna devotees worship a personal God. McBeth, *Strange New Religions*, p. 33; Martin, *The New Cults*, p. 96; Means, *The Mystical Maze*, pp. 151–52; and Sparkes, *The Mind Benders*, p. 95, see these beliefs as hovering between pantheism and theism. Gordon Lewis, *Confronting Religions from the East, Part IV: Hare Krishna*, (Denver, CO: Seminar Study Series, Conservative Baptist Theological Seminary, 1974), p. 3, thinks that in ISKCON the idea of God is contradictory, containing theistic, polytheistic, and pantheistic elements.

29. Means, *The Mystical Maze*, pp. 156–157; Louis Hughes, "Krishna Consciousness—I Was Wrong About Them," *Doctrine and Life* 24 (1983): 317–20.

30. Sparkes, *The Mind Benders*, p. 105.

31. Ronald Enroth, *Youth, Brainwashing and the Extremist Cults* (Grand Rapids, MI: Zondervan, 1977), p. 26; Philip H. Lochhaas, "Gurus' Gospel: Breaking the Chains," *The Lutheran Witness* (22 May 1977): 11–12.

32. Isamu J. Yamamoto, "Hare Krishna (ISKCON)," in Enroth et al., *A Guide to Cults and New Religions*, pp. 91–102.

33. Petersen, *Those Curious New Cults*, p. 170.

34. Cf. McBeth, *Strange New Religions*, p. 39, and Verghese, *Search for Inner Peace*, p. 53. There seems to be some difficulty in understanding, as well as lack of knowledge about, the way children are raised in ISKCON. Some think that the children of devotees are deprived of their parents' love and care (see Sparkes, *The Mind Benders*, p. 107); others however, assert that schoolchildren see parents on a regular basis (see Mark Sandlin, "Krishna Consciousness in West Virginia," *Beliefs of Other Kinds*, ed. E. Hullum [Atlanta, GA: Home Mission Board, Southern Baptist Convention, n.d.], p. 142). Jewish writers in particular are worried about the way children are treated in all cults.

35. Johannes Aagaard, "Has ISKCON Two Faces?" *Update* 7, no. 3 (September 1983): 20–21.

36. Dov Aharoni Fisch, *Jews for Nothing: On Cults, Intermarriage and Assimilation* (Jerusalem, NY: Feldheim Publishers, 1984), p. 154; and M. Yanoff, *Where is Joey? Lost Among the Hare Krishnas* (Athens, OH: Ohio University Press, 1981), p. 119.

37. Yanoff, *Where is Joey?*, pp. 208–10.

38. Silver and Pash, "Cults," pp. 32–33.

39. Rudin and Rudin, *Prison or Paradise?* pp. 17–18.

40. Almost every Christian writer on ISKCON mentions this reason. See, for example, Petersen, *Those Curious New Cults*, p. 171; William J. Whalen, *Strange Gods: Contemporary Religious Cults in America* (Huntington, IN: Our Sunday Visitor, 1981), p. 90; Earl Schipper, *Religions of the World* (Grand Rapids, MI: Baker

Book House, 1982), p. 49; Ed Senesi, "Hare Krishna Starved my Soul," *Escape from Darkness,* compiled by James R. Adair and Ted Miller (Wheaton, IL: Victor, 1982), p. 92; Boa, *Cults, World Religions and You,* p. 180; McBeth, *Strange New Religions,* p. 29; Paul Oxley, "Hare Krishna: It's Dogma and Delusion, Part I," *Advocate* (November 1976): 4; and Yamamoto, "Hare Krishna (ISKCON)," pp. 91–92.

41. Judah, *Hare Krishna and the Counterculture,* pp. 160–61.

42. Lochhaas, *How to Respond to the Eastern Religions,* pp. 29–30.

43. Harvey Cox, "A Christian Tribute to KRSNA Consciousness," *Back to Godhead* 12 (June 1977): 22.

44. Whalen, *Strange Gods: Contemporary Religious Cults in America,* p. 90; and Stephen J. Gelberg, ed., *Hare Krishna, Hare Krishna: Five Distinguished Scholars on the Krishna Movement in the West* (New York: Grove Press, 1983), p. 91.

45. Streiker, *The Cults are Coming,* p. 72; Boa, *Cults, World Religions and You,* p. 181.

46. McManus and Cooper, *Dealing with Destructive Cults,* pp. 45–46.

47. F. H. Touchet, "Cults: A Psycho-Social Overview," *Journal of Psychology and Theology* 8 (Winter 1980): 339–40.

48. Lochhaas, "Gurus' Gospel: Breaking the Chains," p. 39.

49. Yamamoto, "Hare Krishna (ISKCON)," p. 99.

50. Howard A. Wilson, *Invasion from the East* (Minneapolis, MN: Augsburg, 1978), p. 135; John A. Saliba, "The Christian Church and the New Religious Movements: Towards Theological Understanding," *Theological Studies* 43 (1982): 483; and Louis Rambo, "Door Interview," *The Wittenburg Door* (February–March 1981): 24.

51. Aloysius Fonseca, *"Gli Hare Krishna ela Bhagavad Gita,"* La Civilta Cattolica (3 July 1982): 45–46.

52. Solomon J. Spiro, "Probing the Cults," *Jewish Spectrum* 45 (Winter 1980): 31; Yanoff, *Where Is Joey?,* p. 122.

53. Ya'aqov Haramgaal, "Deprogramming: A Critical View," *The American Zionist* (May–June 1977): 18.

54. Gordon J. Melton and Robert Moore, *The Cult Experience: Responding to the New Religious Pluralism* (New York: Schocken, 1969), p. 93; and Bradley Hanson, *Isms and Issues: Religious Movements of our Times* (Minneapolis, MN: Augsburg Publishing House, 1977), p. 15.

55. The literature on the Christian theology of religions is voluminous. See, for example, the works of Donald Dawe and John B. Carman, eds., *Christian Faith in a Religiously Plural World* (New York: Orbis, 1978); Alan Race, *Christians and Religious Pluralism* (New York: Orbis, 1982); Arnulf Camps, Partners in Dialogue: Christianity and Other World Religions (New York: Orbis, 1980); Paul Clasper, *Eastern Paths and the Christian Way,* (New York: Orbis, 1980); and Knitter, *No Other Name?.* Francis Arinze, "The Urgency of Dialogue with Non-Christians," *Origins* 14, no. 39 (14 March 1985): 641–50, gives an excellent summary of the Roman Catholic position and of the work carried out by the Secretariat for Non-Christians since Vatican Council II.

56. Moses Mendelssohn, *Jerusalem* (New York: Schocken, 1969), pp. 66, 107.

57. Emile Fackenheim, *Encounters Between Judaism and Modern Philosophy* (New York: Basic Books, 1973), p. 173.

58. Abraham Heschel, *Man is not Alone: A Philosophy of Religion* (New York: Harper and Row, 1951), p. 182; Daniel S. Bresslauer, *The Ecumenical Perspective and the Modernization of Jewish Religion* (Missoula, MT: Scholars Press, 1978), pp. 17–

19; and Jacob B. Agus, *Dialogue and Tradition: The Challenge of Contemporary Judeo-Christian Thought* (New York: Schuman, 1971), p. 429.

59. Yamamoto, "Hare Krishna (ISKCON)," p. 100.

60. Rev. Edward McCorkell, "A Monastic Encounter," *Back to Godhead* 13 (December 1979): 21; and Gelberg, *Hare Krishna, Hare Krishna*, p. 27.

61. Yamamoto, *"Hare Krishna, (ISKCON),"* pp. 20–21.

62. Silver and Pash, "Cults," pp. 15–16.

Psychiatry and Krishna Consciousness

James S. Gordon

From the time he arrived on New York's lower East Side in 1965, A. C. Bhaktivedanta Swami Prabhupada and the International Society for Krishna Consciousness (ISKCON) that he founded have been controversial. The particular brand of Vaisnavism (Krishna is an Incarnation of the god Vishnu) and Krishna *bhakti* (devotion) he practiced and taught were derived from the millennia-old Vedic scriptures and modeled on the sixteenth-century Caitanyite revival movement in East Bengal. The practices and dress of the Western devotees whom Prabhupada initiated in New York and San Francisco were, however, strange to American eyes. The repetitive public chanting of the Hare Krishna *mantra*, the traditional Indian dress, the shaved heads of the men, the sometimes aggressive fundraising practices, and the ascetic, rigidly regulated lifestyle all seemed bizarre and, to many, repulsive.

As concern about new and deviant religions grew in the early 1970s, ISKCON—along with the Unification Church, the Church of Scientology, the Divine Light Mission and other groups—was labeled a "cult." The word "cult" has traditionally referred in general parlance to devotion to a particular deity, teacher, or religious practice, but has, since its introduction into English five hundred years ago, been given pejorative connotations. Cults and their members have been usually regarded as deviant, deluded, and perhaps dangerous. Consequently, ISKCON members—with their distinctive garb, unusual practices, and high visibility on the street, in shopping malls, and airports—were often viewed as prototypical cultists.

From the beginning there has been much disagreement and little knowledge in the psychiatric and mental health community about the nature of ISKCON and its practices. Many of the early mental health professionals had their attention drawn to ISKCON by parents who were deeply troubled about their children's membership. They examined young people who had been forcibly removed and deprogrammed from ISKCON as well as others who were still in the group. They used existing models of brainwashing and coercive persuasion to characterize ISKCON's techniques of indoctrination, its religious practices—chanting and deity worship—and its collective rituals and lifestyle.[1] On occasion, they testified in court to the pathogenic effects of ISKCON's system of "mind control."[2]

Other clinicians—and sociologists, theologians, historians of religion, and anthropologists—have disputed this perspective. They have stressed the comparison between ISKCON and traditional religious or modern countercultural and therapeutic groups.[3] Some warned against stigmatizing ISKCON and "medicalizing" its deviance.[4] Later, researchers undertook clinical studies to evaluate the mental health of individual ISKCON members.[5]

These diverse perspectives and findings have had very real effects on the lives of ISKCON members and their families and have helped shape public perceptions of the group. The brainwashing/mind control perspective has been used by parents as a justification for kidnapping and "deprogramming" adult children who were ISKCON members and for suing the organization. The therapeutic and religious perspectives have, in turn, been used by ISKCON and individual members to defend themselves.

In this paper I will review the psychiatric and psychological literature on ISKCON, address its limitations, and sketch a larger framework for understanding this group and its members. My perspective is informed by eighteen years of occasional participant-observation of ISKCON and its practices in the United States and India; by lengthy interviews with more than forty present and former ISKCON members of all ages; and by participant-observation studies of a number of other new religions.

The mental health literature on ISKCON may be divided into two categories: surveys of new religious groups and their present and former members in which ISKCON devotees and their practices have been included and, on occasion, specifically discussed; and clinical studies that focus on present members of ISKCON.

Surveys

All the surveys are unsystematic and do not provide much reliable data on ISKCON. They do, however, discuss ISKCON as one of many new religious groups (often simply called cults), such as the Unification Church, the Divine Light Mission, and the Church of Scientology, which it is assumed to resemble in a number of ways. These discussions offer general observations on and information about the character of new religions and those who join them as well as occasional specific observations on ISKCON and its members. One group of surveys views new religions as legitimate alternatives to traditional religious and social groupings and as therapeutic institutions that often provide valuable social and psychological benefits to their members. Opponents usually view new religions in general, and ISKCON in particular, as destructive and coercive institutions, subversive of the established religious, social, and therapeutic order, and deleterious to the mental health of individual members.

Papers by Gordon,[6] Levine,[7] Ungerleider and Wellisch,[8] and Galanter[9] fall into the first category. These generally begin with an attempt to explain the current proliferation of new religions and their attractiveness, particularly to young adults. For example, I wrote ten years ago, "In the religious cults which seemed to arise almost miraculously to meet their needs, they (young people) found both a confirmation of their private longings and a group structure which can help them overcome their isolation. In the web of exotic and highly rationalized theologies they discovered and tenaciously held onto an unerring map, one that could guide them beyond the limitations and uncertainties of secular and political goals."[10] Levine said of those who joined new religions, "They are reactors. They reflected dissatisfaction with contemporary society and particularly with their personal stake in it."[11] Elsewhere he noted new converts' sense of "alienation," "meaninglessness," "powerlessness," and "low self-esteem."

Having established the psychological need that new religions fulfill, this group of surveys goes on to discuss the incidence of various degrees of serious psychopathology among those who join. They vary considerably in their estimates. In his examination of 453 members of a variety of groups, including ISKCON, Levine found "severe psychiatric problems" in 57.[12] He noted that "there is no evidence that devotees are any more disturbed using any psychological classification than comparable peers in the general population." In a similar vein, Ungerleider and Wellisch found no evidence of "insanity or mental illness in the legal sense" among the 50 present and former members whom they interviewed and tested psychologically.[13] By contrast, Galanter in his studies of the Unification Church and Divine Light Mission noted a "higher than average percentage of previous hospitalizations in members than in the general population."[14] "Certain sects," he added, citing studies by Deutsch and Kiev and Francis on "Baba" and "Subud" "attract members with considerable psychopathology."[15]

Although the authors of these surveys vary in their estimates of the incidence of severe psychopathology in members-to-be, all noted the positive psychological benefits for most who joined. Some writers focused on common factors that alleviated distress, enhanced the members' well being, and gave them a feeling of meaning and purpose. I listed transcendent experience, a family feeling, the security of leadership and authority, a sense of community and an overriding world-saving mission as common appealing characteristics of many of the groups.[16]

Other writers drew even sharper analogies between new religions and psychotherapy, the saving of souls and the treatment of illness. Levine noted that "many of the characteristics inherent in these religions—belief, ritual, dogma, hierarchy, sanctioned language, trappings and altered states are similar to some systems of psychotherapy."[17] "The cults," Levine added several years later, "can serve as a haven and even a therapeutic milieu for members with various psychiatric or behavioral disorders."[18]

Kilbourne and Richardson made the comparison most explicit.[19] Citing Frank they listed four common characteristics of psychotherapy and new religions: "a special supportive relationship"; "a special setting imbued with powerful symbols of expertise, help, hope and healing"; "a special rationale, ideology or indisputable myth that explains health, illness and normality"; and "a special set of rituals and practices."[20] To this they added two more common denominators: the ability to provide immediate feedback and a *corrective* experience. The new religions and psychotherapy were, they concluded, structurally similar enterprises competing for a common pool of potential patient-converts.

Galanter, who conducted studies of members of the Unification Church and the Divine Light Mission (but not of ISKCON), described some aspects of the new religions' therapeutic effectiveness. He wrote of a "biological relief effect" that new converts experienced as they identified with and integrated themselves into the group.[21] This relief effect, which he believed to be a common denominator of new religions, was promoted by the groups' "distinctive character" and their isolation from outsiders and their beliefs. Using standardized tests, including the General Well-Being Schedule, he documented "considerable and sustained relief from neurotic distress" among the vast majority of converts. Galanter saw these "charismatic large groups" as analogous in certain ways to Alcoholics Anonymous, drug-free therapeutic communities, and other self-help groups.

In their surveys, Gordon, Levine, and Ungerleider and Wellisch all discussed ex-members' difficulties in leaving groups to which they had committed themselves and from which they had obtained social support, emotional security, meaning, and purpose. "Questions, choices, and ambiguities returned and are," Levine wrote, "often overwhelming to the ex-cultist . . . the difficulties inherent in the process of leaving a closed, cohesive, pressured and unidimensional social system and once again being confronted by the very feelings that made one vulnerable to begin with—alienation, demoralization, low self-esteem—are often more than the ex-cultist can manage on his or her own."[22]

The second group of surveys argues that new religions are pathogenic rather than therapeutic to the individuals who join them. These studies are concerned primarily, though not exclusively, with people who are in transition from new religious groups. They rely, more than the previous group, on retrospective accounts of membership and emphasize the family's perspective on the changes in the individual who has joined the new religion. In contrast to the series that explicitly or tacitly compared new religions with psychotherapy, the frame of reference here is, in Margaret Singer's words, "coercive persuasion and the techniques of 'brainwashing' as they were experienced by former prisoners of war."[23]

Singer, whose work on the destructive effect of "cults" is perhaps most widely known, cites her own studies with Edgar Schein on American prisoners of war in Korea and Lifton's work on Chinese thought reform as paradigmatic.[24] She believes that the physical force used by Korean and Chinese jailors on unwilling captives has its analogy in psychological and social pressure that cults, including ISKCON, apply to vulnerable victims.

Having attracted people who previously "had a sense that life was meaningless," the cults "maintain intense allegiance through their arguments, their ideology and through social and psychological pressures and practices that, intentionally or not, amount to conditioning techniques that constrict attention, limit personal relationships and devalue reasoning."[25] Singer concludes that cults like ISKCON produce significant psychopathology in members and even greater emotional difficulties for those who leave.

In an article that focused on members "Coming Out of the Cults," Singer described the psychological difficulties of ex-members.[26] They suffered from "depression and loneliness," a "blurring of (their) mental acuity," and an "uncritical passivity," which led to their "inability to listen and judge." They were subject to "episodes of 'floating,' like the flashbacks of drug users," when they "returned to the trance-like state they knew in cult days." They experienced "fear of the cults" and guilt at the deceptive practices in which they had engaged while in the group. Many, she reported, felt that as ex-members they had lost their status as part of a world-saving elite.

Like Singer, John Clark and Flo Conway and James Siegelman have relied primarily on retrospective reports from former and deprogrammed members of the new religions and their families to formulate hypotheses about the groups and their effects on the mental status of current members.[27] Clark, a psychiatrist, reported a "clinical study . . . during which 50 individuals" (some of whom were present or former

ISKCON members) *"were directly examined by me as well as over 75 sets of parents."* The study also "includes material from over 150 other subjects seen by other clinicians" (including Singer). Clark identified "deliberate blatant deceit, distortion of reality, and intense group pressure" as factors in the coercive persuasion that ISKCON and other groups used to recruit and maintain members. These, he hypothesized, produced a state of *"narrowed attention"* and high suggestibility, which was, in turn, intensified and sustained "by systematic deprivation of familiar reality and sleep."[28]

Clark separated those whom he interviewed into three groups. Forty percent of those he examined had "no history of any significant prior emotional or developmental problems. The remaining 60 percent were divided between 'seekers' who had tried many unsuccessful avenues to personal comfort such as drugs, other cults, mind control courses, etc." and "delinquent or sociopathic personalities." "Some" of the seekers— he does not specify how many—"had been formerly diagnosed as schizophrenic, borderline state or character disorders" and many had been contending chronically with psychotic thinking. The "delinquents" and "sociopaths" by contrast saw "in cult membership, opportunities to legitimize deviant behavior under the cover of religion."[29]

In his examination of those who had left groups, Clark found "a sameness among these subjects, a smothering smog of drab conformity and shallowness" which he attributed to membership in the group.[30] They were, he noted, "often described by stunned and terrified parents as totally changed . . . drastically altered in personality—a mutilation of the original—with a poverty of memories and hopes and of the richly expressive use of language. . . . In some subjects," he went on, "formal thought disorder had developed, not immediately distinguishable from that of schizophrenia." He noted that many of these signs and symptoms were similar to those observed in "temporal lobe epilepsy, endogenous depression and chronic schizophrenia" and hypothesized that organic changes may have taken place in the brains of people who had been subject to manipulation by the various cults.

In an article in *Science Digest*, Siegelman and Conway—who are social scientists, not clinicians—reported on interviews with "more than 400 former cult members from 48 different groups including the five major international religious cults."[31] Among the latter they list ISKCON. Seventy-one percent of those in their survey had been deprogrammed, forty percent of them after forcible abduction.

Conway and Siegelman saw these former cult members as victims of a "form of mind control," an "information disease" precipitated by the "use—and abuse—of information . . . deceptive and distorted language,

artfully designed suggestion and intense emotional experience, crip-
pling tactics aggravated by physical exhaustion and isolation."

The leaders of cults, they go on, use "calls to surrender," to "let things
float," which serve as "self-hypnotic rituals," to "close off the recruit's
mind to doubts, questions, and disquieting memories of family and the
outside world." According to the reports they later gave Siegelman and
Conway, these members had, while in the group, suffered from "phys-
iological problems," including "extreme weight gain or loss, abnormal
skin conditions such as rashes, eczema, acne, menstrual dysfunction in
women and higher pitched voices and reduced facial hair growth in men
. . . feelings of fear, guilt, hostility and depression, sexual dysfunction,
violent outbursts and self-destructive or suicidal tendencies." Siegelman
and Conway attributed these changes to "intense indoctrination,"
which, they hypothesized, might have brought about "a reorganization
of long-standing synaptic microstructure."[32]

Siegelman and Conway attacked "two groups in particular" that
"showed signs of inflicting the most severe physical and mental and
emotional harm on their members: the Hare Krishnas and the Church of
Scientology."

Clinical Studies

In addition to the surveys that included ISKCON members, there is
also a group of clinical studies of the personality characteristics of present ISKCON members and the effect of membership on them. Some of
these studies are based on case reports and informal surveys. Others are
more sophisticated methodologically and derive from controlled clinical
or experimental studies.

Several of the early anecdotal studies were concerned with analyzing
the specific appeal of ISKCON and its fit with preexisting personality
characteristics of devotees. Kutty offered a case report of a 15-year-old
boy who suffered "narcissistic blows . . . in his attempts at heterosexual
relationships," which "led to a feeling of inadequacy."[33] According to
Kutty, the young man was clearly "running from situations he found
intolerable and was searching for something new. Identifying with the
Hare Krishna movement provided some answers: for example, denial of
sexuality (in ISKCON's celibacy) and, therefore, avoidance of heterosexual narcissistic blows; approval of dependent relationships (in submission to a guru); and anti-materialistic and anti-establishment beliefs
which helped him in de-idealizing his parents in the process of separation."

Looking at Krishna worship from a Jungian perspective, Kenney provided some support for this conclusion. After interviewing three de-

votees at New Talavan, the Krishna temple at Carriere, Mississippi, he noted that "Krishna Consciousness ethical theory (including no gambling, no meat-eating, no intoxicants and no illicit sex) validated the ascetic lifestyle they were living prior to their conversion."[34] In a theoretical paper on sexual sublimation and Krishna Consciousness, Kenney and Poling saw membership as an opportunity for sublimation rather than repression of sexuality.[35] Krishna was a symbol for transformation, love of Krishna a means for "personality recentering and integration."

When Poling used the Myers-Briggs Type Indicator (based on Jung's theory of psychological types) in a study of fourteen ISKCON volunteers, he found a "highly homogeneous group."[36] Thirteen of the subjects "scored high in thinking, sensing and judging with seven favoring extroversion and six introversion." Poling noted the "general behavior and attitudinal features associated with the common elements of these two profiles include: a preference for working with known facts rather than possibilities or relationships; use of impersonal analysis and logic rather than personal values for making judgments; and a strong preference for a planned orderly way of life rather than a flexible spontaneous lifestyle."[37]

Gerson administered the Minnesota Multiphasic Personality Inventory (MMPI), Rorschach test, the Edwards Personal Preference Schedule, an IQ test, the Cornell Index of Medical History and Symptoms, and a Neuroticism Scale to fifty-two ISKCON volunteers in Southern California.[38] He noted that seventy-three percent of the "people that I tested fell within normal range of functioning on the MMPIs." On the Rorschach test, long-time devotees were found to be "assertive, meticulous and expansive," whereas newer devotees were "more insecure, impulsive, and lacking social confidence." The IQ of the entire group fit the normal bell-shaped curve.

More recently, investigators have undertaken more methodologically rigorous studies. In a 1983 paper, Michael Ross reported on a study of the entire population of the Hare Krishna Temple, in Melbourne, Australia.[39] He administered the MMPI, the General Health Questionnaire, and the Eysenck Personality Questionnaire, then randomly selected six subjects to take the "present-state examination." Ross noted that in all cases the mean scores on the MMPI were well within the normal range; the mean F-K ratio did, however, suggest there was a moderate attempt for both men and women to "look good."

When Ross presented his forty-two profiles to two outside assessors who did not know that the profiles were those of Krishna devotees, they "found no clear evidence of pathology" in the subjects. Similarly, all results on the Eysenck Personality Questionnaire and the General

Health Questionnaire were in the normal range. Ross did note that those who had been in the movement for more than one and one-half years were "less secure and more intolerant of suggestions that they were less than perfect . . . less expansive and outgoing than those who had been in the movement for less than one and one-half years." On the other hand, those who had been in the movement longer than three years scored as "more conventional and less rebellious." He concluded that the Hare Krishna devotees, "although clearly engaging in an unusual movement from a Western point of view, are well within the normal range of psychological adjustment."

In a follow-up study four years later, Ross readministered the MMPI to the fifteen devotees—out of the original forty-two—who remained in Australia.[40] This sample did not differ from those who were not available for retest either on initial MMPI scores or demographic variables. There were, Ross noted, "seven changes of personality profile and all but one of these were in a positive direction." In particular the F-K ratio was significantly different, going from -15.7 in 1979 to -10.9 in 1983. The respondents, Ross concluded, were less concerned about looking good, and, according to his interpretation, "probably had an increase in self-confidence as a result of an additional four years in the Hare Krishna movement." Before he concluded this study, Ross published a case history of one devotee whose testing was illustrative.[41]

In 1985, Lilliston, a child psychologist, spent two weeks studying seventy children at ISKCON's Lake Huntington *Gurukula* (school). He observed the children in dormitories and classrooms, during worship services and mealtimes, at play and during fund raising activities in neighboring communities. He interviewed teachers, caretakers, administrators, and, where possible, parents and other visitors to the *gurukula*.

Thirty of the children were selected by the headmaster of the school for a "complete clinical assessment including the Wechsler Intelligence Scale for Children–Revised, the Bender Visual Motor Gestalt Test, the Draw-a-Person Technique, a moral dilemma measure, a projective story-telling technique and a clinical interview."[42]

After reviewing the data, Lilliston concluded that "the rate of psychiatric symptomatology was not greater than that found in the general population. Of the thirty children, one child displayed greater than normal anxiety and one was clinically hyperactive." The children also "performed well intellectually on both the information subtests of the WISC-R . . . and the comprehension subtest." Similarly, the "scores on the wide range achievement test were, on the average, three grades above appropriate age level on reading and spelling and one grade above appropriate age on arithmetic." Although the stories the children elected to tell "generally involved Krishna Consciousness themes, the numbers and types of themes produced were consistent with typical findings and cognitive flexibility was high."[43]

Lilliston found no deficit in the children's "moral reasoning," in their "self-monitoring" (awareness of one's thought processes, bodily feelings, and one's role in a given situation) and "self regulation" in the "spontaneity in classroom situations or play." He concluded that ISKCON's assumptions about childrearing (an emphasis on obedience, integration into the group, and service to others), and on education primarily as preparation for spiritual growth had not in any way impaired children "emotionally, cognitively, or behaviorally."[44]

Weiss's 1985 dissertation study of (226 individuals: 132 males and 94 females) adult Hare Krishna "devotees and sympathizers (people who have not yet been formally initiated into the group)" at eight different sites in the United States is the most extensive so far done and most methodologically sophisticated.[45] He used the Rand Corporation Mental Health Inventory, the Comrey Personality Scales, and a scale that he developed called the "Hare Krishna Acculturation Scale," which measured degree of immersion and acculturation into the movement. He used large control groups for each scale and a sophisticated factor analysis to demonstrate their applicability.

Weiss concluded that the mental health and the "rate of disturbance" of devotees and sympathizers were not significantly different from those of Americans matched for sex, age, and education.[46] Using factor analytic techniques to compare the mental health of long-term and recent members, he found no negative effects from "immersion and acculturation" in the movement. He did note a tendency for males to score more positively on the "well-being" scales than females in the movement but found the same tendency in his control groups.

Discussion

Each of the categories and vitually all of the papers within them shed some light on ISKCON. At the same time the methodology and the observations and conclusions to which they lead are either flawed or limited.

All of the surveys have inherent limitations. In lumping widely disparate groups together, the surveys inevitably blur distinctions among the groups. Findings obtained in a careful study of one group, like Galanter's study of the Unification Church,[47] do not necessarily apply to a group like ISKCON, which shares certain formal characteristics with the Unification Church but from which it differs in many important respects. Nor are conclusions about any group based on interviews with a small number of adherents particularly reliable. Finally, insufficient distinctions are made between the experiences of present and former members and inadequate attention is paid to the influence of their social milieu—as loyal group members or disillusioned ex-members—on their responses.

Those surveys that tacitly or overtly compare new religions to psychotherapeutic groups—like Levine's, Ungerleider and Wellisch's, and Galanter's—and cite the positive effect of membership on mental health are useful but myopic and potentially misleading. A group that improves the mental health of its members, whether according to self reports or before and after measurements, is not necessarily a healthy group. An obvious example is provided by nazism in Germany in the 1930s. Membership in the Hitler Youth may have reduced anxiety and helped young people to resolve an identity crisis, but it encouraged them to participate unquestioningly in heinous acts. Some perspective on the aims and results of a particular group and the lifestyle and ideological basis or context of membership must provide the context for evaluating the information gained from the measurements of mental health of their members.

Similarly, the fact that there are formal similarities between new religions and psychotherapy does not mean that new religions should be studied as if they were psychotherapies or that their effects on members should only be measured by conventional psychometrics. The religious experience has its own dimensions and produces changes in individuals that are not necessarily amenable to easy psychological analysis. Is St. Francis's talking to the birds indicative of a psychotic, deluded man, or has he, through prayer, meditation, and grace come to apprehend and live in an altered state of consciousness in which he and the birds are joined in a common participation in the natural or, indeed, God's created world?

The surveys of Singer, Clark, and Conway and Siegelman that assume that the techniques of conversion of an individual (indoctrination into a group and maintenance of allegiance) are analogous to the techniques used on unwilling captives are equally limited and even more misleading. Psychological pressure, information overload, and induced guilt are, perhaps, unpleasant, coercive, and obnoxious but they are not analogous to physical force. Without physical compulsion to join or force applied to make people stay, the analogy to Korean brainwashing and Chinese thought reform breaks down.

Similarly, analogies drawn between cult membership and medical illness are spurious. There is, at least at this time, no evidence for the biochemical changes that Clark and Siegelman and Conway postulate. Nor, contrarily, is there any evidence that the postulated biochemical changes are any different from those experienced by participants in mainstream religious groups or any other enthusiastic experience.

This survey research is flawed in other ways. It is based largely on interviews with ex-members. From their retrospective accounts, sometimes obtained years after they have left the groups, the investigators draw conclusions about their mental status while they were members. Such a procedure ignores both the effect of the intervening years and the bias that leaving a movement usually creates. All available studies including Singer's and Clark's demonstrate the difficulties that *leaving* ISKCON and other groups create for the ex-devotee. It does not necessarily follow that prior membership created these difficulties. If we assume this is so, it is analogous to finding that marriage creates the individual and personal difficulties of a divorced spouse.

Many of those interviewed—more than seventy percent in Siegelman and Conway's work—have been deprogrammed. Often deprogrammers admonish ex-members to view "the cult"—ISKCON in this case—and its practices as malignant and themselves as its victims. People who have been encouraged to see themselves in this light may well reinterpret retrospectively experiences that once seemed comprehensible and enriching. If they are to perpetuate the belief that they were victims, they may disparage their intelligence, stability, and free will while in the group, and attribute to the group a coercive power that they did not experience at the time. Most of the rest of the subjects of these studies are self-selected volunteers, many of whom felt the need for counseling to deal with problems encountered on leaving ISKCON.

Finally, most of the subjects in the negative studies are reporting their experiences to investigators who are known publicly for their "anti-cult" position. Like subjects of other clinical studies, they will, perhaps unconsciously, shade their perspective to fit that of the investigator. Nor can the investigators themselves help but bring their bias both to the interview situation and the interpretation of the data.

The anecdotal studies of present ISKCON members, though they provide useful information, are limited in their significance both by the size of their samples and their selection procedures. Their outcomes are also, obviously, shaped by the theoretical perspective of the researcher: a Freudian[48] sees repression in ISKCON's approach to sexuality, whereas Jungians[49] find sublimation.

There is also some bias in the generally favorable and better designed clinical studies. The increased F-K ratio in Ross's first study suggests, as he notes, "an attempt to look good."[50] The same reservation must be applied to the results of all the other studies of present ISKCON members. These are people whose behavior and beliefs are under constant attack, who in the course of missionary and fundraising efforts must seek to explain and justify incomprehensible and often offensive practices to people who are, at best, indifferent, and often hostile to them. Clearly, they have learned to look as good as they possibly can—both to buttress their own sense of self-esteem and to shape the responses of those with whom they are speaking. There is no question that, insofar as they are able, they will try to "look good" for researchers whose findings may well affect the public's attitude toward them and, indeed, the outcome of legal proceedings against them. Kuner's work demonstrates that this was, in fact, true for Unification Church members.[51]

The same caveat must be applied to any studies that permit ISKCON leadership to select, supervise, or administer interviews or questionnaires that researchers have designed. Thus, the selection of the thirty children who answered Lilliston's questions and of the devotees who responded to Weiss's questionnaires may have been influenced by ISKCON leaders' preferences for those who would do well or "look good."

Still, taken together, these clinical studies offer a statistical confirmation of the surveys on the possible psychological benefits of membership in new religions and a response to those on the deleterious effects of membership on mental health. Membership in the admittedly authoritarian, highly structured, culturally distinct society of ISKCON does not appear to induce mental illness or decrease the intelligence of adults; nor, so far as we can now determine, does the schooling ISKCON gives its children diminish their creativity or inhibit their intelligence.

The major limitations of these studies are not so much in their findings and methodology as in their scope and perspective. An adequate understanding of ISKCON and its members requires phenomenological investigation as well as sociological, anthropological, and psychological analysis, a temporal and developmental perspective as well as carefully isolated and analyzed glimpses.

ISKCON is a religion imported from India; an attempt to create monastic and lay communities modeled on the prescriptions of millennia-old Vedic texts. In these communities, every aspect of daily life is sacralized and all effort is directed to creating and propagating a God-centered devotionalism, which is called Krishna Consciousness. Any comprehensive investigation has first to assess ISKCON on its own terms. What is the ideal of Krishna Consciousness? How successful is ISKCON in bringing it about in its members? Why is it appealing now to young Westerners? What kinds of experiences—religious as well as psychological and social—do they have while in the group? What are the roles of chanting, dance, prayer, and radically changed diet in bringing about this devotional consciousness? What problems do members who try to achieve Krishna Consciousness face? How does the structure of the group and its ideology help to resolve—or compound—these problems? Only after answering these and other questions can analysis and judgment be justified and authoritative.

At the same time, it is important to evaluate the accusations made by psychiatric studies and ex-members, to take a critical look at conditions and practices that shape life in ISKCON. For example, how have the sometimes deceptive fundraising practices, which critics have noted and which more sympathetic observers confirm, affected the worldview of devotees? Are these practices a temporary aberration of a new movement, born of unchecked zeal, or are they a more permanent and basic fixture encouraged by and encouraging of a sense of superiority? Is ISKCON, in fact, creating a self-serving and arrogant religious elite that may justify any means, including deception, to achieve its ends?

There are other questions that deserve attention as well. For example, are the prohibitions against sexuality repressive or conducive to the kind of successful spiritual sublimation that Kenney and Poling only sketchily described; or are they, as I see it, repressive for some, and life-enhancing for others? Is obedience to the authority of the guru-Prabhupada and his successors a device for spiritual maturation? Or does it foster a regressive dependence on an all-powerful authority figure? Are guilt and shame and threats of eternal damnation used to promote adherence to group norms and prevent defection? And, if so, what are their consequences? These are subtle questions that cannot be answered by facile generalizations or, indeed, conventional psychometrics. They require prolonged study of the group, in-depth interviews with leaders and disciples, and a disciplined subjectivity that admits to and seeks to transcend its own bias.

ISKCON, like other new religions, must be seen as an evolving organization whose members are themselves maturing emotionally and spiritually. To judge the group by practices and attitudes that it has now outgrown is uninformative as well as unfair. My own impression, for example, is that some—but not all—of the fanaticism and dogmatism, the rigid separation of the spiritual elite within the group and the enlightened ones outside, may be dissipating. There is, at present, more intercourse with the outside world, less fear of group boundaries being broken, and more self-criticism. Changes in the children's diet have been made and schooling has improved greatly. A new laity committed to the practices of ISKCON, but not the monastic lifestyle, is forming. Increasingly, the group has opened itself to outside scholarship and enlisted the aid of consultants—educators and medical and mental health practitioners—to help them develop their programs. On the other hand,

deception in fundraising—and the self-righteousness and secretiveness
that justify and perpetuate it—continues.

Any comprehensive attempt to understand and appreciate ISKCON
and its effect on the mental health of its members must move beyond the
initial impetus to condemn or justify a new and deviant movement. In
short, we need to achieve a phenomenological approach to the organization and its members' aims and goals: respect for religious life as a
legitimate option, and spiritual development as an avenue for self-
development, must inform and balance psychological evaluation and
organizational criticism. Only then will we have a fair picture of the
movement, its effects on its members' lives, and its lessons for the larger
society. Only then will we, informed by our study of ISKCON and other
new religions, have developed a psychology that includes and honors
the religious dimension of experience.

Notes

1. M. Singer, "Coming Out of the Cults," *Psychology Today* (1979): 72–82; L. J.
West and M. T. Singer, *Cults, Quacks and Non-professional Psychotherapies: Com-
prehensive Textbook of Psychiatry,* 3rd ed., ed. H. Kaplan and B. Sadock (Baltimore:
Williams and Wilkins, 1980), pp. 3245–58; J. C. Clark, M. D. Lagone, R. E.
Schecter, and R. C. B. Dailey, *Destructive Cult Conversion: Theory, Research and
Treatment* (Weston, MA: American Family Foundation, 1981); J. C. Clark, "The
Manipulation of Madness" (Paper presented in Hanover, West Germany, Febru-
ary 1978, graphic copy pp. 1–22; J. Conway and F. Siegelman, *Snapping: America's
Epidemic of Sudden Personality Change* (Philadelphia: Lippincott, 1978); and F.
Siegelman and J. Conway, "Information Disease: Have Cults Created a New
Mental Illness?" *Science Digest* 90 (January 1982): 86–92.

2. *George* vs. *ISKCON et al.,* Santa Ana, California, 3 May 1983.

3. J. S. Gordon, "Kids and the Cults," *Children Today* 24–27 and 36 (July–
August 1977); S. V. Levine, "Youth and Religious Cults: Societal and Clinical
Dilemma," *Adolescent Psychiatry* 6 (1978): 75–89; S. V. Levine, "Cults and Mental
Health: Clinical Conclusions," *Canadian Journal of Psychiatry* 26 (December 1981):
534–39; J. F. Ungerleider and D. K. Wellisch, "Coercive Persuasion and Brainwashing: Religious Cults and Deprogramming," *American Journal of Psychiatry*
136, no. 3 (1979): 279–82; M. Galanter, "Charismatic Religious Sects and Psychiatry: An Overview," *American Journal of Psychiatry* 139 (December 1982): 1539–48;
M. Galanter, "The Relief Effect: A Sociobiological Model for Neurotic Distress
and Large Group Therapy," *American Journal of Psychiatry* 135 (1978): 588–91; M.
Galanter and P. Buckley, "Evangelical Religion and Meditation: Psychotherapeutic Effects," *Journal of Nervous and Mental Disease* 166 (1978): 685–91; J. S.
Judah, *Hare Krishna and the Counterculture* (New York: Wiley Interscience, 1974);
and J. S. Gordon, "The Cult Phenomenon and the Psychotherapeutic Response," *Journal of the American Academy of Psychoanalysis* 11 (1983): 603–15.

4. T. Robbins and D. Anthony, "Deprogramming, Brainwashing, and the
Medicalization of Deviant Religious Groups," *Social Problems* 29 (1982): 283–93.

5. J. T. Richardson and B. Kilbourne, "Psychotherapy and New Religions in
a Pluralistic Society," *American Psychologist* 39, no. 3 (1984): 237–51.

6. Gordon, "Kids and Cults."

7. Levine, "Youth and Religious Cults," and "Cults and Mental Health."

8. Ungerleider and Wellisch, "Coercive Persuasion and Brainwashing."

9. Galanter, "Charismatic Religious Sects and Psychiatry," pp. 1539–48; Galanter, "The Relief Effect," pp. 588–91; and Galanter and Buckley, "Evangelical Religion and Meditation," pp. 685–91.

10. Gordon, "Kids and the Cults," pp. 24–27 and 36.

11. Levine, "Youth and Religious Cults," pp. 75–89.

12. Levine, "Cults and Mental Health," pp. 534–39.

13. Ungerleider and Wellisch, "Coercive Persuasion and Brainwashing," pp. 279–82.

14. Galanter, "Charismatic Religious Sects and Psychiatry," pp. 1539–48.

15. Ibid.

16. Gordon, "Kids and the Cults," pp. 24–27 and 36.

17. Levine, "Youth and Religious Cults," pp. 75–89.

18. Levine, "Cults and Mental Health," pp. 534–39.

19. Richardson and Kilbourne, "Psychotherapy and New Religions," pp. 237–51.

20. Ibid.

21. Galanter, "The Relief Effect," pp. 588–91.

22. Levine, "Youth and Religious Cults," pp. 75–89.

23. Singer, "Coming out of the Cults," pp. 72–82.

24. E. Schein, *Coercive Persuasion* (New York: Norton, 1961) and R. J. Lifton, *Thought Reform and the Psychology of Totalism* (New York: Norton, 1961).

25. Singer, "Coming Out of the Cults," pp. 72–82.

26. Ibid.

27. Siegelman and Conway, *Snapping*.

28. Clark, "The Manipulation of Madness."

29. Ibid.

30. Ibid.

31. Siegelman and Conway, *Snapping*.

32. Ibid.

33. I. N. Kutty, A. P. Froeze, and Q. A. F. Ray-Grant, "Hare Krishna Movement: What Attracts the Western Adolescent?" *Canadian Journal of Psychiatry* 24 (1979): 604–9.

34. J. F. Kenney, *ISKCON Ethics as a Significant Factor of Conversion to Krishna Consciousness* (University of Arkansas at Little Rock, 1979), 1–4.

35. J. F. Kenney and R. Poling, *Sexual Sublimation in Krishna Consciousness* (University of Arkansas at Little Rock, 1979), 1–9.

36. T. H. Poling, *Personality Variables in Krishna Consciousness* (University of Arkansas at Little Rock, 1979), 1–4.

37. Ibid.

38. A. Gerson, "Psychological Tests and Psychiatric Evaluation of Group Members" (Paper presented at the ACLU Conference on Deprogramming, University of Toronto, Toronto, Ontario, 19 March 1977).

39. M. W. Ross "Clinical Profiles of Hare Krishna Devotees," *American Journal of Psychiatry* 140, no. 4 (April 1983): 416–520.

40. M. W. Ross, "Mental Health in Hare Krishna Devotees: A Longitudinal Study," *The American Journal of Social Psychiatry* 5, no. 4 (Fall 1985): 65–67.

41. Ibid.

42. L. Lilliston, "Children in ISKCON: A Clinical View," 1985, Department of Psychology, Oakland University, Oakland, Michigan 1985, (graphic copy).

43. Ibid.

44. Ibid.

45. A. Weiss, "Mental Health and Personality Characteristics of Hare Krishna Devotees and Sympathizers as a Function of Acculturation Into the Hare Krishna Movement" (Ph.D. diss., California School of Professional Psychology, 1985).

46. Ibid.

47. M. Galanter, "Psychological Inductions into the Large Group: Findings from a Modern Religious Sect," *American Journal of Psychiatry* 137 (1980): 1574–1579.

48. Kutty, Froeze, and Ray-Grant, "Hare Krishna Movement," pp. 604–9.

49. Kenney, *ISKCON Ethics as a Significant Factor.*

50. Ross, "Clinical Profiles of Hare Krishna Devotees," pp. 416–520.

51. W. Kuner, cited in J. T. Richardson, "Psychological and Psychiatric Studies of New Religions," in *Advances in the Psychology of Religion, Vol. II, International Series in Experimental Social Psychology,* ed. L. B. Brown (New York: Pergamon, 1985).

Hare Krishna and the Anti-Cult Movement

David G. Bromley

Any chronicling of the history of ISKCON in the United States would be incomplete without a chapter on the public reaction to the motley assortment of religious groups alternatively referred to as new religious movements (hereafter, NRMs) and as cults. Essays in preceding sections of this book have comprehensively documented ISKCON's theology, history, cultural transplantation, role in the 1960s counterculture, and appeal to young Americans. All of these essays thus elucidate the process by which ISKCON arrived and carved out a niche in America. However, the niche that ISKCON currently occupies also has been significantly shaped by the public response to it. Neither ISKCON's development to the present nor alternative scenarios for its future can be understood without some perspective on its interaction with the sociocultural environment in which it has evolved.

Saliba's essay in this volume describes in detail the chilly reception Christian and Jewish groups gave to ISKCON, which was characteristic of the reaction to other NRMs as well.[1] Although there has been some interaction between the religious and secular groups opposing NRMs, the two can be analyzed independently and the secular movement has been more significant in its overall social impact and implications.

The secular response to NRMs, both at the individual and collective levels, has been shaped largely by the Anti-Cult Movement (hereafter, ACM), which arose in opposition to NRMs. It is therefore important to interpret the societal reaction to Hare Krishna in the context of the response to NRMs in general, for the public reaction was not to Hare Krishna but rather to a whole series of groups that came to public attention at about the same time. Thus, the relationship between Hare Krishna and the ACM is illustrative of but not determinative of the controversy over NRMs.

In this chapter we shall examine the impact of the ACM on ISKCON by tracing the development of the cult scare, the formation of the ACM, and the development of a social control strategy that relied heavily on casting the cult controversy in mental health terms. Two major legal cases involving ISKCON will be used to illustrate the structure and dynamics of the cult controversy as it impinged upon the development of the Hare Krishna movement in America.

The Cult Scare

As the essays by Hopkins, Elwood, and Melton in this volume reveal, the historical development of Hare Krishna, its migration to the United States, and the enthusiastic reception it received among youth in the early 1970s constitutes a complex vignette. This historical and developmental perspective on Hare Krishna specifically and NRMs in general has largely been obscured amid the development of a social scare in which NRMs came to be perceived as a set of groups that were both dangerous and destructive. The reaction was triggered by conflicts of interest between major social institutions and NRMs. A social scare is defined as (1) a sociocultural climate characterized by heightened tension as a result of (2) intense conflict between two (or more) social groups in which (3) the more powerful group mobilizes control claims by (4) denigrating the moral status of the less powerful group through (5) construction of a subversion mythology.

Through history a common correlate of intense conflicts in which important cultural values or institutional arrangements have been perceived to be at risk has been the emergence of subversion myths.[2] These myths, which frequently form the ideational framework for social scares, offer systematic explanations that bring together otherwise apparently unrelated groups and events in such a way as to account for the perceived danger to the existing social order. Subversion mythologies are premised on the existence of a conspiracy. They posit a specific danger and a group associated with it, one or more conspirators who have planned and direct the plot, a set of base impulses that motivate the conspiracy leaders, a manipulative process through which the conspirators involve others in their conspiracy, an imminent danger for the entire society, and a remedial agenda that must be followed if catastrophe is to be avoided.

Historically there have been extended national scares over religious groups such as the Catholics and Mormons.[3] Currently it is widely believed that there exists a class of groups called "cults" that can be distinguished from any other type of group.[4] The distinguishing characteristics of cults putatively include authoritarian leadership, suppression of rational thought, deceptive recruitment techniques, coercive mind control, a totalistic group structure, isolation from conventional society and former relationships, and exploitation of group members by leaders.

Malevolent gurus are thought to be the driving force behind these pseudoreligious groups that have been cynically created to take advantage of religious liberty guarantees as a means of maximizing these leaders' wealth and power. The membership of such groups is comprised of young adults from the middle class whose naivete and idealism is being systematically exploited by these gurus. According to the anti-cultists, cultic groups employ a combination of deception and sophisticated, coercive mind control techniques to subvert individual autonomy and free will. Thus, the danger is rapidly growing and proliferating cults, and gurus are the conspirators; the motives are power and money; the subversion mechanism is coercive mind control techniques; the imminent danger is legions of unquestioning followers in the service of unscrupulous leaders; and the remedy is formal or informal extrication of individuals from these groups along with revision of laws behind which they hide.

Sociocultural Sources of Anti-Cultism

The question immediately presents itself, of course, as to what precipitated this scare. Clearly it was not simply the existence of new religious groups because several of the diverse array of groups that later came to be perceived as cults (such as Hare Krishna, the Unification Church and Shiloh Youth Revival Centers) had been recruiting members from the drug subculture or other marginal populations for some time without great opposition.[5] Rather, it was when recruitment began to move to college campuses and other centers of middle-class youth subculture that the visibility of these groups to families, the media, and political and religious leaders increased; a concerted public reaction then developed. At first it was families of new converts that organized to combat NRMs; only gradually did the broad-based institutional reaction to NRMs emerge.

The source of the reaction to NRMs can be traced to their challenges to the interests of major institutions, including government, family, media, and churches. Certain developmental qualities of NRMs also contributed substantially to the reaction as some movements sustained their symbolic identity and internal cohesiveness by rejecting conventional institutions and creating separate, encapsulating communities. It was out of the dynamics of the interactions between these NRMs and major institutions that the cult scare developed.

NRMs and the Societal Reaction

The ACM formed around and the most intense opposition was directed at groups such as the Hare Krishna, Children of God, and the

Unification Church. In varying degrees these NRMs were organized communally; professed millennial, apocalyptic expectations; and recruited from the ranks of young, middle-class individuals. There were some important organizational corollaries of such characteristics.

First, each of these groups functioned during the mid-1970s with an imminent expectation of world transformation.[6] To prepare themselves for and contribute to this anticipated transformation, these groups withdrew from conventional society, which they deemed corrupt and moribund, and established spiritually based communities designed to be as independent of the larger society as possible. The outside world was primarily a source of converts, economic resources, and a model of immorality against which these movements' own utopian social orders could be contrasted. Second, recruitment was pursued aggressively as these groups perceived that world transformation was at hand. Total commitment was required to ensure salvation, and it was this type of total involvement that was so often interpreted as evidence of brainwashing. In this circumstance of heightened mobilization and absolute commitment there was little tolerance for questioning or dissent. Third, consistent with many other communal, utopian communities, these movements frequently employed familial metaphors (for example, referring to fellow members as brothers and sisters and leaders as fathers and mothers) to organize and articulate normative interpersonal relations. Finally, their contempt for conventional society led to a lowered level of concern about conformity with the established normative order. The existing social order was perceived to be fatally flawed and crumbling under the weight of its own decadence.

In the case of Hare Krishna, various characteristics of the movement contributed to the image of NRMs as dangerous cults. For example, in some quarters outsiders were rhetoricaly referred to as "karmi demons." Mobile witnessing teams created the potential for individuals to affiliate with the movement in one location and then move suddenly to a distant temple. The combination of this mobility and the encapsulation produced by the communal lifestyle in Hare Krishna temples was a key element in family anxiety about their offsprings' membership in the movement. In addition, several scholars have noted that members of Hare Krishna involved in fundraising utilized deceptive practices such as disguising their identity, misrepresenting the quality and value of artwork offered for sale, and engaging in "change up" (for example, having gotten agreement to pay for a religious book, the devotee then tried to obtain a large bill; with the bill in hand, the devotee was then able to bargain further for a higher price).[7] Finally, a maverick West Coast guru, who ultimately was excommunicated from the movement, apparently was involved in much more serious violations. A police raid on Hansadutta's temple yielded a number of firearms, and he was later arrested with other weapons in his automobile. Based on his own careful field research, Shinn says that there were allegations of other violations that contravened Krishna as well as mainstream norms:

> Devotees I interviewed accused Hansadutta of allowing drug use in his temple, a blatant violation of the Krishna vow to use no intoxicants. Some of his godbrothers suggested that Hansadutta's disciples were possibly selling drugs to fund his zone's activities. One devotee I interviewed even accused Hansadutta of encouraging some of his disciples to engage in prostitution when funds got really tight.[8]

It was precisely these types of incidents that led to the public furor over NRMs. The media tended to sensationalize these incidents, which created the impression that exploitation and lawlessness were the modal pattern in NRMs. In fact, there has been great internal discussion and conflict over more controversial and radical practices. Currently, for example, there is intense political conflict within Hare Krishna over the official handling of a few cases in which it was discovered that gurus were involved in illicit sexual relations with devotees or in drug use. The cult scare, with its emphasis on brainwashed membership, has largely ignored these very real crises and political divisions.[9]

Families and New Religions

Although NRMs would certainly have engendered opposition from other quarters, it is unlikely that the intensity of controversy would have transpired without the family conflict as its driving force. It was individual families and groups of families that banded together to form anti-cult organizations that coordinated the opposition to NRMs.[10]

A principal function of the contemporary American family is preparation of offspring for occupational and domestic careers. Mobility opportunities for offspring are the linchpin in family financial planning, residential location, and career management. Families seek to provide social and educational opportunities for sons and daughters so as to maximize the range of choices of career options and partners for family formation. Although families have retained both a real and perceived responsibility for socialization, managing this responsibility has become increasingly problematic as a result of the extended period of financial dependency, the increased importance of higher levels of education for achieving mobility opportunities, and the ambiguous boundary between adolescence and adulthood, which has reduced the control parents retain during the latter stages of the socialization process. Of course, parental feelings of efficacy and family prestige also are involved in the successful negotiation of childrearing objectives.

Given the enormous investment families have in the outcome of socializing sons and daughters for career and family formation and the tensions inherent in that process, it is not surprising that decisions affecting future mobility opportunities are of the greatest consequence to parents. It is in this context that decisions by college-aged youth to join NRMs must be understood. When some of the more prominent NRMs began aggressive recruitment campaigns on college campuses and centers of youth subculture, many of the new recruits were at precisely the stage of career and family formation preparation for which their parents had so long prepared. When these individuals, often with little if any prior consultation with their families, decided to join a NRM and abandon their domestic and occupational plans, the reaction of parents was predictably negative.

As Beckford has observed, the most common response was anger and urgency. This reaction occurred in situations where parents felt unable to understand "how their best efforts to bring up children in what they regarded as a firm and fair fashion had resulted in an apparently sudden and unexpected rejection of the parental home and all that it represented."[11] This group of parents, in the absence of any other explanation for unfolding events, was most likely to resort to the explanation that both recruitment and subsequent membership were the product of manipulation. This group is particularly significant in understanding the controversy over NRMs because these families possessed the motivation and determination to establish the organized opposition to new religions. Parents of members of NRMs quickly formed a series of voluntary associations with names such as the American Family Foundation, Citizens Freedom Foundation, and Love Our Children. These organizations served as support groups for families, networks through which offspring with whom contact had been lost might be located, and lobbying vehicles (which sought to bring pressure on NRMs by enlisting the support of political, economic, religious, media, and educational institutions possessing greater resources and sanctioning power).

The Structure and Impact of the Anti-Cult Campaign

The campaign against "cults" coalesced at two levels, organizational and interpersonal, although the levels were not independent but rather mutually reinforcing. At an organizational level the anti-cult campaign incorporated a broad range of activities such as conducting "educational" programs in schools and churches warning of the dangers of cults, seeking to gain media coverage of their perspective, and lobbying state legislatures to adopt legislation that would impose various types of legal restrictions on NRMs. In these initiatives the ACM coordinated much of its activity with elements of the media, political, religious, and educational institutions.[12] At an interpersonal level, the ACM developed a procedure termed "deprogramming," which presumably reversed the effects of cultic "programming," as a means for extricating individual family members from NRMs. Essentially, deprogramming entailed separating NRM members from their groups, voluntarily or forcibly, and then confronting them with whatever assortment of allegations of movement improprieties, testimonies from former members, emotional appeals from family members, or theological arguments was effective in persuading individuals to renounce their group membership.[13] A motley assortment of individual moral entrepreneurs coalesced around the family-generated market for recovering errant youth.

However, a number of major institutions also opposed NRMs in an independent defense of their own respective interests. There were conflicts with local communities over public solicitation of funds, purchases of property, establishing church-related businesses or centers in local communities; state concerns with health care, child care, and educational practices; federal investigations over issues such as requests for tax-exempt status, immigration status of members of certain groups, various types of political practices and involvements potentially inconsistent with church status. Michael's essay in this volume provides an illustrative case study of some of these types of conflict in which the Hare Krishna movement became embroiled at New Vrindaban. Even though individual NRMs were involved in only certain of these conflicts, the constant flow of high-visibility allegations and conflict from the mid-1970s to the mid-1980s both contributed to and sustained the persistence of the cult scare.

Hare Krishna and the Cult Controversy

Although NRMs came into conflict with a number of institutions, we shall focus here on the conflict between NRMs and the family-based ACM and its allies in the mental health professions. This particular conflict most significantly shaped the structure and direction of the cult controversy. This conflict often took the form of a public drama in which families were pitted against NRMs with individual members supporting one side or the other and often each side at different times. The outcomes of these cases influenced strategies employed in the subsequent conflicts. Thus, these individual cases illuminate the interests and worldviews of the partisans as well as the developing course of their respective strategies. Here we shall utilize the two most significant legal conflicts involving the Hare Krishna movement to examine the development of the ACM.

The Shapiro and George cases both revolved around allegations of brainwashing and in this sense contributed to the cult scare. However, the two cases occurred nearly a decade apart, were handled rather differently, and yielded opposite legal outcomes. Thus these cases are particularly useful in illustrating the structure and development of the ACM.

THE SHAPIRO CASE

Edward Shapiro, son of a Boston University Medical School physician, became interested in Hare Krishna while a high school junior.[14] He visited a local temple during his remaining years in high school and even considered dropping out of school to join the movement, but his parents persuaded him to complete the degree. In 1972, after one year at Brandeis University, he did drop out of college and moved into the local Hare Krishna temple.

Shapiro's decision to adopt a culturally divergent lifestyle and to distance himself from his family predictably precipitated in his parents anxiety and a concern that he had somehow been manipulated. An article authored by Shapiro's father and published in a 1977 issue of a medical journal indicates that he saw his son's affiliation with Hare Krishna in terms of ACM ideology. Indeed, he "concluded that a distinct syndrome of destructive cultism can be defined" and that "destructive cultism is a sociopathic illness which is rapidly spreading through the U.S. and the rest of the world in the form of a pandemic."[15] According to the elder Shapiro, the characteristics of "destructive cultism" included change in personality, loss of personal identity, change in mannerisms, and intense psychologic fear.[16] His mother appeared to share a similar perspective. As she later stated:

> I think you should know that we are not trying to get Ed back into the fold; we are just trying to get him back to sanity. . . . To them, thinking is mental speculation. . . . You're not allowed to think, to doubt, to question. This is why we feel Eddie is being controlled. He's not thinking for himself. We are trying to get him the proper attention he needs.[17]

His father asserted that young Shapiro had stated that "I was not really his father, and that he was not really Ed Shapiro, just a spirit that inhabits the body."[18] His parents also expressed concern that he might fail to continue to get appropriate ongoing treatment for his long-standing diabetes problem.

In 1974 his parents decided to take unilateral action. Shapiro at this juncture was twenty years old. On 5 August Shapiro's father and the father of another devotee, Lee Roth (then twenty-five years old), arrived at the Hare Krishna Temple in Newton, Massachusetts. The four then went to the Shapiro residence, on the pretext that both devotees were to receive medical attention, where deprogrammer Ted Patrick and a contingent of family, friends, and members of the deprogramming team were waiting.

According to Shapiro, he initially expressed willingness to discuss his Hare Krishna affiliation with the assembled contingent until he recognized that his own positive sentiments were not open to consideration. Shapiro then attempted to exit the situation but was physically restrained. During one of the ensuing confrontations Shapiro's *sikah* (hair-tuft) was cut off and his neck beads and devotional beads were taken away from him.

Late that night Shapiro gained access to a phone and called members of the local temple who, in turn, called the police. Shapiro asserts that he told the investigating officer that he was an adult, being held against his will and wanted to leave the premises. The officer decided to leave Shapiro at the family home overnight and to return the following morning. By the next morning all those involved in the deprogramming had left the house and moved to a local motel where the deprogramming continued. Shapiro acknowledged that he "began doubting then . . . but I was simply confused and bewildered, that's all. They isolate you from the movement and torture you and get you to believe anything for a little while."[19] Shapiro was subsequently moved again to Toronto, Canada, and then to various places in Ontario. There Canadian deprogrammers attempted to involve him in various types of recreational activities and offered him liquor and cigarettes, substances specifically proscribed by Hare Krishna theology. Shapiro was flown back to Newton, where he reported to authorities that he had not been held against his will. He avers that these statements were made out of "fear" because "my father pleaded with me. He said his life and reputation were on the line."[20]

By his own account, Shapiro at this point did not intend to return to Hare Krishna. However, while changing planes on a flight to rejoin his parents he apparently serendipitously encountered a devotee in the airport and decided on the spur of the moment to return to the temple. In the wake of the now unsuccessful deprogramming and Shapiro's return to the temple, family strain increased further. Shapiro requested and his family rejected placing under his control $20,000 in inheritance over which his parents had earlier gained conservatorship to prevent his giving the money to Hare Krishna. There was considerable ill-feeling over this issue, and at one point Shapiro considered initiating legal action. Further, throughout his membership in Hare Krishna he had continued to visit his father each week to receive insulin shots for his diabetic condition. He now discontinued those visits.

The case took a new turn again in October 1976. Another devotee, twenty-three-year-old Merylee Kreshower, attempted to press kidnapping charges in a Queens, New York, court against her mother and deprogrammer Galen Kelly, following an unsuccessful deprogramming. The Assistant District Attorney prosecuting the case clearly saw the matter from a different perspective. As he put it: "The thing that frightens me is that a group like this . . . can use mind control to create an army of zombies or robots who could undermine the government and law enforcement." He later stated, "Mind control has nothing to do with religion. It's a question of free will. I don't think an individual in his right state of mind would allow someone else to control his mind. Just think of it in terms of hypnosis."[21] Instead of a probe of Kreshower's abduction and deprogramming, the case quickly became an investigation of Hare Krishna. Shapiro's parents, former members of Hare Krishna, and ACM activists eventually testified in the grand jury proceedings at the prosecution's invitation. As a result, the grand jury ultimately dismissed the charges against the two defendants and instead indicted two local Hare Krishna leaders for using mind control to unlawfully imprison Shapiro and Kreshower. Shapiro was detained as a material witness in the case. Shapiro and one of the Krishna leaders also were accused of attempting to extort $20,000 (which constituted the amount of the trust fund under dispute between Shapiro and his parents).

Dr. John Clark, ACM affiliated psychiatrist, interviewed Shapiro at the Queens police station for fifteen minutes and then observed Shapiro for another hour and a half after Shapiro refused to talk with him any longer. Based on that brief interview-observation, Clark issued a certificate to place Shapiro in a mental hospital, which then refused to admit him in the face of potential litigation. However, Shapiro's father obtained a temporary guardianship order over his son in a Boston court. The presiding judge ruled that the guardianship order issued in Massachusetts was legal in New York. Shapiro thereupon returned to Massachusetts in the custody of deprogrammer Galen Kelly and was signed into McLean Hospital, a psychiatric institute at which Clark was a staff physician, by his father. Clark stated that in his professional opinion:

> Edward David Shapiro demonstrates psychotic thinking and extremely poor judgment which renders him incapable of managing his very severe and long-standing juvenile diabetes; thus he is in

immediate and constant danger to himself because he is mentally ill.[22]

Shapiro spent two weeks undergoing psychiatric evaluation by Clark as well as other staff physicians. At the end of that period, despite a recommendation by Clark that additional testing be conducted, the court dissolved the conservatorship order and Shapiro was released. Criminal charges against the two Hare Krishna leaders were later dismissed by the New York State Supreme Court.

Edward Shapiro remained a member of Hare Krishna for several more years. However, at twenty-six years of age, nearly ten years after he joined Hare Krishna, Shapiro voluntarily left the movement. By his own account he had begun smoking and drinking (theologically proscribed activities), and his marriage with another devotee had proved unsatisfying. These longer-term sources of conflict appear to have been exacerbated by what he came to view as interpersonal callousness and dishonesty within the movement. His last public statements on his involvement in the movement reflected disillusionment, acknowledged the basis for his parents' original opposition to his involvement, but did not allege brainwashing or psychological manipulation.

THE GEORGE CASE

Prior to her first contact with Hare Krishna at age fourteen, Robin George had been experimenting with alternative religious, meditative, and dietary practices.[23] Raised a Lutheran, George reported being "disillusioned" with her religion. She and her mother attended a Billy Graham Crusade where she found a "living spirit" that she felt was absent in her own church; she also attended a number of churches including Catholic, Jewish, Baptist, and Seventh Day Adventist. In addition, she and her father practiced yoga, and she experimented with vegetarianism. In July 1974, George initially visited a Hare Krishna temple with an older girlfriend. Shortly thereafter her friend joined the movement. By September George had begun to alter her style of dress and wear the traditional Krishna sari. Her mother went to the temple with her in September, and George began visiting the temple regularly during the next two months with her parents' knowledge. She appears to have spent most of her time at the temple involved in ritualistic and temple maintenance activities. Parental concern with her involvement grew as she began to rise early in the morning to chant Hare Krishna, established a small shrine in her room at home, adopted Krishna dress and dietary practices, and lost interest in school. Her parents began trying to limit her devotional activities and insist on better school performance. There was conflict over these issues.

On 16 November, without telling her parents and simply leaving a goodbye note (which read: "I love you both very much but I've got to leave. I'll be in touch later"), George left home and moved into the temple. She asserted that local Hare Krishna leaders had urged her to leave home in full knowledge that her parents were opposed to this move. When she joined the movement she was quickly moved from California to a temple in New Orleans, specifically to conceal her location from her parents, and spent several months at Krishna centers in that area. In April her parents finally discovered her whereabouts and her father brought her back home. She immediately attempted to run away but was caught by her parents and was physically confined for a period of several days to prevent another attempt. On 1 May she ran away from home again. With the assistance of Krishna members she went this time to a temple in Canada where she remained for several months. Finally, through George's girlfriend, who by now had left the movement, George's parents once again were able to discover her whereabouts.[24] Her father then traveled to Canada in an attempt to find her.

This trip to Canada was simply the last event in a continuing effort the Georges had waged to locate their daughter. During the period when she was in Louisiana and Canada George's parents conducted an unrelenting campaign to locate her themselves and to bring pressure on Krishna leaders to reveal her location. These efforts included picketing temples; writing letters to police officials, the FBI, ambassadors of foreign nations, Krishna temple leaders around the country and Prabhupada himself; appearing on radio and television shows and giving interviews with the print media; and traveling to temples where they thought she might be found. Krishna leaders consistently denied knowing George's whereabouts and at one point arranged for a letter (written by George) with a photograph of George with some "hippies" to be postmarked from Mexico and sent to her parents in order to throw them off the trail. Finally, Krishna leaders began to fear that legal charges would be brought against them and decided that George should remain at home until she reached legal adulthood.

It seems clear that George did not wish to leave the movement at that time. She reported that "I was perfectly content to stay there (in Ottawa) the rest of my life."[25] Her disillusionment with the Krishnas began when leaders began pressuring her to return home in order to avoid litigation. Her account was as follows:

> It was traumatic for me. . . . I had totally depended on them to tell

me what to do, to bring me my food, to answer all my questions. All of a sudden the support wasn't there. I was crushed. By turning me in to the police they were ignoring everything they had taught me. Women are supposed to be protected. . . . They were pushing me to my limit. I wanted to live there, but I was being forced to leave. . . . I was losing all my faith in them.[26]

Even after her return home and her disillusionment with the Krishnas, Robin's public accounts did not stress the brainwashing allegations that became a centerpiece of the ensuing civil litigation.

Robin said she was not coerced to join or remain in the Krishna movement. She attributed her dedication to the movement to subtle pressure from devotees and her own frame of mind when she was first exposed to the Krishnas as she was about to enter high school. At that time, she said, the thought of entering the job market after high school and accepting adult responsibilities frightened her. "I was confused about what I was going to do with my life," she explained. "I thought all I had to do was join this and everything would be taken care of. It was an escape."[27]

Following her return home in November 1975, George experienced continued turbulence. In March 1976 her father experienced a heart attack from which he never fully recovered. A combination of additional strokes and heart attacks caused his death the following September. George reported that for several years she daily experienced nightmares, anxiety attacks, fear of strangers, crowds, and Krishna members. She also reported feelings of confusion, bewilderment, and depression. Behaviorally, she reported an inability to read or concentrate for more than a brief period, which resulted in academic problems; a series of unsatisfactory relationships with men; and an inability to retain jobs for more than brief periods.

George also became involved in the anti-cult network after her return home. Her mother served as the Chair of the Orange County Citizens Freedom Foundation, one of the two largest national ACM organizations. George herself attended meetings, met with apostate Hare Krishna members, and discussed her problems with anti-cult psychiatrist Marvin Galper. In addition, she had a born-again experience and joined a fundamentalist-oriented Christian church. As Saliba's paper in this volume indicates, fundamentalist churches have been particularly outspoken in their opposition to "cults."

Both George and her mother began to conclude that the Krishnas were responsible for George's subsequent problems as well as her father's death. George began utilizing ACM terminology in recounting her experiences in Hare Krishna. For example, she told one of the examining psychiatrists that "she felt like she was in a continual hypnotic state and this alteration of her consciousness was reinforced by her rhythmic repetition of the *mantra* throughout the day."[28] Her mother also reflected ACM thinking in her analysis of Hare Krishna and clearly blamed the movement for her daughter's post-Krishna problems. For example, she stated:

> The strains of living up to, then trying to overcome the cult's false teachings, the Hare Krishna slave-type lifestyle, the diet poor in protein and heavy in sugar for energy, the lack of proper rest and sleep in her adolescence, has left a dark groove in Robin's life which she may never overcome. . . . Contrary to her former love and respect for family and friends, she came out of the Hare Krishna cult with a lack of respect for her parents, relatives, friends and other people outside of the cult. In the cult she was made to think all were ignorant bcause they did not accept the teachings of the Hare Krishna cult. Robin felt superior to everyone because of her false Hare Krishna knowledge . . . as written and preached by their self-proclaimed Hindu guru, Prabhupada, who wanted to be known as a God among his people in India.[29]

The Georges first initiated legal action against Hare Krishna in October 1977; however, the case did not actually reach trial until 1983. In 1981, when George was twenty-one years old and more than five years had passed since she left Hare Krishna, she was interviewed for several hours by anti-cult psychologist Margaret Singer. Two other clinicians also presented evidence supporting George's case. Psychiatric testimony for the prosecution supported the brainwashing allegations. One expert witness for the defense observed that the essence of the trial was a brainwashing/mind control charge upon which all of the other charges (false imprisonment, infliction of emotional distress, wrongful death, and libel) rested.[30] Indeed, the Georges' attorney had asserted in his closing argument that "If there was not false imprisonment, then the rest of this stuff is a lot of hogwash because that means that Robin decided to run away from home and torment her parents."

In contrast to the Shapiro case in which attempts to win support of the legal system were unsuccessful, the George case constituted a major victory for the ACM. The jury awarded a total of $32,500,000 to the George family for false imprisonment, for intentional infliction of mental distress on George and her mother, for contributing to the wrongful death of George's father, and for libeling George and her mother. Approximately $29,000,000 was in punitive damages. The ultimate outcome still remains in doubt as the case currently is on appeal, and the original award was reduced to $9,700,000 by the trial judge.

It is clear from post-trial interviews with some of the jurors that the jury was outraged by what it perceived to be a coordinated effort by members of Hare Krishna to conceal Robin George from her parents. The investigating agency reported the jury foreman as stating that the jury was unanimous in its view that "the importance of the family came first." He went on to assert that the jury felt

> the Hare Krishnas should have at least notified Mr. and Mrs. George as to Robin's location, and even entered into a discussion with the parents regarding her return. This was the main issue on which this jury focused. . . . (The) jury, based on that issue, made the award for punitive damages as large as they could to express their outrage against any organization that would do this type of thing . . . (and) the jury was sending a message to other groups.[31]

Another jury member put the matter in a slightly different way. He stated that "the jury was in total agreement that Ms. George had never been physically restrained by any member of ISKCON, and that the award was made solely on the basis that she had been concealed from her parents rather than held against her will."[32] He went on to report that Robin's willingness to remain concealed had not been a factor brought up during the deliberations. This juror also emphasized that the award "should be very substantial as a warning or a message to other similar cults or groups, whom the jury wanted to understand that they cannot treat members of their group like Robin George was treated."[33] The jury foreman also stated during the interview that

> jurors expressed the opinion that Robin George had been influenced to the point where she could not make a rational decision by herself. . . . Ms. George obviously felt that based on the feelings of the Hare Krishna about her and her relationship with her parents, she did not have the right to contact or return to her parents, as members of the group stated that all she needed was the Krishna group itself.[34]

Given the complexity of the case, it is difficult to isolate the effect the anti-cult psychiatric testimony had on the jury's deliberations. However, the brainwashing testimony probably was instrumental in freeing the jury's sense of outrage. The jury was presented with a variety of facts (running away from home prior to her involvement with Hare Krishna, a pattern of religious experimentation, running away from home on several occasions to participate in the Krishna movement, the influence of her best friend joining the movement, resentment against the Krishna movement for abandoning her in the face of legal action by her parents, strong connections with the ACM and a theologically hostile fundamentalist church) that conceivably could have yielded a more mixed attribution of responsibility in the case. The evidence of Krishna complicity in concealing George from her family clearly overrode these other factors. The brainwashing testimony had the effect of inviting an interpretation in which these various actions on George's part had less relevance because she had a reduced decisional capacity.

Commonalities in the Shapiro and George Cases

In a number of significant respects the scenarios in the Shapiro and George cases were very much alike and illustrate the patterning of family–NRM conflicts discussed earlier. Both Shapiro and George were discontented with their familial religious affiliations and experimented with alternative religions while living at home. Neither Shapiro nor George was initially recruited by the Hare Krishnas, as anti-cult descriptions of cultic recruitment imply. It was when the involvements with Hare Krishna began interfering with scholastic achievement and family solidarity that parents began to express concern and opposition. In neither case was religion per se the primary basis for conflict. It seems evident from the public statements of the families that both accepted the brainwashing explanations and were closely connected with the ACM.

Both George and Shapiro encountered parental opposition by acting unilaterally—George by running away from home and Shapiro by dropping out of college—after a period of acceding to parental constraints. Parents then intervened decisively, Robin George's father traveling across country on two occasions to retrieve his daughter and Shapiro's father arranging to have him abducted, deprogrammed, and committed to a mental institution. Both youthful converts resisted initial attempts at parental control, George by running away from home after her father forced her to return home and Shapiro by returning to the Hare Krishna temple following his deprogramming and again later following his commitment to a mental institution. Shapiro remained a member of Hare Krishna considerably longer than George; however, whether George would have remained a member longer is not clear, her parents' resistance notwithstanding, had not the Krishnas insisted that she return home. In the end both Shapiro and George became disillusioned with the movement relatively independently of their parents' efforts. George's disillusionment stemmed from what she perceived to be Krishna leaders' failure to support her in her conflict with her parents whereas Shapiro tired of lifestyle restrictions, found his endogamous marriage unsatisfying, and came to question the moral rectitude of the temple devotees and leaders. This sequence of intense commitment followed by disillusionment and withdrawal is, of course, one of the most frequent patterns in NRM affiliation/disaffiliation.[35]

The public pronouncements and actions of the pair following disaffiliation are not surprising. The results of Shapiro's deprogramming are somewhat unusual because overall deprogramming success rates have been estimated at approximately sixty-five percent.[36] Nonetheless, this outcome is significant in interpreting Shapiro's subsequent statements and actions. Shapiro's resistance to deprogramming and to additional attempts at parental control, which caused further alienation, may well have been a factor in his mild public accounts following defection. These accounts acknowledged parental concern but stopped short of embracing the brainwashing ideology. George, by contrast, was extensively involved in ACM activities and one element of her reunification with her family became allocating blame for her affiliation with Hare Krishna and her father's untimely death to the Krishna movement. This stance is consistent with those of other former NRM members who have been significantly influenced by the ACM.[37]

In both cases the families sought assistance from clinicians in pressing their claims of deleterious mental health effects of membership in Hare Krishna for their offspring as a result of coercive persuasion techniques. In each case the clinicians who were most supportive of the family positions were closely linked to the ACM. It seems clear in retrospect that the Georges received much greater public support, in large measure because Robin was a minor and hence was regarded by jurors as appropriately under the domain of her parents.

Ideological Orientation of the ACM

It was precisely out of family conflicts such as the Shapiro and George cases that ACM ideology evolved. These two cases were more publicly celebrated, dramatic, and precedent-setting than countless others involving a wide range of NRMs, families, and individuals, but the substance and dynamics of the conflicts were relatively typical. It now remains to outline the major components of ACM ideology and to trace the development of legal tactics based on it.

Because ACM ideology was developed by families of converts to NRMs and allied clinicians, it was predictable that the ideology would emphasize a commitment to established institutions and the value systems underpinning them. This commitment was reflected in a defense of the family unit (and other established institutions), rejection of religiously based alternatives to the secular/rational worldview, and explanation of commitment to alternative institutional arrangements and worldviews as the product of a coercive mind-control process.[38] From an

ACM perspective religious commitments that would threaten family solidarity, remove individuals from domestic/occupational networks, and reject secular rationalism have little to recommend them.

West and Singer clearly sounded the ACM concern with family integrity. As they put it, "While protecting religious freedom, how can society protect the family as a social institution from the menace of the cults as a competing superfamily."[39] This issue came up in both the Shapiro and George cases. In his testimony in the Shapiro case, Clark stated, "If someone is loved as a natural parent, the cults generally say that biological parents are not important. It is now some aspect of religion."[40] In her assessment of Robin George, Singer used adjectives such as talented, outgoing, self-directed, self-motivated and mentally gifted in describing the girl during the period before her Krishna affiliation. Her family life was also described in very positive terms. Singer's assessment, then, was that George was "on course" and the Hare Krishna movement was to be held responsible for diverting her from a conventional lifestyle and developmental sequence. Singer concluded, "It is my opinion that a 23-year-old woman, who is as attractive and pleasant as Robin George, would normally, at age 23, be able to get jobs and hold them, and be making plans to either live independently or be thinking about possibly meeting a person, and marrying them and starting her own family."[41]

SECULAR, RATIONAL VALUES

The most interesting and telling evidence of the ACM commitment to secular values is the persistent reference to rational, abstract thinking as the norm by which appropriate human functioning is to be judged. There is good evidence that the social psychological relationships that are normative in contemporary secular society and in some NRMs proceed from different premises. Such differences have been observed empirically. For example, based on a review of Rosen and Nordquist's research on Ananda Cooperative Village, Richardson notes that these researchers concluded that there was a conflict of values between Ananda and conventional society: aestheticism and mysticism versus technology and bureaucracy and an orientation toward self-realization and altruism versus accomplishment and achievement. Responses to the Rokeach Value Survey indicated that:

> Highest ranked "terminal" values were (in order), "self-realization," "inner harmony," "happiness," "wisdom," and "freedom." Lowest

ranks were given to "pleasure," "national security," "social recognition," "a comfortable life," and "an exciting life" . . . Highest ranking "instrumental" values were "loving," "cheerful," "honest," "forgiving," and "self controlled." Lowest rankings were assigned to "logical," "clean," "intellectual," "polite," and "obedient."[42]

Inferences that secular rationalism is the normative mode of functioning abound in work of ACM proponents. Singer, for example, stated that her concern about new religions was heightened in part after she observed "many young adults turning to extremely authoritarian social groups, dropping this world of science, liberalism, and rationalism and entering a world of magic and primitive thinking."[43] From this liberal/rational perspective, "cults pare down multidetermined reality into an oversimplified pastiche of cosmic truths and clichés that explain everything."[44] Clark concurs. In applying Robert Lifton's theory to interviews with clients, he observed that this type of manipulated dependence inappropriately returns a presumably adult individual to a childlike status.

> What distinguished these themes was their contrast and non-congruity to adult, trained perceptions of reality and relationships, and the imposition of a strange, foreign climate of congruous, simplistic and closed ideologies. Group pressures and expectations along with ideological instruction are clear analogues of early relationships with parents, having no relevance to real problems of adult living. The lies of designated authorities, supported by group assent, forced a suspension of critical judgement and enabled new belief.[45]

This perspective was reflected in both the George and Shapiro cases. In diagnosing George as suffering from atypical dissociative disorder, Margaret Singer asserted that one source of this condition came from ritualistic chanting.

> She has her mind get off the track. . . . (One reason is) the impact of the continuous chanting where she was trained not to think while she was with the Krishnas. This was very reinforced and conditioned into her, and it has stayed as a kind of overlearned habit in her thinking so when she gets a little bit anxious she starts spacing out. She no longer does the chanting, but that part of the chanting, the spacing away from and not thinking and not reflecting, turns on now. So that she does sort of space out a bit.[46]

Clark emphasized the Krishnas' rejection of secular rationalism in the Shapiro case: "They accept all reality, excluding any scientific reality as a common course, which they themselves do not test."[47] Thus, from the ACM viewpoint, the personal qualities and interpersonal dynamics integral to the religiously based lifestyles of NRMs were judged to be intrusive and deleterious to normal human functioning.

BRAINWASHING/COERCIVE PERSUASION

ACM ideology has depicted NRMs as subverting legitimate social institutions and individual functioning through brainwashing. To view NRM affiliations as psychologically coerced, ACM ideology has portrayed NRMs as exploiting social conditions and the stress associated with such conditions. Margaret Singer has been particularly clear on this point. With respect to individual adjustment to social tensions, she observed that "the cult's supposedly sublime principles and ultimate states of awareness offer clear-cut, black-and-white answers to young adults who are seeking relief from *many age-appropriate developmental crises*" (emphasis added).[48] She did acknowledge that "this period in history may make certain quests more prominent in the lives of young adults: the loose social structures, the feelings of alienation, and the promise of what turning inward may bring to modern man."[49]

However, it is clear that the problem was cult seductiveness and individual vulnerability:

> The general crisis of young adulthood usually centers around career, sex, marriage, what values to hold or develop, where and how to live, and how to make friends. The common pressures of the late teens and early twenties have been exacerbated by current social influences; cults offer a lure of simplistic answers that some cannot resist.[50]

Further, whatever consequences contemporary social instability might have for individuals, the notion that young adults actively have sought alternative meaning systems through NRMs has been roundly rejected. Zerin quoted Singer on this point.

> After talking with over 700 ex- and current cult members, none have told me that they set out to find a guru or a messiah who would set them up in prostitution, flower-selling, cocaine-dealing, gun-smuggling, child abuse, or living off garbage. These were merely naive, friendly, trusting, altruistic people hoping to make friends and to help make a better world.[51]

ACM ideology has contained some recognition that vulnerability may vary. For example, Singer asserted that middle- and upper-middle-class youth are most vulnerable because they "have not had enough experience with the street hustlers in growing up and knowing how artful deceivers on the street can operate."[52] West and Singer have argued that some family backgrounds are more conducive than others and that "some families unwittingly foster a combination of indecisiveness and rebelliousness that makes the cult seem like a perfect solution to the young person seeking escape from the frustrations of that family situation."[53] Clark's work contains the same implication as he has divided NRM converts into two categories: individuals who had been "chronically disturbed and unhappy for many years" and "essentially normal, maturing persons" whose "susceptibility to conversion was either an artifact of the aggressive manipulation of a proselytizer or the result of a normal painful crisis of maturation."[54]

Although some acknowledgment has been given to sociocultural factors, ACM ideology has made it clear that the primary factor accounting for NRM affiliations was the recruitment, socialization process. There is frequent mention in ACM literature of deceptive recruitment practices; however, this issue was not central to ACM clinicians' analyses in the Shapiro and George cases, as both individuals had sought out the Hare Krishnas and, given the Krishnas' distinctive appearance, it is difficult to argue that they concealed their identity. Thus the major stress was on the socialization process.

Clark's formulation was considerably less sophisticated than Singer's. He identified nine mind-control techniques that result in "mental harm" to converts: relative to complete separation from families; intense group pressures; isolation from familiar places, associations, and ideas; sleep deprivation; severe dietary restrictions; continuous chanting and bizarre rituals; frequent coercion and terror; ultrastrict rules of chastity, poverty, and obedience; other means designed to maintain a totalistic society.[55] Working from this perspective, he asserted in the Shapiro case that:

> The cults themselves in many, many ways impose their will to the point where individuals can no longer be taken up about anything. Their actions are a stereotyped, controlled obedience to the leader and to anything that is said by the leaders.[56]

He identified several symptoms of mind control which he observed in Edward Shapiro.

> Constant need for reinforcement, contact with persons of his cult, a compulsive use of language of the cult, even in some situations which are not altogether appropriate under slight stress. A wandering away from stressful situations, a return back to the rituals by chanting and a complete turning away from the established, well-organized intellectual understanding of reality and as investment of

all the emotions essentially in one major factor that is religion of a certain kind, or what is defined as religion.[57]

Singer has gradually abandoned the term brainwashing for the concept "systematic manipulation of social influence" (SMSI). She has defined SMSI as involving six elements: gaining control over a person's physical and social environment and time; creating a sense of powerlessness in the individual; manipulating rewards, punishments, and experiences so as to suppress the former self; manipulating rewards, punishments, and experiences to elicit the new, desired behaviors; presenting the individual with a closed system of logic in a totalitarian atmosphere; and maintaining the individual in ignorance about the process in which he or she is involved.[58] The individual who has undergone SMSI experiences what Singer refers to as the five d's: *deception* of the person, *dependence* on the organization, *debilitation* of the individual through group controls and routines, *dread* (both within the group and of the outside world), and *desensitization* such that individuals no longer utilize their "old conscience."[59]

Singer's testimony in the George case was framed around the SMSI explanation. George was described as "a very naive girl. She was not street smart."[60] Further, the other factors operant in the environment (Robin's religious seeking, her girlfriend's joining Hare Krishna, Robin's running away from home) all were dismissed as significant causal factors. It was the SMSI process that was the source of George's leaving home and subsequent involvement in Hare Krishna. Singer opined:

> It's my opinion that she was not at that point freely using her own will and volition, but being influenced and manipulated and made to comply with the wishes of the various Krishna organization representatives.[61]

CULTS AS SUBVERSIVE AND CONSPIRATORIAL

In light of the ACM view that NRMs were, on a social level, subverting crucial social institutions and, on an individual level, undermining individual intellectual functioning, it was hard to conclude other than that these groups were subversive and conspiratorial. This orientation is reflected in the work of ACM clinicians. (Emphasis is added in the following quotations.) For example, West avers that cults are "as much a *perversion* of the meaning of religion as the quack is a perversion of the meaning of the medical oath."[62] Clark, in discussing the motivations for joining NRMs, refers to "seekers" as individuals who are trying to restore themselves to some semblance of comfort in a fresh, though *false*, reality."[63] Singer observes that "cults offer certain *pseudo*-philosophical, spiritual, and psychological dimensions of the life of these persons."[64] West and Singer attribute a "lack of sincerity" to cults and assert that "many cults demonstrate *extreme* interest in finanical or political *aggrandizement*, rather than the spiritual development of the faithful."[65] Such qualities distinguish cults from more legitimate religious groups that proceed from "theological or moral motives, rather than avarice, personal convenience, or a desire for power."[66]

Despite these types of statements in their written work, in their role as expert witnesses, ACM clinicians have studiously attempted to steer around any evaluations of religious belief or practice, as these would constitute constitutional grounds for reversal of trial verdicts. Naturally, defense attorneys have always probed this area in search of precisely these types of evaluations. In general the ACM position has been that it is deleterious group practices and not religious content that is at issue. In the Shapiro case, for example, Clark asserted that:

> In the course of this study it slowly became pressingly obvious that it was the quality of the experiences and not so much the content that was the crucial factor. It did matter if the cult were religious, terrorist-political of either left or right, rich or poor in intellectual or doctrinal outlook.[67]

Early in her testimony in the George case, Singer attempted to diffuse this issue in the same fashion, asserting that:

> I have studied 75 different groups that in one way or another meet the criteria I have outlined of . . . the SMSI. And they vary in content. Some of them have religious themes, some are political themes, some are psychological themes. The content of the organization is not crucial at all.[68]

However, as the subsequent section on the development of ACM strategy will demonstrate, this issue has constituted a continuing point of ACM vulnerability.

Strategic Development of the ACM

The basic structure of ACM ideology has been shaped by a confluence of three major interest groups within the movement: individual families, such as the Georges and Shapiros, who were actively trying to resolve family conflicts over their offsprings' religious affiliations; entrepreneurial deprogrammers, who acted on behalf of families to extricate individuals from NRMs; and a small group of clinicians, who helped both to construct the brainwashing ideology and to provide access to social control mechanisms (through medically based psychopathological definitions of NRM membership). The ACM's dual goals of retrieving individual family members from NRMs and combatting the groups themselves were limited by two factors. First, the adult status of NRM members impeded parental efforts to exert control over their offsprings' affiliation decisions. Second, the religious status of NRMs impeded ACM efforts to mobilize state sanctions against NRMs. ACM strategy developed gradually over a decade on a trial-and-error basis and became an effort to meld the three interest groups comprising the movement and to overcome the obstacles posed by adult status of adherents and first-amendment limitations on regulation of religious expression.

For heuristic purposes three stages of development are identified here: formative, expansionist, and institutional. The Shapiro and George cases were temporally spaced so as to be useful in documenting the evolution of anti-cult strategy through these three stages. The Shapiro case in fact involved two discrete incidents, the coercive deprogramming in 1974, which illustrates the formative stage, and the conservatorship proceedings in 1976, which illustrate the transitional stage. The George case illustrates ACM strategy during the institutional stage as it did not actually reach trial until 1983.[69]

THE FORMATIVE STAGE

The first wave of growth among NRMs occurred during the late 1960s. By the early 1970s the "cult problem" began to take shape as awareness of various NRMs increased and new groups appeared on the scene. Recruitment rates to Hare Krishna and other groups increased rapidly as NRMs entered their growth phase. The ACM began as loosely organized local and regional networks of family members of individuals affiliated with NRMs. Within these networks there quickly developed a simultaneous effort to conceptualize what had happened to their offspring and to retrieve them from the groups with which they had affiliated. In this highly emotionally charged context, the notions of brainwashing and deprogramming began to be developed.[70]

The early conception of brainwashing simply constituted a wholesale transfer of the popular stereotype of the Korean prisoner of war brainwashing model in which imprisonment (captivity) formed the basis for attempting to effect ideological conversion. This model, which enjoyed widespread acceptance in American society despite the fact that there was little confirming evidence to support it, offered distraught family members a convenient conceptual schema for interpreting the changes in behavior and expressed values of converts to NRMs that they found so incomprehensible and disturbing.

Based on the captivity model of brainwashing, at an individual level ACM strategy became to "rescue" NRM members from their imprisoning environments. ACM proponents came to believe that NRM members had been "programmed" and required "deprogramming" in order for their former, normal personalities to be restored. Ted Patrick serendipitously initiated the practice of deprogramming in the early 1970s, and his tactics soon were cloned by a coterie of other moral entrepreneurs who responded to the families anxious to retain their services.

It was Patrick who deprogrammed Edward Shapiro in 1974. His description of the programming process and the tactics he used in attempting to deprogram Shapiro reflect the relatively primitive stage of ACM ideology and strategy during this stage. The following constitutes a capsule summary of Patrick's view of his deprogramming process.[71]

> Typically cult street recruiters approach an individual. The technique is to make eye contact and to get their attention and their trust. Frequently this takes the form of initiating a conversation on some subject of mutual interest. The objective is to get the individual thinking in a "single frame of mind." . . . Then with just eye contact, the cult member can place the individual in a complete hypnotic trance, without, of course, the individual's knowledge or permission. This capacity physically comes from brainwaves which are projected outward through the cult member's eyes and fingertips. The individual's mind then switches from conscious to unconscious and a post-hypnotic suggestion is placed. . . . The individuals may continue to do what they are doing or to say what they are saying but the suggestion has been placed in their minds, which leaves them open to brainwashing. They may even walk away from the recruiters, totally negative toward the recruiters and the groups. However, they find themselves returning to meetings and cannot understand why.

From Patrick's perspective, once cultic programming had been induced, the objective of deprogramming was to break the "hypnotic trance." Anything that would shake the individual sufficiently to break through the cult-imposed barrier was incorporated as an element of deprogramming. Tactics included efforts to demonstrate that NRM theologies were false, testimony from former members that they had indeed been brainwashed but they too had been incapable of recognizing that fact, making allegations about abusive leadership and financial practices within the NRM, and emotional pleas from family members to consider the effects of membership on family solidarity. Particularly early in the history of deprogramming more physical shock tactics also were employed. For example, in the Shapiro case, faced with strenuous resistance from Shapiro, Patrick reported the following incident.

> Then I picked Ed up by the front of his robes and marched him backwards across the room, slamming him bodily against the wall. You listen to me! You so much as wiggle your toes again, I'm gonna put my fist down your throat! His eyes got bigger and bigger with fear. He sat down abruptly. I had a picture of Prabhupada and I tore it up in front of him and said, "There's the no-good son of a bitch you worship. And you call him God!" The usual line of approach.[72]

As a defense against the ensuing onslaught of criticism, Shapiro began chanting Hare Krishna. Obviously Patrick saw this as an effort by Shapiro to hypnotize himself. To prevent him from chanting at one point the deprogrammers started tickling him. At another point Shapiro recounted that

> people started to yell, scream, make funny noises, gurgle, make animal noises—anything. They were trying to freak me out completely. One would make faces. Another would race into the room, scream in my face, and race out again. And in the background was Ted Patrick, playing strange combinations of music and discordant sound on his tape recorder.[73]

Patrick's confidence that he simply had to break the programming code was evident in his account of his initial success.

> Inside of an hour, he was out of it. The Krishnas are easy. I think the reason they're easy is that they don't really study anything like some of the other sects do. They're simply into self-hypnosis. They are programmed to chanting and their beads and once you prevent them from doing that, it's a snap to make them see how they've been deceived. . . . With Ed, it was like he was waking up. His personality changed in an instant, and suddenly he was laughing and joking with his parents, relaxed, sensible, and friendly.[74]

When Shapiro subsequently returned to ISKCON, Patrick indicated that he was "firmly convinced that he was bodily abducted."[75]

One early legal strategy associated with the conception of cultic capture involved obtaining writs of habeus corpus requiring an NRM to produce an allegedly brainwashed member in court.[76] The implication was that, if the individual could be separated from the group and reunited with family members, he or she would elect to leave the NRM. This tactic failed both because NRMs argued that, as churches, they could not be held accountable for the whereabouts of individual members and because it became apparent that individuals who did appear were likely to assert that their religious affiliation was a conscious voluntary choice.

Early ACM strategy posed several problems for the movement. First, coercive deprogrammings invited criminal prosecution. Indeed, Merylee Kreshower did seek to have Ted Patrick indicted on kidnapping charges. Although the Kreshower initiative was not successful, NRMs and unsuccessfully deprogrammed individuals succeeded sufficiently often in prosecuting deprogrammers to raise the stakes of employing this tactic substantially. Although ACM activists did gain considerable support from public officials during the early phases of the cult controversy, as reflected in the actions of the police officer rejecting Shapiro's request for assistance and the Assistant District Attorney's transformation of the Kreshower kidnapping complaint into an indictment of Hare Krishna, such overt partisanship declined rather rapidly.

Second, evidence of physical restraint, a vital element in the POW brainwashing model, was absent. Had such evidence existed, of course, it would have provided the ACM with strong legal grounds for criminal prosecution under well-established legal principle and precedent. The absence of evidence of physical restraint eliminated the possibility of prosecutions of the type brought against Krishna leaders in the Shapiro case. This problem was evident in the New York Supreme Court's dismissal of the false imprisonment charges brought against Krishna leaders in the Shapiro case. In that decision Judge John Leahy observed that:

> The said two individuals entered the Hare Krishna movement voluntarily and submitted themselves voluntarily to the regimen, rules and regulations of said so-called Hare Krishna religion, and it is also conceded that the alleged victims were not in any way physically restrained from leaving the defendant organization.[77]

Finally, there was a persistent problem in attempting to attack NRM practices without that attack explicitly or implicitly involving theologically based practices. Judge Leahy concluded:

> The Hare Krishna religion is a bona fide religion with roots in India that go back thousands of years. It behooved Merylee Kreshower and Edward Shapiro to follow the tenets of that faith and their inalienable right to do so will not be trammeled upon. . . . The entire and basic issue before this court is whether or not the two alleged victims in this case and the defendants will be allowed to practice the religion of their choice—and this must be answered with a resounding affirmative. . . . The freedom of religion is not to be abridged because it is unconventional in its beliefs and practices

or because it is approved or disapproved by the mainstream of society or more conventional religions.[78]

It was precisely this kind of judicial rebuff that led the ACM to revamp the brainwashing ideology to rely on the concept of psychological rather than physical coercion and to rely more heavily on the expertise and power base of clinicians.

EXPANSIONIST STAGE

The expansionist stage constituted a transitional phase between the entrepreneurially organized formative and more professionally oriented institutional stages of ACM development. The rate of conversions to NRMs reached its zenith during the mid-1970s; however, because the average length of NRM membership was relatively short, the rate of defection also increased rapidly. With NRM growth, of course, came more deprogrammings as well. During the latter half of the 1970s, the cult controversy was at its peak. The increase in conversions swelled the ranks of the ACM, family conflicts over NRM affiliation became common journalistic fare, the paroxysm at Jonestown focused national attention on the "cult problem," and deprogrammings yielded a sizable cohort of former members who recounted atrocity tales about their usually brief cultic careers.[79]

Toward the end of the decade NRM recruiting success declined, primarily as a result of changing social and economic conditions. The number of deprogrammings fell off both because of the greater legal risks involved and because there were fewer new NRM recruits. The ACM, however, developed greater sophistication and coherence as a result of further development of its ideology and closer linkages with mental health professionals. In addition, the growing emphasis on psychological manipulation rather than physical coercion in ACM ideology encouraged the ACM to expand the range of groups considered cultic far beyond the communal, apocalyptic NRMs against which it first mobilized.

The expansionist stage of development was becoming evident by the time of the 1976 attempt to have Edward Shapiro hospitalized for psychiatric evaluation. Rather than insisting that individuals were physically imprisoned, the ACM was moving toward the notion that cult membership was the product of psychological manipulation (although the term "brainwashing" was still frequently employed) that had deleterious and incapacitating consequences for individual NRM members. The legal strategy associated with this ideology of NRMs was acquiring conservatorship orders that would remand individuals to the custody of their parents. Once in parental custody, NRM members often were "deprogrammed," given "exit-counseling" by former members or counseled by ACM-oriented clinicians.

During this stage the role of mental health practitioners in the cult controversy grew, but it still was not pivotal. Clinicians could testify in support of the issuance of a conservatorship order although at first such orders frequently were issued in *ex parte* hearings in which parental assertions constituted the only testimony. More important, clinicians could more easily become involved in counseling an individual immediately after separation from the NRM if that separation were occasioned by a court-authorized conservatorship order rather than by a coercive deprogramming. Of course, the availability of conservatorships also extended the life of traditional deprogramming as well.

Although obtaining conservatorships offered distinct advantages over the rough-and-tumble deprogrammings of entrepreneurs like Ted Patrick, this strategy too proved to be problematic. First, conservatorship orders became increasingly more difficult to obtain as NRM attorneys began objecting to their unilateral use in this novel and unintended fashion.

Second, if ACM clinicians were going to present court testimony, they needed to be able to link, in some fashion, allegations of mind control with some disorder on which they could offer expert testimony. The Shapiro case demonstrated the ACM's vulnerability on this point. John Clark diagnosed Edward Shapiro as a "borderline personality" and attempted to link this disorder to Shapiro's membership in Hare Krishna. The problems they encountered, of course, were gaining collegial acceptance of the brainwashing allegations and providing supporting evidence that could be corroborated by other clinicians. On these points, ACM clinicians were likely to find themselves in conflict with other clinicians. In the Shapiro case Dr. Hopkins, representing McLean Hospital in which Shapiro had been committed and undergone psychiatric testing, testified that "I was in agreement with the other people who had presented evidence; there was no mental disorder."[80] He further testified, "that phrase, mind control does not appear to be in my standard nomenclature for diagnosing" and denied that "it is an emerging psychiatric field."[81]

Third, in cases where family members were in conflict it was difficult for ACM clinicians to gain access to the NRM members as the latter were hardly disposed to cooperate with conservatorship hearings. Thus, conservatorship orders had to be based on parental assertions of personality change and on more observable changes in behavioral patterns. However, basing actions on behavior changes ran directly into constitutional problems associated with inquiry into religious practice. These difficulties were obvious in the Shapiro case where, for his handling of the Shapiro case, Dr. John Clark was informally reprimanded by the Massachusetts Board of Registration and Discipline in Medicine in a letter sent to his attorney. The letter stated in part that there "is no recognized diagnostic category of mental illness of 'thought reform and mind control.'" The Board further admonished Clark that "witnessing a conversation was not a basis upon which such strong medical judgements could be made." The letter observed that the certificate Clark signed "invites the concern that the judgements were based entirely on the subject's religion." Finally, the letter concluded that "it is also improper and unlawful to base a finding of mental illness solely on membership in a religion regardless of one's personal opinion as to the merits of the religion."[82] This type of resistance led to further reformulation of ACM strategy.

Professionalization Stage

The 1980s brought mixed fortunes to NRMs. On the one hand, several NRMs weathered the initial reverberations following the death of the founder, as did Hare Krishna, and several developed more sophisticated, stable organizational structures that increased the probability of longer-term survival, and found means of generating a modicum of credibility for the movements (such as New Vrindaban). On the other hand, in general there was further erosion of the membership bases of several of the NRMs that sparked the cult controversy, several movements experienced major schisms (as may be now occurring in Hare Krishna) or complete collapse (Rajneesh, Love Israel). In general, the negative developments outweighed the positives and took much of the luster off expectations that these groups would soon achieve the radical social change that had been so ebulliently envisioned only a few years earlier.

The ACM also was experiencing mixed success in its public crusade. No headway had been made in gaining legislative leverage on NRMs, deprogrammings were decreasing and journalistic interest in apostate accounts was declining just as rapidly, and the events at Jonestown did not produce the outpouring of public support that the ACM had hoped. Like the NRMs, however, the ACM developed a much more sophisticated organization, secure funding base, and broad range of activities that kept the cult controversy alive. Coercive deprogramming was largely replaced with voluntary "exit counseling," which appears to have yielded about the same results but avoided the stigma associated with the coercive interventions. Finally, the ACM kept discovering new "cults" or groups with cultic tendencies, which maintained a large supply of target groups.

At this juncture the ACM clearly needed a major new strategic initiative if the cult controversy was not to deteriorate into a long-term stalemate. Two important developments took place that promised to change ACM fortunes. First, ACM activists were successful in achieving inclusion in DSM-III (the Diagnostic and Statistical Manual used by clinicians in making diagnoses of mental disorders) new language that made reference to cult-induced disorders.[83] The revised definition of atypical dissociative disorder reads as follows:

> A residual category to be used for individuals who appear to have a Dissociative Disorder but do not satisfy the criteria for specific Dissociative Disorder. Examples include trance-like states, derealization accompanied by depersonalization, and those more prolonged dissociated states that may occur in persons who have been subjected to periods of prolonged and intense coercive persuasion (brainwashing, thought reform, and indoctrination while the captive of terrorists or cultists).

This new language directly linked the putative brainwashing procedures of NRMs to an established category of mental disorder and hence created the basis for clinical evaluation of the consequences of NRM membership. In addition, ACM clinicians utilized the already established "post-traumatic stress syndrome" category and interpretively extended it to include members of NRMs.

Second, the ACM began relying on civil suits filed by apostate members against their former groups as a strategy for attacking NRMs. There was an ample pool of apostate members, some of whom were disenchanted with their former groups and willing to testify that they had been subjected to brainwashing techniques. This new strategy circumvented the problem of gaining means of extricating individuals from NRMs, which the ACM had not been able to solve satisfactorily. Instead, civil suits were initiated by individuals who had already left NRMs and now sought compensation for allegedly abusive practices to which they were subject while they were members. Rather than being allied with NRMs, these individuals had realigned with family members against their former groups. Not only was their testimony available but also ACM clinicians could evaluate them and present expert testimony in legal proceedings.

These two elements of the new ACM strategy dovetailed nicely. Former members of NRMs filed civil charges against NRMs, typically under such generalized legal provisions as infliction of mental distress. They were then examined by ACM clinicians who diagnosed the distress in terms of atypical dissociative disorder and post-traumatic stress syndrome. ACM clinicians and the plaintiff then would testify that affiliation with the NRM had not been voluntary but coerced, that the brainwashing process and subsequent group practices and conditions were the proximate cause of the mental disorders, and that the diagnosed disorders were the source of the emotional distress. The brainwashing explanation linked membership with the disorders and assigned responsibility to the group rather than the member because a voluntary decision to join had never been made.

This was precisely the scenario in the George case. Margaret Singer testified that George had suffered from three mental disorders—atypical dissociative disorder, post-traumatic stress disorder, and an identity disorder—and that these were "a direct and near result from her time spent in the Krishna organization."[84] Affiliation with Hare Krishna had not been voluntary as George had been subjected to the SMSI process. Indeed, Margaret Singer explicitly testified that prior to running away from home to the Krishna temple, Robin George's "will had been overcome" and thus the decision to run away could not have been voluntary.[85] The damage that resulted from her time in Hare Krishna, Singer concluded, created a need for "prolonged psychological or psychiatric treatment, and by persons who are familiar with and have worked with people who have been exposed to similar types of trauma that she has had."[86]

Only the pattern of trial and appellate decisions ultimately will determine the viability of this new strategy. The ACM still confronts a number of problems in long-run implementation. Given the absence of physical coercion, ACM clinicians had to argue that coercive persuasion is more effective when force is not used. This argument raises questions about the necessary and sufficient conditions for the coercive persuasion they allege is operant. The length of time between defection from NRMs and filing of legal complaints by apostates often has been several years, and thus ACM clinicians have had to contend that the passage of time does not diminish the accuracy of a diagnosis. The mounting body of psychological and sociological research by behavioral scientists has not supported ACM allegations, as Gordon's review of that literature with respect to ISKCON indicates. Thus, ACM clinicians have adopted the position that brainwashing effects do not appear in the standard diagnostic tests used by clinicians and that only those who have worked with populations subjected to coercive persuasion are in a position to understand and interpret this condition fully. Nevertheless, the fact that the ACM was able to score some striking victories in civil trials (and the George decision was among the more noteworthy) was significant. Such outcomes constituted symbolic victories for the movement, drew media attention, generated financial resources within the ACM network, and held the potential for creating legal precedents that might influence outcomes in future litigation.

Conclusions and Discussion

There is a tendency in recording the history of social movements to treat the sociocultural environment as merely the backdrop that frames movement action. In a very real sense, however, the history of movements like Hare Krishna *is* the history of the society and its culture. As various essays in this volume have demonstrated, the appearance and growth of Hare Krishna in the United States can be understood only in terms of the longer history of Asian religions in America, cultural availability of converts, the development of viable communities and an integrated lifestyle, and, as we have argued here, the societal reaction to the movement.

This chapter has outlined the structure and evolution of the organized opposition to Hare Krishna (and other groups that appeared about the same time), using two major ISKCON–ACM confrontations as illustrative cases. It is clear that the controversy in which Hare Krishna became embroiled reflected more profound cultural tensions between secular/individualistic and sacred/communal lifestyles. In this sense, Hare Krishna was caught up in a conflict that far transcended the movement itself, although some of the more radical beliefs and practices characteristic of the movement's early stages of development certainly contributed to the emergence of the cult scare. In this conflict the ACM served as a proxy for established institutions and the values on which they were erected. The ACM's campaign had significant implications for the survival and development of Hare Krishna through its impact on such key movement resource mobilization processes as recruitment/defection, financial resource generation, public image management, and commitment to articulated movement goals rather than self-protection. From this perspective, a significant element in the evolution of the movement has been the implications of the parallel development of the ACM.

The cult scare was played out in public dramas involving conflicts among converts, families, and NRMs, as the chronology of events in the Shapiro and George cases has demonstrated. The conflict was not a static one, however, as the ACM sought means of linking its subversion ideology to an effective means of gaining control over individual converts as well as NRMs as organizations. In this sense, the evolution of ISKCON must be understood dialectically: Hare Krishna was shaping the social order even as the social order was shaping the movement. The transition from coercive deprogrammings during the formative stage to civil suits in the professional stage illustrates that process. The underlying premise, that conversions to Hare Krishna were involuntary, was increasingly cast in medical/psychological terms. Ultimately, a specific mental disorder was linked to membership in Hare Krishna and this diagnostic category created the basis for legal action against the movement.

The medicalization of religious conversion surely constitutes the most significant development in ACM strategy, one with far-reaching implications for a wide array of religious groups. Because the cult controversy is still in flux, the longer-term implications of this medicalized construction of a social conflict remain indeterminate. However, it is clear that the evolution of Hare Krishna cannot be understood outside the context of its interaction with the ACM and that there is a continuing trend toward interpreting and evaluating the sacred in secular terms.

Notes

1. See also Anson Shupe and David Bromley, *The New Vigilantes* (Beverly Hills, CA: SAGE Publications, 1980), pp. 63–70; and Anson Shupe, David Bromley, and Donna Oliver, *A Bibliographic History of the Anti-Cult Movement* (New York: Garland Publishers, 1983), pp. 51–80.

2. David Bromley and Anson Shupe, *Strange Gods: The Great American Cult Scare* (Boston: Beacon Press, 1981); David Brian Davis, "Some Themes of Counter-Subversion: An Analysis of Anti-Masonic, Anti-Catholic, and Anti-Mormon Literature," *Mississippi Valley Historical Review* 47 (1960): 205–22; Harvey Cox, "Deep Structures in the Study of New Religions," in *Understanding New Religions,* ed. Jacob Needleman and George Baker (New York: Seabury, 1978); Thomas Robbins and Dick Anthony, "Cults, Brainwashing and Counter-Subversion," *The Annals of the American Academy of Political and Social Science* 446 (1979): 78–90; Rodney Sawatsky, "Moonies, Mormons and Mennonites: Christian Heresy and Religious Toleration," in *A Time for Consideration,* ed. M. Darroll Bryant and Herbert Richardson (Lewiston, NY: Edwin Mellen Press, 1978), pp. 22–40.

3. Ray Billington, *The Origins of Nativism in the United States, 1800–1844* (New York: Arno Press, 1974); Charles Cannon, "The Awesome Power of Sex: The Polemical Campaign Against Mormon Polygamy," *Pacific Historical Review* 43 (1974): 61–82.

4. Willa Appel, *Cults In America: Programmed for Paradise* (New York: Holt, Rinehart and Winston, 1981); A. James Rudin and Marcia Rudin, *Prison or Paradise? The New Religious Cults* (Philadelphia: Fortress Press, 1980).

5. Gregory Johnson, "The Hare Krishna in San Francisco," in *The New Religious Consciousness,* ed. Charles Glock and Robert Bellah (Berkeley: University of California Press, 1976), pp. 31–51; James Richardson, Mary Stewart, and Robert Simmonds, *Organized Miracles: A Study of a Contemporary Youth, Communal Fundamentalist Organization* (New Brunswick, NJ: Transaction Press, 1979).

6. Bromley and Shupe, *Moonies in America,* pp. 27–29.

7. E. Burke Rochford, Jr., *Hare Krishna in America* (New Brunswick, NJ: Rutgers University Press, 1985), pp. 171–89; David Bromley and Anson Shupe,

"Financing the New Religions: A Resource Mobilization Approach," *Journal for the Scientific Study of Religion* 19 (1980): 227–39.

8. Personal communication from Larry Shinn, 1987.

9. For example, in recent years the Rajneesh, Love Israel, and Divine Light Mission have all experienced organizational collapse.

10. Shupe and Bromley, *The New Vigilantes*, pp. 87–120.

11. James Beckford, "A Typology of Family Responses to a New Religious Movement," *Marriage and Family Review* 4 (1981): 41–56; Anson Shupe and David Bromley, "The Moonies and Anti-Cultists: Movement and Countermovement in Conflict," *Sociological Analysis* 40 (1979): 325–36.

12. See, for example, Shupe and Bromley, *The New Vigilantes*, pp. 169–206; David Bromley and Anson Shupe, "The Dynamics of Repression," in *Research in Social Movements, Conflict and Change*, ed. Lewis Kriesberg (Greenwich, CT: JAI Press, 1982), pp. 25–64; David Bromley, "Cults, Crusaders and the Constitution," in *Laws of Our Fathers: Popular Culture and the U.S. Constitution*, ed. Ray Browne (Bowling Green, OH: Popular Culture Press, 1986), pp. 167–86.

13. David G. Bromley, "Ted Patrick and the Development of Deprogramming," paper presented at the annual meeting of the Society for the Scientific Study of Religion, Savannah, 1985. Available evidence suggests that deprogrammings have been successful. See David G. Bromley, "Deprogramming as a Mode of Exit from New Religious Movements: The Case of the Unification Church," in *Falling From the Faith*, ed. David G. Bromley (Beverly Hills, CA: SAGE Publications, 1988).

14. The composite description of the Edward Shapiro case presented here was derived from the following sources: "Testimony of Dr. John Clark," Commonwealth of Massachusetts, "In the Matter of: Petition of Guardianship of Edward David Shapiro," Middlesex Probate Court, 3 November 1976; Dave O'Brian, "Krishna Calls Deprogramming Mental Torture" *The Boston Phoenix* (3 September 1974): 3, 13; Lindsay Miller and Lendsy Van Gelder, "Dad Gets Krishna Disciple for Deprogramming," *New York Post* (20 October 1976): 5, 16; Martin King, Thomas Pugh, and Harry Stathos, "Cult Witness Sent to Mass. Hospital" *Daily News* (21 October 1976): QL7; Michael Matza, "The Battle for Krishna Minds," *The Boston Phoenix* (16 November 1976): 1, 27; New York Civil Liberties Union, "Defend Religious Freedom of Harassed Hare Krishnas" *N.Y. Civil Liberties* 25 (November–December 1976): 1, 7; Mary Thornton, "The Hare Krishna Puzzle," *Boston Globe* (23 January 1977); Murray Schumach "Judge Dismisses Charges in Hare Krishna 'Brainwashing' Case," *New York Times* (18 March 1977).

15. Eli Shapiro, "Destructive Cultism," *American Family Practice* 15 (February 1977): 83.

16. Ibid.

17. Matza, "The Battle for Krishna Minds."

18. Ibid.

19. O'Brian, "Krishna Calls Deprogramming Mental Torture."

20. Ibid.

21. New York Civil Liberties Union, "Defend Religious Freedom of Harassed Hare Krishnas."

22. "Testimony of Dr. John Clark."

23. The composite description of the Robin George case presented here was derived from the following sources: "Summary of Marcia George Deposition;" "Transcript of interview with Robin George by Dr. Margaret Singer;" Marcia George, "Evaluation of Robin George, by her Mother, Marcia George, n.d.;"

"Testimony of Dr. Margaret Singer," in the case of *Robin George and Marcia George* vs. *International Society of Krishna Consciousness,* Superior Court of the State of California, County of Orange, 3–4 May; "Letter from Dr. Raymond Cameron to Milton J. Silverman, Attorney at Law," 3 September 1982; "George vs. ISKCON," Report from L. M. Alter, Stein Investigation Agency to ISKCON, 6 July 1983; Sherry Angel, "Girl Finds No Escape in the Year-Long Krishna Odyssey," *Los Angeles Times* (7 April 1976); Lu Blindbury, "Girl, Mother Describe Cult Experiences," *Temple City Times* (13 January 1977); Sheryl Johansen, "PTA Defies Cultist Threat," *Burbank Daily Review* (15 March 1977); "$32.5 Million Awarded in Hare Krishna Case," *Los Angeles Times* (18 June 1983); Timothy Carlson, "Landmark Case Awards Cult Victim $32.5 Million," *Los Angeles Herald Examiner* (18 June 1983); Jerry Hicks and Pam Steinriede, "Judge Cuts Payment in Krishna Suit," *Los Angeles Times* (11 August 1983): 1, 2.

24. It is interesting to note that Robin's girlfriend independently disaffiliated from Hare Krishna without becoming involved in the kind of brainwashing allegations so central to the George case. Robin George's mother accounted for this process as follows: "It's difficult to get out of the cults by yourself. Robin's friend Karen never really gave her complete attention to the Krishna. She told us she only listened to what the Krishna said with the top of her brain" (Johansen, "PTA Defies Cultist Threat").

25. Angel, "Girl Finds No Escape in the Year-Long Krishna Odyssey."

26. Ibid.

27. Ibid.

28. Letter, "Robin George vs. ISKCON et al." from Raymond Cameron to Milton Silverman, 3 September 1982, p. 10.

29. Marcia George, "Evaluation of Robin George, by her Mother, Marcia George."

30. Larry D. Shinn, *The Dark Lord: Cult Images and the Hare Krishnas in America* (Philadelphia: Westminster Press, 1987), p. 123.

31. Alter, "George vs. ISKCON."

32. Ibid.

33. Ibid.

34. Ibid.

35. Stuart Wright, "Leaving New Religious Movements: Issues, Theory and Research," in *Falling from the Faith,* ed. David G. Bromley (Beverly Hills, CA: SAGE Publications, 1988).

36. David G. Bromley, "Deprogramming as Mode of Exit," in Bromley, *Falling From the Faith.*

37. James Lewis and David Bromley, "The Cult Withdrawal Syndrome: A Case of Misattribution of Cause?" *Journal for the Scientific Study of Religion* 26 (1987): 508–22; Trudy Solomon, "Integrating the 'Moonie' Experience: A Survey of Ex-Members of the Unification Church," in *In Gods We Trust: New Patterns of Religious Pluralism in America,* ed. Thomas Robbins and Dick Anthony (New Brunswick, NJ: Transaction Books, 1981), pp. 275–96.

38. The work and testimony of Dr. John Clark and Dr. Margaret Singer will be used to document the values underpinning ACM ideology because Clark was the primary advocate of the ACM position in the Shapiro case and Singer was a central ACM expert witness in the George case.

39. Louis West and Margaret Singer, "Cults, Quacks, and Nonprofessional Psychotherapies," in *Comprehensive Textbook of Psychiatry/III,* ed. Harold Kaplan,

Alfred Freedman, and Benjamin Sadock (Baltimore: Williams and Wilkins, 1980), p. 3252.

40. "Testimony of Dr. John Clark," pp. 25–26.

41. "Testimony of Dr. Margaret Singer," p. 68.

42. James Richardson, "Psychological and Psychiatric Studies of New Religions," in *Advances in the Psychology of Religion*, ed. L. B. Brown (New York: Pergammon Press, 1985), 2: 213–14.

43. Singer, "Therapy with Ex-Cult Members," p. 14.

44. Ibid., p. 16.

45. Clark, "The Manipulation of Madness," p. 10.

46. "Testimony of Dr. Margaret Singer," p. 76.

47. "Testimony of Dr. John Clark," p. 26.

48. Singer, "Therapy with Ex-Cult Members," p. 16.

49. Ibid.

50. Ibid.

51. Marjory Zerin, "The Pied Piper Phenomenon and the Processing of Victims: The Transactional Analysis Perspective Re-examined," *Transactional Analysis Journal* 13 (1983): 175. It should be noted that although Zerin makes several references to a 1982 source attributed to Margaret Singer, no corresponding item appears in the list of references.

52. Singer, "Therapy with Ex-Cult Members," p. 16.

53. West and Singer, "Cults, Quacks and Nonprofessional Psychotherapies," p. 3250.

54. John Clark, "When Friends or Patients Ask About Cults," *Journal of the American Medical Association* 242 (1979): 279–81.

55. Letter "To Whom It May Concern," accompanying John Clark, "Investigating the Effects of Some Religious Cults on the Health and Welfare of Their Converts." Statement to the Vermont State Legislature, 12 August 1976.

56. "Testimony of Dr. John Clark," pp. 25–26.

57. Ibid., p. 35.

58. "Testimony of Dr. Margaret Singer," pp. 20–21.

59. Ibid., p. 26.

60. "Testimony of Dr. Margaret Singer," pp. 30–31.

61. Ibid., p. 29.

62. Louis West, "Contemporary Cults—Utopian Image, Infernal Reality," *The Center Magazine* (March/April 1982): 13.

63. "Testimony of Dr. John Clark," p. 3.

64. Margaret Singer, "Therapy with Ex-Cult Members," *National Association of Private Psychiatric Hospitals Journal* 9 (1978): 16.

65. West and Singer, "Cults, Quacks, and Nonprofessional Psychotherapies," p. 3252.

66. Ibid.

67. John Clark, "The Manipulation of Madness" (Paper presented at the Deutsche Gesellschaft für Kinder und Jugendpsychiatric und Bundeskonferenz für Enzienlhungersvertung, Hanover, West Germany, February 1978), p. 5.

68. "Testimony of Dr. Margaret Singer," p. 39.

69. A discussion of these stages is included in David Bromley and Anson Shupe, "The Future of the Anti-Cult Movement," in *The Future of New Religious Movements*, ed. David Bromley and Phillip Hammond (Macon, GA: Mercer University Press, 1987).

70. See Shupe and Bromley, *The New Vigilantes*, for a more detailed history of the Anti-Cult Movement.

71. Bromley, "Ted Patrick and the Development of Deprogramming," pp. 9–11.

72. Ted Patrick and Tom Dulack, *Let Our Children Go!* (New York: Ballantine Books, 1976), pp. 170–71.

73. O'Brian, "Krishna Calls Deprogramming Mental Torture," p. 3.

74. Patrick and Dulack, *Let Our Children Go!*, p. 171.

75. Ibid., p. 178.

76. This tactic was not appropriate in the Shapiro case because Shapiro was visiting his physician/father on a weekly basis in order to receive treatment for his diabetic condition.

77. Schumach, "Judge Dismisses Charges in Hare Krishna 'Brainwashing' Case," p. 1.

78. Ibid.

79. David Bromley, Anson Shupe, and Joseph Ventimiglia, "The Role of Anecdotal Atrocities in the Social Construction of Evil," in *The Brainwashing/ Deprogramming Controversy*, ed. David Bromley and James Richardson (Lewiston, NY: Edwin Mellen Press, 1983). pp. 139–60.

80. "Testimony of Thomas Hopkins."

81. Ibid.

82. Letter from George Annas to William Homans, "Re: John G. Clark, Jr., MD," 16 January 1980.

83. Brock Kilbourne and James Richardson, "Anti-Religion Bias in the Diagnostic and Statistical Manual-III: The Case of Cults" (Paper presented at the Annual Meeting of the Society for the Scientific Study of Religion, Chicago, October 1984), p. 7.

84. "Testimony of Dr. Margaret Singer," p. 50.

85. Ibid., p. 46.

86. Ibid., p. 81.

Notes on Contributors

DAVID G. BROMLEY (Ph.D), Professor in the Department of Sociology and Anthropology at Virginia Commonwealth University, has authored or edited numerous books and articles on new religious movements and the various controversies surrounding them. His books include "Moonies" in America: Cult, Church and Crusade (with Anson Shupe, 1979), The New Vigilantes: Deprogrammers, Anti-Cultists, and the New Religions (with Anson Shupe, 1980), Strange Gods: The Great American Cult Scare (with Anson Shupe, 1981), The Brainwashing/Deprogramming Controversy (edited with James Richardson, 1983), The Future of New Religious Movements (edited with Phillip Hammond, 1987), and Falling From the Faith (1988).

CHARLES BROOKS is a doctoral candidate in the Department of Anthropology at the University of Hawaii at Manoa, where he is completing a dissertation examining the social and economic impact of ISKCON upon Vrindaban, India ("Change and Continuity in the Land of Krishna: A Symbolic Interactional Study of Western Devotees in a Traditional India Pilgrimage Town"). He served as president of the Hawaiian Anthropological Association in 1984.

WILLIAM H. DEADWYLER, III (RAVINDRA-SVARUPA DAS) (Ph.D.), a member of ISKCON since 1971, received his doctoral degree in religion from Temple University with a dissertation on the theology of Charles Hartshorn (1980). He is author of "The Devotee and the Deity: Living a Personalistic Theology" in Gods of Flesh/Gods of Stone: The Embodiment of Divinity in India, edited by J. Waghorne and N. Cutler (1984), and a collection of his articles from ISKCON's monthly magazine Back to Godhead is published under the title Encounter with the Lord of the Universe: Collected Essays, 1978–1983 (1985).

ROBERT S. ELLWOOD (Ph.D.), Bishop James W. Bashford Professor of Oriental Studies at the University of Southern California, has made many important contributions to the historical and comparative study of religion, and alternative religion in particular, as the author of many books including Religious and Spiritual Groups in Modern America (1973),

Alternative Altars: Unconventional and Eastern Spirituality in America (1979), and *Mysticism and Religion* (1980).

STEVEN J. GELBERG (Subhananda dasa), a member of ISKCON since 1970, is the society's director for interreligious affairs, and a senior editor of the Bhaktivedanta Book Trust. He has edited a number of volumes including, most recently, *Hare Krishna, Hare Krishna: Five Distinguished Scholars on the Krishna Movement in the West* (1983). His article, "The Future of Krishna Consciousness in the West: An Insider's Perspective," appears in *The Future of New Religious Movements*, edited by David Bromley and Phillip Hammond (1987). In addition, he edits *ISKCON Bulletin*, a journal of ISKCON studies.

JAMES S. GORDON (M.D.), is Clinical Associate Professor in the Departments of Psychiatry and Community and Family Medicine at the Georgetown University School of Medicine. He has written several books in the areas of holistic medicine and adolescent psychiatry, as well as articles on the cult issue including "The Cult Phenomenon and the Psychotherapeutic Response" in the *Journal of the American Academy of Psychoanalysis* (1983). He is currently working on a book on new religious movements to be published by McGraw-Hill.

THOMAS J. HOPKINS (Ph.D.) is Professor and Chairman of the Department of Religious Studies at Franklin & Marshall College, where he teaches Asian religious traditions. His publications include "The Social Teachings of the Bhagavata-Purana" in *Krishna: Myths, Rites and Attitudes*, edited by Milton Singer (1966), and the widely used college text, *The Hindu Religious Tradition* (1971). Professor Hopkins discusses ISKCON at length in *Hare Krishna, Hare Krishna*, edited by S. Gelberg (1983).

J. GORDON MELTON (Ph.D.) is founder and Director of the Institute for the Study of American Religion located in Santa Barbara, California, and an authority on alternative religious groups in American history. He is author and editor of many books including *The Encyclopedia of American Religions* (1978), *A Directory of Religious Bodies in the United States* (1977), and coauthor, with Robert Moore, of *The Cult Experience: Responding to the New Religious Pluralism* (1982).

R. BLAKE MICHAEL (Ph.D.) occupies the Swan-Allan-Collins Chair of World Religion and Christian Mission at Ohio Wesleyan University. He is also an adjunct associate professor of world religion at the Methodist Theological School in Ohio. His publications in *JAAR, JAOS, JAS, NVMEN*, and other journals focus primarily on the Virassaiva tradition in South India, but he also maintains a keen interest in contemporary American religion, particularly in developments at New Vrindaban, West Virginia.

JOHN A. SALIBA (S.J.) is Associate Professor of Religious Studies at the University of Detroit. His publications in the area of new religious movements include "The Christian Response to the New Religions" published in the *Journal of Ecumenical Studies* (1981), "The Christian Church and the New Religious Movements: Towards Theological Understanding (*Theological Studies*, 1982), and *Religious Cults Today: A Challenge to Christian Families* (1983).

LARRY D. SHINN, formerly Danforth Professor in History of Religions at Oberlin College, is now Dean of Arts and Sciences at Bucknell University. He is author of *Two Sacred Worlds: Experience and Structure in the World's Religions* (1977), coauthor with Roy Amore of *Lustful Maidens and Ascetic Kings: Buddhist and Hindu Stories of Life* (1981), and associate editor of the *Abingdon Dictionary of Living Religions* (1981). He has also edited *In Search of the Divine: Some Unexpected Consequences of Inter-faith Dialogue* (1987). He recently finished a book on ISKCON, *The Dark Lord: Cult Images and the Hare Krishnas in America* (1987).